Thomas Jefferson

Roots of Religious Freedom

John H Peach

John Harding Peach

CROSSBOOKS

CrossBooks™
A Division of LifeWay
1663 Liberty Drive
Bloomington, IN 47403
www.crossbooks.com
Phone: 1-866-879-0502

© 2012 John Harding Peach. All rights reserved.

No part of this book may be reproduced, stored in a retrieval system, or transmitted by any means without the written permission of the author.

First published by CrossBooks 8/31/2012

ISBN: 978-1-4627-2052-1 (sc)
ISBN: 978-1-4627-2054-5 (hc)
ISBN: 978-1-4627-2053-8 (e)

Library of Congress Control Number: 2012915720

Printed in the United States of America

This book is printed on acid-free paper.

Any people depicted in stock imagery provided by Thinkstock are models, and such images are being used for illustrative purposes only.

Certain stock imagery © Thinkstock.

Because of the dynamic nature of the Internet, any web addresses or links contained in this book may have changed since publication and may no longer be valid. The views expressed in this work are solely those of the author and do not necessarily reflect the views of the publisher, and the publisher hereby disclaims any responsibility for them.

Dedication

I dedicate this book to the following Americans:

- To those who educate their children to follow the principles that made our nation exceptional over others.

- To parents who dedicate themselves tirelessly to raise their children to become physically, mentally, spiritually and morally fit to become the promising future of America.

- To women who were refused the right to vote, to go to school, to own property, or to hold public office in early America.

- To African Americans who suffered the abominable torments of slavery and to their descendants.

- To children of all ages and races in America, that they will have an intense interest in their nation's founding fathers and all they endured to establish our great nation.

- To those who are fighting to keep the truth alive that America is a Christian nation founded on the truths located in the Bible.

Contents

Preface – A Man Ahead of his Time ix
Introduction – Jefferson's Religion xiii
1. The Teacher Who Lit His Fire 1
2. Life Wasn't Fair 17
3. The Way it all Began 25
4. Returning to Shadwell 33
5. Dying Embers of the Loyal Company 47
6. College of William and Mary 61
7. Patrick Henry 71
8. Leaning toward Liberty 83
9. The Power of the Pen 99
10. Declaration of Independence 113
11. Keeping the Dream Alive 123
12. Governor of Virginia 133
13. The French Connection 145
14. First Secretary of State 163
15. Early Retirement 173
16. Adams-Jefferson Ticket 183
17. Jefferson as President 195
18. Meriwether Lewis 219
19. Louisiana Purchase 235
20. Beginning of the Expedition 247
21. Back at the White House 265
22. Sacajawea 277
23. Jefferson's Dream Come True 289
24. The First Dog in the White House 301
An Addendum – The Thornton Legacy 319
References Consulted 323
Index 335

Preface

A Man Ahead of his Time

Prior to the Revolution, colonial America in the eighteenth century was hopelessly stagnant. As she was still tied to England's archaic laws and medieval traditions, she found herself imprisoned by a tyrannical king on the other side of the Atlantic. Whatever meager efforts of new ideas she attempted to introduce, she found them ruthlessly squashed by King George III or his unrelenting Parliament.

Although many Americans eagerly yearned for freedom from the oppressive rule of the British, they had few ideas what to do with the liberty they so ardently craved. Yes, they wanted independence. However, what would they do with it once they had it? They were like teens that can't wait to leave their secure nests in their parents' homes. So anxious to leave, but they have no plan how to survive on their own.

At the end of the Revolutionary War, America was crying for George Washington to be her king! England had her King George. Why not America? Had he accepted the citizens' coronation, he would have destroyed what would make America a shining light on the hill. Instead, George Washington decided on the meager title of "President" and even chose to serve his nation with no salary.

Enter Thomas Jefferson. He was a man full of new ideas and an unwavering compulsion to sell them to his country's leadership. However, change was not easy, even with those who so desperately craved independence from British rule. Jefferson was obsessed with his father's dream to somehow, someday, capture the West all the way to the Pacific. However, his active mind was filled with many other dreams. Although he proposed all these during his lifetime, many of them were not realized until after the flowers he always cherished deteriorated on his grave. Those propositions accepted while he was alive took years after he had fought for them before they became the law of the land.

Jefferson had held the highest offices of the United States. Besides serving two terms as president, he was also vice president and Secretary of State. Earlier, he served as both Governor of Virginia and Minister to France. Repeatedly he served in the Virginia House of Burgesses and the Continental Congress. Yet with all that fame and glory, Thomas Jefferson wanted to be remembered primarily for his grandiose dreams and revolutionary ideas.

He personally designed his own tombstone to memorialize only his three most cherished accomplishments. Those were as: "Author of the Declaration of American Independence, of the Statute of Virginia for Religious Freedom, and Father of the University of Virginia". Although those were the most significant to Jefferson, yet they only represented a small sampling of that which portrayed him as a man ahead of his time. These are numbered as follows, but not necessarily in the order of importance to Jefferson.

1. **The Abolition of Slavery**
   That was one of Thomas Jefferson's life-long goals, which will be revealed repeatedly throughout this biographical novel.

2. **The Education and Training of Slaves**
   In colonial America, it was against the law to teach slaves to read and write. Jefferson believed that education was the key to freedom. For slaves eventually to be free, they must be educated.

3. **Free Public Education**
   Jefferson proposed a tax-supported elementary education for all. He felt that girls, as well as boys, should attend school at least three years of their childhood. He proposed scholarships to attend college for aspiring youth.

4. **Free Public Library**
   His love for books and libraries compelled him to believe they should be available freely to all. Jefferson's possessed one of the

largest private libraries and used it to help supply the shelves of the Library of Congress.

5. **Land changes to break America's ties to Pseudo- aristocracy.**
Jefferson knew that to break the stranglehold of the outmoded medieval system in England; he had to abolish both the laws of entail and primogeniture. Entail required property always to remain in possession by the same family or group. Primogeniture was the requirement that the firstborn son inherited all the land of his deceased father. Jefferson believed that law unfairly treated the rest of the members of the family.

6. **Change the monetary system**
Jefferson proposed that the new republic leave the British pound, replacing it with the American dollar. He believed that was necessary to complete the nation's independence from England.

7. **Declaration of Independence**
When Jefferson was given the responsibility of drafting a document that would officially cut ties with England, he willingly accepted the challenge. He considered the *Declaration of Independence* to be one of his most significant achievements.

8. **The Statute of Virginia for Religious Freedom**
Jefferson believed each person should have the freedom to worship whenever, wherever and whoever he or she chooses. The Church of England required people to attend church, mandated parents to have their children baptized, and assessed property owners to be taxed to support her ministry. Although he was a vestryman for his Anglican church, Jefferson fought tenaciously for each individual's right to choose his or her own religious preference.

9. **Father of the University of Virginia**
His crowning achievement was the founding of a university that was able to absorb all his ideals for education, the first secular university in America. He conceived it, planned it, designed it, and supervised both her construction and the hiring of her faculty.

10. **Capturing the West all the way to the Pacific**
   That was his father's dream. For that to happen, he had to become president. When he authorized the Louisiana Purchase, he doubled the size of the United States and provided the mandate for him to send an expedition to explore the Louisiana Territory. Because of his father's dream, he decided to go beyond that, all the way to the Pacific Ocean.

What follows is a biographical novel of Thomas Jefferson from his birth through his presidency. Although it is a novel, all historical events and places were provided as they factually occurred. Over a hundred books and articles were researched to assure its authenticity. As an ardent genealogist, this author was meticulous to make sure that all dates, names and family relationships were historically accurate. The same careful precision was given to those who were slaves, at least as far as any of their genealogy was known.

On January 6, 1821, Thomas Jefferson sat down to write the autobiography of his life until 1776, the year he wrote the *Declaration of Independence*. He introduced his beginning in life with these words. "At the age of 77, I begin to make some memoranda, and state some recollections of dates and facts concerning myself, for my own more ready reference, and for the information of my family."

This autobiography will be followed with exact detail, quoted throughout this book, as the primary source for Thomas Jefferson's own recollection of the first 33 years of his life.

Introduction

Jefferson's Religion

The religious views of Thomas Jefferson were as complex as the man himself. He was a man who has confused critics and historians for centuries due to his all-encompassing religious views from one end of the spectrum to the other. The reason so much has been known about Jefferson's spiritual aspirations is because he was an avid writer, and much of his correspondence has been preserved for the ages. During his 83 years of life, like most people his views on the Bible and religion changed from one period of his life to the other.

Although he studied extensively every book he could get on religion, including the works of deists, infidels, atheists and Unitarians, he practiced his core convictions of basic Protestantism throughout his lifetime. His parents had him baptized in the Church of England, in which later he became a vestryman. On his deathbed, he petitioned an Anglican rector to perform his funeral sermon and burial, as he had done for the burials of all his loved ones.

Was he a Christian? There is no evidence in Thomas Jefferson of a dramatic born-again experience. As a private person, if he had such an awakening, he would have tended to keep it to himself. His theology was filled with doubts about the Trinity and the supernatural. However, whatever deviations he may have had with core Biblical concepts, he more than rectified by his actions as the author of religious liberty in America. His writings and actions inspired the new nation to break the chains of state-sponsored churches prevalent in the European countries.

Was he a Christian? He claimed he was. On April 21, 1803, he wrote to noted physician, Dr. Benjamin Rush, "I am a Christian, in the only sense in which he *(Jesus)* wished any one to be; sincerely attached to his doctrines, in preference to all others; ascribing to himself every human excellence, and believing he never claimed any other."[1] Thomas Jefferson proved his Christian values from his childhood and all through his presidency, as shown by these decisive actions.

- When he was 14, he chose to be tutored by Rev. James Maury, his ardent Huguenot pastor who passionately taught him the Scriptures. Prior to that, for the past five years he had been taught by Rev. William Douglas, another of his pastors. If Thomas Jefferson was adamant against Christianity, why did he personally choose to be tutored by his pastor?
- When he was 26, his home at Shadwell was burned to the ground. When this happened, Jefferson was 120 miles away in Williamsburg, where he was practicing law. When he finally arrived to see the charred remains of Shadwell, he wrote to his friend, John Page, bereaving his loss of "every paper I had in the world, and almost every book." When he asked a Shadwell slave about his books, he was told, "No master, all burnt, but we save your fiddle."[2] However, his family Bible he inherited from his father and his Book of Common Prayer survived. These remain in mint condition at the Special Collections Library of the University of Virginia. The only way for them to be saved from the fire was for Jefferson to have transported them 120 miles to Williamsburg when he set up his law practice. His family Bible is rather large, weighing about ten pounds. Why would he have gone to the trouble of transporting it and the Book of Common Prayer to Williamsburg if he wasn't using them? The Bible must have been used for study and referencing while his prayer book was needed for worship when he went to church. Does this sound like someone who was an infidel or an atheist, as he was labeled by his enemies?
- When he was 31, he proposed a *Resolution for a Day of Fasting, Humiliation & Prayer* in Virginia. This, his first public document, was presented to the Virginia House of Burgesses on May 24, 1774 and was quickly passed with unanimous consent. If Thomas Jefferson was not a Christian, then why would he see the necessity to call on all citizens to fast and pray to God for his intervention in their affairs? To amplify his belief that

prayer and fasting was vital to call on God's favor, he took his resolution back to his own Albemarle County and proposed another day of fasting for his local parish.

- When he was 34, in writing the *Declaration of Independence*, he began with these words. "When in the course of human events, it becomes necessary for one people to dissolve the political bands which have connected them with another, and to assume among the powers of the earth, the separate and equal station to which **the laws of nature and of nature's god** entitle them, a decent respect to the opinions of mankind requires that they should declare the causes which impel them to the separation. We hold these truths to be self-evident, that **all men are created equal, that they are endowed by their Creator** with certain unalienable Rights, that among these are Life, Liberty and the pursuit of Happiness." He left no doubt he believed in God being the Creator and that those in America were his creation. Furthermore, he believed that God afforded Americans "certain unalienable rights."

    According to Bo Perrin of the Black Robe Regiment, "The Declaration of Independence's principles stem from Judeo-Christian principles, alone….So many people have wasted hundreds of gallons of ink as well as millions of man-hours proving that the Founders' epistemology is Deistic and secular. It can't be done! Why? The phrase 'laws of nature and nature's God' historically stretches back hundreds of years from Jefferson's pen to the writings of Locke, Blackstone, Coke, Aquinas and the Apostle Paul. The phrase 'laws of nature' refers to the natural law (Law of the heart) which God placed into mankind. The 'laws of…nature's God' refers to the Scripture. The two are different sides of the same coin. These two phrases cannot be traced back to the Romans or the Greeks! The Declaration committee made sure that the Bible would legally be a part of the American system. This explains the Secularist's unyielding, undying, inexhaustible obsession to rewrite history, invent meanings that did not at the time exist and put words, ideas and thoughts into the Founders' mouths impossible for them to have at the time."[3]

- When he was 37, he wrote *The Virginia Act for Establishing Religious Freedom* as his original plan to give everyone the liberty to worship as they will. Jefferson was quick to assert, "that Almighty God hath created the mind free, and manifested his supreme will that free it shall remain . . ."[4] Jefferson was the first to propose religious liberty in America, and he based it upon the sovereignty and supreme will of Almighty God.

These are only a few examples of how Thomas Jefferson proved his Christianity. In this biographical novel, one will find many more illustrations of this. Although he never spoke of having a born-again experience and harbored irrational ideas about the teachings of Scripture, his faith was proven by his historic deeds. Without Jefferson, America may never have gained religious liberty or possessed the *Declaration of Independence*. In his public documents, Jefferson made certain that God was properly honored as both the Creator and the One who guided the affairs of mankind. Throughout his lifetime, he was branded a deist, an infidel, and an atheist. However, according to Jefferson himself, he boldly asserted, "I am a Christian."

The Teacher Who Lit His Fire

"Maury was a correct classical scholar"
Thomas Jefferson

1757

Thomas Jefferson quietly entered his log-cabin classroom, arms loaded down with an assortment of books. Some were written in English; some in French; some in Latin; and others in Greek. At 14 years old, he read and spoke fluently in all four languages. Other boys his age bragged about their coon hounds, their hunting prowess, their latest river adventures, or their ways with the girls. But he was more into books and flowers.

Jefferson seemed sort of weird to the others. They all liked him, but they didn't quite understand him. For a teenager, they thought he should be more about having fun than spending days and nights reading boring books. They had plenty of wild oats to sow, and this was time to prepare for their harvest.

Jefferson was taller than the others, and his red hair and freckled face made him look stranger yet. Furthermore, his eyes watered from overwhelming sorrow. The dirt on his father's grave was still fresh on his mind. He was a father's boy. No one loved his Pa more than he. Being Peter Jefferson's only son for twelve years gave Thomas his father's undivided attention whenever they were together. The young boy's mind kept recalling the memorable times they spent hunting, fishing, boating, horseback riding, and hiking together. His Pa was a surveyor and loved teaching Thomas all his unique skills in laying out the land. Among all the things he inherited from his father, what he liked the most was his Pa's surveying instruments. He would use them often, and whenever he did so, those exceptional times spent with his father would reappear.

The young teenager also carried an overwhelming burden since his Pa's unexpected death just a month ago. Why did God take his father home at such an early age? He hadn't even seen his fiftieth birthday yet! Thomas was told that God takes the best home with him, but he felt Peter Jefferson was needed more on earth than in heaven. Pa left the staggering responsibility for the care of a wife and eight children in the hands of his teenage son. His father also left behind several plantations with thirty slaves, all inherited by young Thomas Jefferson.

He knew the reputation of red heads to explode quickly in a rage. However, Thomas believed his anger toward God had nothing to do with the color of his hair. What did the Creator need from his father? Did he have some unique surveying job in the hereafter that only his Pa could complete? Since his father made maps, perhaps he was needed in heaven to create a comprehensive drafting of the pearly gates. The young teen had tons of questions for Father God, but he had no answers. In all the books he was reading, he kept searching for some solution to his dilemma.

Once Thomas got firmly planted in his hand-crafted wooden desk, he heard the carefree voices of his fellow schoolmates approaching the one-room school. He readily recognized the tone of Jack Walker's speech, since he was his closest friend and neighbor. However, he was not sure about the others, as they all were new to him. He realized two of them would be the teacher's sons, 13-year-old Matthew and 11-year old James Maury, Jr.

Tom had been properly introduced to each of the boys, but he hadn't sorted them in his mind yet. Tom was the oldest of the six. Dabney was next in age, also 14. (He was from Bear Castle, a prosperous thousand-acre plantation in Louisa County owned by John and Barbara (Overton) Carr). Jack Walker was next at 13. The youngest was eight-year-old James, the son of John and Agatha (Strother) Madison of Augusta County near Staunton. (Not to be confused with his second cousin, James Madison, who was to become fourth president of the United States).

Although their ages varied, they all were in the same class, there being only one room and one teacher, Rev. James Fontaine Maury. Long before Tom lost his Pa, he had pleaded with him to be taught by Maury. Finally, his father gave his consent. Sorry to say, Tom's Pa would not be around to see how this humble teacher could play such an influential part in turning Thomas Jefferson into a man who could turn his world upside down.

Jack Walker was the first to open the creaking wooden door to the rustic classroom. Right away he spied Jefferson.

"Where have you been, Tom? I have been looking all over for you. I thought we would come to school together."

"You know me, Jack. I wanted to get here early and get settled. That way I could prepare my mind for the teacher's lesson."

"Tom, you never cease to amaze me. You seem never to get enough of school and of learning."

Once again, Tom heard the creaking of the door again, and the other three boys came in together.

"Well, I guess you found Tom." Dabney yelled out to Jack.

"That I did. He was right here, buried in his books."

"We saw a bear in the woods, Tom, and we wanted you to see how big it was," Matthew said rather coyly.

Little James Maury was more excited about it than the others. He quickly climbed upon his desk and reached his right hand to the ceiling to show how tall the bear was. "He was a real monster, Tom. He scared me half to death. He was this tall, or perhaps taller."

About that time, in marched the teacher. That was the first time Tom would sit under his tutelage, and he could hardly wait. Tom knew what to expect because Reverend Maury was the rector of his church. The youngster had fallen in love with the passionate sermons of his preacher, giving him the longing to hear more from his role model. He could tell from the pulpit how well-rounded Maury was in the delivery of his messages. Tom wanted to go much deeper than on Sunday mornings. Maury had preached his father's funeral with such fervor that the minister had a significant place in Tom's heart.

Although Thomas Jefferson had been left with the burden of caring for his mother and seven siblings, he knew he must continue his education. Fortunately, he had guardians like Jack's father, Dr. Thomas Walker, to take the oversight of his four plantations and the thirty slaves. To go to Maury's school meant he must leave home. He would spend the week with the other students who lived there, where he would lodge and eat his meals. Arriving the day before school began, Tom was taken on a tour of Maury's house. Being introduced to his teacher's library overwhelmed Tom so much he was speechless.

"Reverend Maury, I've never seen that many books in my whole life." Tom finally uttered his amazement. "How many are there?"

"The last I counted, Tom, there are over four hundred volumes."

"My father had over twenty books in his library, and I thought that was a lot. But yours is beyond comprehension. I didn't know there were that many books in the whole world."

"While you are here, Tom, I hope you will read many of them. They are available for the use of all you boys during your schooling."

"Reverend Maury, you know how much I love books, and I plan to read every one of these."

"Yes, Tom, every time I see you, you have a book open in front of you. Even when I am preaching, I look down from the pulpit to see you are reading a book. Hopefully, it is the Bible or the *Book of Common Prayer*."

"Usually that's what it is, Reverend Maury, but I must confess that sometimes I am tempted to read another book I brought with me to church. My favorite is *The History of Tom Thumb*."

"Now that you are my student, Tom, I will see if I can help remove that temptation. When in church, your mind should only be on God and on the spiritual applications I am sharing."

"I assure you that I will do better at that," Tom ran his finger through his red hair and looked at his teacher rather sheepishly.

Rev. Maury then showed the boys the room where they would sleep during the week. On Saturdays and Sundays, they were told they would be going home to be with their families.

Thomas Jefferson noted that Maury was a short man who was fairly quiet. He only spoke when he had something worthwhile to say, and when he did, his students knew they better listen. He was a man with curly brown hair and piercing green eyes. Whenever he asked a question of one of his disciples, he would point his bony finger toward the boy and look him squarely eyeball to eyeball. Tom's teacher was a strict taskmaster, but he was well respected. They knew he did not have a sense of humor. Jack Walker quickly learned that his foolishness wouldn't be allowed in his presence.

"Now our class will come to order and begin our day with prayer." Rev. Maury announced rather matter-of-factly as he faced his boys.

"In respect of God, we will always stand for prayer." The boys wasted no time rising to their feet.

"I will lead us in prayer this morning, but from henceforth, I will ask each of you to take a stab at it."

Rev. Maury prayed earnestly for each of his students, their lessons and their families at home. Following his prayer, he read from the Bible beginning at Matthew chapter five, referring to the beatitudes of Jesus. When he came to verse three, he asked his oldest son, Matthew, to explain the meaning of "Blessed are the poor in spirit; for theirs is the kingdom of heaven."

After Matthew gave his answer, his brother, James, was asked to explain the second beatitude found in verse 4. Next it was Tom's turn, followed by Jack, Dabney, and finally little Jimmy Madison.

"We will follow that procedure every day until we get through the end of that chapter," said the professor rather sternly. I want you boys to memorize each of these beatitudes, as you will be tested on them.

The remainder of the day was focused on the languages of Latin and Greek, both of which Tom felt he had mastered.

"I have some books in my library which are written in the original tongues of Greek and Latin. You will be expected to read them as part of your assignment here." Rev. Maury walked around the room as he talked, but always kept the boys utmost attention. "Latin and Greek are the classical languages that form the basis for the other languages you will be using. French, Spanish and Italian all come from the roots of Latin. They are called romantic languages, not because they make you appealing to the young ladies. It's because they have their roots in Rome and its Latin foundations. Greek is the language of the New Testament, which you will need to know to be properly educated."

By the time the class was over for the day, the boys were relieved. Although they enjoyed learning, they did not seem to like it as much as Rev. Maury enjoyed teaching it. Mrs. Maury had dinner prepared for the boys as soon as they washed up. She had the five students plus her other five children to feed. They ranged in ages from one to eight. Jack Walker was familiar with them, being they were his cousins. So he felt right at home.

After a delicious meal of Virginia ham with all the trimmings, the boys excused themselves for the evening. They went to the stable to saddle their horses for a jaunt around the base of the Southwest Mountains. Tom's horse, Footloose, was a painted filly mostly brown with white accents. Dabney's was a dapple grey stallion named Dominion. Jack's horse, Wanderer, was a black Arabian filly with white feet. Matthew's and James' mounts were both Appaloosas, one primarily brown, Newby; and the other predominantly white, Milky. Little Jimmy Madison stayed behind, where he was playing with Maury's youngest son, 5-year old Walker. After trotting around a bit, they talked about racing.

Tom decided to challenge Dabney to a race, his filly against Dabney's stallion. He knew he did not stand a chance against Dabney's faster horse. However, he took a lesson from the tomfoolery of Jack

John Harding Peach

Walker, deciding to play a prank on his new friend. Dabney was quick to accept the challenge and wanted to know when he wanted to race. Tom chose to pick a date far enough in the distance so that everyone in both Albemarle and Louisa counties would be able to attend. Tom told Dabney he would race him on the thirtieth day of February. He bet him money his smaller horse would beat Dabney's thoroughbred.

The Carr boy was so excited to accept the bet that he failed to realize that February did not have thirty days in its calendar. No one told him differently until the day approached for the showdown. Finally, it dawned on him that Thomas Jefferson had pulled a practical joke on Dabney Carr that he never allowed him to forget.

Tom and Dabney grew to become the closest of friends, doing everything together. Whether it was taking their long guns hunting, canoeing in the Rivanna River, riding horses or just climbing the mountains, they were inseparable.

One day shortly thereafter, Rev. Maury brought some more of his books to class and told his boys they were going to learn something different.

"The educational ideas of Virginia major on the languages. The belief is the more you know Latin, Greek and French, the more successful you will be in life." He paced the room with a cane in his hand he pivoted on whenever he changed direction. Back and forth he went, marching as if on a mission. Tom's head kept turning to see where he would go next. He knew he must be prepared whenever his teacher stuck out his bony finger and pointed it at Tom. At that point, Tom would see his teacher's piercing green eyes staring right at him. Then there came a question Tom was required to answer immediately. The juvenile's plan each day was to be prepared for whatever Rev. Maury threw at him. After a brief pause, the teacher continued.

"I believe there is more to proper schooling than the classics and languages. We need to understand mathematics and literature. However, equally noteworthy are the subjects of history, science and geography." Tom could tell he was leading up to a question.

"Thomas Jefferson, what is the name of the ocean due west of us?"

"The Pacific, sir." Tom answered without any hesitation.

"That is correct, Thomas. Now can anyone tell me what grand river is in the west that leads to the Pacific Ocean?"

"Yes, Pa, that's the Missouri." Tom was shocked at first that Matthew Maury knew the answer. But then it dawned on him that he was the teacher's son, who had heard that before.

Then Rev. Maury referred to a book written by Daniel Coxe called *A Description of the English Province of Carolana*. From that source, he began a series of lessons which were based on Coxe's travels to the southern and western part of North America. Those were used to help establish English colonization beyond the thirteen colonies. What was so inspiring to Jefferson was that his professor didn't own a copy of the book, only borrowing one for his lectures. Maury claimed he only knew of one copy of the book, and that was one owned by the deceased Colonel Joshua Fry, of which he was fortunate to read in his earlier years.

As Maury continued teaching this lesson, he reminded Tom of his father's dream. His Pa was one of five men who had the vision to capture the West, going all the way to the Pacific. Col. Joshua Fry, Col. Thomas Meriwether, Rev. James Maury and Dr. Thomas Walker (Jack's father) were the other four. Although Colonel Fry and Peter Jefferson were deceased, three other men worked to keep the dream alive. Tom decided to take his father's torch to make sure his long-held vision would be fulfilled.

Thomas Jefferson yearned to know all he could about his teacher. What made him so zealous about what he was teaching? Why did it seem like everything he taught was not just book learning, but it was a matter of life and death? As he discovered the haunting images of his troubled past, he better understood his teacher's consuming passion.

Reverend James Fontaine Maury was born in Dublin, Ireland on April 8, 1718, the son of Matthew and Mary Anne Fontaine Maury. They were Huguenots, who fled France after the overturning of the Edict of Nantes. Tom had read about how King Henry IV of France first authorized that ruling in 1598. It was one of religious liberty in a nation ruled by Roman Catholicism. Finally, the Protestants were free to worship the way they believed would best honor their Creator. That law primarily favored the Calvinistic-oriented Huguenots.

However, on October 22, 1685, King Louis XIV signed into law "The Revocation of the Edict of Nantes." That horrid declaration totally nullified all the religious freedom the Huguenots had experienced for nearly a century. Now, all of a sudden, they were branded by the French government as the "R.P.R. *(Religion prétendue réformée)*. That was translated to mean "the religion called the Reformed." All their religious convictions and freedoms were nullified, making them illegal to worship in France. Reverend Maury passionately reviewed this with his students, firmly implanting these infringements on his religious liberty in their young minds. This was the way the new law read. (Certain words are underlined as Maury emphasized them).

. The Revocation of the Edict of Nantes

"I. Be it known that for these causes and others us hereunto moving, and of our certain knowledge, full power, and royal authority, we have, by this present perpetual and irrevocable edict, suppressed and revoked, and do suppress and revoke, the edict of our said grandfather, given at Nantes in April, 1598, in its whole extent, together with the particular articles agreed upon in the month of May following, and the letters patent issued upon the same date; and also the edict given at Nimes in July, 1629; we declare them null and void, together with all concessions, of whatever nature they may be, made by them as well as by other edicts, declarations, and orders, in favor of the said persons of the R.P.R., the which shall remain in like manner as if they had never been granted; and in consequence we desire, and it is our pleasure, <u>that all the temples of those of the said R.P.R. situate in our kingdom, countries, territories, and the lordships under our crown, shall be demolished without delay.</u>

"II. We forbid our subjects of the R.P.R. to meet any more for the exercise of the said religion <u>in any place or private house</u>, under any pretext whatever, …

"III. We likewise forbid all noblemen, of what condition soever, to hold such religious exercises in their houses or fiefs, under penalty to be inflicted upon all our said subjects who shall engage in the said exercises, of imprisonment and confiscation.

"IV. <u>We enjoin all ministers of the said R.P.R., who do not choose to become converts and to embrace the Catholic, apostolic, and Roman religion, to leave</u> our kingdom and the territories subject to us within a fortnight of the publication of our present edict, without leave to reside therein beyond that period, or, during the said fortnight, to engage in any preaching, exhortation, or any other function, on pain of being sent to the galleys…

"VII. <u>We forbid private schools for the instruction of children of the said R.P.R.</u>, and in general all things whatever which can be regarded as a concession of any kind in favor of the said religion.

"VIII. As for children who may be born of persons of the said R.P.R., we desire that from henceforth they be baptized by the parish priests. We enjoin parents to send them to the churches for that purpose, under penalty of five hundred livres fine, to be increased as circumstances may demand; and thereafter the children shall be brought up in the Catholic, apostolic, and Roman religion, which we expressly enjoin the local magistrates to see done.

"IX. And in the exercise of our clemency towards our subjects of the said R.P.R. who have emigrated from our kingdom, lands, and territories subject to us, previous to the publication of our present edict, it is our will and pleasure that in case of their returning within the period of four months from the day of the said publication, they may, and it shall be lawful for them to, again take possession of their property, and to enjoy the same as if they had all along remained there: on the contrary, the property abandoned by those who, during the specified period of four months, shall not have returned into our kingdom, lands, and territories subject to us, shall remain and be confiscated in consequence of our declaration of the 20th of August last.

"X. We repeat our most express prohibition to all our subjects of the said R.P.R., together with their wives and children, against leaving our kingdom, lands, and territories subject to us, or transporting their goods and effects therefrom under penalty, as respects the men, of being sent to the galleys, and as respects the women, of imprisonment and confiscation.

"XI. It is our will and intention that the declarations rendered against the relapsed shall be executed according to their form and tenor.

"XII. As for the rest, liberty is granted to the said persons of the R.P.R., pending the time when it shall please God to enlighten them as well as others, to remain in the cities and places of our kingdom, lands, and territories subject to us, and there to continue their commerce, and to enjoy their possessions, without being subjected to molestation or hindrance on account of the said R.P.R., on condition of not engaging in the exercise of the said religion, or of meeting under pretext of prayers or religious services, of whatever nature these may be, under the penalties above mentioned of imprisonment and confiscation. This do we give in charge to our trusty and well-beloved counselors, etc.

"Given at Fontainebleau in the month of October, in the year of grace 1685, and of our reign the forty-third."[5]

The teacher's passion for religious liberty burned deep into Tom's heart and soul. Maury kept reminding his students how his family lost everything when they fled France in fear of their lives. If they and their children agreed to be baptized in the Roman Catholic Church and practice all her teachings, they and their property would have been spared. Knowing their passion for what they believed about the Bible, they risked everything as they stood their ground against the French authorities.

Reverend Maury often told how he was born at sea as his parents sailed to Ireland. Not long after his birth, his parents made another boat trip, and that one to America. There they found many other Huguenots who also fled from French persecution. One of those was Rev. Francis Fontaine, brother to James Maury's mother. He was rector at St. Margaret's Parish in King William County when they arrived in 1718, and that was where they settled.

Rev. Maury's father, Matthew, was known to be a passionate Christian, willing to die for his Biblical convictions. He was recognized as a` virtuous man and a tireless worker. He came from Ireland with nothing but the clothes on his back, but through his unwavering desire to eke out a living for his family, he eventually acquired a piece of property in King William County at the mouth of the York River, where he built a modest home he called "Hickory Hill." Through his tireless work ethic, his continued education and his honest reputation, he was elected justice of King William County in 1732, a position which he held until 1744. He also served as sheriff in of the same county in 1739. He lived a long life, dying in 1752.

Rev. Maury's mother was the daughter of Reverend Jacques "James" Fontaine. He was another ardent Huguenot, who also fled France in 1685 due to an earlier persecution from the Catholic-controlled government. Fontaine's fiancée, Anne Elizabeth Boursiquot, escaped by boat with him to England. This was where they later married. In 1694, they moved to Dublin, Ireland, where they were reunited with their daughter, Mary Anne, and new grandson, James Maury.

Mary Anne Fontaine, the mother of Rev. James Maury, was the daughter of a preacher who dared to risk his life for his firm Calvinistic convictions against Catholicism. She was also the wife of a minister who was just as excited about what he believed about the Bible. Although Reverend Maury never suffered persecution himself from the French Catholics, he often said he feared the "papists" more than he did the Indians. That was the legacy of Rev. James Maury.

When a man named Colonel Joshua Fry started the Grammar School for Boys at the College of William and Mary, the Maurys sent James to be a student. That Oxford graduate from England whose major was mathematics made an indelible impression upon young Maury. Among all the things he learned from the colonel, his passion to capture the West, going all the way to the Pacific Ocean, was what he remembered most.

James Maury learned as a child how a caring, dedicated and knowledgeable teacher could help mold the sculpture of a young man's mind and soul. This he used as a model when teaching his students, such as Thomas Jefferson, at his Maury's Classical School for Boys. Hopefully, he would be able to light a fire under his students that would help make the world a better place to live.

After Maury had completed grammar school, he received his college education at William and Mary, where he trained to be a minister. Following his graduation, he travelled to London to receive his ordination into the Church of England. Then he returned to America, where he carried out his ministry in Virginia. In 1754, he was appointed to be the rector of the Fredericksville Parish in Albemarle County. That was the parish of the Jeffersons, the Walkers, and the Meriwethers.

Tom found that Rev. Maury's relationship with the Walkers began when the preacher fell in love. In 1743 he married Mary "Mollie" Walker, the niece of Dr. Thomas Walker (She was the daughter of Capt. James Walker). Thus, Jack Walker was the first cousin of his teacher's wife. Tom was getting used to all the intermarrying of those who were considered "married well and often" among the class of gentile with large plantations.

His church provided him with a Glebe Farm of four hundred acres, where a parsonage was built. Later, he built his log cabin schoolhouse on the same property, where James and Mollie Maury raised their seven children.

At the end of the week, the preacher sent the boys home to be with their families. However, Tom and Dabney seldom didn't make it. Closer to their homes was Castle Hill, the home of the Walkers -

strategically situated between Maury's School and the Shadwell and the Bear Castle homes of Tom Jefferson and Dabney Carr.

• Jack usually encouraged them to stay at his home for the weekends. Dr. Thomas Walker and his wife, Mildred Thornton, always let their guests know they were welcome in their home. They had a house full of children, with Jack having seven siblings all the way from two to fifteen years of age. Jack's mother was pregnant again with another one due in May.

Tom preferred to stay at the Walkers for several reasons. Jack's father was his guardian and became more like a father to him. He also knew the burden awaiting him at Shadwell was too overbearing for him to handle. He wasn't close to his mother and didn't think she would miss him. Besides, he preferred being with his two friends, Dabney and Jack.

Whenever Tom returned home, he usually convinced Dabney Carr to join him. Tom's favorite spot on the Shadwell plantation was what he called "Tom's mountain," believed to be the highest point on the Jefferson property. Tom and Dabney established a tradition of stealing off together to ride Footloose and Dominion to the top of the hill. Dabney's horse being faster usually arrived first. On top of the world, they wandered through the wild flowers, trying to identify each one of them. Tom got excited when he saw a work of nature that was new to him.

Dabney was his soul brother who shared Tom's aspirations. He was like no other friend he ever had. All the other boys considered Tom rather aloof and introverted. They failed to understand why he preferred to read up to 15 hours a day or practice his fiddle for three hours at a time. Why couldn't he have more fun? He was often left behind with a book in his hand while others would take their dogs and go hunting or find ways to play pranks on each other.

Jack Walker fancied himself as the best trickster. Since his father was the local physician, he encouraged his patients to come to his home for their medicine. On at least one occasion, Jack went to the field to gather some lamb manure. Then he rolled the pellets into little balls, covering them with flour. When one of the neighbors came for his medicine, Jack gave him a pillbox with his creation looking like his prescription. Later, the patient returned for more, claiming those pills did more good for him than any he had taken before. It seemed Jack never tired of telling this story to anyone who cared to listen.

One day Tom was with Dabney Carr when they dismounted and tied up their horses atop Tom's mountain.

"Dab, I brought a book along for us to study together." Tom proudly pulled the manuscript from his saddle bag.

"That doesn't surprise me, Tom. I've never seen you without a book to read." Dabney swatted at a horse fly as it buzzed around his ear. "I guess you're waitin' for me to ask you which one it is."

As the two boys strolled to their favorite majestic oak tree, Tom opened up to the beginning pages of the book, "That is *The History of Fortunatus*. It is one of my favorites."

"Why do you like it so much, Tom?"

"It's about a man who received from the goddess of Fortune a purse that never ran out of money."

"How did that happen?" Dabney's excitement grew as the boys sat together under the shade of the grand ol' oak.

"Whatever he took from the purse always was replenished. So he never ran out of money. He could do anything his heart desired."

"Boy, Tom, wouldn't it be awesome to have one of those?"

"Dab, he also had a magic cap. Whenever he put it on, wherever he wished to go in the world, he would be immediately transferred there."

"If you had a cap like that, where would you want to go?" Dabney reached for the book and looked through its pages with Tom.

"I wish I could go to England without having to journey by sea. I've learned enough French that I would love to go to France."

"What do you think about what Reverend Maury's teaching about going to the Pacific?"

"If I had a magic cap, Dab, that's the first place I would go. I wish I could travel there now and return to tell our teacher what I found."

"Why would that be so important to you?"

"It was my father's dream. He helped establish the Loyal Company our teacher shares with us. Jack's father is also a member of that. Pa died young, never realizing what he envisioned. One day I want to see his dream come true."

Tom and Dabney lost track of time as they took turns reading the book aloud to each other. Later, Tom stopped suddenly as he told Dabney his plans to build a house one day on that mountain. As they talked about that, they decided they both wanted to be buried right there under their favorite oak tree. They then made a vow to each other that whoever died first, the remaining one would bury his friend under that tree. Whenever they were home on the weekends, the two would find a reason to steal away together to their secret hideaway. It was there that they would read books like *Robinson Crusoe* or Aesop's *Fables* to the delight of each other.

Another day came for Tom at Maury's school. His teacher entered the room quietly and carefully arranged his books and notes on his desk. The boys all watched patiently and remained quiet. They knew they didn't want to agitate him, getting him in a sour mood. The class was started as usual, except on that day Rev. Maury had the war on his mind. His lesson was from Matthew 5:5 where Jesus said in the Beatitudes, "Blessed are the meek, for they shall inherit the earth."

As the master of the school began shuffling his feet around the room, he started his discourse. "Jesus taught us that if we are meek, we shall inherit the earth. To be meek means that we need to be humble and not think too highly of ourselves. You boys know the colonies have been at war with France. We are now into its fourth year. What you didn't know is that I am the chaplain to the militia in our area. Whenever a soldier comes home dead or wounded, I am the one who must meet with the grieving families. Thus, that war has a profound effect upon me, and I wish it would end soon." He then reached his desk and picked up his Bible before he continued.

"Now, young men, Jesus said the meek would inherit the earth. We're fighting the French to inherit a portion of the earth on that side of the Atlantic. According to the Scriptures, whether England or France wins the war, in the end if we are meek we shall inherit the earth. What Jesus was telling us is that he will reward those who put him first with prosperity and blessing. We have been taught to believe the more possessions we have, the richer we are. According to the words of Christ, our wealth is found in our character rather than in our property. We need to realize that we need to be honest, trustworthy and diligent in all our dealings with others in a humble manner. If we do that, we will be blessed by God beyond measure."

That evening after supper Tom went on a stroll through the woods with Jack Walker and Dabney Carr. Tom picked a yellow daffodil from among the first fruits of that spring's blossoms. That was his favorite time of the year. He couldn't wait until he saw the first blooms of the redbuds and the dogwoods, following the sprouting of the crocus and the tulips. As Jack and Dabney were talking about their plans for the weekend, they turned to see Tom smelling the fragrance of his daffodil while he was lost in serious thinking.

"What's going on inside that head of yours, Tom?" Dabney slapped at a mosquito that had been annoying him.

"I'm just thinkin' about the war. If that doesn't end soon, we might be dragged into that. Jack, what's the latest with your cousin, William Peachey?"

"The last I heard he's still at Fort Cumberland in Maryland. He's now been promoted to Major Peachey by George Washington." Jack's attention was drawn to a squirrel running up an oak tree. "Boy, I sure wish I had my gun now. I'd shoot us some yummy squirrel stew."

"Reverend Maury sure has a full plate," Tom continued his line of thinking. "He's a planter with four hundred acres of land to manage. He's a father of seven children, with his wife Mollie Walker, ready to deliver another one shortly. He's the rector of our church and teacher at our school. Now we hear he's the chaplain of the militia. Is there anything else I've failed to mention?"

Dabney promptly asked, "What about the Two Penny Act? He is vigilant about that. He tries not to talk about it in class, but I can tell it's downright bothering him."

"Well, pray tell, that is the first I've heard about it." Jack admitted he must have been daydreaming when it was mentioned.

"I don't understand it," Tom said as he scratched his head, "but I know it has something to do with the Virginia clergy not receiving the full amount of their salary promised them."

"I think our teacher will not rest until that matter is settled," said Dabney. "He says it's going to court soon, and he will be there to represent the rectors."

Dabney and Jack continued to discuss the matter, as Tom's mind wandered back to the beginning of his life with his dear father. According to his autobiography, this was what he knew about his ancestry.

"The tradition in my father's family was, that their ancestor came to this country from **Wales**, and from near the mountain of **Snowdon**, the highest in Great Britain. I noted once a case from Wales, in the law reports, where a person of our name was either plaintiff or defendant; and one of the same name was secretary to the **Virginia Company**. These are the only instances in which I have met with the name in that country. I have found it in our early records; but the first particular information I have of any ancestor was of my grandfather, who lived at the place in Chesterfield called Ozborne's, and owned the lands afterwards the glebe of the parish. He had three sons; Thomas who died young, Field who settled on the waters of Roanoke and left numerous descendants, and Peter, my father, who settled on the lands I still own, called **Shadwell**, adjoining my present residence. He was born February 29, 1707-8, and intermarried 1739, with **Jane Randolph**, of the age of 19, daughter of **Isham Randolph**, one of the seven sons of that name and family, settled at Dungeoness in Goochland. They trace their pedigree far back in England and Scotland, to which let every one ascribe the faith and merit he chooses.

"My father's education had been quite neglected; but being of a strong mind, sound judgment, and eager after information, he read much and improved himself, insomuch that he was chosen, with **Joshua Fry**, Professor of Mathematics in William and Mary college, to continue the boundary line between Virginia and North Carolina, which had been begun by Colonel Byrd; and was afterwards employed with the same Mr. Fry, to make the first map of Virginia which had ever been made, that of **Captain Smith** being merely a conjectural sketch. They possessed excellent materials for so much of the country as is below the Blue Ridge; little being then known beyond that ridge. He was the third or fourth settler, about the year 1737, of the part of the country in which I live. He died, August 17th, 1757, leaving my mother a widow, who lived till 1776, with six daughters and two sons, myself the elder. To my younger brother he left his estate on James River, called Snowdon, after the supposed birth-place of the family: to myself, the lands on which I was born and live."[6]

Life Wasn't Fair

"Bigotry is the disease of ignorance, of morbid minds."
Thomas Jefferson

1743

Two boys were born at the Shadwell plantation in the shadow of the Blue Ridge Mountains of Virginia in 1743. One was black, and the other white. One was the son of a slave, while the other was the son of a slave master. One lived in a dreary, dirty, rat-infested slave shack while the other lived in the spacious well-furnished great house overlooking the shacks.

The slave baby's name was Jupiter, the son of a compassionate black woman named "Sall". Nothing was known of her ancestry from Africa. To be a slave, who needed any proof of parentage? She would give birth to five children, all born in that dingy squalid one-room shack she called home. Sall was a diligent hard-working woman who not only nursed and raised her five children, but also spent many hours every day laboring in the fields or assisting her master's wife. Sall spent her tedious life under the dreadful threats and barking commands of the plantation's strict overseer. She woke every morning filled with the crippling fear that someone in her neighborhood would be whipped or that she might be raped. Her worst nightmare would happen if one of her children was to be snatched from her arms and sold to another plantation owner.

Born in the master's house at Shadwell was Thomas Jefferson, whose destiny it was to become President of the United States. Unlike Jupiter, he was born in a meticulously sterile room with the blazing rays of the radiant sun pouring though the large eighteen-pane windows. In her delivery of baby Thomas, his mother was given the finest of care to ensure both her safety and that of her newborn. With her mother and sisters present, she had her family physician, Dr. Thomas Walker, to deliver her first-born son on April 13, 1743.

As a white boy from a prestigious planter family in colonial Virginia, baby Thomas Jefferson was provided with the tools to rise to the highest office of the land. His father, Peter Jefferson, owned two plantations totaling fifteen hundred acres. He was the assistant county surveyor and a maker of maps. He held the distinguished title of "Colonel" as the leader of his local militia. Peter Jefferson's grandfather, also named Thomas Jefferson, was his immigrant ancestor from Wales, who came to Henrico County, Virginia, prior to 1679, where his son, Thomas Jefferson, Jr. was born. Peter Jefferson was born on Osborne's plantation in that same county on February 29, 1708. His mother was Mary Field, daughter of Major Peter Field and Judith Sloane, another planter family of colonial Virginia.

The mother of Thomas Jefferson had a richer heritage than her husband. She was the former Jane Randolph. Her roots were traced back to one of the earliest and most notable families in Virginia. Her grandfather was Colonel William Randolph, who immigrated from Moreton Morrell, Warwick, England to Turkey Island in Henrico County, Virginia in 1674. He rose through the ranks of power from the county clerk to the House of Burgesses. Then he took higher steps becoming Virginia's Attorney General and later the Speaker of the House of Burgesses. He married Mary Isham, the daughter of Captain Henry Isham, the high sheriff of Henrico County.

One of their sons was Isham Randolph, born at Turkey Island in Virginia. As a mariner, he traveled back to England to find his wife, Jane Lilburne Rogers. They were married at St. Paul's Church, London in 1717. Their daughter, Jane, was born on February 9, 1721, at Shadwell parish, Tower Hamlets, London.

Jane migrated to Virginia with her parents sometime before 1725. When Peter Jefferson married her in 1739, he named their plantation of residence "Shadwell" in honor of her birthplace.

When Thomas Jefferson was born, he was destined to be successful. Being the first-born son, by rights of primogeniture, he would inherit his father's entire estate. Without any effort, he would become a prominent planter of colonial Virginia. That would give him the right to vote, the right to go to school, the right to lead the militia, the right to be a vestryman in his church, and the right to become one of the political leaders of his nation.

When Jupiter was born, he was destined to become nothing but a slave. He would have no right to vote, no right to own property, and no right to go to school. It would be forbidden for him to be taught how to read and write. He would never be able to lead a militia, as he wasn't allowed even to join one. He would never be a vestryman in a church because he wasn't even allowed to become a member. Jupiter was destined to be raised in a crowded one-room shack with his mother and all his siblings. As a young boy, he would be required to labor in the fields with the other black children of Shadwell. He would live in fear of the overseer's rebukes, insults and the sounds of his blistering whip. He saw no hope for his future, as his fate was doomed into the bonds of slavery.

As was customary in colonial Virginia, many white infants were nursed by a slave woman. For her to wet nurse another child, she must have a child of her own about the same age. Who better to accommodate Thomas Jefferson as a baby than Sall, the mother of Jupiter? Both boys were born the same year at Shadwell and were believed to be nursed by the same woman. She would feed little Jupiter in the slave cabin and then later head to the great house to nourish baby Jefferson.

Whenever little Tommy cried for food, Sall would come running to his house. Whether it was in the middle of the night or throughout the day, Sall was willing and able to give him his anticipated meal.

Throughout his lifetime, Thomas Jefferson was troubled by the bigotry that was shown toward those of African heritage. When Jefferson's father died, he as a child of 14 would inherit Jupiter as his slave. He also would become the owner of Sawney, Tom's father's personal black servant. As a middle-aged man, Sawney was expected to teach young Thomas Jefferson the basics on how to be a slave master. That was necessary because the young teen received thirty slaves from his father's inheritance, including Jupiter and Sawney.

When he was only 14, Thomas Jefferson had no interest in farming and running two plantations, especially when they involved the practice of slavery. Furthermore, when Peter Jefferson died, he also left his teenage son with the burden of caring for Tom's mother and seven siblings ranging from ages 17 down to twins under two years old. Fortunately, Thomas also had some guardians who temporarily assumed that unbearable burden.

Meanwhile, Tom and Jupiter formed a strong bond with each other. At 16, when he enrolled in college, he asked his black soul mate to join him. Thomas Jefferson once again saw the inequality of the races, realizing Jupiter could not enroll as a student because of the color of his skin. In fact, it was against the law in colonial Virginia for blacks to be taught to read and write. As a child, Tom ignored that discriminatory law, teaching Jupiter most everything he learned himself.

Tom and Jupiter spent most of their lives together. As Tom's personal servant, Jupiter knew more about Tom than anyone else. He got his wash tub filled with cold water by 5:00 a.m. every day and served as Tom's alarm clock. He helped the future president get dressed and made sure he prepared his meals. He washed his clothes, cleaned his rooms and helped him with his bathing. He fed and cared for his horse, even making sure it was brushed and shoed. Jupiter served as his right hand man everywhere he went, helping to protect him from danger.

The older Thomas Jefferson became, the more he grew to realize that life wasn't fair to those of African descent. As a lawyer, he occasionally defended slaves who wanted their freedom. Since they had no money, they received their services from Jefferson pro bono.

In one of his cases in 1770 on behalf of a slave, he argued:

> "Under the law of nature, all men are born free; every one comes into the world with a right to his own person, which includes the liberty of moving and using it at his own will. That is what is called personal liberty, and is given him by the Author of nature, because necessary for his own sustenance." [7]

When Jefferson was elected to the prestigious House of Burgesses in 1768, one of his first actions was to file a grievance to abolish slavery. That was quickly squelched. He was informed by that ruling body of Virginia that King George III of England mandated slavery, and it was the law of the land.

When Thomas Jefferson wrote the *Declaration of Independence* in 1776, he declared those immortal words in his final draft "that all men are created equal, that they are endowed by their Creator with certain unalienable rights, that among these are life, liberty and the pursuit of happiness."[8] In his rough draft that he sent to Congress for approval, he proposed once again the abolishment of slavery. He blamed King George III for the cruel, abominable practice of enslavement of the Africans. Since America was declaring its independence from England, why not use that opportunity to prove that all men were truly equal? That would include the Africans and the Indians, as well as the European whites. Thomas Jefferson was furious when Congress voted to remove the paragraph abolishing slavery. He stood in full agreement with his black personal servant, Jupiter, that life wasn't fair for all people.

Women also suffered the brunt of inequality. In early America, women were not allowed into politics and were discouraged to discuss the subject. Since they were forbidden to vote, then why concern themselves with those who would lead their counties, states and nation? Women were neither required nor expected to go to school or to get educated. Their place was in the home trying to see how many male children they could produce for the next generation. Most women of that era were either pregnant or recovering from pregnancy during most of their married lives. Many women died either during or shortly after childbirth, and some suffered an early death due to giving birth to more children than their bodies could endure.

The custom of primogeniture banned a woman from inheriting property from her father. That medieval practice could be traced back to those in Normandy prior to 1066. When William the Conqueror crossed the English Channel to conquer England, he brought with him that tradition that kept women from receiving equal and fair treatment in life. Seven hundred years later, the medieval practice was carried to the shores of America, where it remained unchallenged until the likes of Thomas Jefferson.

Although he benefitted from the custom of primogeniture by receiving his father's entire estate, Jefferson saw how it was flawed. He had two sisters older than he, and they received no property from their father. It wasn't due to their father's lack of love for them, but simply because of that custom of inequality.

That was another practice that Jefferson wanted to see abolished. As early as 1767 when he was only 24, he began arguing against primogeniture. A year later as a Virginia Burgess, he continued to promote his abhorrence for that medieval custom. Although it took 17 years, in 1785 the Virginia assembly finally accepted Thomas Jefferson's recommendation to reject primogeniture. Georgia and North Carolina abolished the same before 1785, and other states followed Virginia's lead. In 1798, Rhode Island became the last state to adopt its abolishment. Although Jefferson worked diligently to make life fairer for all, when he was President of the United States, he could still see the prejudice that pervaded his new nation.

His father had a dream to capture the West going all the way to the Pacific. Thomas Jefferson made it his life's ambition to fulfill his father's dream. Before he could do that, he had to become president and purchase the Louisiana Territory. He next appointed his personal secretary, Meriwether Lewis, to lead the next-to-impossible journey.

Among those who teamed together for the Lewis and Clark Expedition was a slave man named "York" and an Indian squaw name "Sacajawea." Both of them were instrumental in making the dream come true for Jefferson. In fact, without Sacajawea, the Indians probably would have massacred all of those on the expedition. Either that or they would have died on the Rocky Mountains due to the lack of horses which Sacajawea would arrange for them to obtain.

At the end of the expedition, each man received his reward. Most of them were compensated with 320 acres of land plus payment for their services. What did York, the slave of Captain William Clark, receive? Nothing. Likewise, what was Sacajawea's reward for her labors? Nothing. York asked Clark for his freedom. That would be the greatest gift he could have received from his master. Sorry to say, it was not granted. Thomas Jefferson offered free trips to Washington for all the Indian chiefs, but there would be no such trip offered to an Indian squaw. As much as he fought against the inequality of people of different races and genders, towards the end of his presidency, life still wasn't fair for most of those who lived in the United States.

The Tuckahoe mansion of Jefferson's early childhood

The Way it all Began

"A room without books is like a life without meaning."
Thomas Jefferson

1745

Sawney, the personal slave of Peter Jefferson, carried his master's two-year-old son, Thomas, to the gentlest horse in Shadwell's prestigious stable. The black man then carefully climbed on his mount as he secured the boy to a pillow attached to the horse's neck. Little Thomas Jefferson's first memory as a child was the lengthy trip Sawney rode east with him to Tuckahoe. His cousins, the Randolphs, lived in a majestic home on the James River.

Colonel William Randolph, who owned the house and its plantation, died in 1745, leaving his three children as orphans. (Randolph's wife, the former Maria Judith Page, had died several years before). Peter Jefferson's wife, Jane Randolph, was first cousin to the Randolph children's father, and Peter was his close friend. When he died, the following was read to the Jeffersons.

> "Whereas I have appointed by my will that my dear only son Thomas Mann Randolph should have a private education given him in my house at Tuckahoe, my will is that my dear and loving friend Mr. Peter Jefferson do move down with his family to my Tuckahoe house and remain there till my son comes of age with whom my dear son and his sisters shall live."[9]

Although the Jeffersons had a plantation at Shadwell with 60 slaves, they accepted Randolph's request to move to Tuckahoe and care for his children. The house was larger and more accommodating for two families than their home at Shadwell. Besides, Peter knew there was no way he could turn down his dear friend's request.

As the Jefferson family arrived at the James River plantation, they were excited to see all the smiling faces awaiting their procession. From the front step of the Tuckahoe mansion, the three orphan children of the William Randolph family, all ran to greet their cousins and their new guardians.

The oldest was Judith, who was nine. Although she was merely a child, she had been the matriarch of the family since her mother died three years ago. She had been like a mother hen watching over her baby chicks when it came to caring for her younger brother and sister.

Next there was Mary. At seven, she was just the opposite of her older sister. She was full of fun and play. To her, life was no burden at all. Being that she had a younger brother, she became a tom boy. The two of them were always scampering outdoors and getting into mischief. More often than not, she came running into the house filthy and bruised, often crying to Judith with a bloody arm from another clumsy accident.

The youngest of the clan was Thomas Mann Randolph, who was four. He was too young to remember his mother, being only an infant when she died. However, his father's death hit him hard. Pa had tried to spend as much time as he could afford with little Thomas. He was the son whom every planter needed to make his life fulfilled. Without a son, who would carry on his name? Without a son, who would inherit his property? The law of primogeniture in colonial Virginia required that a man's estate would be left to his oldest son. Thus, whenever his wife was to deliver a new baby, her husband paced the floor hoping to hear the cry from the midwife, "It's a boy!" If not, then he would hope for something better the next time around. Col. William Randolph, had to suffer two disappointments before he finally got his needed son.

The main reason Colonel Randolph requested the Jeffersons to move to Tuckahoe was to provide home schooling for his son. Nothing was mentioned about his daughters because they weren't expected to go to school. For his education, the boy's father refused to send him to England or to the grammar school at William and Mary. He also didn't want little Tommy to be sent to a boarding school. He believed the best education opportunity for his son would be teaching him at home.

The Jeffersons brought four children of their own to Tuckahoe. Jane was the oldest at five; Mary (whom they called "Polly") was turning four; Thomas was two; and Elizabeth (nicknamed "Bet") was still a baby. Being cousins, they took no time being warmly received into the Randolph household.

Their mother, Jane (Randolph) Jefferson, assumed the role of mother and matriarch over all seven children, while being pregnant with another. She also assumed the daily responsibility for supervising the household staff of slaves at Tuckahoe. The mansion had four bedrooms, as well as rooms for a parlor, a living room, a dining room and an office. The home was built as two separate residences joined by a long room in the middle to accommodate social gatherings. The kitchen, the overseer's room and all the slave cabins were scattered throughout the plantation. Jane knew she took on quite a heavy burden when she moved to her new home.

One of Peter Jefferson's first tasks was to have a meeting with the overseer of the Randolph slaves, coordinating their activities. By that time, Jane had her "honey-do" list prepared for her husband. All their furnishings and belongings brought with them must be properly arranged with what was already in the Tuckahoe house. To prepare for the education of the Randolph boy, Peter Jefferson oversaw the construction of a one-room schoolhouse adjacent to the Tuckahoe mansion. Thomas Mann was four years old when the Jefferson's arrived, and in one year, he would begin his education.

Thomas Jefferson was two years younger than "Mann", but he was too impatient to wait his turn for being tutored. Whatever Mann was learning was also taught to young Jefferson. As a child, he was an avid reader and an enthusiastic student. His father, as a surveyor and mapmaker, had a library of over twenty books. Before Tom was six years old, he had read every one of them. Although some were law books and some more scientific, they were all the same to Tom. When he was six, he began reading them all anew. He never tired of reading. That led him to tell others, *"A room without books is like a life without meaning."*

The one-room schoolhouse was a rather simple wood frame. However, Peter Jefferson wanted something in it that would make it unique as he designed the ceiling in the shape of a dome. Whenever Tom would day dream in school, he would look up at the domed ceiling and think about its creative design. At an early age, he developed an interest in architecture that would lead to the creation of the some of the most masterful buildings in America.

Fellow students were his two sisters, together with the Randolph children. Since girls were not expected to be educated, they went to school only when Mrs. Jefferson had nothing else for them to do. The only one Tom knew would be with him each day was his cousin, Mann. Pa hired a local tutor to instruct them.

Tom always loved school. He was anxious to learn and soaked up what he was taught. His only problem was that his mind went ahead of the teacher's. That caused him to appear to be bored because he knew what the tutor was going to say many times before he opened his mouth. Once, the teacher found him behind the schoolhouse on his knees praying that his school day would soon be over.

His father's office was his favorite room in the house, and whenever he visited another home, he always wandered purposefully until he fastened himself onto the bookshelves of newly discovered nuggets he could devour. His hunger and thirst for knowledge was extraordinary. His conviction was: *"A mind always employed is always happy. That is the true secret, the grand recipe, for felicity."*

The Peter Jefferson family was faithful in attendance at their St. James-Northam Parish in Goochland County, where Peter served as a vestryman. His son, Thomas, soaked up everything he heard from the rector, Rev. William Douglas, all of which helped to form his religious ideas throughout his life.

While a young boy at Tuckahoe, Thomas Jefferson recalled many occasions when Col. Joshua Fry, Col. Thomas Meriwether, Rev. James Maury and Dr. Thomas Walker met at his home with his father. Obsessed with their dream to one day capture the western part of America, they decided to extend their aspirations all the way to the Pacific Ocean. That was the ultimate goal of what was called the "Loyal Company" by some and the "Loyal Land Company" by others.

When Thomas Jefferson was nine, he returned with his parents to their plantation home at Shadwell in Albemarle County. Seven years earlier Peter and Jane Jefferson had arrived at Tuckahoe with four children. Upon their return to Shadwell, they had two more: Martha, whom they called "Patsy" and Lucy. (Mrs. Jefferson had lost one son at birth and another shortly after birth while at Tuckahoe).

The historic plantation house of Tuckahoe and its schoolhouse have been preserved in their original location with many of the dependencies (outbuildings) and graveyard. The Daughters of the American Revolution (DAR) have honored Tuckahoe with a historical marker underneath one of the trees in front of the house.

> "Over these grounds and to the schoolhouse came the child, Thomas Jefferson, and here the discipline of his noble mind began."[10]

The Tuckahoe one-room schoolhouse

Thomas Jefferson's immediate family

1. **COL. PETER[1] JEFFERSON** *(CAPT. THOMAS[A], THOMAS[B])* was born 29 Feb 1708 in Osborne's, Henrico Co., VA, and died 17 Aug 1757 in Shadwell, Albemarle Co., VA. He married JANE RANDOLPH 03 Oct 1739 in Goochland County, VA, daughter of ISHAM RANDOLPH and JANE ROGERS. She was born 09 Feb 1721 in Shadwell parish, Tower Hamlets, London, and died 31 Mar 1776 in Monticello, Albemarle Co., VA.

Children of COL. JEFFERSON and JANE RANDOLPH are:

   i. JANE[2] JEFFERSON, b. 17 Jun 1740, Shadwell, Albemarle Co., VA; d. 01 Oct 1765, unmarried.
   ii. MARY "POLLY" JEFFERSON, b. 01 Oct 1741, Shadwell, Albemarle Co., VA; d. 1804; m. JOHN BOLLING, 24 Jan 1760, Shadwell, Albemarle Co., VA; b. 1737; d. 22 Apr 1800, Chestnut Grove, Chesterfield County, VA.
   iii. THOMAS JEFFERSON, b. 13 Apr 1743, Shadwell, Albemarle Co., VA; d. 04 Jul 1826, Monticello, Albemarle Co., VA, on the 50th anniversary of the Declaration of Independence, which he authored.; m. MARTHA EPPES WAYLES, 01 Jan 1772, The Forest, Charles City County, VA; b. 28 Oct 1748, The Forest, Charles City County, VA; d. 06 Sep 1782, Monticello, Albemarle Co., VA;
   iv. ELIZABETH "BET" JEFFERSON, b. 04 Nov 1744, Shadwell, Albemarle Co., VA; d. 01 Jan 1773, mentally handicapped (unmarried).
   v. MARTHA "PATSY" JEFFERSON, b. 29 May 1746, Tuckahoe, Goochland County, VA; d. 1811; m. DABNEY CARR, 20 Jul 1765, Shadwell, Albemarle Co., VA; b. 26 Oct 1743, Bear Castle plantation (1000 acres), Louisa Co., VA; d. 16 May 1773, Charlottesville, VA.
   vi. PETER FIELD JEFFERSON, b. 16 Oct 1748, Tuckahoe, Goochland County, VA; d. 29 Nov 1748, infancy.
   vii. SON JEFFERSON, b. 09 Mar 1750, Tuckahoe, Goochland Co., VA; d. 09 Mar 1750, at birth.
   viii. LUCY JEFFERSON, b. 10 Oct 1752, Tuckahoe, Goochland Co., VA; d. 1784, Monteagle, Kentucky; m. CHARLES LILBURNE LEWIS, 12 Sep 1769, Shadwell, Albemarle Co., VA; b. 1747; d. 1831.
   ix. ANNA SCOTT "NANCY" JEFFERSON, b. 01 Oct 1755, Shadwell, Albemarle Co., VA; d. 1828; m. HASTINGS MARKS, Oct 1788, Shadwell, Albemarle Co., VA; d. 1811.
   x. RANDOLPH JEFFERSON, b. 01 Oct 1755, Shadwell, Albemarle Co., VA; d. 1815; m. (1) ANNE JEFFERSON LEWIS, 30 Jul 1780; d. 1808; m. (2) MITCHIE B. PRYOR, 1809.

W 202
SHADWELL, BIRTHPLACE OF
THOMAS JEFFERSON

Thomas Jefferson -- author of the Declaration of Independence, third president of the United States, and founder of the University of Virginia -- was born near this site on 13 April 1743. His father, Peter Jefferson (1708-1757), a surveyor, planter, and officeholder, began acquiring land in this frontier region in the mid-1730s and had purchased the Shadwell tract by 1741. Peter Jefferson built a house soon after, and the Shadwell plantation became a thriving agricultural estate. Thomas Jefferson spent much of his early life at Shadwell. After the house burned to the ground in 1770, he moved to Monticello, where he had begun constructing a house.

DEPARTMENT OF HISTORIC RESOURCES, 2001

Returning to Shadwell

*"Friendship is precious, not only in the shade,
but in the sunshine of life."*
Thomas Jefferson

1753

Young Thomas Jefferson recently celebrated his tenth birthday on April 13 at his father's Shadwell estate in Albemarle County, Virginia. Of all the presents he received, the one he loved most was his new geography book. Although to most boys, a horse, a saddle or a gun would have given them the greatest joy, to Tom it was a book. All through his childhood, he cherished the moments he would sneakily tip toe into his father's study and borrow another scintillating manuscript for his eager delight.

The irritating crow of the roosters awakened Tom from a deep sleep. All snuggled up in his featherbed, he laid there planning that special day. What made it significant was that he had not lived that day before, and he could not wait to see where it would take him. He viewed the first rays of the sun beaming in his open window and decided to stealthily slip out of his chambers with his precious new book in hand. By the time the morning sun had begun showing its image on the horizon, Tom was sitting among the wildflowers on his favorite hillside that overlooked his father's massive plantation.

The tall, lanky boy, his red hair glistening, opened his new book for the first time with eager anticipation. Immediately, pages magically opened that displayed a vast assortment of maps. His addiction to these illustrative drawings of surveys came from his father, whom Tom loved and admired dearly.

Although Peter Jefferson was essentially a planter with five thousand acres to manage, his passion was in surveying new lands and making maps illustrating his findings. How well Tom remembered his father spending many days and nights with Colonel Joshua Fry, as they mysteriously created "The Fry-Jefferson Map." When the drawing was published in 1751, Tom thought how novel an idea it was to name the map after its designers. That way no one would ever doubt who created it.

Joshua Fry was an Englishman who received his title of "Colonel" from his distinguished leadership of the Virginia militia. However, Tom always thought of him as a teacher. The grammar school at College of William and Mary appointed him its first master. Whenever Tom was in Fry's presence, he welcomed Colonel Fry's lesson for the day. He was a budding lad when he first recognized his Pa and Fry were close friends, and he quickly absorbed all he could glean from them. When he saw them working together with their surveys and creating maps, he wanted to follow in their footsteps.

He witnessed them feverishly laboring together two years earlier. They were given the authority and responsibility to extend the boundary line between North Carolina and Virginia. He believed his father was chosen for that task because he was of strong mind and sound judgment. That was combined with an intense desire to learn and establish absolute truth.

Colonel Fry taught Tom without even trying. Tom eagerly learned just from listening to all Fry would share with his father. Fry taught mathematics to the college students at the College of William and Mary. The problem-solving equations young Jefferson learned from Fry added to the skills he would need throughout his career.

After Tom had browsed through the maps in the book, he returned to the beginning and read every detail of his newest prized possession. As he did so, he bathed in the wildflowers all around him. They were his friends and his sheer delight. He admired how God made each of them so unique and beautiful, with their different sizes, vibrant colors and scintillating aromas. Whenever he spied a strange flower new to him, he would feel goose pumps popping up all over his freckled skin. He would stop in his tracks and meticulously observe the exquisite detail of his newly discovered blossom. He always carried a writing tablet with him to record the details of each handiwork of creation.

As Tom tried to divert his attention from his flower friends to his new book, he heard a rustling in the grass that startled him. At first he was frightened, thinking it might be a bear, but rather out from behind a tree popped his close friend and neighbor, Jack Walker. When he saw how startled Tom was, Jack chuckled. He loved playing tricks on folks, and no one was a better target than Tom because he was always so studious and sober-minded. Jack, the agitator, always seemed to catch Tom by surprise and lived for the next moment he could try another trick on his bosom friend.

Jack, whose birth name was "John", lived on the next plantation over from the Jeffersons. His father, Dr. Thomas Walker, owned the fifteen-thousand acre Castle Hill estate, making the Jefferson's five thousand-acres a small farm in comparison. Tom and Jack shared a lot in common, Tom being one year older. They went to school together where they were tutored by the strict Scotsman, Rev. William Douglas. There they studied Greek, Latin and French. Douglas was the rector of St. James-Northam Parish in Goochland County, where Tom's father had served on the vestry.

Both Tom and Jack were the oldest sons in their households, although they each had an older sister to try to keep them on the straight and narrow. Tom was doubly-blessed with two older sisters – Jane and Mary (called "Polly") whereas Jack only had one – Mary, whom he called "Molly."

What contributed to Tom and Jack's close friendship was their fathers' partnership in a venture they called "The Loyal Company." It seemed to Tom they had been working on that project most of his lifetime. Tom also had a bonding affinity to Jack Walker because Jack's father was the personal physician of the Jeffersons, responsible for delivering newborn Thomas Jefferson into the world. Occasionally, the doctor would bring Jack with him to visit at Tuckahoe for a spell, where Tom lived until he was nine.

Jack just had startled Tom from his silence and deep introspection. As he heard the muffled laughter from Jack, Tom suddenly jumped to his feet to turn around. Then he spied Jack trying to hide behind a tree, noticing he had his gun in his hand.

"What ya' doin', Tom?"

"What does it look like I'm doin'? Haven't you ever seen someone readin' a book before?" Tom appeared to be upset with Jack's line of questioning.

"Yeah, I've read a few myself, but I've never seen anyone who was a book worm like you."

"What do ya' mean, Jack?"

"You know what I mean, Tom. You always have a book in your hand. I've seen you from sun up to sun down always with your eyes magnetized to those pages."

"What's so wrong with that? You know I cannot live without books."

"You're only a child, Tom, and you should have more fun in your life. While the rest of us are huntin' or fishin', you're lost in your silly books."

"Don't say such a thing, Jack, because I cherish the times we spend together huntin' turkeys, possums, and bears."

"Then go get your gun, and let's be on our way."

"Would you sit down here and rest a spell before we go huntin'?"

"Sure, Tom, what's on your mind?" Jack splattered himself in front of his friend, stirring up his nest in the wildflowers and tall grass.

"It's about my father's dream. Ever since I can remember, he's been talking about how he somehow wants to explore the western part of that nation, going all the way to the Pacific Ocean."

"Tom, you know how my Pa is all fired up about that too. Since he returned from the Cumberland Gap and what's beyond it, he's never been the same."

"Come to think of it, Jack, you're right. How long ago was that?"

"It's goin' on three years now. I was only six at the time. Pa was gone more often that year than he was home. I hated him goin' away and leavin' us so long."

"But Jack, just imagine what he accomplished. He discovered so much of the western part of Virginia, goin' into the Tennessee territory and discoverin' the Cumberland Gap and all that is on the other side of that vast mountain range."

"Yeah, yeah, yeah, I've heard it all – time and again. Frankly, I'm sick of hearin' about all that. He's a hero to many folks, but to me, he's my Pa, and I don't want to share him with the world."

Tom was stunned by Jack's sense of remorse about his Pa's significant accomplishments. As he glared at Jack, he searched the features of his face and tried to look into the depths of his soul. That brunette, brown-eyed boy had a distinctive pointed nose and a relatively long face. After several moments of silence, Tom said rather slowly,

"Jack, I think you should be mighty proud of your Pa. He and my father and some other men have been chasing that dream of theirs for years, and I think they're onto somethin'."

"Who are the others, Tom? Who else has been taking my father's time from me?"

"Colonel Joshua Fry is one of them. He's the oldest and most educated of the bunch. He must be over fifty now. He teaches mathematics at William and Mary. He was the one who worked with my Pa to make the Fry-Jefferson Map. Did I ever show that to you, Jack?"

"Oh yeah, I've seen that map hangin' in my Pa's office and your house. Frankly, I'm tired of seein' the thing. Who else has teamed up with my father on that far-fetched dream of theirs?"

"Thomas Meriwether is the richest in the group. His plantation is one of the largest around here and the most successful."

"Isn't he the one from Cloverfields?"

"That's right."

"I heard that farm is larger than our Castle Hill. Is that true, Tom?"

"I've been told your Castle Hill is some fifteen thousand acres, but Cloverfields is nearly three thousand acres larger than that. I bet you'll never guess who the fifth man is in that inner circle of dreamers."

"That has to be Reverend James Maury, the rector of our church."

"How did you figure that, Jack?"

"When he gives his sermons, that scheme you keep talking about sounds as if he's obsessed by it as well."

"That's right. In fact, I believe he's the one that keeps stirrin' the pot. Whenever he comes to the house to meet with those men, he leaves with my Pa all stirred up again. His French blood seems to boil in his veins and spill over to the others."

"Wasn't his daddy one of the Huguenots?"

"Sure enough, Jack. Reverend Maury tells how his Ma and Pa had to flee from France due to all the Huguenots being persecuted, tortured, raped and killed when they were under the Catholic rule. If they would have recanted and become Catholic, their lives would have been spared and their property restored. However, they adamantly refused to abandon their religious convictions."

"You have to admire them for that, Tom."

"Oh, indeed I do. I believe everyone should be free to worship as they so desire. Why should anyone be tortured or killed because of his religion?"

"How come our preacher was born in Ireland if he came from France?"

"Reverend Maury told me his Pa was Matthew Maury, and his Ma was Mary Anne Fontaine. They fled France around 1716 and landed in Dublin, Ireland, where our pastor was born. Although he thinks he was born on the boat before they arrived there."

"Is his mother related to the other Fontaines here in Virginia?"

"Surely, she must be. I heard they all have French Huguenot heritage."

"Tom, does anyone else share that so-called dream to capture the West?"

"I understand the one who started the Loyal Company is John Lewis, another Irishman whose ancestors also fled France as Huguenots. then had to flee Ireland because he murdered two men, including his landlord, who wounded his wife and killed his brother."

"Where is he? I've never seen him visit Castle Hill."

"He lives somewhere in the Shenandoah Valley just west of here. He's not in the inner circle with our fathers because he doesn't go to our church or retain business dealings in our neck of the woods."

All of a sudden, Jack jumped to his feet and grabbed his gun. "Tom, I'm tired of all these stories. Bears are out there just waitin' to get a load of this gunshot in 'em. Fetch your gun, and let's get out o' here."

With that Tom decided to join his friend for a few hours away from his first love. That was studying and learning about what was beyond the small world where he lived. Once they started, though, Tom forgot about his books and wildflowers, as the two boys frolicked in the woods until early in the afternoon.

Tom never passed a tree he did not recognize, and if he did, he would stop to take detailed notes about it in his writing tablet. He loved spring, when all his species of trees burst asunder with a newly found splendor of leaves and blossoms. He was excited to see both the redbuds and the dogwoods bringing new life into the world with their impressive blooms.

When they arrived at the Rivanna River bordering Tom's Shadwell estate, they suddenly forgot about the bears. As soon as they laid eyes on their canoes, they grabbed their paddles and ran to their boats. Without boyhood frivolity, they raced each other upstream and downstream and back and forth across the river. Jack loved the times when he would draw Tom out of his doldrums and tedious books. Then, he could see the sunny side of Tom with his rather dry sense of humor and his face all aglow with smiles. Being the trickster that Jack was, he worked hard to get Tom to laugh out loud, believing laughter was a medicine for the soul. He got the feeling that Tom, even at ten years old, was too dignified to utter such trivial sounds from his lips.

When Thomas Jefferson returned home in the early afternoon for dinner, he saw his sisters playing on the front porch. They were like stair steps, with Jane going on thirteen; Mary was eleven; Elizabeth was eight; and Martha would soon be seven. His youngest sister, Lucy, was born last October and was still being cared for by one of the slave ladies. Tom finally got some brothers he wanted, but they both died in infancy. So Tom felt like a thorn in the midst of a rosebush with his five sisters capturing most of the affection from his mother.

Jane and Tom had a strong bond between them. Tom admired his oldest sister's mature demeanor. He could always count on her to be faithful and true to her word. She was like a lighthouse to him, one whom he could always turn to when he was in a dilemma or dangerous water. Tom developed his passionate love for flowers and all kinds of vegetation from Jane. As early as he could remember, Jane took him on adventurous strolls through the woods where she enlightened him about those glorious marvels of God's creation.

Their shared passion for music also brought them together hours upon end - she with her harpsichord and he with his violin. Tom was thrilled whenever Jane sang. She seemed to have the voice of an angel. With her leading the way, Tom loved trying to harmonize with her as they made music together.

After Tom had greeted his playful sisters, he went into the house looking for his father. "Pa, where are you?" He called out several times as he moved quickly through the house. His father was nowhere to be found.

Tom's mother entered the parlor, where she found her wayward son. "Thomas, where have you been? I've been worried sick about you. You weren't in your bed this morning, and now it's nearly dinner time before you come traipsing in here smelling as if you've been out in the pigpen."

"I'm sorry, Ma, I took my new geography book out to read on the hillside among my favorite wildflowers. Along came Jack, and he insisted we go hunting. I should have come to tell you where I was going."

"That's right, Thomas; you know I don't want you to be running off without my permission. Your Pa's been out all day surveying, and hopefully he will be home in time for supper. Now you go wash up and change into something that smells better."

Tom's mother, Jane Randolph, never seemed to bond well with Tom. Perhaps, it was because she had such a noble affluent upbringing causing her to relate more to the prim and proper ways than the rambunctious outdoorsman that Tom had become. After all, she came from the celebrated Randolph family of Virginia, who traced its bloodline to nobility in England. (The Randolphs had held influential positions in Virginia, where they accumulated vast land holdings. Being raised with a silver spoon in her mouth might have contributed to her aloofness to Tom).

Perhaps his mother was so busy having children and preparing to conceive more that she was preoccupied with childbearing. That kept her from giving Tom much individualized attention. (In the thirteen years of her marriage to Peter Jefferson, she gave birth to eight children. She may have lost her last two children after birth because she wearied from bearing so many children in a short period of time).

Perhaps, she related more to girls than to boys. After all, she had five daughters in her care and only one son. Tom's father took Tom under his wings from the time he was born. Therefore, Tom did not seem to need his mother as much as the girls. Then there was Elizabeth (whom he called "Bet"). She had something wrong with her that required lots of his Ma's attention. There was some mental condition that Tom never quite understood. Although he knew she needed more of his mother's time and effort, he somehow felt cheated that his Ma might have stolen some precious moments with Tom to contribute to Bet.

Although Tom was distant to his mother, he loved and respected her. She managed the home well, making sure her children were raised in the nurture and admonition of the Lord. She provided the discipline to confirm they did their chores and learned all their manners. She loved music and dance and taught those talents to her children. She insisted those skills would increase their status as they socialized with the distinguished planter families of Virginia. Tom realized his Ma did whatever she could to raise her children properly, but he was still felt a loneliness in her presence.

After a bountiful feast of wild turkey with all its trimmings, Tom searched in his closet for his father's hand-me-down surveying tools. Next to his books, those had the most value of any of his belongings. Out came the compass, the chains and the steel-tipped pen he needed to practice measuring the land.

Tom then marched down toward the Rivanna River which bordered his father's estate. As he found the place he wanted to begin his measurements, he saw one of the slave boys in a distance. He yelled out to him, "Hey, boy, would you come here for a moment?"

As the black disheveled child instantly obeyed, within seconds, he was standing in front of Tom with his tools. Tom noticed the boy was perfectly black, not mulatto like some. His kinky hair was cut short, and he had the largest brown eyes Tom had ever seen. "Don't be shy, boy, tell me what's your name."

"Name's Jupiter, Massa." The boy's eyes turned away as he spoke, showing his timidity.

"Jupiter," Tom repeated with emotion. "I like that name. It suits you, boy, because it means you are out of this world." Tom paused a moment, waiting for the slave's response. "My name is Thomas Jefferson, but you can call me 'Tom'."

"Yessa, Massa Tom, I know who you are 'cause my mammy done tole' me."

"Who's your mammy, Jupiter?"

"Her name's Sall. I have a sis, whose name is Nan. She's also like a mammy to me."

"Where were you born, Jupiter?"

"I's born right here at Shadwell, Massa Tom."

"You were! How about that? How old are you?"

"I's ten years, Massa Tom."

"That's how old I am too, Jupiter. I also was born here at Shadwell, but for the past seven years, I lived in a place called Tuckahoe. I was born in 1743, and if you are ten, then you were too."

"I don't recollect none what you say, Massa Tom. But if you say I was born then, then that's when it must be."

"Jupiter, see these tools here."

"Yessa, Massa Tom, if that's what you call them."

"They're surveying tools. I was wondering if you could help me as I'm laying off some land."

"Glad to do so, Massa Tom."

"If you are going to help me, please stop calling me 'Massa'. Just call me 'Tom'.

"Yessa, but my mammy say I got to have respect."

"I don't want to be your Massa, Jupiter. I want to be your friend."

"What ev'r you say, Massa..." the black boy had caught himself before he finished. Then he looked at Tom with his first smile. "Sorry, Tom. I's just have to get used to not calling ya 'Massa'."

"That's quite all right, Jupiter."

The boys barely got started surveying when Tom heard the supper bell ringing. That would mean his Pa would be home, and so he hurried to gather up his things quickly. As they walked together back toward the great house, Tom had Jupiter point out the slave cabin where he lived. The black boy was all smiles when he saw how much interest his master's son had shown in him, a lowly slave.

By the time supper was ready, Peter Jefferson walked in the door. Tom was there to wrap his arms around him letting him know how much he was missed. Peter shared his same feelings with Tom, returning the hug and placing a kiss on the top of his carrot top hair. Tom's Pa stood head and shoulders above everyone and was a strong backwoodsman. Descending from Welsh ancestry, Peter had a disciplined work ethic. Whereas Tom's Ma was born into a wealthy family; his Pa had to work hard for everything he received. Tom admired and sought to follow his father's structured role model.

From the time Tom was born, Peter Jefferson tried to teach his son everything he knew about hunting, fishing, paddling a canoe, riding horses and swimming. Although he bore the responsibility of running plantations both at Tuckahoe and Shadwell, separated by sixty five miles and a two-day journey, he always found time for Tom. Peter taught him how to use his surveying instruments, how to sketch maps and how to keep his account books for his farms. Indians always felt welcome at Shadwell as they made their way to Williamsburg. Peter showed them warm hospitality and courtesy, which rubbed off on his son.

Tom was like a magnet to his Pa when they were together – following him to the stables, the harness rooms and the blacksmith's shop. He could never imagine life without having his caring father around.

Because Peter Jefferson learned everything the hard way, he wanted his son to be successful by being properly trained and educated. Therefore, under his father's tutelage, by the time he was five, he could read and write. That's when Tom began devouring all the books in his father's large library. By the time he left Tuckahoe, he had been prepared to take another step up the educational ladder.

Therefore, when the Jeffersons moved back to Shadwell, at nine years old, his father sent him to Reverend William Douglas' Latin School. Being fifty miles from Shadwell meant he boarded with the Douglas family during the school year. When it came time for Easter, Tom travelled home and reunited with his family.

"Where have you been, Pa?" Tom asked as soon as he got his hugs from his father.

"Thomas, I spent the morning meeting with the overseer of Shadwell, and then I had some surveying to do. You know what I always tell you."

Then they both harmoniously quoted Peter's favorite rule, "Never ask another to do for you what you can do for yourself."

Tom was proud of himself that he could say those words as assuredly as his father, even matching the pitch of his Pa's voice when quoting them with him.

Supper to Tom was merely leftover dinner, but he enjoyed it more than he had earlier because his Pa was available to eat it with him. After supper, they both went into Peter's office, where Tom shared what he had learned from his new geography book.

As Tom went to bed, he envisioned what the next day would hold. Being Easter Sunday, all his family would be decked out in their newest outfits. Several carriages would be needed to get them all to the Fredericksville church to hear another one of Reverend Maury's inspiring sermons. His mind reflected on the meaning of Easter and all he had learned from Reverend Douglas about it. He knew that without Christ's resurrection, there would be no freedom from sin. Freedom was a concern that became near and dear to his heart – a passion that would ultimately endanger his personal life and all his worldly possessions.

After Easter Sunday was over, Tom slipped off to the slave cabins searching for Jupiter. With thirty slaves on the plantation, Tom passed by several shacks before he found his black friend. He greeted each one of the slaves he encountered. Although he knew they were bonded servants to his Pa, he still recognized they were human and were created by God. He felt as if they deserved more respect than the white folks gave them.

When Tom arrived at Jupiter's cabin, a rather attractive slave girl opened the door. She appeared to be in her teens with the same stunning brown eyes as Jupiter. He couldn't tell anything about her hair because it was wrapped in cloth. Tom addressed her politely as the girl appeared to be startled. "You must be Nan."

"Tha's right, Massa, but how'd ya know?"

"Jupiter told me about his older sister who was like a mammy to him. I figured you must be the one. May I come in?"

As Tom entered the slave quarters, he was visibly shaken by the dark, dingy, downright filthy room all that family shared together. Equally shocking was the mouse that ran across the dirt floor right in front of him. After he had gathered his emotions, he looked up to see a slave lady smiling at him. "Welcome to our cabin, Thomas Jefferson. I'm so glad to see ya."

"You must be Sall, Jupiter's mammy."

"Tha's right, sir." She was still all smiles.

"How did you know my name?" Tom asked, being a little bewildered.

"Thomas Jefferson, I knew ya when ya was born, about the same time as my lil' Jupiter. I knows ya well."

"Ma'm, I just met Jupiter a few days ago, and that is the first time I have met you. How do you know me so well?"

"Thomas, when ya were born, your mammy needed someone to nurse ya. I was nursin' Jupiter at the time, and I had enough milk for ya too."

Tom grew speechless, as he thought back to those early days at Shadwell. Putting the pieces of the puzzle together in his mind caused him to realize his closeness to his father's slaves. As a baby, he was fed by a black lady, and as a toddler, he was transported so carefully by a black man to Tuckahoe. As he pondered these thoughts, Jupiter stumbled into the room. He must have been running outside, as he was nearly out of breath.

"Jupiter, I'm so glad to see you again." Tom reached out to steady him, so he wouldn't fall. The black boys captivating brown eyes matched Tom's, pleasantly surprised to see him in his cabin.

"Yessa, Massa…." And then Jupiter caught himself again before he finished his addressing Tom. "Sorry, Tom, I almost called you 'Massa' again."

"Don't worry yourself about it, Jupiter. I'm so glad to meet your mammy and your sis." Tom then turned to Sall and asked, "Ma'm, would you mind if your son and I take a walk together?"

"Thomas, my son is here for ya whenever ya want him. No need to ask me any okay." Sall then grabbed her broom and gently swept Jupiter out the door.

From then on, Jupiter and Tom became soul mates, spending many hours together in play and study. What Tom liked most about Jupiter was that he was a devoted listener. After Tom would read a book, he would sit down and tell Jupiter what excited him most about his research. The slave boy always waited in eager anticipation to what Tom would share with him next. As a slave, Jupiter was not allowed to go to school and get a proper education. He was forbidden to learn to read and write. However, Tom taught him so much that Jupiter became more educated than many of the white children. Whenever Tom returned from being away to school for awhile, he found Jupiter waiting to catch up on a week's worth of lessons. Tom always had his notepad in hand and would stand and lecture Jupiter just like Reverend William Douglas did to Tom at his Latin School. That time, Tom took his new geography book to show Jupiter. He found the slave boy appreciated it more than Jack Walker.

Brief Biography of Colonel John "Jack" Walker

Born at Castle Hill plantation in Albemarle Co., Virginia, on Feb. 13, 1744, he was the son of Dr. Thomas Walker and Mildred Thornton. After graduating from College of William and Mary in 1764, he married Elizabeth "Betsy" Moore, daughter of Bernard Moore and Ann Spotswood. Thomas Jefferson served as his groomsman at their wedding. They established their residence at Belvoir plantation in Albemarle County. Jack Walker donated the acreage for Maury's Fredericksville church from a parcel of this Belvoir estate. (This was why the congregation was later called "Walker's Parish").

His father represented Albemarle County in the House of Burgesses from 1761 to 1771, when he turned over his burgess seat to his son, John, who continued to serve until 1775. Thomas Jefferson served with Dr. Walker and later with John Walker as a burgess from Albemarle County from 1769 through 1775. When the Continental Congress convened in 1775, both Dr. Thomas and John Walker were there with Thomas Jefferson.

He worked as a clerk with his father negotiating peace treaties with the Indians. On Nov. 15, 1768, The Treaty of Stanwix revived the dreams of Virginia's speculators for westward expansion, as Six Nations of Indians granted the British a vast expanse of land that included Tennessee and Kentucky.

In 1775, at Fort Pitt he demonstrated his own negotiating skills in a successful meeting with the Shawnees and other tribes.

During the Revolutionary War, he served as an aid-de-camp to Gen. George Washington in 1777 with the rank of Colonel, leading Washington to call him "a very respectable Gentleman." He served as a Delegate to the Continental Congress in 1780, and in 1790, he became a U. S. Senator. John Walker died in December 2, 1809, and was laid to rest at his Belvoir estate in Albemarle County, Virginia

Dying Embers of the Loyal Company

"Here lies the good, the noble Fry."
George Washington

1754

Thomas Jefferson and Jack Walker were nearing their year's session at Reverend William Douglas' Latin School. By now, Tom was bored with his Scottish teacher. He felt the Latin he was learning was inferior, feeling about the same when it came to the Reverend's Greek. The only spoken language he was learning was French and that with a Scottish twang.

After school one April day in 1754, Tom could not wait to quiz Jack about what just happened. As he chuckled aloud, he asked,

"Jack, are you sure you weren't the one that put the frog in the teacher's desk drawer?"

"Why Tom," Jack said with a slightly sheepish grin, "would you think I would do such an awful thing?"

"Because I know you only too well. Whenever you're around, foolishness is rampant. That's why you were the number one suspect when it happened. You didn't fool the teacher, and you don't fool me."

"I must confess, Tom, but I sure felt sorry for that frog. He must've croaked when Reverend Douglas jumped out of his skin."

"Enough of that, Jack, have you thought about what you will be doing that summer?"

"I know one thing. I can't wait to get home to my gun and huntin' dogs. I truly miss 'em."

"You've got to be kiddin', Jack. Don't you realize the danger out there with all that fightin' goin' on?"

"What do you mean, Tom?"

"If you had been listening to our professor, you would know what has broken out between the British and the French. They both want the Ohio Valley because it is so valuable for their fur-trading industry. Young George Washington was sent by Virginia Governor Robert Dinwiddie to Fort Le Boeuf to warn the French they were on English property."

"Tom, I guess the French didn't like what he had to say."

"That's what I heard. They told the English to move out. That land was theirs. Washington returned to Dinwiddie defeated."

"Tom, you tell that story more excitin' than our teacher. If he told us that, it went right over my head."

"That's because you were too busy day dreamin' about the next prank you'd play on him, Jack."

"What happened after Washington returned?"

"Colonel Joshua Fry was chosen by our governor to lead the Virginians to war against the French."

"Tom, is that the same Joshua Fry that keeps meetin' with our fathers about their Loyal Company adventures? Why was he chosen? I thought he was busy surveyin', makin' maps and teachin' at William and Mary."

"True, but at the same time, he was the colonel of the Virginia militia, a position he's held almost as long as you've been born." Jack's face looked bewildered as he listened intently to Tom's story. It was hard to imagine one man could accomplish so many things at the same time.

"How old do you think he is, Tom?"

"He must be in his fifties. I know he's the oldest of the Loyal Company."

"Where is the war happenin'?"

"I understand its focus is Fort Duquesne near the forks of the Ohio River. Colonel Fry has been chosen to be the commander in chief of the Virginia forces, partly due to his familiarity with the Indians."

"Why is that important, Tom?"

"We need the Indians to side with us against the French, Jack."

"I've had enough of that frightful talk. Let's take our guns and go find us a turkey to eat."

"I'll join you, Jack, if you agree to study with me when we get back."

What the boys didn't realize was that Colonel Fry wouldn't be with them much longer. As he would lead his troops of three hundred to Fort Duquesne the following month, somehow he broke his neck falling off his horse and died near Fort Cumberland, Maryland May 31, 1754. 22-year-old George Washington, who was second in command under Fry, came to officiate at Fry's funeral, buried in the vicinity where he died. Washington carved in the oak tree above his grave, "Here lies the good, the noble Fry."[11]

Joshua Fry was bigger than life itself, achieving success quickly. Born about 1700 in Somersetshire, he was properly educated at Oxford University. After receiving a 14,000-acre royal land grant in Spotsylvania County, Virginia, he made his way to America. In 1729, he became the first master of the grammar school at College of William and Mary. Later, he accepted the position of math professor for the young adult students there. Before he ever married, he had become a planter, a house builder, a grammar school teacher and a college professor. He was a vestryman of his church and therefore, a member of the parish's governing body.

Sometime before 1736 he married Mary Micou Hill, a wealthy widow, who came from a family of French Huguenots. She gave Joshua six children, three of whom were sons. One of his sons, Henry, later would marry Jack Walker's sister, Sukey, and one of his grandsons would marry Peachy Walker, another sister of Jack.

Being a planter, a school teacher, a church leader, a husband and a father was not enough for Joshua Fry. It wasn't long before he was elected a member of the House of Burgesses. (Peter Jefferson was chosen to accept Fry's position as a burgess from Albemarle County upon Fry's death).

Fry also was commissioned to be King George II's royal surveyor and in 1738, he was given the assignment to make a map of Virginia showing all its navigable waters. It wasn't until he later teamed up with another surveyor, Peter Jefferson, that he was able to create what became known as the "Fry-Jefferson Map." For a century, that became the official map of Virginia.

When he formed that partnership with Jefferson, he had moved to Goochland County, which later became part of Albemarle County, Virginia. There, he built his house called "Viewmont" on eight hundred acres bordering the Hardware River.

Fry and Jefferson not only worked together as surveyors and map makers but also as leaders in their church, their county and their state. Both were vestrymen, magistrates and burgesses. Fry also became the first presiding judge of Albemarle County.

On July 12, 1749, Jefferson and Fry joined forces with Thomas Meriwether, Dr. Thomas Walker and Reverend James Maury to receive an 800,000 acre land grant from King George II, which they called the "Loyal Company." After Doctor Walker had made the first wilderness journey to discover Kentucky, he returned to prepare for his next assignment. That time he was destined to expand his expedition all the way to the Pacific Ocean - the dream that would capture the West.

Joshua Fry also rose to the top in the military, quickly becoming the colonel in the Virginia regiment representing his county. By 1754 Gov. Robert Dinwiddie promoted him to Commander of all the troops in Virginia.

His credentials for that assignment tilted in his favor due to his understanding of the culture of the American Indians and the harmonious relationship he had formed with them. In 1752, Colonel Fry was one of four chosen to negotiate a treaty with the Six Nations of Indians at Logstown, (near present-day Pittsburgh, Pennsylvania. That gave England permission to build two forts on the Ohio, enabling them to settle southeast of that river.

Thomas Jefferson had been living with Reverend William Douglas and his wife many months before he returned to Shadwell for his summer break. Every day without his family had grown longer than the day before. Before he returned home, he knew his father was determined to teach Tom how to become a surveyor like himself.

Early one summer morning, Peter Jefferson and Tom lit out together toward the Shenandoah Valley, where there was a surveying opportunity awaiting them. Peter's personal valet was Sawney, a slave who had been attending him all Tom's life. Tom believed that Sawney was the one who moved him as a little boy on a horse from Shadwell to Tuckahoe.

Sawney knew by experience exactly what tools would be needed for the job and already had them loaded on one of the Jeffersons' pack mules. As father and son mounted their horses, they were followed by Sawney walking behind pulling the mule. After they had climbed over the Blue Ridge mountain range, they stopped and set up camp at their starting point.

"Thomas, please bring me my compass," requested his father. Although Peter was over six feet tall with broad shoulders that overpowered most strangers, he was generally quite harmless and understanding when he dealt with his only son.

"Yes, Pa. Are you goin' to need your chains at that time?"

"Go ahead, son, and bring those with you. Sawney will help you. Have him also bring those steel-tipped pens."

Peter Jefferson set his compass in position, carefully showing Tom exactly what he was doing and why it was necessary. Then he gave Tom and Sawney each a chain and had them walk forward with them in hand.

"Thomas, remember the mathematics Colonel Fry has taught you. You will need that when you start surveying." Tom was eagerly watching his father's every move and following his directions intently. He always wanted to be a surveyor just like his Pa.

"Son, do you see the carving in that tree?"

"Yes, father. I wonder who made that."

"What you see are the letters 'P.J.'. This is my mark, Thomas. I made it the last time I surveyed that area. We use these carvings to mark the corners of each of our surveys. What we need to do now is start at this point and move forward. You and Sawney take the chains and march down the hill."

Tom realized he must make a straight line with his chain. Sawney did not need any further instructions because he had worked with Peter through most all his surveying expeditions.

As Tom tried to make a straight line, he immediately encountered a bush in his way, full of briars. "What do I do now, Pa? There's no way I can get the chain through that."

"Oh, yes there is, Thomas. You get your axe out and chop it down and get all the underbrush cleared."

"I sure wish I had brought Jupiter with me. He could have done this hard work."

"Son, remember I have told you. 'Don't ask someone else to do something you can do yourself.' Now get your axe and clear the way for the chain."

As Tom was removing the bush in front of him, he saw Sawney having to move a large tree branch that had fallen across his path.

Both of them continued going forward climbing over rocks and crawling under trees. They worked together with their pack mule when they pulled their chains across the creeks and rivers. In some places, the ivy was so thick that they would have to struggle to keep it from strangling them.

Whenever Tom would come to another corner of the survey, Peter would have him take his steel-tip pin and whittle his initials in the tree that marked the spot. Before long, there were many trees that bore the initials "T.J." indicating young Thomas Jefferson had been there. Although Tom did not care for all the obstacles in his way to make his straight line survey, he was always rewarded when he got to make his mark on the tree.

In late summer of 1755, Peter Jefferson heard that his close neighbor and family physician, Thomas Walker, had guests visiting at his Castle Hill estate. They were the Peacheys from Richmond County on the Northern Neck. Following breakfast, Peter enticed his son away from one of his books long enough to visit their neighbors.

"Thomas, come now, our carriage is ready to roll."

"Pa, why don't we ride our horses to the Walkers?"

"No, I want us to go in style this morning. Besides, your mother is going with us. We need to make a favorable impression on the Peacheys."

"Pa, are the Peacheys any kin to the Walkers?"

"Yes, Susanna Peachey was Dr. Walker's mother. That is her nephew, William Peachey, and his family."

"So that would make Jack Walker the grandson of Susanna Peachey."

"That's right, Tom. Now let's get on our way before they leave Castle Hill."

As the Jefferson coach arrived at the Walker's spacious great house, it reminded Tom how much he missed Tuckahoe. The Randolph mansion of his childhood was so much larger and extravagant than his home at Shadwell. Dr. Walker and Jack came out to greet the Jeffersons as they stepped down from the carriage.

"Welcome to Castle Hill, Peter. To what do we owe the honour of your visit?"

"You told me that you would have your kinsfolk visiting you, and I thought we might come to get to know them." Peter Jefferson responded.

"That was quite thoughtful of you, Peter. What a pleasure to see you brought your wife and son. I want all my family to meet them." Dr. Walker greeted each one of them individually before inviting them into his home, where he introduced them to his guests.

"Come here, Peacheys. I want you to meet the Jeffersons." After they all had stood together as in a reception line, the doctor gave the following announcement.

"I hereby present to you Peter and Jane Randolph Jefferson and their twelve-year old son, Thomas."

"And to the Jeffersons, I introduce you to William and Million Glascock Peachey, their young children, Samuel and Winifred; and Will's three brothers, Samuel, Thomas Griffin, and LeRoy."

"I just call them Sam, Tom, and Roy," William smiled and gave the Jeffersons a wink of his eye.

After they politely greeted each other, Dr. Walker escorted Peter and Jane Jefferson to the parlor, along with William and Million Peachey and Walker's wife, the former Mildred Thornton Meriwether. A Negro house slave served them tea with plum pudding and sweet bread rings. The doctor started asking how Peter's health had been. That was when the Peacheys found that Peter Jefferson was not only one of Walker's friends, neighbors and colleagues, but he was also one of his regular patients.

Thomas Jefferson chose to head outside, where Sam, Tom and Roy Peachey joined him. "How are you fellows related to Doctor Walker?" Young Jefferson asked as he strolled down a winding path leading away from the house.

"He's our uncle." Sam replied, as he and the others followed in stride.

"Thomas, you live out here in the woods. What excitement do you have around here?" They waited a moment for the tall red-head youth to answer.

"You wouldn't believe all the important people who come our way." Tom stopped for a moment in his tracks and assumed a teaching posture. "When I was just a lad of six, a young man named George Washington came to Shadwell. He spent the night at our house. Lord Fairfax, who controlled all that Shenandoah area, sent Washington to survey his property. My father was one of those who led the expedition team. The other was Joshua Fry, who was both the professor of mathematics at William and Mary and the royal surveyor."

"You mean the George Washington who is the son of Mary Ball?" Roy was stirred with emotion.

"That's right. I didn't know that at the time, and at six years old, I didn't much care. However, when I got older I was aware of all the adventures of that young officer. I heard he had a letter from the governor he was to deliver to the French authorities at Fort Le Boeuf

John Harding Peach

on the Ohio River. I know you boys have a lot more questions than that. So please just let me tell you the whole story, and hopefully your questions will be answered."

The Peachey boys' eyes glanced toward each other in apparent disbelief. That Jefferson fellow was quite witty for a twelve-year old. They could tell he was more mature than those they knew who were much older. They found he was an avid reader and spent a lot of time with their uncle. He said Dr. Walker's expeditions gave him the desire to explore all the way to the Pacific. George Washington, as well as his father, stirred his aspirations of being a surveyor and an explorer. He was anxious to find out how much land was available between the Atlantic and the Pacific oceans.

"I was surprised to know that Washington would be trusted with such an awesome responsibility in only his early twenties." Jefferson continued.

"The letter was telling the French they were on English property and to leave immediately. Well, I didn't hear any more from Washington until the following spring. He was ordered by Gov. Dinwiddie to go to Fort Duquesne and take it by force. Later on that year, I heard the French got the better of him, and he was forced to surrender."

"That doesn't sound good for us." Sam offered.

"I'm afraid your right, Sam. I predict it won't be long before we are at all-out war with the French. You mark my words. That day is sure to come."

During the lengthy stroll around the grounds of Castle Hill, Thomas Jefferson asked many questions about how the Peacheys and Glascocks got their start in Virginia. They told him about how their great grandfather, Samuel Peachey, came to America about 1659 from Mildenhall, Suffolk, in England. He acquired a six-hundred acre plantation on the banks of the Rappahannock River in what became known as Richmond County, Virginia. There, he built his great house he called Milden Hall, named after his place of birth. That has been the homestead for five generations of Peacheys.

The Glascocks had their origin in America when Thomas Glascock came from St. Mary's Whitechappell, Middlesex in England before 1639. Among his children were two sons, Gregory and Thomas. They passed on their family name to their sons and grandsons in Virginia. Million Glascock, wife of William Peachey, is the great great granddaughter of her immigrant ancestor, Thomas. She was born and raised at Indian Banks, built in 1699 by her grandfather, George, which was also on the banks of the Rappahannock River in Richmond County.

"How are the Walkers related?" the young Jefferson quizzed them.

"We've been told his grandfather, John Walker, came from Staffordshire, England to Virginia sometime before 1650," Sam said with practical certainty. "His son, Thomas, married Susanna, daughter of William and Phebe Peachey of Milden Hall. Their oldest daughter, Mary Peachey Walker, married Dr. George Gilmer, a noted physician in Williamsburg, where he also served as mayor."

"Dr. Thomas Walker was one of his sons," added Roy, "and he was trained in medicine by his brother-in-law, Dr. Gilmer, a Scottish graduate of the renowned Edinburgh University,"

"Dr. Walker then married Mildred Thornton, the widow of the wealthy Nicholas Meriwether," said Tom Peachey, "That is how they acquired that large plantation."

"Your Uncle Walker has certainly made a name for himself," responded Jefferson. "I'm so glad he's doing all he can to fulfill the dream of capturing the West."

After he returned to Milden Hall in Richmond County, William Peachey received his orders from George Washington to serve as a captain and to organize a regiment for battle. On Sept. 3, 1755, Washington's mandate came from Williamsburg, Virginia, directing each captain to "raise thirty men" to serve in his regiment. Capt. William Peachey had been anticipating that assignment since the inception of the war. Thankfully, he had completed his visits to his kinfolks in the backwoods country before Washington needed him. After he had selected his men carefully, he was ordered to proceed to Fort Cumberland. He already was familiar with that garrison, as he recalled it was near the burial site of Col. Joshua Fry. George Washington referred repeatedly in his letters to Will Peachey as "Capt. Peachy", leaving the "e" out of his surname. Will got used to the change and continued its use thereafter, as found in the names of his descendants. His primary duty during the French and Indian War was to guard the garrison at Fort Cumberland (now in Maryland).

Within a month of Capt. William Peachey's receiving his orders to lead his regiment to battle, Thomas Jefferson finally welcomed into that world his first brother, Randolph, born on October 1, 1755. Amazingly, not only did he get a brother, but at the same time a new sister, Anna, was born as his twin. Now his parents had eight children at Shadwell, all less than sixteen years of age and all but two being girls.

The Loyal Company team of five within a few years lost several members. Col. Joshua Fry died in 1754. Toward the end of 1756 or early 1757, Col. Thomas Meriwether said his final adieus to the world at the early age of 43. That left his wife, Elizabeth Thornton, as a widow with the charge of ten children under twenty one. They were all unmarried, the youngest being a newborn infant. Her husband left for his inheritance an estate of over two thousand acres.

That left Col. Peter Jefferson, Dr. Thomas Walker and Rev. James Maury to carry on the mission of the Loyal Company. As summer drew near in 1757, soon one of these would no longer be around.

Thomas Jefferson and Jack Walker returned from Reverend Douglas' school for the summer. Tom let Jack know he did not intend to return. He had enough of Douglas and his wife's moldy pies. Tom believed he learned all he could from the ol' Scotsman. His father already had granted his permission for Tom to move to Reverend James Maury's Classical School for Boys next year.

During the summer, Peter Jefferson became seriously ill. He called for his trusty neighbor, Dr. Thomas Walker, to attend to his needs. Whatever the doctor was doing for Jefferson, it did not seem to cure him. Repeated visits were made to Shadwell by Dr. Walker in which Tom overheard one of their conversations.

"Doc, I am distressed over what is happening to our plans to reach the West." Peter said rather weakly as he lay on his bed of affliction, Dr. Walker monitoring his condition.

"That's right, Pete, you can't expect me to journey to the Missouri River and beyond with all this war going on."

"Well, Doc, It shouldn't take long. Soon we should be able to proceed."

"I sure hope you're right. I believe this is going to be quite a lengthy engagement." When the doctor said that, he could see his patient had slumbered into temporary unconsciousness. He decided to leave for the time and let him get some needed rest.

During the time of his long bereavement, Peter Jefferson received comfort whenever he heard the music from his children. Tom and Jane played and sang together, he on his fiddle, and she on her harpsichord. He was so proud of his wife and children. When he heard his son's and daughter's melodious harmonies, he was reminded how much he loved them.

Thomas Jefferson

All his loved ones spent a lot of time praying about Peter's ongoing illness and were distraught that he wasn't improving. Dr. Walker stayed close at hand and came to Shadwell regularly during the summer. On another occasion, Tom overheard his father saying to the doctor,

"Doc, if I don't pull through this, I want to ask if you will do me a favor."

"Whatever you wish, consider it granted."

Peter Jefferson struggled to lift himself up on his left elbow, as he looked into Dr. Thomas Walker's eyes noticing his bushy grey eyebrows. "Doc, can I trust you to become the guardian of my son, Thomas?"

After a moment of silence and reflection, the doctor said with a smile and a twinkle in his eye, "Your wish is granted, Pete. I would be proud to be your son's guardian. I swear I will do my best to raise him to follow in his father's footsteps."

With that, Jefferson settled himself back in his prone position and relaxed. "That would mean everything to me, Doc. Thank you so much."

Soon thereafter, on August 17, 1757, Colonel Peter Jefferson took his final breath and left this world behind. Being ill for the past two months, he had time to make his peace with God. His legacy included surveying tens of thousands of acres in the wilderness frontier and, with Colonel Fry, he accurately mapped Virginia. Eventually, his son, Thomas, would prove to be the greatest legacy Peter gave to his country.

His pastor, Reverend James Maury, preached his well-attended funeral and committed his body to the grave at Shadwell.

Peter's wife, Jane, was only 36 when she became a widow, with eight children to raise at Shadwell. Following his funeral, all his family and friends remained in a state of shock and disbelief for several months.

"How could such a staunch, muscular, seemingly healthy man lose his life at the early age of 49?" That was the question people kept asking themselves. There was never an answer to their dilemma.

Peter Jefferson left Thomas, his oldest son, his plantations which had accumulated to 7500 acres. The young teenager now bore the responsibility of caring for his Shadwell estate, for his mother, and for his seven siblings.

That was a staggering responsibility heaped upon a fourteen-year old child. It was not one he accepted willingly. His father specified in his will that his desk of cherry wood, his extensive library of about fifty books, his surveying instruments, notes and journals and his account books would be given to Tom. What was the most precious to him was his father's family Bible and prayer book. However, none of that would replace his father. Life would never be the same without the man whom he dearly loved.

Following his father's death, Tom found no pleasure in reading. When he tried to play his violin, the music he tried to create was in grating discord. When he took his Pa's instruments and tried his hand at surveying, he found it was pointless. When he tried to use his quill on his father's account books, he found nothing to write. Rather than grow closer to his mother, he seemed to grow more distant and aloof. His sister, Jane, did her best to console him, but even his love and respect for her was of little consolation.

When Peter died, he also left his trusted Negro servant, Sawney, to become his son's property. That provided Tom with a man who knew how to care for his father in every detail. Sawney was the man who helped his Pa bathe, shave, get dressed, cook his meals, and keep him on his schedule. He also cared for his horse and saddled it for his master's riding. He knew all about Shadwell and the other slaves and how to manage them. To Thomas, Sawney would be an invaluable asset. However, even he could not arouse Tom from his doldrums.

Although Jupiter knew Tom's feelings, nothing he could say would touch the lost boy's soul. Jack Walker, Tom's good friend and neighbor did his best to cheer him, even trying some of his practical jokes to distract him from his remorse. Still Tom would not budge.

Finally, one day shortly thereafter, the doctor paid a visit to Tom. Dr. Thomas Walker had been his father's physician and the one who helped bring Thomas Jefferson into the world. Now he came as one of Tom's guardians because of his father's dying wish. (Peter Randolph, his mother's cousin; and John Harvie, were executors of Tom's father's will. They, along with Dr. Walker, also were charged with the guardianship of Tom).

The doctor's call came shortly after breakfast. Sawney spied his carriage coming up the dusty road to Shadwell. He tried to get everyone prepared to warmly welcome Dr. Walker.

When the two white horses from Castle Hill pulled the coach to a stop, the slave driver opened the door for the doctor to step out. Once Walker's feet hit the ground, he turned around to help a young lady appear. Stepping out of the carriage in her blue dress wearing her white mob cap was Mrs. William Peachey, the former Million Glascock. She came to the funeral of Tom's father, all the way from Richmond

County. Since her husband was away in the war, she found it necessary to visit his Walker cousins without him.

While Tom awaited their arrival, he was questioning the purpose of their visit. When Sawney escorted them into the Shadwell home, Tom followed them to greet his mother and sisters. Jane was always the first to come forward, being the friendliest of the Jefferson children. Tom tried to remain aloof from the visitors, not wishing to reveal his feelings of deep depression. After they all had socialized around some homemade apple cider, Dr. Walker broke the formalities when he asked to meet with Tom alone in his father's office.

"Thomas, as you know by now, your father placed on me the staggering responsibility of being your guardian. I only agreed to do that because of the fondest respect and admiration I had for your father. I know you had a strong bond with your father, and you haven't been the same since he left us. However, it's time to move ahead with your life. Your mother and family need you. Shadwell needs you. Your father's primary order for you was that you should continue your schooling. He always considered that to be of paramount importance from the time you were only a lad of five."

"Doc, I don't want to go back to Reverend Douglas' school," Tom asserted himself as he sat up and looked into Dr. Walker's eyes.

"Tom, your Pa and I agreed you will now go to Reverend James Maury's school. Is that what you want?"

"Oh, yes, that's what I want. I like our Pastor Maury. His sermons always seem to inspire me. I long to hear more from him."

"That's settled then. You will need to move to Maury's school soon to begin your new school year. Since that isn't that far away, you will be able to come home on the weekends to tend to your Ma and your family."

"I'll be glad to get back in school, Doc."

"I was hoping this would encourage you. I have been quite concerned with the way you've been acting. You need a change of scenery, and I believe that will help you."

"Will Jack be going to Maury's school also?"

"Yes, he will be joining you. The two of you seem to be inseparable, and there's no way I would want to come between your friendships."

That brought a long-awaited smile to Tom's lips, causing Dr. Walker assurance that Tom's passion for life would be restored as soon as he was off to school. After Christmas and the New Year of 1758 in the dead of winter, Tom and Jack began their studies in Maury's school.

In the beginning, there were five men who had a dream to capture the West. With Peter Jefferson, Thomas Meriwether and Joshua Fry now deceased, only two of the visionaries still remained. They were Dr. Thomas Walker, the guardian of Thomas Jefferson, and Rev. James Maury, who was Tom's tutor. With these men around, there was little chance the dream of Jefferson's father would be extinguished from Tom's thinking.

College of William and Mary

"Nothing can stop the man with the right mental attitude from achieving his goal; nothing on earth can help the man with the wrong mental attitude."
Thomas Jefferson

1760

When Christmas arrived in 1759, Thomas Jefferson was nowhere to be found at his home in Shadwell or with his family. Instead, he accepted an invitation to a party where he was introduced to Patrick Henry. That stalwart of a man was seven years Tom's senior, but he failed to show the maturity Tom was expecting. While Tom tried to engage him in discussion and debate about vital issues, Henry was having the time of his life dancing and telling dramatic tales to whomever would listen.

The only thing the two of them seemed to have in common was they both loved to fiddle, and both brought their instruments. They were the delight of the party as they played their merry tunes on their fine-crafted violins. Since Tom was studious and sober-minded and Patrick was a happy-go-lucky carefree soul, only destiny would bring them back together to help change the world.

Following Christmas, Tom was found at Chatsworth, the majestic great house of his uncle Peter Randolph, who was one of his three guardians. He was paving the way for the opportunity to go to college. Tom convinced his uncle he needed to reach a higher level of his education. He had spent two years of inspirational teaching under Reverend Maury, and now he was 16. He believed if he was in

Williamsburg, the capital of Virginia, he would acquaint himself with many of the influential leaders of the colony.

When he returned to Shadwell after New Year's Day in 1760, he wrote to a second guardian, John Harvie, pleading his case. Once he received his permission, he had two others to contact. Having only one other guardian, he cleared his proposal with Dr. Thomas Walker. Although Walker approved that, he did so reluctantly, as he hoped Tom could wait until the doctor's son, Jack Walker, could join him the following year.

Tom realized the most difficult one to convince would be Rev. James Maury, who had been like a father figure to Tom. Although he admired his teacher and grew like a weed under his tutelage, he knew he must take the next step up the educational ladder. By now Tom had read most, if not all, the books in the preacher's library. He kept hearing of the bustle of the city and came to realize he would never advance in society unless he moved to Williamsburg.

After the Christmas break, Tom returned to Maury's School, where he waited for the ideal time to meet with his teacher. Finally, the day came when James Maury and Tom were together alone.

"You asked to see me privately, Thomas." Maury took his seat behind his desk, with Tom sitting across from him.

"Yes, Reverend Maury, I am here to inform you I am planning to go to college." Tom tried to match the sober-mindedness of the man he was facing.

"That's wonderful, Tom, I am only too pleased for you. When do you plan to go?"

"Right away, sir." Tom looked away, finding he couldn't peer into his teacher's piercing eyes. He was sure Rev. Maury wouldn't want him to go.

"What?" Maury stood to his feet immediately, pushing his chair away from the desk. "You are only 16 and too young to go to college!"

"Well, sir, I have received permission from all three of my guardians. They believe I am old enough to further my education and have agreed for me to begin attending William and Mary."

"Then there is nothing I can say to discourage you," Maury pranced the room striking his can on the wooden floor as he moved about. "I have been privileged to be your teacher, and I was looking forward to the opportunity to help you learn more."

"I figured that is the way you felt and thus, I found it difficult to approach you about this." Tom ran his fingers through his reddish blonde hair as he started to stand to his feet.

"Thomas, before you leave, I have three requests of you."

"What are those, sir?"

"When you began school here, I asked you to keep a notebook of all you learned in and out of school. That was a way for you to keep track of the new things you discovered and how you felt about them. Have you done so, Thomas?"

"Oh yes, sir, I have my notebooks all completed up to date. I truly appreciate you encouraging me to do that. I plan to continue this practice for the rest of my life."

"I am pleased to hear that. One other concern I have for you. Remember what I have been teaching you about the Loyal Company."

"Yes, sir, that is a subject that is dear to my heart. As a child, I first heard about that company and the dream you men had from my father. That was to go beyond the Alleghenies all the way to the Pacific Ocean."

"That's right, Thomas. Do you remember the others who were leaders in that Loyal Company?"

"They would each come to my father's home and meet with him regularly. One was Colonel Joshua Fry, who died in 1754. Another one was Thomas Meriwether, who died just before my Pa."

"Right again, Thomas. When your father died, that left only two to keep the dream alive."

"One was my guardian, Doctor Walker, and the other was you, my beloved teacher." Tom told his teacher rather proudly.

"Thomas, the two of us left have been trying to keep that vision alive within you, and if you go to college, I feel you may forget your father's dream."

"I promise you, Reverend Maury, I never will forget it. My ambition is that soon that war will come to an end so that your company can continue its goal to capture the West."

"Now for my last request, Thomas. I have saved the best 'til last."

"What might that be?" Tom was all ears.

"I want you to remember what I taught you faithfully about Jesus and his Sermon on the Mount. If you follow those words, you will never go wrong."

"I'm glad you brought that up, sir. I wanted to let you know how much I have learned from all you have taught, especially your words that came from the Bible. They will follow me all the days of my life."

"That being said, young man, there should be no barriers left for you to enroll at College of William and Mary. I give you my utmost blessing. Be sure to take your Bible and your prayer book with you."

"I'll be sure to always have them with me. My father left me both his family Bible and his *Book of Common Prayer.*

"Do you remember why I have taught you their purpose?"

"Yes, sir. I will need the Bible for study and the prayer book for worship. These will be my constant companions."

With that Rev. Maury bowed his head and offered an earnest prayer for the safety and well-being of Thomas Jefferson.

On March 25, 1760, Williamsburg welcomed a new student to its college. The boys there saw in Tom a boy who at six feet was taller than others his age. His reddish-blonde hair was a dead giveaway. Tom was a country boy who was rather shy and naïve when it came to the social affairs of Virginia's capital. He brought his personal servant, Jupiter, with him. He knew that by being a slave, he wouldn't be allowed to enroll in classes. But he would be able to stay with Tom to assist to his needs and those of Footloose, his horse.

Although Tom enrolled in College of William and Mary for his education, he found himself sidetracked by the night life of the others. Quickly, he befriended a student his own age named John Page, who helped introduce him to his new adventures.

John was born four days after Tom in the majestic manor home of Rosewell in Gloucester County. He came from the influential lineage of planters, which began with the marriage of his great grandfather, Mann Page, to Judith Harrison Carter, the daughter of Robert "King" Carter. (He was called "King" because as the chief proprietary of the Northern Neck of Virginia, he accumulated 330,000 acres of land and owned a thousand slaves). When he died in 1732, also in his estate was 10,000 pounds sterling. He and his first wife, Judith Armistead, had four children who survived adulthood, including Judith Harrison Carter, the great grandmother of John Page.

When Mann Page married into the Carter wealth, he brought some riches of his own. His father, Matthew Page, came to Virginia from England about 1650 and was remembered as the one who donated the land on which to build Williamsburg's historic Bruton Parish Church.

Every time Tom and John went to church, they passed by the tomb of Matthew Page next to the front door.

After the two boys became friends, John Page invited Tom to his home. His father, Mann Page II, sent a chariot pulled by four white horses to escort the boys to Rosewell. Tom was speechless when he saw the slave drive the carriage right up to the steps of the college. He was fancifully dressed wearing white gloves and boots with a brilliant shine. When he saw the method of transportation, he could only imagine what splendor was awaiting them. The chariot took them as far as Yorktown, where there was a sloop awaiting them, attended by Negro men in more rustic garb. As they sailed across the York River, Tom couldn't wait to see where they would land. It pleased John to keep him in suspense. No matter how many questions Tom asked, he would have to wait until he arrived at his destination before they were answered.

When they landed on the other side, another carriage was awaiting them with yet another slave driver. After the boys entered the coach, they were transported to Rosewell, one of the most majestic homes in Virginia. Tom thought Dr. Walker's Castle Hill home was immense, but John's Rosewell home dwarfed any house Tom had seen before. After his parents warmly welcomed the boys, they turned them loose so John could give Tom the royal tour. Rosewell was three stories high with twenty-three rooms. What Tom saw at Rosewell was a home fit for a king.

Although Tom was impressed with all the carved mahogany covering the walls, he was even more excited with the majestic staircase wide enough for eight boys to walk side-by-side from one floor to another. When he saw the unique carvings on the handrails of the staircase, he was reminded of Tuckahoe. He paused to remember that his cousin, Thomas Mann Randolph, was the son of Maria Judith Page, who was born at Rosewell. Thus, when she married and moved to Tuckahoe, her father instructed his craftsman to match the engravings of the handrails at Rosewell with those of Tuckahoe. After all these years, Tom beheld the maternal heritage of Thomas Mann.

John Page continued to be the dearest friend of Thomas Jefferson, not because of his wealth, but because of their common interests. John's father sent his son to William and Mary's grammar school for boys when he was 14. Thus, by the time Tom arrived several years later, he found John was well rooted in the activities of Williamsburg. Although that was advantageous to Tom, it became a distraction to him during his first year of college. The boys regularly took part in the social affairs where Tom began flirting and dancing with many of the finest young women around. He often took his fiddle, where he played for their minuets and reels and joined in the singing at the parties. Tom, though truly an introvert, became one of the friendliest, most likeable young men of the college.

Dr. William Small taught science, mathematics and philosophy at the college, and Tom became one of his prized students. Although he was only his teacher for two years, he became like a father to Tom. George Wythe was his law professor. Tom was amazed whenever he saw Wythe walk because he always held his hands behind him, one hand holding the other. He also admired how splendidly he dressed, appearing to be a disciplined person as a man of conviction.

Both Small and Wythe were best friends with Governor Francis Fauquier, who had been sent from England to represent King George III. The two professors invited Thomas Jefferson to join their threesome at the Governor's Palace, where he was warmly accepted by the governor. There Tom enjoyed delectable dinners of wild duck and oysters as he learned the latest political news and events in the colonies, as well as abroad. Tom claimed those three men "fixed the destinies of my life."

After his first year at William and Mary, Tom realized he had been going the wrong direction. His close friends, Dabney Carr and Jack Walker, arrived on campus as new students and helped bring him back to reality. He knew if he continued with his jovial ways he would become, in his own words, "worthless to society." John Page, Jack Walker and Tom were among six boys who were members of the first college fraternity of the colonies, the F.H.C. society, derived from the Latin "fraternitas, humanitas et cognito."

Organized in 1750, it was identified with a silver badge and a secret handshake as it held parties in the upper room of both the Crown and Raleigh Taverns. Years later Tom despairingly remarked about the fraternity that "it had no useful object."

Tom, being an extremist, decided he must make up for lost time in his second year of college. Although he was glad to be reunited with Dabney and Jack and continued his friendship with John Page, he started a new life for himself.

Every morning he would arise at five o'clock and have his personal slave, Jupiter, bring a wash tub of cold water where Tom soaked his feet. He believed that would keep sickness away from his door. He would then hit his books, studying as long as fifteen hours a day. His daily routine also included a two-mile run, his violin practice and a horseback ride on Footloose. As much as he cherished education, he valued his health more. He was quoted as saying, "Leave all the afternoon for exercise and recreation, which are as necessary as reading. I will rather say more necessary because health is worth more than learning."

His disciplined physical exercise routine and healthy eating habits contributed to his longer-than-usual lifespan. Early in life, he learned to eat healthy, preferring vegetables and fruits rather than meats and fattening foods. He refused to use tobacco or to gamble and tried not to become entangled with questionable activities of needless quarrels.

Without Jupiter's constant assistance, Tom knew he never could keep such a schedule. He depended on personal servant, with whom he was raised, to wake him up each morning, to prepare his meals, to help him get dressed, to clean his clothes and to care for his horse. Dabney, Jack and John also depended heavily on the slave boys their fathers sent with them to Williamsburg.

Tom studied every subject available including agriculture, astronomy, calculus, chemistry, history, the languages and physics. He was personally tutored by Dr. Small in math, science and philosophy because the teacher saw in Tom one who was destined for greatness. Whenever Tom wanted to learn more about the laws of the land, he would turn to George Wythe, the first and finest law professor in the colonies.

Although Tom was deeply involved in his daily routine of study and exercise, he still found time to look at the young ladies who passed his way. One of these was Rebecca Burwell, one of the most beautiful women in Williamsburg, of whom he fell in love. He tried repeatedly to propose to her, but his shyness caused him to stumble with his words each time. He wrote romantic poems to her, but he lacked the courage to send them. Before he could bring himself to let her know his true feelings, she gave her hand in marriage to another man. Although Tom tried to keep his emotions in check, from that point on, he had experienced what it was like to live with a broken heart. The loss of his first love led to the beginning of excruciating headaches he experienced in times of crisis throughout the rest of his life.

Thomas Jefferson would never have achieved greatness if he hadn't developed strong bonds with some of the brightest minds of successful men. Beginning with his school days at the College of William and Mary, he surrounded himself with skilled and loyal friends whom he developed over his lifetime. He was quoted as saying, "Friendship is precious, not only in the shade, but in the sunshine of life; and thanks to a benevolent arrangement of things, the greater part of life is sunshine."

Years later in his autobiography, he summarized all his years of education. "He (my father) placed me at the English school at five years of age; and at the Latin at nine, where I continued until his death. My teacher, Mr. Douglas, a clergyman from Scotland, with the rudiments of the Latin and Greek languages, taught me the French; and on the death of my father, I went to the **Reverend James Maury,** a correct classical scholar, with whom I continued two years; and then, to wit, in the spring of 1760, went to **William and Mary College**, where I continued two years.

"It was my great good fortune, and what probably fixed the destinies of my life, that **Dr. William Small** of Scotland, was then Professor of Mathematics, a man profound in most of the useful branches of science, with a happy talent of communication, correct and gentlemanly manners, and an enlarged and liberal mind. He, most happily for me, became soon attached to me, and made me his daily companion when not engaged in the school; and from his conversation I got my first views of the expansion of science, and of the system of things in which we are placed. Fortunately, the philosophical chair became vacant soon after my arrival at college, and he was appointed to fill it per interim: and he was the first who ever gave, in that college, regular lectures in Ethics, Rhetoric and Belles Letters.

"He returned to Europe in 1762, having previously filled up the measure of his goodness to me, by procuring for me, from his most intimate friend, **George Wythe**, a reception as a student of law, under his direction, and introduced me to the acquaintance and familiar table of Governor Fauquier, the ablest man who had ever filled that office. With him, and at his table, Dr. Small and Mr. Wythe, his *amici omnium horarum*, and myself, formed a partie quarrée, and to the habitual conversations on these occasions I owed much instruction. Mr. Wythe continued to be my faithful and beloved mentor in youth, and my most affectionate friend through life."[12]

Thomas Jefferson decided to cut his college education short of receiving a degree. Dr. Small left Virginia to live in England, and in the spring of 1762, Tom chose to study law under the personal tutelage of George Wythe. The more Tom saw of George, the more he liked. He admired his large aquiline nose and high forehead graced with his dark brown hair. Set in his well-shaven face was his prominent blue eyes. Since he was of medium height, Tom being over six-foot tall was forced to look down on him when standing together.

Although George was supremely intellectual, yet he had a kind, compassionate heart that magnetized Tom to him. He always was cheerful and had a positive attitude that became molded into Tom's character.

Tom also saw in George Wythe a man after his own heart. Whereas Tom was arising early each day to bathe his feet in a tub of cold water, he found George customarily rose at dawn and took a shower in his back yard. He had rigged a large bucket over his bathing stall, which his slave filled with cold water from his well. When George was ready, his slave pulled the rope, releasing the ice cold water on his shivering body. If that wasn't enough to wake a soul from slumber, nothing would.

George lived next door to Bruton Parish Church in Williamsburg and owned one of the grandest homes in the city. Designed and built by architect Richard Taliaferro, it became George's when he married the architect's daughter, Elizabeth. George took Thomas Jefferson into his home to live and gave him access to his library, believed to be the largest of the land. For two years Tom feasted sumptuously at Wythe's table and was named his personal clerk. With that honor Tom was like a thirsty sponge as Wythe taught him while on their travels throughout the colonies. When they arrived at their individual assignments, Tom would record all Wythe's court cases and his political meetings as a burgess of Virginia.

Young Thomas Jefferson diligently made notes of all he was taught and the things he learned. He wrote his notes in five different languages, and his bookshelves were filled with books – all before he reached the age of 21. According to Tom, "a lawyer without books would be like a workman without tools." Wythe was another father figure to Tom. Not only did Tom absorb all he could from Wythe's teachings, but also from his wise counsel. This gave him a distinct advantage over others throughout his illustrious life.

While Tom was in Williamsburg between 1760 and 1764, he missed many special occasions of his family and friends, which included births, marriages and deaths. Some of these were members of Dr. Thomas Walker's family. Col. William Peachey, Walker's first cousin, returned from the war in time to see his daughter, Mary, born before he suffered the death of his wife, the former Million Glascock. Tom also missed the marriage of Col. Joshua Fry's oldest son, John, to Sarah Adams, as well as the birth of three of their children - William, Tabitha and Joshua.

While he was in college, his cousin Thomas Mann Randolph at Tuckahoe, who was more like a brother to him, got married to Anne

Cary in 1761, whose mother was also a Randolph. The following year, Tom was absent at the marriage of Peachy Ridgway Gilmer, son of Dr. George Gilmer, to Mary, daughter of Thomas Meriwether, one of the Loyal Company five.

In 1762, Dr. Thomas Walker donated land to build the courthouse in Albemarle County. The following year, he laid out a gridded town plan as the Trustee of the county in order to sell and convey the lots which became known as the city of Charlottesville.

What Thomas Jefferson didn't miss was the *Treaty of 1763 of Paris* signed on February 10, which officially ended the French and Indian War. It was agreed by England, France and Spain that all the North American territory east of the Mississippi would be put under the control of Great Britain. That was quickly followed on October 7 with the *Proclamation of 1763* issued by King George III, which forbade the colonists from settling land beyond the Appalachian Mountains.

When Tom received word about the *Proclamation*, he was devastated. Such an imposing act thrust a dagger into the depths of his heart because it dealt a death-blow to his father's dream. How could Virginians capture the West if they couldn't settle land beyond the Appalachians? That effectively nullified the Loyal Company grant provided by King George II in 1749.

When Dr. Walker discovered Kentucky in 1750 under the commission of the Loyal Company, he returned to make plans for his next excursion. His proposal was to locate the Mississippi and Missouri Rivers and hopefully go all the way to the Pacific Ocean. However, with the French and Indian War followed by the *Treaty of Paris in 1763*, western explorations were deadlocked.

Patrick Henry

> *"It is not now easy to say what we should have done without Patrick Henry"*
> Thomas Jefferson

1763

Thomas Jefferson left Reverend Maury's Boys School in 1760. Over three years later, Tom heard his former teacher. Rev. James Maury was pleading his case against the church's vestry called "The Parson's Cause" in, Hanover Court House. A fledging rookie lawyer named Patrick Henry would be defending the vestry against Maury.

George Wythe, who helped admit Henry to the bar, decided to attend the trial. He would take his clerk, Jefferson, with him to advance his legal training.

The two men prepared for their lengthy assignment as Wythe's most trusted slave went to the stable to retrieve the carriage. When Tom saw two dapple gray horses passing by the Bruton Parish Church next door, he knew they would soon be fastened to Wythe's coach, and they would be on their way. Their seventy-mile journey allowed them plenty of time to discuss the importance of the occasion. After they left the outskirts of Williamsburg, Wythe began telling Tom the purpose of the trip.

"Thomas, you've told me a lot about Reverend Maury, your former teacher. Did he ever tell you about the Two Penny Act?"

"Yes he did, Mr. Wythe, but he tried to keep it to himself. Therefore, I never quite understood it."

"It's a long story that began in 1758 and now five years later we hope to reach the conclusion of that conflict between the Anglican clergy and the planters of Virginia." George paused momentarily as he covered his face to keep the dust from road inflaming his nostrils.

"As you know, all the Anglican clergy receive their wages from the taxpayers. We used to give each minister 16,000 pounds of tobacco for their annual salary."

"I remember hearing that figure." Tom sat with his eyes intensely glued on George, although he struggled whenever the coach hit some bumps in the jagged road.

"When an economic crisis hit the land, the Virginia General Assembly passed the Two Penny Act in 1758. Rather than pay the clergy in tobacco, the planters would give them two pence per pound of tobacco that was sold. That meant the ministers would get a drastic cut in wages." Wythe continued to cough as he struggled with the dust coming in the windows.

"No wonder Reverend Maury was upset about that." Tom replied. "That all happened while I was in his school."

"Well, Thomas, the law was only supposed to be for one year. But it was never changed. So here we are five years later, and the ministers want their wages to be paid retroactively back to 1759."

"I guess that's what this court trial will be about."

"Right, Tom, your Reverend Maury is representing the Anglican clergy in a lawsuit against the planters called 'The Parson's Cause.' We've been invited to bring some assistance to Maury's side. It won't be long before you will see your good friend and former teacher."

Tom sat in shock at what he heard. George never had seen him so speechless. Tom couldn't imagine what it would be like to see his favorite teacher in the middle of a court battle. He knew Maury was one of the two still alive who shared his father's dream.

George Wythe, being a stickler for punctuality, arrived with Thomas Jefferson well ahead of the trial. What they were about to behold was the likes of which Tom never had seen before. He was quick to seek out Reverend Maury and offer him his full support. Maury told him the best support he could offer was that of earnest prayer for him.

With George and Tom seated in the gallery, they saw the prestigious attorney, Peter Lyons, representing Maury's cause. He was one of the ablest prosecutors around, and they knew the minister was in good hands. They noticed that Colonel John Henry was the presiding judge. Tom thought it was a conflict of interest for the justice to be the father of Patrick Henry arguing for the defense. How could an impartial judgment be reached in this situation?

As the participants of the trial entered the courtroom, one-by-one they introduced themselves to Jefferson and Wythe. Finally, one of the clergymen on Reverend Maury's side came to meet Tom. Dressed in his clerical robe, he said, "I am Patrick Henry."

Tom thought he was trying to trick him. "Wait a minute, isn't Patrick Henry defending the vestry against Reverend Maury, whom you support?"

The minister gave Tom a big grin. "That's right, but that man is my nephew, who just happens to bear my name. I am the judge's brother."

Tom sat rather befuddled throughout the trial trying to sort out all the Henrys involved. He expected more of them would be in the gallery or perhaps sitting on the jury.

The prosecution felt like it had an open and shut case because the Church of England was brought in question, and King George III was the head of the church. How would the defense stand a chance going against Britain's ruler?

John Lewis was the lead defense attorney, but he didn't stand a chance against a stacked deck. He used the Two Penny Act to prove his case, but Peter Lyons insisted the law never was legal. Judge Henry ruled for the defense, saying the Two Penny Act was null and void. However, they still must have a hearing to award damages to the clergy. (Rev. Maury was claiming he was due three hundred pounds back wages). The defeated lawyer, John Lewis, left in disgust and turned the hearing over to his colleague, Patrick Henry, the son of the judge and nephew of his namesake who represented the opposing side.

Tom looked in disbelief as Patrick entered the courtroom. He hadn't seen him since four years ago when they fiddled together at the Christmas party. He looked on him as being too carefree and undisciplined to be a lawyer. But here he was, nonetheless. After Lyons argued his case for Maury, Patrick Henry stood to his feet and gave a rousing oratory that lasted nearly an hour. Tom saw that the courtroom was quiet as a mouse, the jurors were spellbound, and the judge was weeping at his son's splendid speech.

Throughout the stem-winding summation, Tom heard some cries from the gallery of "treason." That was because Patrick Henry was taking his charge against the king's institution, the Church of England. He even accused the king of degenerating into a tyrant. Henry also attacked the Anglican clergy, accusing them of greed:

"Do they feed the hungry and clothe the naked? Oh, no, gentlemen! These rapacious harpies would, were their power equal to their will, snatch from the hearth of their honest parishioner his last hoe-cake, from the widow and her orphan children her last milk cow! the last bed - nay, the last blanket from the lying-in woman!"[13]

Patrick Henry asked the court to award Reverend Maury one farthing for his back wages. The jury was more gracious, but still the one penny they offered was a slap in the face to Maury. Henry, in one prolific speech, alienated the Anglican clergy and the King of England. However, he became a hero in the sight of all those who sought freedom from tyranny. The raucous, rejoicing men in the gallery pulled Patrick Henry up to sit on their shoulders as they carried him across the street to Shelton's Tavern, where they drank the night away.

At the expense of the dejected Rev. Maury, Patrick Henry became an instant success. From that point on his law business boomed with new clients and significant court cases. Amazingly, that trial helped ignite the American Revolution. King George III reacted both in rage and humiliation, but hadn't heard the last from young Patrick Henry.

As George Wythe and Thomas Jefferson made their departure for Williamsburg, they had mixed emotions. George was pleased with Patrick Henry's performance in the court room. That was the best closing argument he ever witnessed. However, Tom was visibly upset at the way Henry belittled and embarrassed his dear friend, Rev. Maury.

"To be frank with you, Thomas, I never thought he had it in him. Did you know he barely passed his bar exam? I was one of those who tested him. I understand he studied no more than six weeks for my questioning, which made him quite inadequate. However, what he lacked in knowledge he made up with his tenacity. I just saw something in that 24-year-old fellow that made me sit up and take notice. When I saw his moving oratory today, I realized my questionable reservations of him were unfounded."

"Mr. Wythe, I wished I shared your feelings, and perhaps, one day I will. I feel if his father was not the judge, he may not have won his case. Peter Lyons kept objecting that his speech was treasonous, and that gives me some food for thought."

"Both you and I, Thomas," said Wythe. "Both you and I."

Thomas Jefferson returned to his home in Shadwell for his 21st birthday on April 13, 1764. All his family welcomed him with open arms. He could see the love of his mother in her magnetic brown eyes, realizing she missed him more than he had missed her. Standing on each side of her was his youngest sister and only brother, twins, eight-year old Anna and Randolph. They ran up to jump in his arms in delight. His sister Lucy was now eleven, and he could still see his 19-year old sister, Bet, was still not right in her head, but he loved her all the more because of it. Sister Mary came out to greet Tom on the porch with her husband, John Bolling. They were married before Tom left for William and Mary, and now they had two sons, Jack and Tom.

His sister, Martha, came up the stairs on the porch with her new fiancé, Dabney Carr.

"Well, I'll be darn, I never expected you to be here, Dab." Tom yelled out excitedly as he gave his best friend a crushing bear hug.

"What did you expect, Tom? Do you think you could keep me away from your birthday?" Dabney returned the embrace with a chuckle of delight.

"I can't believe you and Sis are goin' to tie the knot. That's just beyond my wildest dreams."

"How could that be, Tom? You know I've always had eyes for Martha."

After the noise of the greetings mellowed, Tom heard the melodious sound of the harpsichord coming from the upstairs window. What sweet music to his ear to know his sister, Jane, must be the one playing one of his favorite hymns? He rushed up the stairs and, finding her door open, began matching his voice with hers in musical harmony. Jane had always been his special sister and his soul mate. She knew him better than anyone else, appreciating his creative mind, his studious habits and his love for music. He was delighted she still was single. That would give them extended time together.

"Welcome home, Tom, my how I've missed you." Jane threw her harpsichord aside and swung her arms around her brother.

"I'm glad to be back at Shadwell, and even more delighted to see you once again." Tom assured her as she rubbed her hand through his strawberry hair.

"Did you bring your fiddle with you?"

"I wouldn't dare to see you again without it."

After dinner, Tom and Jane became the life of the party as they played their instruments before all the Jefferson's family and friends. There was a mixture of sing-along hymns and dance-along minuets and reels.

After the party started, Tom's old friend, Jack Walker, walked in the door. He was greeted by all, even more so by Tom. They talked about how busy it was going to be at neighboring Castle Hill in June. Jack was marrying Elizabeth Moore, and he asked Thomas Jefferson to be his groomsman. Jack's sister, Susanna, was holding her wedding to Henry Fry the same month. Henry was the son of Col. Joshua Fry, one of those who shared Tom's father's dream. Another one who shared that vision was Dr. Thomas Walker, father of both Jack and Susanna. With her marriage to Henry Fry, Peter Jefferson's dream was sure to be kept alive for another generation.

Although Tom enjoyed his party immensely, he was overwhelmed by the added burden that was placed on his shoulders. Now that he had become an adult, he was responsible to run his five thousand acres, which included four adjacent plantations - Shadwell, Monticello, Tufton and Lego. That included overseeing some thirty slaves and caring for his mother and five of his siblings. Sister Jane was nearly 24 and still unmarried. Tom could depend on her to care for his family while he lived in Williamsburg. Although he had learned enough to be a lawyer, he wanted to continue his life with George Wythe and the upper crust of society in the capital. His father's overseer of the slaves was still around, and Tom knew he could depend on him to keep the farm productive with the tobacco and corn crops. Sawney, his father's personal slave, was also available to help keep the other slaves settled. If there was ever any hint of an uprising among them, Sawney would squelch it.

The following day, Dabney and Tom were back to their old tricks – canoeing down the Rivanna River, riding their horses and running up to the top of Tom's mountain. They recalled the vow they made to each other as they sat under their big oak. They had no idea how soon it would be before one of them would die, and they would have to open the first grave at what would be called Monticello.

Tom hung around Albemarle County for the next few months as he helped organize the affairs of his house and plantation. That gave him a lot of time to spend with Jane, talking about old times and making music together.

Jack Walker also required some of his attention as he prepared for his wedding. It would be held at his fiancée's majestic home, Chelsea, on the Mattaponi River in the distant King William County. Jack would be married to the girl he called "Betsy" on June 6, 1764. Tom was envious of his dear friend because Jack was younger than him and had already found in Betsy the mate for his life. Tom felt like love was going to pass him by. Since he failed to make his feelings known to Rebecca Burwell years ago, he questioned whether he would ever find another woman who would spark up his life like she did.

Whenever Tom was at Jack's house at Castle Hill, he saw all the elaborate arrangements being made for Jack's sister, Susanna, whom Jack called "Sukey". Her marriage to Henry Fry would join the strong bloodlines of the Walkers with the Frys. Henry became a born-again Christian as the result of the preaching of Presbyterian evangelist, Samuel Davies, and others during the Great Awakening. Since that time, he felt called by God to become a preacher.

Jack's oldest sister, Mary, held her wedding at Castle Hill in 1758 to Col. Nicholas Meriwether Lewis, first cousin of Thomas Meriwether, one of the five who carried Tom's father's dream. She had already given him four children. When Tom saw the two together, he was reminded how Thomas Meriwether and Tom's father, Peter Jefferson, both died within months of each other. Now the two of them, along with Col. Joshua Fry, must keep their dream alive on the heavenly shores above. The Frys, Walkers and Meriwethers intermarrying with each other kept them motivated to one day capture the West all the way to the Pacific Ocean.

The next occasion Thomas Jefferson encountered the carefree, unprofessional and unlearned Patrick Henry was on May 29, 1765. Henry recently had been elected to the House of Burgesses representing Louisa County. As a newly-elected congressman, he was expected to take a back seat to his elder statesmen. Those wealthy and well-born men included George Washington, Thomas Nelson, Jr. and Landon Carter, son of Robert "King" Carter. Five of the Lee family was burgesses including brothers - Francis Lightfoot, Richard Henry and Thomas Ludwell Lee - and their cousins, Henry and Richard Lee.

Burgesses whom Tom knew personally were his cousin, Peyton Randolph; his former guardian, Dr. Thomas Walker; and Henry, son of Col. Joshua Fry and now the son-in-law of Dr. Walker. Mann Page and his brother, John Page, also were members of that prestigious assembly. Mann was the father of Tom's close friend, John Page; and the elder John Page was his friend's uncle. With George Wythe also being a burgess, Tom felt even more justified being present at the sessions, being under his tutelage and living with him in Williamsburg.

Jefferson knew the meetings would be controversial and thus quite emotional. All Virginia was ablaze with the recent passage on March 25, 1765, of the Stamp Act by England's Parliament. That required all the colonists in America to pay a tax to England for every piece of paper they purchased. Whether it was legal documents, newspapers, licenses or playing cards, they were all to be taxed. To add insult to injury, Parliament followed that with the Quartering Act, requiring the colonists to pay for the lodging of ten thousand troops of British soldiers sent to defend and protect the American frontier.

Thomas Jefferson concealed himself in the doorway of the lobby as he waited for the fireworks to proceed. The Stamp Act was presented to the assembly the day before. A motion had been made and seconded to bring the motion to the floor. However, it faced such stiff opposition that many of the burgesses were stirred to anger. Tom knew that would be an exciting day, to say the least. Sure enough, he was not to be disappointed, thanks to the likes of Patrick Henry.

Tom didn't have long to wait to find what was stirring in Patrick Henry's soul. During the night, Henry had scribbled on a blank leaf of an old law book seven resolutions against the abominable Stamp Act. When Tom saw him enter the chambers, he could tell he was on fire. What was on his mind, Tom didn't much care, for his mind was set against him. The blasphemous words uttered against his beloved Rev. James Maury at the "Parson's Cause" trial festered in him like a malignant tumor.

Tom noticed John Robinson, the Speaker of the House, wasn't present, and so Tom's cousin Peyton Randolph had taken his chair. He knew Randolph and many of the others disliked the Stamp Act, but they had too much to lose if they rebelled against British law. Their wealth, their position in society, and their lives would all be in jeopardy if they stood against King George III.

Tom didn't have long to wait. Soon Patrick Henry took his scribbled page from his pocket and began reading his seven controversial resolutions against the Stamp Act. Right away, Tom noticed the stirring of opposition coming from many of the burgesses. His eyes were glued on his cousin Randolph in the Speaker's chair, who was trying his best to find a way to rule Henry out of order. Although he didn't much care for Henry, Tom was awe-stricken at Henry's creation of such a well-worded document. He was moved further by Henry's passionate, soul-stirring delivery of it. What he said in his rousing oratory was controversial and considered treasonous, but it shook the rafters where the burgesses met. Tom couldn't believe what he saw, but it was an event he would remember forever.

Patrick Henry read his first four propositions, which asserted the colonists' rights and privileges and the belief they should not have taxation without representation. After a bitter exchange of opinions coming from both sides, those four resolutions narrowly were adopted.

Thinking that grievous matter was settled, Patrick Henry continued on his feet. He had three more resolutions, each one more controversial than the others. Those asserted that Virginia reserved the right to levy taxes on its subjects and that they were not bound by the British government to pay taxes. The last one was the most controversial. Henry proposed that anyone holding a contrary opinion would be an enemy of the Virginia Colony.

The fifth one passed by only one vote. Only 39 of the 116 members were present, many having left earlier thinking nothing important would be held at the end of the session. Peyton Randolph was so upset the motion passed, Tom heard him cry out, "By God, I would have given one hundred guineas for a single vote."

The last two were shouted down by the angry members. Henry refused to sit down and be quiet. As he stood his ground, passionately he spoke with such sublime eloquence that Tom's adamant feelings toward Patrick Henry completely reversed. On May 30, 1765, the day following his 29th birthday, Henry proclaimed, "Tarquin and Caesar had each his Brutus, Charles the First, his Cromwell; and George the third . . . ."

"Treason!" cried Peyton Randolph, as he banged his gavel on the podium. Many members of the assembly followed the Speaker as they railed against Henry. Tom couldn't help notice that even his mentor, George Wythe, was adamant against that young whippersnapper.

After the fury died down, Henry continued. "...and George the Third may profit from their example. If that be treason, make the most of it!"[14]

That was the last Tom would see of the young revolutionary for awhile, as Henry left town before the next day. What was to follow was the vote on the sixth and seventh resolutions, which failed, and the fifth was nullified by another vote. However, all Henry's seven resolutions were reported as law by some newspapers. That burgess, still wet behind the ears, had stirred the colonies like no one ever had before or will again.

In Tom's own words, "Call It oratory or what you please, but I never heard anything like it. He had more command over the passions than any man I ever knew."[15] Later in life Tom recalled, "I heard all the celebrated orators of the National Assembly of France, but there was none equal to Patrick Henry."[16] His resolutions stirred the beginning of the American Revolution. By his own admission, later Patrick Henry claimed his controversial speech and Stamp Act resolutions "brought on the war which finally separated the two countries & gave independence to ours."[17]

Where in the world did Henry learn how to speak so passionately? Tom found out it began when he was a child. Although Henry's Pa was a vestryman for his Anglican church, his mother took to young Patrick to hear preachers involved in the Great Awakening. He was only nine when he sat under the preaching of George Whitfield. His maternal grandfather, Isaac Winston, became a born-again Christian under the preaching of Presbyterian preacher, Samuel Davies. As a young teen, Henry sat under the stirring sermons of Rev. Davies, which apparently rubbed off on him. In his autobiography, Tom remembered the indelible impression Patrick Henry made on his life that day.

"When the famous Resolutions of 1765, against the Stamp Act, were proposed, I was yet a student of law in Williamsburg. I attended the debate, however, at the door of the lobby of the House of Burgesses, and heard the splendid display of Mr. **Patrick Henry**'s talents as a popular orator. They were great indeed; such as I have never heard from any other man. He appeared to me to speak as **Homer** wrote. Mr. Johnson, a lawyer, and member from the Northern Neck, seconded the resolutions, and by him the learning and the logic of the case were chiefly maintained. My recollections of these transactions may be seen on page 60 of the life of Patrick Henry, by Wirt, to whom I furnished them."[18]

The Adopted Stamp Act Resolutions of Patrick Henry

Resolved, that the first adventurers and settlers of His Majesty's colony and dominion of Virginia brought with them and transmitted to their posterity, and all other His Majesty's subjects since inhabiting in that His Majesty's said colony, all the liberties, privileges, franchises, and immunities that have at any time been held, enjoyed, and possessed by the people of Great Britain.

Resolved, that by two royal charters, granted by King James I, the colonists aforesaid are declared entitled to all liberties, privileges, and immunities of denizens and natural subjects to all intents and purposes as if they had been abiding and born within the Realm of England.

Resolved, that the taxation of the people by themselves, or by persons chosen by themselves to represent them, who can only know what taxes the people are able to bear, or the easiest method of raising them, and must themselves be affected by every tax laid on the people, is the only security against a burdensome taxation, and the distinguishing characteristic of British freedom, without which the ancient constitution cannot exist.

Resolved, that His Majesty's liege people of that his most ancient and loyal colony have without interruption enjoyed the inestimable right of being governed by such laws, respecting their internal policy and taxation, as are derived from their own consent, with the approbation of their sovereign, or his substitute; and that the same has never been forfeited or yielded up, but has been constantly recognized by the kings and people of Great Britain.[19]

Leaning toward Liberty

*"We hold these truths to be self-evident,
that all men are created equal."*
Thomas Jefferson

1765

Thomas Jefferson had experienced many crises, but none was more personally devastating than when his dear sister, Jane, died on October 1, 1765. She was only 25 and still unmarried when Tom's kindred spirit was suddenly taken from him. Most children that Tom knew thought him a bit odd when he would choose to read and study and play his fiddle rather than frolic and spend his time in idleness and tomfoolery. Jane knew Tom's heart and soul. They shared the same deep intuitive passions. They spent many an hour together, she on her harpsichord and he on his violin. Although she was not as well read as Tom, she shared his love for books and learning. Tom relished the hours they spent together in the woods collecting wildflowers and singing together. She was the only one who seemed to love botany more than he. Tom recalled how he was introduced to the world of flowers by Jane when as small children they strolled in the meadow together.

When Jane died, Tom's song seemed to die with her. His fiddle was put away as he turned to his books to detract from his grievous heart. Life would never be the same without his dear Jane. Now his mother was left with four children under her care, without Jane's dependable aide - Elizabeth "Bet" at 21, Lucy at 13, and Anna and Randolph at 10. Jane's death ironically occurred on the tenth birthday of the twins. What was to be a day of celebration was instead a day of sorrow. Although Bet was now the oldest, she was still a child at heart, being mentally challenged, and would be of little help to her mother.

George Gilmer, Jr., the son of Dr. George Gilmer and the former Mary Peachey Walker, began the practice of medicine and midwifery in December, 1766. Now licensed as a new doctor, he accepted Thomas Jefferson as one of his first patients, Prior to Gilmer's putting out his medical shingle in Williamsburg, he had arranged for Tom to get his smallpox vaccine. To get the inoculation, Tom needed a letter of introduction to Dr. John Morgan in Philadelphia, which Gilmer graciously provided in 1766. Gilmer would marry his first cousin, Lucy, daughter of Dr. Thomas Walker, on August 27, 1767, and would move his practice to Charlottesville by 1771. Eventually, he would settle on his spacious Pen Park plantation three miles north of town.

During the winter following Jane's death, Tom continued studying the law books for his future bar exam. However, after spring arrived, he decided he wanted to see what the rest of the world was like outside Virginia. Knowing he was going to have to go the Philadelphia to get his smallpox inoculation, he made plans to spend time during the summer visiting cities in the north. He had just received news that the abominable Stamp Act had been repealed, and he wished to celebrate that glorious occasion with the rest of the patriots.

On his way to Philadelphia, he made a prolonged visit to Annapolis, Maryland, where he observed the Maryland State House and how the delegates there had ordered their assembly. Then he made his way to Philadelphia, where he met Dr. Morgan to get his inoculation. Tom was excited to see such a large city, and to him it would always be the most beautiful in the world. He was awestruck by the spacious harbor on the Delaware River, which accommodated hundreds of ships at a time.

Next, Jupiter chauffeured Tom in his coach to New York, where he was welcomed by Elbridge Gerry. Gerry, a native of Marblehead, Massachusetts, had invited Tom to visit and lodge with him while they discussed politics. They were both thrilled with the repeal of the Stamp Act and shared their feelings of rebellion against England. Physically, they were in direct contrast, Tom standing at six foot two, while Gerry at a mere wisp of a man was much shorter. But philosophically, they were both patriots. Ten years later they would meet again to sign the *Declaration of Independence.*

When Tom returned to Virginia, he passed his bar exam and began practicing law. He and Footloose, his painted filly, travelled hundreds of miles each month to cover his circuit, his trusted Jupiter by his side. Most of these were cases covering debt, divorce or land disputes.

Thomas Jefferson was first elected a burgess representing Albemarle County in December, 1768, but his first session wasn't held until the following May. Tom was relieved to take a breather from his itinerant circuit. Ever since he had witnessed Patrick Henry arguing his case before the burgesses in 1765, Tom yearned for the day he could join that elite group. In his autobiography, he recalled how his aspirations for leadership developed.

"In 1767, he (George Wythe) led me into the practice of the law at the bar of the General court, at which I continued until the Revolution shut up the courts of justice.

"In 1769, I became a member of the legislature by the choice of the county in which I live, and so continued until it was closed by the Revolution. I made one effort in that body for the permission of the emancipation of slaves, which was rejected: and indeed, during the regal government, nothing liberal could expect success. Our minds were circumscribed within narrow limits, by an habitual belief that it was our duty to be subordinate to the mother country in all matters of government, to direct all our labors in subservience to her interests, and even to observe a bigoted intolerance for all religions but hers. The difficulties with our representatives were of habit and despair, not of reflection and conviction. Experience soon proved that they could bring their minds to rights, on the first summons of their attention. But the King's Council, which acted as another house of legislature, held their places at will, and were in most humble obedience to that will: the governor too, who had a negative on our laws, held by the same tenure, and with still greater devotedness to it: and, last of all, the Royal negative closed the last door to every hope of amelioration."[20]

At the early age of 26, Thomas Jefferson made his debut into the prestigious Virginia House of Burgesses as her youngest member. From his beginning in 1768, he remained a valuable member of that powerful ruling body until it was angrily dissolved permanently by British Governor Lord Dunmore in 1774. Throughout that six-year time span, Virginia's governing body was on the road to revolution. Jefferson found himself in the midst of the hornet's nest he was helping to stir.

Tom already had experienced a similar crisis when he was first elected. One of his first actions as a burgess was to file a grievance to abolish slavery. That was quickly squelched because he was informed by that ruling body of Virginia that King George III made slavery mandatory, and it was the law of the land. Jefferson was shocked speechless and inwardly disappointed.

When Tom returned to his room that night, he was visibly shaken. Jupiter, Tom's servant and soul mate, was tuned into his master's gloomy feelings. No one knew Tom better than he. Wherever Tom went since leaving Shadwell ten years ago, Jupiter was close by his side. From four in the morning when he began preparing Tom's cold tub of water for his feet to the late night hours when he helped put him to bed, Jupiter was always around.

"Wha's the matter, Tom? I've never seen you dis sad."

"My dear friend, Jupiter, you've seen me in all my highs and lows, but I think you're right. That is about as bad as I've ever felt."

"What came over you, Tom?"

"Today, the governor shut us down. Because we were trying to assert our rights as colonists, he dissolved our assembly."

"Tha's right bad, sir."

"That's not as bad as what happened in the days before that. Remember, I told you how much I detested slavery and what I wanted to do about it?"

"Yassa, Tom." Jupiter was busy trying to get Tom comfortable by propping his legs up and getting him relaxed in his favorite chair.

"I made an effort in the burgesses for the emancipation of slaves, but it was rejected. I can't believe the leaders of Virginia are so blind!" Tom refused to sit still, preparing to arouse himself to a standing position. "Don't they know God created all men equal, whether they are white, Negro or Indian? That is a fatal stain upon Virginia. What nature had bestowed on us of her fairest gifts, we have cast asunder and trampled it under our feet." Tom left his chair to stand in front of the warm fire of the hearth. Jupiter knew his master was deep in thought and must not interrupt him.

"Under the law of nature," Tom continued his exhortation, "all men are born free. Everyone comes into the world with a right to be his own person, which includes the liberty of moving and using it at his own. That is what is called personal liberty, and is given him by the God Almighty, because it is necessary for his own sustenance."[21]

Tom couldn't be stopped, as he pranced back and forth like a tiger on the loose. "Jupiter, we have been born and raised together, both on the same plantation. The only difference between the two of us is the color of our skin. Yet, I am a wealthy planter and a burgess of Virginia, and you are simply someone's slave. There's something terribly wrong with that. I know it is a horrific sin in the eyes of Almighty God.

Sooner or later, I feel America is going to have to pay the price, and it's going to be heavy." Tom had adopted the similarities of George Wythe, as he put his hands behind his back, one hand in another, and strolled methodically across the room.

"Here's the reason my motion to free the slaves was rejected. Years ago King George II made a law....let me see, I have a paper here that gives it exactly. *'No Negro, mulatto or Indian slave shall be set free upon any pretence whatsoever, except for some meritorious services, to be adjudged and allowed by the Governor and Council.'*"[22] Tom threw the wrinkled paper into the fire. "That is what I think of England's vagrant law! Let it burn, and let America be free from such unbridled tyranny. Oh, for the day when we can be loosed from these chains!"

The following year, the Virginia governing body was once again disbanded by British rule. After only one session of the burgesses beginning on May 8, 1769, it came to a crashing halt on May 17. On the preceding day the House of Burgesses adopted vigorous resolutions asserting colonial rights. Royal Governor Lord Botetourt, an agent of King George III, declared their actions treasonous with this declaration - "Mr. Speaker and Gentlemen of the House of Burgesses, I have heard of your resolves and augur ill of their effects. You have made it my duty to dissolve you, and you are dissolved accordingly."[23] Within ten days after their session opened, the Governor of Virginia dissolved it.

What was meant as defeat for the patriots turned into a victory. As a result of Virginia's government being disbanded, her leaders were passionately stirred toward freedom from tyrannical rule. On the following day, Thomas Jefferson met with burgesses like Patrick Henry; Richard Henry Lee; Thomas Nelson, Jr.; Speaker of the House Peyton Randolph; Attorney General John Randolph (another cousin of Jefferson); and his former guardian, Dr. Thomas Walker. Their contrived convention met in the Apollo room of the Raleigh tavern. Tom vividly described those significant events in his autobiography.

"In May, 1769, a meeting of the General Assembly was called by the governor, Lord Botetourt. I had then become a member; and to that meeting became known the joint resolutions and address of the Lords and Commons, of 1768-9, on the proceedings in Massachusetts. Counter-resolutions, and an address to the King by the House of Burgesses, were agreed to with little opposition, and a spirit manifestly displayed itself of considering the cause of Massachusetts as a common one. The governor dissolved us: but we met the next day in the Apollo of the Raleigh tavern, formed ourselves into a voluntary convention, drew up articles of association against the use of any merchandise imported from Great Britain, signed and recommended them to the people, repaired to our several counties, and were re-elected without any other exception than of the very few who had declined assent to our proceedings."

After the meeting Dr. Walker invited Tom to meet with him and another burgess named Thomas Glascock from Richmond County. He lives at Indian Banks and was the brother of Million Glascock, who married Col. William Peachey.

"Tom, Peachey is my first cousin, which makes Thomas Glascock my cousin through marriage."

"Doctor Walker, I recall the time when my father and I came to your house. I must have been about twelve at that time. I remember meeting Colonel Peachey and his wife, Million, and their three sons."

"Yes, Tom, I recall that occasion well. Now meet Million Peachey's brother, Thomas Glascock."

"I'm so pleased to make your acquaintance, sir." Tom reached out his hand to the man who was his senior. "I heard you were the Justice of Richmond County. Is that correct, Mr. Glascock."

"That's right, Mr. Jefferson, you are quite observant."

"Being a traveling lawyer, I try to get acquainted with all the county justices. I guess you know why."

"I do my best not to show partiality. So just being on my good side won't curry you any favors."

"As well as it should be, your honor. You won't find me seeking preferential treatment," Jefferson looked at him with a gleam in his eye. "However, I am pleased to welcome you as a fellow burgess."

The next month Tom was stricken again with grief. He received word of the death of his former teacher and father-figure, Rev. James Fontaine Maury. On June 9, 1769, the preacher departed to his heavenly reward at the age of fifty one. His wife, Mollie Walker Maury, and a dozen children surviving him mourned their loss. He was buried in honor beneath the chancel of Walker's Church in Fredericksville Parish where he pastored for 18 years (1751-1769). During the funeral, Tom kept wondering if that was the death of his father's dream. Once there were five men who held it. Four of them were now deceased, Dr. Walker being the only survivor. Tom vowed in his heart to help Walker keep his father's dream alive, still hoping and praying one day the western frontier could be captured for America.

Thomas Jefferson kept refreshing his memory with the parting words he heard from his mentor when he left Maury's School many years ago.

"I want you to remember what I taught you faithfully about Jesus and his Sermon on the Mount," Maury asked for a promise from Tom. "If you follow those words, you will never go wrong."

Tom remembered the vow he made to the preacher. "Jesus words will follow me all the days of my life." He hoped and prayed he would be able to keep that commitment he made to the man who stirred within him the passion to help change his world for the better. He was reminded of the religious freedom Maury's forefathers, the Huguenots, had lost in France, and all the horrendous consequences they experienced. Jefferson would vow to do whatever he could to bring about the religious liberty in America that Rev. Maury instilled within him.

The preacher's two oldest sons, Matthew and James Maury, Jr., were friends and fellow students of Tom when he was at Maury's School. Matthew followed his father into the ministry serving as his assistant before his Pa's death. Tom was pleased to know he would continue to serve the church as her rector in his father's stead.

Tom learned from Matthew that his father taught James Madison and James Monroe at his school. (With Thomas Jefferson, that would be three future presidents Rev. Maury had trained). Matthew shared with Tom a letter his father left him regarding "The Parson's Cause." It was from Patrick Henry, who won the case against Rev. Maury years ago. Tom read the following words from the preacher's own handwritten note. "Mr. Henry apologized to me, alleging that his sole view in engaging in the cause was to render himself popular." That was sweet music to Tom's ears, as he still carried a kernel of revenge about the way Patrick Henry treated Tom's dear friend, Maury, at the "Parson's Cause" trial.

During the past year, Thomas Jefferson kept his slaves busy leveling the top of Tom's Mountain. There he planned his future home he would name "Monticello," little mountain in Italian. He carefully laid out his plans for his new home and left them with his craftsmen on his plantation. Although he hoped to have a home for a future bride, at that point he had no one in mind. His younger sister, Lucy, had just been married to Charles Lewis on September 12, 1769, at Shadwell, reminding Tom that he was still left behind in the marriage cycle.

As he worked busily in Williamsburg the following February, he received the frightful news about Shadwell. A messenger announced to Thomas Jefferson that his boyhood home went up in flames and burned to the ground. Immediately, Tom inquired about the welfare of his family. Did mother survive? Was she hurt in any way? What about his brother and sisters? All these plaguing questions were thrust haphazardly to the messenger. According to the answers, all his family made it out of the house safely. Once he had this assurance, he thought about personal possessions of his in the charred remains.

His father's desk, surveying instruments and library left in his will for Tom would be destroyed, together with most of the books Tom had acquired during his lifetime. Then he remembered his notebooks, in which he had recorded everything he had learned and observed in life. Tom was overwhelmed with the realization that some of the most significant events and ideas of his life, would be lost to the ages. The only things he had left were those things he had brought with him to Williamsburg. Fortunately, that included his family Bible and the *Book of Common Prayer*, which he tried always to keep with him. Needing his Bible for study and his prayer book for Sunday worship was a constant for him. Although the Bible was quite large and cumbersome, it was his father's, and safe by Tom's side it would remain.

Jupiter was with Tom when he heard the devastating account. While trying to bring comfort to his master, he was concerned about his own family. Were his Ma and brother and sisters in the house? After all, some of them were house servants. Could any of them have been killed or injured? Without being told, Jupiter immediately went to the stable and quickly prepared the horses for the 120-mile trek to Shadwell. Having spent most of his life with Jefferson, he usually knew how he would respond to situations like this. By the time Tom decided he must leave as soon as possible, he saw Jupiter and the horses all ready to go.

When Tom and Jupiter arrived to find what remained of the burning embers of Shadwell, they both searched for their families. Tom was told they were in safe hands, staying at the homes of their kinfolk. Jupiter found his family all safe in their undisturbed slave shack. As Tom was carefully combing through the ruins in desperation, looking for any token of his past life, he saw one of the slave boys running to meet him. From a distance, Tom could see he carried something in his hand. All of a sudden, Tom recognized the object was his prized fiddle.

"Massa, I's ga' somefin' for ya!'"

"What is that, boy?" Tom was garnering a broad smile.

'I's ga' ya' fiddle!"

Thomas Jefferson

"Indeed, you do. Where did you get that?"

"When I's see far' comin' out ya' house, I run in to get ya' fiddle." The little slave boy showed his full set of white teeth and his eyes all aglow.

"You are my hero, boy." Tom reached down to give the boy a big hug and pat him on the head.

"Here's ya' fiddle, Massa," said the boy as he gave it to Tom.

"You know, boy, I don't like to be called 'Massa', but I will gladly receive your gift. I will put in a good word for you with my overseer."

"Thanks ya', Massa...uh, I mean 'Sir.'" The boy ran off back into his humble cabin.

* Tom now needed a new place to live, not only for him but for his mother and family as well. He had been preparing to build his new home up on the mountain, where his slaves worked from sun up to sun down days leveling a place for it. They also had been laying bricks and digging a cellar to build a mansion he called "Monticello."

Jefferson learned he could get more production from his slaves by giving them incentives instead of discipline. Therefore, he let them know he would reward them with money if they performed above his expectations. He knew, though they worked all day long, they could move faster and get more accomplished if there was a carrot dangling at the end of the stick. He also bought vegetables from his slaves they grew in their personal gardens around their slave shacks. Although slavery was still the law of the land and Tom reluctantly accepted it, nevertheless he was compelled to soften the blow against his subjects as much as possible. Sorry to say, he had some problems with a runaway or two and some who were persistently defiant toward the overseer. Those suffered lashings and other punishments for their behavior. But Jupiter and his family knew Mr. Jefferson was kinder to his slaves than most other plantation owners.

As Tom returned to his legal practice, he received another surprised assignment. This came in the form of a letter, which he opened to his amazement. It was addressed as follows: "His Excellency The Right Honourable Norborne Baron de Botetourt, his Majesty's Lieutenant and Governor General of the Colony and Dominion of Virginia, and Vice Admiral of the same. To Thomas Jefferson, Esquire." When Tom began reading the proclamation, he was shocked by the governor's new assignment for Jefferson. He was appointing him, "Thomas Jefferson to be Lieutenant of the County of Albemarle and Chief Commander of all his Majesty's Militia, Horse and Foot, in the said County of Albemarle..."[24]

All of a sudden, Tom's focus was on his new title. Although he had never soldiered before, he now would be responsible to lead a militia of soldiers whenever needed. Just like his pro bono cases he argued on behalf of the poor and those in slavery, he knew he would also have no financial benefit for this assignment. However, he was honored to be designated an officer in the military. His father would be proud of him, as his Pa bore the title, "Lieutenant Colonel Peter Jefferson" in the same militia.

Meanwhile, back in Williamsburg, Tom finally met the woman of his dreams. Martha Wayles Skelton was a young widow of 22 with a three-year old son. Her father, John Wayles, knew Tom, being a lawyer himself. Martha's first husband, Bathurst Skelton, died two years after their marriage, leaving her available since 1768. Her striking beauty combined with her joyful personality attracted several courting men her way. However, it was Tom's love for music that drew him particularly to that auburn-hair, hazel-eyed lady. She, like Tom's favorite sister, Jane, loved playing her harpsichord and pianoforte. When they were courting, Tom brought along his fiddle, as they played their instruments and sang the night away.

They started their relationship in the fall of 1770 before he moved into his one-room bachelor's quarters at Monticello. He envisioned his home by this time to be much grander and larger, but he had to take one step at a time. Martha's four-year old son, John, died during her courtship to Tom, causing her sorrow that festered like an open wound. Tom's mind returned to the way he and Martha's life began in his autobiography.

"On the 1st of January, 1772, I was married to Martha Skelton, widow of Bathurst Skelton, and daughter of John Wayles, then twenty-three years old. Mr. Wayles was a lawyer of much practice, to which he was introduced more by his great industry, punctuality, and practical readiness, than by eminence in the science of his profession. He was a most agreeable companion, full of pleasantry and good humor, and welcomed in every society." [25]

When Martha and Tom married on New Year's Day of 1772, the wedding took place at her majestic home, The Forest, in Charles City County, near Williamsburg. They were in close proximity to the prominent planters along the James River. The wedding was a gala affair with the most distinguished citizens of Virginia in attendance.

Since the bride's father had a large mansion and lots of money to throw their way, he continued the celebration at The Forest for two whole weeks.

When the wedding finally ended, it was mid-January and in the dead of winter. The newlyweds began their honeymoon travelling in a horse-drawn carriage to Monticello, a one-hundred mile journey. After having to stop several days while their coach was under repair, a prolific snow storm came their way. Eight miles before their destination, they were forced to leave their carriage, its wheels stuck in the ice and snow. They then released the two horses from the coach and rode them the remaining distance to Monticello at the top of Tom's Mountain.

The Jeffersons' Honeymoon Cottage at Monticello

When they finally arrived at Tom's one-room bachelor's quarters, it was late in the evening. The slaves had gone to bed and were not available to assist them. There was no fire burning in the hearth, and they were drenching wet and bitterly chilled. After Tom stabled the horses, he got a fire started in their 18-by-18 foot cottage. Remembering he had a half bottle of wine hidden behind his books, he opened it as a gesture of celebration for their honeymoon night. They joined together singing a few merry tunes, rejoicing that they were finally safe and secure together "'til death do them part."

Their honeymoon was short lived because within two weeks, Tom was required to be back in Williamsburg. Tom reported for duty at the February 10 session of the House of Burgesses. That time he traveled to Williamsburg with two of his best friends, newly elected burgesses, Jack Walker and Dabney Carr. Dr. Thomas Walker had been a regular fixture at the House for the past ten years. When he retired after the 1771 legislature, he passed the baton down to his son, Jack, who was elected as one of two of the burgesses of Albemarle County, Thomas Jefferson being the other. Dabney Carr was from neighboring Louisa County. Besides being Tom's close friend, he was his brother-in-law, being married to Tom's sister, Martha. The two of them had given Tom two nephews and three nieces.

When they arrived at the February, 1772, session, Tom took Jack and Dabney under his wings, introducing them to the rest of the burgesses. Right away, they spied John Page, another of Tom's best friends; and Thomas Mann Randolph, his childhood friend and cousin. During the session in Williamsburg, the five friends spent their spare time together reminiscing about their college days. They each displayed their silver badge and greeted one another with their secret handshake. Those symbols of the first college fraternity in America, which three of them helped organize, bound them together with a strong chord throughout their days as fellow burgesses.

On September 27, 1772, the Jeffersons welcomed into their tiny bungalow their first child, Martha, whom they nicknamed "Patsy." She was a special blessing to her mother because of Martha's loss of her only child, John Skelton by her first marriage, a year ago.

About that time, Tom began his lifetime infatuation with mockingbirds. In November, he purchased his first one from one of John Wayles' slaves at the Forest. He fell in love with his feathered friend's melodious warbling and began to teach it some tunes of his own. Throughout her childhood, little Patsy was always serenaded by the music of one of Tom's pet birds.

Although Tom was a burgess, his main occupation involved his trade as a lawyer. Repeatedly, he found himself drawn to cases where he defended the rights for a slave to be liberated. Jupiter always traveled with him to these trials, and they freely discussed Tom's inner feelings about the injustice of slavery.

Thomas Jefferson acted as attorney pro bono in two Virginia legal suits for freedom by enslaved mulatto children. In *Samuel Howell v. Wade Netherland*, April 1770, Jefferson unsuccessfully argued that Samuel Howell's grandmother was a white woman. He further argued that "under the law of nature, all men are born free."[26] Using the law of *partus sequitur ventrum*, in which the child held the mother's status, Tom was devastated when the judge ruled against him. (Samuel Howell lost his case in the 1770 session of the General Court and ran away shortly after the verdict).

In 1772, he agreed to represent George Manly, the son of a free woman of color. Tom argued for his freedom from his servitude. The law stated that as an illegitimate son of a free woman, he was bound as an indentured servant until he reached 31 years. He was now three years overdue. That time Tom won the case, and as was his custom with these cases, he represented him at no charge.

As much as Tom wanted to give the slaves their freedom, he found he could not change British rule. Besides, the planters knew they must keep their slaves in order to make their massive plantations productive. He knew that as an institution, slavery was immoral. He later wrote about this abominable dilemma saying "we have a wolf by the ears and we can neither hold him nor safely let him go."[27]

Although Dabney Carr served in that prestigious assembly for a short time, he proved himself to be a powerful orator, only second to Patrick Henry. Tom said Dabney "was one of the earliest and most distinguished leaders in the opposition to British tyranny." The new Royal Governor of Virginia was egotistical, haughty Lord Dunmore. As was the custom, he had been sent by King George III from England to rule the colony. In a rebellious tone against the governor, on March 12, 1773, Dabney Carr introduced a resolution to the House of Burgesses to create a Committee of Correspondence. The first purpose was to provide an avenue for the colonies to keep in touch with each other to unify their cause against tyranny and taxation. The second purpose was to find out what the Parliament and the Crown was up to in England so that all colonies would be alerted of actions that might negatively affect them. As the result of the passage of Dabney's resolution, Lord Dunmore angrily dissolved the House and locked the burgesses out of their chambers.

Not to be stifled, Tom and Dabney met the next day at the Raleigh tavern with three other burgesses – Patrick Henry, Richard Henry Lee, and his brother, Francis Lightfoot Lee. Those four formed a nucleus of patriots who would lead the colonies to rebellion and revolution. They methodically planned how they would communicate with the other colonies through their standing Committee of Correspondence. That meeting was the predecessor of the Continental Congress of 1774.

Sorry to say, the one who tenaciously fought for that resolution never would live to see its results.

Tom's world was turned upside down when on May 16, 1773, he said goodbye to his bosom buddy, 29-year old Dabney Carr. Dr. George Gilmer, Jr., Tom's physician had been called to the bedside of Dabney as he was having violent vomiting spells with a high rate of fever. Tom's soul mate had left the House of Burgesses heading home, but before he got there, he died suddenly in Charlottesville. Tom had remained in Williamsburg on business, only hearing of his dear friends passing days later.

Dabney Carr's body was first laid to rest at Shadwell until Tom could prepare a proper burial ground for him at Monticello. Tom hired his pastor, Rev. Charles Clay, rector at Saint Anne's Parish in Albemarle County, to officiate at the funeral. When it came time for Tom to fulfill his sacred vow to Dabney to bury him on Tom's Mountain beneath the great oak tree, Tom remembered him with the following inscription on his tombstone.

> *Here lie the remains of Dabney Carr*
> *Son of John & Barbara Carr*
> *of Louisa County*
> *Who was born___, 1744.*
> *Intermarried with Martha Jefferson,*
> *Daughter of Peter & Jane Jefferson, 1765*
> *And died at Charlottesville, May 16, 1773*
> *Leaving six small children.*
> *To his Virtue, Good Sense, Learning and Friendship*
> *That stone is dedicated by Thomas Jefferson,*
> *Who, of all men living, loved him most.*[28]

While Tom was grieving over the loss of Dabney, he took on the awesome responsibility of caring for Dabney's wife, who was Tom's sister, Martha, and her six children. Fortunately, Monticello was now large enough to accommodate them, with little elbow room to spare. Jean was the oldest at seven; Lucy and Mary were five-year old twins; their three sons were Peter at three, Samuel at two and Dabney being born just before his father's death. He would join the nursery with Tom and Martha's Patsy, who was only seven months old when Dabney died.

To add insult to injury, Tom's situation became more stressful when one week after he buried his best friend, his father-in-law, John

Wayles, died on May 23, 1773. While that left Martha grieving the loss of her father, it added to Tom's burden because of Martha's inheritance. Her father left her all his estate of 11,000 acres of property spread throughout Virginia, a huge debt of £4,000 and 135 slaves. Overnight, with a total of 187 slaves, Tom became the second largest slave owner in Albemarle County. As much as Tom tried to fight the institution of slavery, this new inheritance would place a greater strangle hold on him to accept slavery as a present fact of life. In his autobiography, Tom highlighted how this negatively affected his life.

"He (Martha's father) acquired a handsome fortune, and died in May, 1773, leaving three daughters: the portion which came on that event to Mrs. Jefferson, after the debts should be paid, which were very considerable, was about equal to my own patrimony, and consequently doubled the ease of our circumstances."[29]

Before 1773 came to an end, Jefferson would hear of the news from Boston that shocked the world. On the cold night of December 16, irate Bostonians stormed three British ships, tossing 342 chests of tea into the harbor. That gave Tom the reassurance that the rebellion in Virginia toward England had helped ignite the northern colonies against British taxation and tyranny.

The Power of the Pen

"The God who gave us life gave us liberty at the same time."
Thomas Jefferson

1774

Tom had retired from legal practice by the time he reached his 31st birthday. In October, 1773, he became the County Surveyor of Albemarle. When he took Jupiter with him to survey new lands, he was reminded how he and his father would spend their days together doing the same.

During that time, he purchased 157 acres of property in the Shenandoah Valley, which included the Natural Bridge. He called it "the most sublime of Nature's works." The initials of George Washington (G.W.) were carved into its limestone wall, showing that he had surveyed it earlier. Tom would use the natural wonder as one of the reasons America was superior to England.

Tom also bore the responsibility to care for his wife and young daughter and his sister and her six children, all living at Monticello. The fields of his properties had to be cultivated by his slaves, providing tobacco, wheat and corn to keep his plantations productive. At the same time, Jefferson was representing his Albemarle County as a burgess in Williamsburg.

1774 marked the year of the birth of Jane Randolph Jefferson, Tom and Martha's second child. The joy he had in April at her birth helped him recover from the sorrow he experienced several months before when his sister, Bet, died. On February 21, a rare earthquake had occurred at Monticello described by Tom in his account book as

John Harding Peach

one that ". . . shook the houses so sensibly that everybody ran out of doors."[30]

Tom's mentally-challenged sister, Bet, became a victim of that violent tremor because following the quake, she came up missing. Her personal servant was little Sall, who was Jupiter's sister. (She was called "little Sall" to differentiate her from her mother, known as "big Sall"). Since the earthquake, she also was nowhere to be found. Tom organized a search party for the two girls, which included his family and his slaves. Jupiter was by his side day and night as they left no leaf unturned to find both their sisters.

To make matters worse, the nearby Rivanna River had flooded its banks. When Bet and little Sal were discovered several days later, their bodies had turned blue, frozen from the bitter cold of winter. Tom surmised the two girls in their apparent confusion tried to cross the raging waters in a makeshift boat and drowned in the process.

Bet was only 29, but apparently her mental deficiency contributed to her fear and confusion. As for little Sal, her Ma, her brother, Jupiter, and all their family were given time off from their labors as they outwardly agonized their loss. Once again, Tom called on his pastor, Rev. Charles Clay, to perform the ceremony. This time both blacks and whites mourned together in a combined funeral, an unusual sight on any plantation. Tom buried both of the girls near his father in the Shadwell graveyard.

Martha found it difficult to comfort Tom after that. He refused to eat or sleep.

"I can't handle this guilt I'm carrying, Patty." Tom shared with his wife. (Although her first name was "Martha", he called her "Patty").

"Thomas, what do you feel guilty about?" She was standing beside him as he slumped over in his wing chair, with her arm around his neck.

"It's all my fault. I was so busy trying to look after my books and things in the house after the quake that I failed to keep an eye on Bet."

"Dear, you can't blame yourself for that. Little Sal was there to care for her."

"I know, Patty, but that didn't help. Now they are both dead."

"Is that all that's bothering you, dear?" Patty sat down on the stool in front of Tom to hold his hands.

"No, I also feel guilty because of the lack of time I have spent with Bet when she was alive. I never quite understood her with her quirky ways. Rather than try, it was easier for me to stick my head in another book or wander off with the flowers."

"Thomas, you're beating yourself to death over that. Let me fix you some corn chowder to help you with your gloominess. I'll also bring you a mess of your favorite peas."

As Martha went to the kitchen, she left Tom sitting in front of the hearth, where he continued to mope in his sadness and guilt. Several days later, he was back to his old self, putting the burials behind him.

Soon thereafter, Tom found time to separate himself from all his commitments. He took his quill in hand as he discovered a new calling in his life. All the years of making meticulous notes of everything he did in life prepared him for his future as a writer. Reverend Maury had taught him the importance of doing his journals when he was a teenager. Tom realized how these had helped him develop his writing skills.

As he thought about Reverend Maury, he remembered both his fiery sermons on Sunday as well as his passionate lessons at school during the week. Because he made extensive notes on them all, he was able to quickly bring them out of his mental filing system. Although the journals themselves were burned at Shadwell, their messages were burned indelibly into Jefferson's heart and soul.

All the revolutionary ideas of Maury caused Tom to do some intensive research on his own. A new church started in town, and he decided to go for a visit. The people assembled there called themselves the Lewis Mountain Baptist Church. Andrew Tribble was their pastor. When Tom entered their make shift of a building, he was in shock. What a stark difference from the Church of England buildings of which he was accustomed. This church didn't even look like the architecture of a church, with not even a sign in front indicating it was a place of worship. As he entered, he saw no prayer books in the rustic pews, nothing showing an order of worship and no religious symbols or stain glass windows.

What Tom saw seemed to be completely spontaneous. There was no rhyme or reason what would happen next. But he witnessed an excitement and enthusiasm in the congregation that was unique. He could tell the people were filled with exuberant joy when they sang, reminding him more of those who would sing and dance when he played for them on his fiddle.

The preacher then got up with his Bible in hand and had a fire in his voice as he railed against sin and abomination. Tom hadn't seen any emotion among the ministry like that since Reverend Maury.

After their church service ended, they held their monthly business meeting. Although Tom was not a member, he decided to find out what it was all about. As a vestryman for his church, he knew the twelve members of the vestry made the decisions for his Anglican church. In this little Baptist church, every member had a vote, as well as a voice. He didn't hear any women speak because they respected the leadership of their husbands. But no restrictions were held regarding time or subject when it came to the men's deliberations.

Jefferson was so impressed with what he saw that day that he returned again and again. He arranged to meet personally with Pastor Tribble, inviting him to Monticello for dinner. He learned right away the minister didn't want to be called "reverend" or any titles normally associated with the clergy.

After the scrumptious meal, the pastor was interested to find out what Jefferson thought of the services. By this time, he knew how significant a man was sitting before him. What his guest said in response never escaped the memory of the preacher.

"Pastor Tribble, as I carefully observed your business meeting, I believe it would be the best plan of government for the American colonies."[31]

At that point neither man knew how that little dinner meeting would possibly lead to the rights for religious liberty or for the *Declaration of Independence*. One thing was for sure. All the services Thomas Jefferson attended at that little Baptist church in Charlottesville made an indelible impression upon what he was destined to write.

Since the Baptist church only met once a month, Tom began attending Sunday meetings at the Albemarle County Courthouse. He called it "the common temple", as there was a different denomination represented each week. This introduced Jefferson to many styles and methods of worship. He saw they all believed in the same God and the same Jesus as did the Church of England. During that time, he continued to pursue his struggle against the state church concept that came from the British.

While Patrick Henry stirred the embers that ignited the fires of insurrection with his tongue, Thomas Jefferson accomplished the same with his trusty pen. With quill in hand, he found his proficient writings of rebellion and independence would do more to initiate the American Revolution than the finest of captivating oratory. Like George Washington, Tom preferred to keep silent in the burgess meetings. Both of them chose not to lead with their speeches, but with their constant commitment to their goal of overthrowing the British tyranny.

When Dabney Carr and Tom originated the idea of the Committee of Correspondence, Dabney believed Tom should be the one designated to present it to the House of Burgesses. Between the two, Tom was the senior member of the prestigious assembly. However, Tom insisted that Dabney make the speech. He believed speech-making was his best friend's talent, and he wanted to see him put it on display. When Tom saw how Dabney captivated his audience with his persuading oratory, he knew others should do the speaking. Tom would accomplish more if he used the power of his pen.

England's coercive reaction to the Boston Tea Party on December 16, 1773, was Parliament's passing of the Boston Port Bill on March 31, 1774. That was the first of a series of "Intolerable Acts" from British rule, which ignited the American Revolution. According to the new law, the port of Boston would be closed to shipping on the first day of June.

When Patrick Henry, Richard Henry Lee, and Francis Lightfoot Lee received word of that, they assembled with Tom and several other members. Tom later wrote their reaction in his autobiography.

"Not thinking our old and leading members up to the point of forwardness and zeal which the times required, Mr. Henry, **Richard Henry Lee**, **Francis L. Lee**, Mr. Carr and myself agreed to meet in the evening, in a private room of the Raleigh, to consult on the state of things. There may have been a member or two more whom I do not recollect. We were all sensible that the most urgent of all measures was that of coming to an understanding with all the other colonies, to consider the British claims as a common cause to all, and to produce a unity of action: and, for this purpose, that a committee of correspondence in each colony would be the best instrument for intercommunication : and that their first measure would probably be, to propose a meeting of deputies from every colony, at some central place, who should be charged with the direction of the measures which should be taken by all. We, therefore, drew up the resolutions which may be seen in Wirt, page 87.

"The consulting members proposed to me to move them, but I urged that it should be done by **Mr. Dabney Carr**, my friend and brother-in-law, then a new member, to whom I wished an opportunity should be given of making known to the house his great worth and talents. It was so agreed; he moved them, they were agreed to nem. con. and a committee of correspondence appointed, of whom **Peyton Randolph**, the speaker; was chairman. The governor (then Lord Dunmore) dissolved us, but the committee met the next day, prepared a circular letter to the speakers of the other colonies, inclosing to each a copy of the resolutions, and left it in charge with their chairman to forward them by expresses." In his autobiography, Thomas Jefferson recalled the following images burned into the depths of his memory.

"The next event which excited our sympathies for Massachusetts, was the Boston port bill, by which that port was to be shut up on the 1st of June, 1774. This arrived while we were in session in the spring of that year. The lead in the House, on these subjects, being no longer left to the old members, Mr. Henry, R. H. Lee, Fr. L. Lee, three or four other members, whom I do not recollect, and myself, agreeing that we must boldly take an unequivocal stand in the line with Massachusetts, determined to meet and consult on the proper measures, in the council-chamber, for the benefit of the library in that room.

"We were under conviction of the necessity of *arousing our people from the lethargy into which they had fallen, as to passing events*; and thought that the appointment of a day of general fasting and prayer would be most likely to call up and alarm their attention. No example of such a solemnity had existed since the days of our distresses in the war of '55, since which a new generation had grown up. With the help, therefore, of Rushworth, whom we rummaged over for the revolutionary precedents and forms of the Puritans of that day, preserved by him, we cooked up a resolution, somewhat modernizing their phrases, for appointing the 1st day of June, on which the portbill was to commence, for a day of fasting, humiliation, and prayer, to implore Heaven to avert from us the evils of civil war, to inspire us with firmness in support of our rights, and to turn the hearts of the King and Parliament to moderation and justice.

"To give greater emphasis to our proposition, we agreed to wait the next morning on Mr. Nicholas, whose grave and religious character was more in unison with the tone of our resolution, and to solicit him to move it. We accordingly went to him in the morning. He moved it the same day; the 1st of June was proposed; and it passed without opposition.

"The governor dissolved us, as usual. We retired to the Apollo, as before, agreed to an association, and instructed the committee of correspondence to propose to the corresponding committees of the other colonies, to appoint deputies to meet in Congress at such place, annually, as should be convenient, to direct, from time to time, the measures required by the general interest: and we declared that an attack on any one colony, should be considered as an attack on the whole. This was in May. We further recommended to the several counties to elect deputies to meet at Williamsburg, the 1st of August ensuing, to consider the state of the colony, and particularly to appoint delegates to a general Congress, should that measure be acceded to by the committees of correspondence generally. It was acceded to; Philadelphia was appointed for the place, and the 5th of September for the time of meeting.

"We returned home, and in our several counties invited the clergy to meet assemblies of the people on the 1st of June, to perform the ceremonies of the day, and to address to them discourses suited to the occasion. The people met generally, with anxiety and alarm in their countenances, and the effect of the day, through the whole colony, was like a shock of electricity, arousing every man, and placing him erect and solidly on his centre."[32]

Before the colonists took that proposed step, the British sought to checkmate them with three more "Intolerable Acts". On May 20, 1774, Parliament passed the Administration of Justice Act and the Massachusetts Government Act, both of which ended any self-rule by the colonists. On the same day, the Quebec Act was used by England to diminish the size of the thirteen colonies by extending the Canadian borders further south. Massachusetts, Connecticut and Virginia were immediately downsized. England now deemed herself to be in total political control over America.

Thomas Jefferson took out his trusty quill and penned his first public document. When he presented it to the Virginia House of Burgesses on May 24, 1774, it quickly passed with unanimous consent.

Resolution for a Day of Fasting, Humiliation & Prayer

"This House, being deeply impressed with apprehension of the great dangers, to be derived to British America, from the hostile invasion of the City of Boston, in our sister Colony of Massachusetts ... deem it highly necessary that the said first day of June be set apart, by the members of this House as a Day of Fasting, Humiliation and Prayer, devoutly to implore the Divine interposition, for averting the heavy calamity which threatens destruction to our civil rights. ... Ordered, therefore that the Members of this House do attend ... with the Speaker, and the Mace, to the Church in this City, for the purposes aforesaid; and that the Reverend Mr. Price be appointed to read prayers, and the Reverend Mr. Gwatkin, to preach a sermon suitable to the occasion."[33]

George Washington wrote in his diary on that date: "Went to church, fasted all day." Lord Dunmore, Virginia's royal governor, in response angrily dissolved the House of Burgesses once again. Back to the Raleigh tavern Thomas Jefferson and the other revolutionaries marched to convene their meetings following their day of fasting and prayer. This was where they put their heads together to formulate the first Continental Congress.

The Day of Fasting and Prayer was held on June 1, 1774, to coincide with the day the British would close Boston's port. As a result of that special day, a sleeping giant was aroused, and cries of revolution filled the streets.

When Thomas Jefferson saw all the enthusiasm for freedom to unshackle the intolerable chains of Britain, he was moved to call for a separate day of prayer and fasting just for those in Albemarle County. Both he and Jack Walker were members of the vestry of St. Anne's Parish and jointly presented the following resolution so penned by Jefferson.

Resolution of Albemarle County

"To the Inhabitants of the parish of St. Anne, the people are notified of the recommendation by the House of Burgesses to hold a fast day. The purpose of the day was described to the people of St. Anne's parish as such: Fasting, humiliation and prayer to implore the divine interposition in behalf of an injured and oppressed people; and that the minds of his majesty, his ministers, and parliament, might be inspired with wisdom from above, to avert from us the dangers which threaten our civil rights, and all the evils of civil war. We do therefore recommend to the inhabitants of the parish of Saint Anne that Saturday the 23rd instant be by them set apart for the purpose aforesaid."[34]

On July 26, 1774, the freeholders of Albemarle County assembled at the court house where Rev. Charles Clay, rector of St. Anne's Parish, preached an arousing sermon that stirred the cries for revolution. Thomas Jefferson followed his pastor's patriotic message with his bold, controversial resolve to the House of Burgesses, calling for a trade boycott with England. The assembly stood behind Tom, giving him its full approval. As a result, they elected Thomas Jefferson and Jack Walker to be their representatives at the First Virginia Convention to be held in Williamsburg the following month.

A Summary View of the Rights of British America in 1774

Tom returned to Monticello to prepare for the convention. Having found success from his other resolutions, he wrote a much longer and even more caustic document for the burgesses when they met at Williamsburg. What he called a "pamphlet" resulted in a 23-page manuscript. In that historic document, he wrote to justify the violent actions of the Boston and the American Revolution.

Jefferson argued that Parliament meeting in London had no rights to govern the colonies. He claimed they had been independent since their founding. He also insisted that illegal actions were committed by King George III and Parliament.

"Being elected one for my own county," Tom wrote in his autobiography, "I prepared a draught of instructions to be given to the delegates whom we should send to the Congress, which I meant to propose at our meeting. In this I took the ground that, from the beginning, I had thought the only one orthodox or tenable, which was, that the relation between Great Britain and these colonies was exactly the same as that of England and Scotland, after the accession of James, and until the union, and the same as her present relations with Hanover, having the same executive chief, but no other necessary political connection; and that our emigration from England to this country gave her no more rights over us, than the emigrations of the Danes and Saxons gave to the present authorities of the mother country, over England.

"In this doctrine, however, I had never been able to get any one to agree with me but Mr. Withe. He concurred in it from the first dawn of the question, What was the political relation between us and England? Our other patriots, **Randolph**, the **Lees**, **Nicholas**, **Pendleton**, stopped at the half-way house of **John Dickinson**, who admitted that England had a right-to regulate our commerce, and to lay duties on it for the purposes of regulation, but not of raising revenue. But for this ground there was no foundation in compact, in any acknowledged principles of colonization, nor in reason: expatriation being a natural right, and acted on as such, by all nations, in all ages."[35]

Tom prepared to deliver his completed manuscript to the First Virginia Convention meeting in Williamsburg. However, on the first day of the assembly, Jefferson was missing. The delegates questioned his whereabouts, all to no avail.

Shortly after Tom left Monticello with two copies of his manuscript in his duffle bag, he was struck with an uncontrollable bout of dysentery. He knew there was no way he could travel in that condition. But his prized document must get to Williamsburg. He felt like it was a difference maker for America. He turned to his trusted servant, Jupiter, handing him both copies of Jefferson's masterpiece.

"Jupiter, please take these to the courthouse in Williamsburg. Give one to Patrick Henry and the other to Peyton Randolph. He is the moderator of the convention. I know I can trust you to carry out this task."

Jupiter was afraid to leave his master in such a weakened condition. But he knew he must do as he was told. "I's be glad to do it, Sir. Just pray no slave hunters will capture and kill me."

"That's a concern I have, and I will invoke my heavenly Father to guide you there safely. As for me, I must return quickly to Monticello." These are Tom's recollections of this most embarrassing day and the events following it, as he recorded in his autobiography.

"I set out for Williamsburg some days before that appointed for our meeting, but was taken ill of a dysentery on the road, and was unable to proceed. I sent on, therefore, to Williamsburg two copies of my draught, the one under cover to **Peyton Randolph**, who I knew would be in the chair of the convention, the other to **Patrick Henry**. Whether Mr. Henry disapproved the ground taken, or was too lazy to read it (for he was the laziest man in reading I ever knew) I never learned: but he communicated it to nobody. Peyton Randolph informed the convention he had received such a paper from a member, prevented by sickness from offering it in his place, and he laid it on the table for perusal."

Jupiter arrived in Williamsburg safely and delivered the copies as Tom has instructed. Typically, Patrick Henry misplaced his, but Peyton Randolph took Jefferson's *"A Summary View of the Rights of British America in 1774"* and read it to the delegates. At the conclusion of those pungent accusations addressed against King George III, Tom boldly declared,

> "The God who gave us life gave us liberty at the same time; the hand of force may destroy, but cannot disjoin them. That, sire, is our last, our determined resolution; and that you will be pleased to interpose with that efficacy which your earnest endeavours{sic} may ensure to procure redress of these our great grievances, to quiet the minds of your subjects in British America, against any apprehensions of future encroachment, to establish fraternal love and harmony through the whole empire, and that these may continue to the latest ages of time, is the fervent prayer of all British America!"[36]

Thomas Jefferson had written his *"Summary View"* with haste. He was not satisfied that all his words or facts were properly chosen. It was only meant to be a rough draft that could be corrected at the meeting. Since he didn't make it to the Convention, his proposed changes never were made.

When his controversial document was read, the younger members applauded it, while the older, more austere representatives had grave reservations. They had too much to lose to stir up the ire of King George III and Parliament, knowing it could lead to war. Tom expected his essay would be questioned by many. As he expected, his *"Summary View"* was not adopted by the Convention and not authorized to be printed.

Nevertheless, Tom's friends published his manuscript in Williamsburg, which was then circulated throughout the colonies and traveled across the Atlantic. As a result, Thomas Jefferson became recognized as a skillful but controversial, writer with a sharpened pen that would shake the world. His masterful writings kept coming, and they all proved that Tom had revolution on his mind. And he knew how to use the pen to articulate it.

When Jupiter returned to Monticello, he was pleased to know that Jefferson had improved and was feeling much better. After giving him the news in Williamsburg as he heard it, he shared some news of his own.

"Thomas, I's found me the gal I's wanna marry."

"Why, Jupiter, who is she?"

"She's one o' ya' slave women." Tom's servant was finding it difficult to talk about her to her master.

"Well, that's wonderful. You are now 31, and it's about time you fall in love. I always wondered if you had it in you. Tell me about her, Jupiter."

"Her name is Suck. She's one o' ya' slaves you's got from Massa Eppes."

"How well I remember. She was one of about one hundred and thirty five in one day. How old is she?"

"Well, she's only sixteen."

"Jupiter, you rascal. You are old enough to be her father."

"Tha's right, but I knos I love her."

"That's the main thing, Jupe. I think you need to stay at Monticello from henceforth. That way you can see more of your lady. You have always taken good care of my horses, and I need you to manage all those in my stables."

"I'd like tha', Sir. I really 'preciate it."

"I believe I will ask Robert Hemings to take your place. All the Hemings family seems to be trustworthy folk."

The Virginia Conventions began in response to the Boston Tea Party. The first one opened on August 1, 1774, in Williamsburg. Four more would convene, ending on May 6, 1776. During that same time period, the Continental Congress was organized in Philadelphia, holding its first meeting from September 5 to October 26, 1774.

Williamsburg, home of the Virginia Conventions, was about 300 miles from Philadelphia, where the Continental Congress was staged. Since the same political leaders in Virginia were expected to be involved in both Virginia and national assemblies, they found themselves busy traveling back and forth. By horse or carriage, 300 miles in those days could take a week's travel one way.

Sandwiched in between the First and Second Virginia Conventions was the First Continental Congress held at Carpenter's Hall in Philadelphia. Tom and some of his friends wrote a letter to all the colonies suggesting they all meet at a central location to address their apparent conflict with England.

Thomas Jefferson was one of the delegates, but when they arrived in Philadelphia on September 5, 1774, once again Tom was absent. Continuing his sickness of the previous month, he didn't feel up to making a 270-mile trip from Monticello. However, he made detailed notes of his proposals to the First Continental Congress. When Peyton Randolph, Tom's cousin, was elected to be the first president of that prestigious body, Tom felt confident the notes he sent to Philadelphia would be properly read and presented. However, what he wrote stirred division within the assembly because he proposed that England had no right to rule the colonies. Many were patriots who favored independence from British rule. Nevertheless, most came to Philadelphia hoping to resolve their differences with England and stood resolute against those seeking to break with their mother country.

Tom finally recovered from his lingering illness and enjoyed the winter at home in Monticello with his wife, his two-year daughter, Patsy, and his little baby Jane. He continued construction efforts on Monticello and got caught up on things at home. Owning many farms, he found it necessary to check with the overseers and their slaves, making sure his crop would be plentiful the following year. Daily he continued his practice of reading the books in his library and making entries in his garden, farm and account journals at home. His passionate thoughts about the God-given rights of Americans and his feelings against slavery continued to dominate his thinking and writing.

The Second Virginia Convention was held in March of 1775 at St. John's Church in Richmond, having been moved away from Williamsburg for fear of British attacks. This time, delegate Thomas Jefferson was present at the meetings. On March 23, Patrick Henry delivered his dynamic, earth-shattering "Give me liberty or give me death" speech. This time Tom was not caught off guard. He knew Henry's capabilities in dramatic oratory, and Tom wasn't disappointed. Patrick Henry's Richmond speech would go down in history as one of the most significant ones ever delivered.

Within one month, on April 19, 1775, the Revolutionary War began with the Battles of Lexington and Concord, Massachusetts. That was what Ralph Waldo Emerson famously touted as "the shot heard around the world."

In Virginia, Royal Governor Dunmore was having his own conflict with the colonists. First, he issued a proclamation that promised freedom to all slaves who would join his British army. Tom heard that some 800 slaves followed Lord Dunmore's lead. Since Tom had about 200 slaves of his own, he was outraged at the thought that some of them might run away to join the British cause. All the other slave owners were equally upset, leading the Virginia Convention to threaten to execute any rebellious slaves. Even some loyalist planters favorable to England leaned their support now to the American patriots. On June 8, the governor and his family fled from the Governor's Palace in Williamsburg, taking refuge on a British ship in the Yorktown harbor.

Declaration of Independence

"Rebellion to tyrants is obedience to God"
(Motto used on Thomas Jefferson's personal seal)

1775

Thomas Jefferson was in the midst of all the rebellion against British rule in Williamsburg. Meanwhile, he was chosen a delegate for the Second Continental Congress. Leaving Williamsburg for Philadelphia with his new personal servant, Robert Hemings, he arrived for its first session on June 21, 1775. Benjamin Franklin and John Adams were new acquaintances of Jefferson, but they wasted no time recognizing the persuasive power of his trusty pen.

Declaration of the Causes and Necessity of Taking up Arms

* Almost immediately, John Dickinson of Pennsylvania and Thomas Jefferson were handed the awesome responsibility of drafting a resolution called *Declaration of the Causes and Necessity of Taking up Arms*. That took the next step forward from *"A Summary View of the Rights of British America in 1774"*. Tom now advanced the threat that if England didn't change her ways, independence was bound to happen. He also proposed the need for an American army and advanced the necessity to bear arms. Tom's rough draft was too caustic for the moderate-minded Dickinson, and so it was diluted before it was approved by the Continental Congress on June 26, 1775. Although the Second Continental Congress made a gesture for a peaceful solution with England, her delegates were opposed by King George III

When Tom wrapped up that arduous assignment, he knew he must quickly return to Virginia. The Third Virginia Convention began meeting in Richmond at St. John's Church on July 17. With Governor Dunmore hiding out on the British ship, *William*, in the Chesapeake Bay, the convention had become the only government of Virginia. Hence, her delegates managed legislation and decided to organize a military force against England.

They gave their seal of approval that one of their own, George Washington, was chosen to lead the American Army. Realizing their indebtedness to the flamboyant igniter of the revolution, in August, the delegates chose Patrick Henry as Colonel of the 1st Virginia Regiment.

In September, Tom and Martha's youngest child, baby Jane, died before she reached her second birthday. Following her funeral and burial at Monticello, Tom returned to Philadelphia for the next session of the Second Continental Congress.

By the first of the year, Tom returned home, only to witness the unexpected death of his dear mother on March 31, 1776. Being born February 9, 1721, she was only 55 when she died of a stroke, leaving four surviving children - Mary Bolling, Thomas Jefferson, Martha Carr and Lucy Lewis. Although his father was buried at Shadwell, Tom wanted his mother in the new graveyard at Monticello. Sadly, she died of the same malady that ended his famous cousin, Peyton Randolph's life October of last year. Tom called on his pastor, Rev. Charles Clay, to provide a proper eulogy for his mother, preparing her for burial.

After Tom celebrated his 33rd birthday at home, he made plans to return to Philadelphia for the next session of the Second Continental Congress. His carriage ride with all his books took him a week's journey, arriving on May 14, 1776. He carried the mandate that the Virginia Convention proposed independence from England, and he was bent on doing everything he could to accomplish it.

"On the 15th of May, 1776," Tom wrote in his autobiography, "the convention of Virginia instructed their delegates in Congress, to propose to that body to declare the colonies independent of Great Britain, and appointed a committee to prepare a declaration of rights and plan of government."

Richard Henry Lee then took Virginia's proposition to Philadelphia, presenting a resolution in the Pennsylvania State House at the Second Continental Congress, as personally recalled by Tom in his autobiography. "In Congress, Friday, June 7, 1776. The delegates from

Virginia moved, in obedience to instructions from their constituents, that the Congress should declare that these **United colonies are, and of right ought to be, free and independent states**, that they are absolved from all allegiance to the British crown, and that all political connection between them and the state of Great Britain is, and ought to be, totally dissolved; that measures should be immediately taken for procuring the assistance of foreign powers, and a Confederation be formed to bind the colonies more closely together.

"The House being obliged to attend at that time to some other business, the proposition was referred to the next day, when the members were ordered to attend punctually at ten o'clock.

"Saturday, June 8. They proceeded to take it into consideration, and referred it to a committee of the whole, into which they immediately resolved themselves, and passed that day and Monday, the 10th, in debating on the subject. It was argued by Wilson, Robert R. Livingston, E. Rutledge, Dickinson, and others that, though they were friends to the measures themselves, and saw the impossibility that we should ever again be united with Great Britain, yet they were against adopting them at this time.

"That the conduct we had formerly observed was wise and proper now, of deferring to take any capital step till the voice of the people drove us into it: That they were our power, and without them our declarations could not be carried into effect: That the people of the middle colonies (Maryland, Delaware, Pennsylvania, the Jerseys and New York) were not yet ripe for bidding adieu to British connection, but that they were fast ripening, and, in a short time, would join in the general voice of America."[37]

John Adams of Massachusetts; Robert R. Livingston of New York; Roger Sherman of Connecticut; Benjamin Franklin of Pennsylvania; and Thomas Jefferson of Virginia were mandated to complete the challenging assignment in a timely and effective manner. Since Ben Franklin at 70 was the oldest of the group, he was expected to make the rough draft for the *Declaration*. However, because he was ill, he gave the assignment to John Adams. However, Adams passed the baton to Jefferson, saying, "You are ten times the writer I am."[38]

Adams faulted Jefferson for his speaking skills. He said about Tom, "During the whole time I sat with him in Congress, I never heard him utter three sentences together."[39] However, he was quick to recognize that what Jefferson lacked in oratory, he excelled in his writing skills.

In 1822, John Adams wrote a letter to Timothy Pickering describing the heated conversation Adams had with Jefferson in 1776 over who should write the historic document.

"The subcommittee met. Jefferson proposed to me to make the draft. I said, 'I will not,' 'You should do it.' 'Oh! no.' 'Why will you not? You ought to do it.' 'I will not.' 'Why?' 'Reasons enough.' 'What can be your reasons?' 'Reason first, you are a Virginian, and a Virginian ought to appear at the head of this business. Reason second, I am obnoxious, suspected, and unpopular. You are very much otherwise. Reason third, you can write ten times better than I can.' 'Well,' said Jefferson, 'if you are decided, I will do as well as I can.' 'Very well. When you have drawn it up, we will have a meeting.'"[40]

Although Tom argued the point to no avail, he reluctantly accepted the awesome task. During this time, Philadelphia was hot and humid, and the lodging in the city was too unbearable for him to give his total concentration to his arduous assignment. So he found a newly-built house owned by Jacob Graff on the outskirts of town. With open fields surrounding his residence, Tom felt right at home. This reminded him more of his Virginia plantations.

Renting two rooms on the second floor, Thomas Jefferson sat down at his writing desk with a new quill in hand. He began on June 11 and completed his rough draft 17 days later on June 28. However, in his intense perfectionism, Tom struggled with every word and sentence in the proposed *Declaration*. Therefore, before he finalized his work, he had wrestled with the document through trial and error.

What he wrote would be quite shocking to the moderates in the Congress. He asserted that a nation's rights came from God rather than from the king and that all men were created equal. How earth shattering! His perfectionist mind and caustic quill attempted to accomplish what many thought was impossible. Breaking away from England required boldness and firm resolve.

On June 28, Jefferson presented his version of the *Declaration of Independence* to the committee of Dr. Benjamin Franklin and John Adams, who made some minor revisions before submitting it to the Continental Congress.

Upon its initial reading, Tom heard deafening cries from some shouting, "This is treason!" Tom had nothing to say publicly in his defense because all he wanted to say already was written. Tom then suffered through depression and a sense of defeat during the next four days as he witnessed the heated arguments over the content of his masterpiece. Throughout his life Tom suffered with headaches, and all this consternation may have produced his greatest headache ever.

While men argued Tom's proposed *Declaration*, John Adams with his eloquent oratory fought ardently for every word Tom had written. John Adams' rousing patriotism reminded the delegates of Patrick Henry's rally cry in Richmond the year before.

> "Gentlemen may cry, Peace, Peace-- but there is no peace. The war is actually begun! The next gale that sweeps from the north will bring to our ears the clash of resounding arms! Our brethren are already in the field! Why stand we here idle? What is it that gentlemen wish? What would they have? Is life so dear, or peace so sweet, as to be purchased at the price of chains and slavery? Forbid it, Almighty God! I know not what course others may take; but as for me, <u>give me liberty or give me death</u>!"[41]

After several days of quarrelsome debate, on July 2, Congress approved the *Declaration of Independence*. Tom was visibly disturbed that some of his original lines, complete paragraphs and finely crafted words were changed or deleted. Benjamin Franklin sat next to him during these wranglings over Tom's document and did whatever he could to encourage his friend's anxiety. As one who meticulously had chosen and rethought every letter and iota of words he had written, Tom couldn't believe what he was hearing.

Of all the significant documents Thomas Jefferson created, the *Declaration of Independence* would be his greatest. The final draft of that historic document began as follows:

Declaration of Independence

[Adopted in Congress 4 July 1776]

The Unanimous Declaration of the Thirteen United States of America

"When, in the course of human events, it becomes necessary for one people to dissolve the political bands which have connected them with another, and to assume among the powers of the earth, the separate and equal station to which the laws of nature and of nature's God entitle them, a decent respect to the opinions of mankind requires that they should declare the causes which impel them to the separation.

"We hold these truths to be self-evident, that all men are created equal, that they are endowed by their Creator with certain unalienable rights, that among these are life, liberty and the pursuit of happiness. That to secure these rights, governments are instituted among men, deriving their just powers from the consent of the governed. That whenever any form of government becomes destructive to these ends, it is the right of the people to alter or to abolish it, and to institute new government, laying its foundation on such principles and organizing its powers in such form, as to them shall seem most likely to effect their safety and happiness. Prudence, indeed, will dictate that governments long established should not be changed for light and transient causes; and accordingly all experience hath shown that mankind are more disposed to suffer, while evils are sufferable, than to right themselves by abolishing the forms to which they are accustomed. But when a long train of abuses and usurpations, pursuing invariably the same object evinces a design to reduce them under absolute despotism, it is their right, it is their duty, to throw off such government, and to provide new guards for their future security. — Such has been the patient sufferance of these colonies; and such is now the necessity which constrains them to alter their former systems of government."[42]

Jefferson felt a sigh of relief when the *Declaration of Independence* was finally approved. However, he was fuming internally when his argument against the slave trade was stricken from the document. Before, it couldn't be done because the colonies were under British rule. Now, there were other excuses. Although Tom had about 200 slaves he desperately needed, yet he still felt it was time to find an end to what he believed was a curse upon America. Repeatedly, Tom fought for the abolition of slavery, but each time it fell on deaf ears. Later, in his autobiography, he revealed how upset he was at that disastrous decision.

> "The pusillanimous idea that we had friends in England worth keeping terms with, still haunted the minds of many. For this reason those passages which conveyed censures on the people of England were struck out, lest they should give them offence. The clause too, reprobating the enslaving the inhabitants of Africa, was struck out in complaisance to South Carolina and Georgia, who had never attempted to restrain the importation of slaves, and who on the contrary still wished to continue it. Our northern brethren also I believe felt a little tender under those censures; for tho' their people have very few slaves themselves yet they had been pretty considerable carriers of them to others."[43]

When he wrote in the beginning of the *"Declaration"*, "All men are created equal", he meant all men and women, not just white males who owned property. He proved his convictions in the final segment of his rough draft. The following is what was stricken from the finalized version of the *"Declaration"*. Referring to King George III,

> "He has waged cruel war against human nature itself, violating it's most sacred rights of life & liberty in the persons of a distant people who never offended him, captivating & carrying them into <u>slavery</u> in another hemisphere, or to incur miserable death in their transportation thither. this piratical warfare, the opprobrium of infidel powers, is the warfare

of the CHRISTIAN king of Great Britain. determined to keep open a market where <u>MEN should be bought & sold</u>, he has prostituted his negative for suppressing every legislative attempt to prohibit or to restrain this execrable commerce: and that this assemblage of horrors might want no fact of distinguished die, he is now exciting those very people to rise in arms among us, and to purchase that liberty of which he has deprived them, & murdering the people upon whom he also obtruded them; thus paying off former crimes committed against the liberties of one people, with crimes which he urges them to commit against the lives of another."[44]

On the same day the *Declaration* was being approved, Congress received a letter from General George Washington warning British warships were spotted in New York and he needed help with troops and supplies right away. Conflict was still experienced between the delegates until finally they agreed to sign the *Declaration of Independence* on the eve of July 4, 1776.

At noon on Monday, July 8, a multitude gathered in front of the State House (now Independence Hall) in Philadelphia, as the *Declaration of Independence* was read to the eager audience. They showed their unanimous approval by shouting three Huzzas. The soldiers fired salutes from their muskets as the church bells rang day and night. The arms of the King of England were torn down and burned that night in one of the bonfires that evening. As July 8th drew to an end, all the people knew a new nation was born.

The *Declaration of Independence* had to be sent to the printer before it could be signed. By the day of the signing on August 2, several delegates who were at the ceremony had been either elected after its approval on July 2 or were absent on that date. Among the 56 signers who were Tom's friends were fellow Virginians Carter Braxton, Benjamin Harrison, Thomas Nelson, Jr. and the Lee brothers - Richard Henry and Francis Lightfoot. Of course, Tom's mentor and father-figure, George Wythe at 50, was his favorite signer. He was also an abolitionist and helped to steer Thomas Jefferson to take a stand against the practice of slavery.

Signers from Massachusetts also became Tom's favorites – men like John Adams and John's cousin, Samuel Adams, Elbridge Gerry, and John Hancock, the president of the Congress. Of course, in

Philadelphia, Benjamin Franklin and Thomas Jefferson began a longtime mutual relationship that would bridge across the Atlantic.

Only two delegates failed to sign. One was John Dickinson from Pennsylvania, who desired to make peace with England. Robert R. Livingston of New York, a member of the committee to create the *Declaration of Independence,* was recalled by his state before he was able to sign it.

As each member's names were called to step forward to sign, a hush of silence was prevalent in the house as they realized they might be signing their own death warrants. "We mutually pledge to each other our lives, our Fortunes, and our sacred Honour" was their agreement. Benjamin Harrison of Berkeley, Virginia, and Elbridge Gerry of Marblehead, Massachusetts, were two of the honorable delegates. Harrison was tall and obese while Gerry was thin and lean. The silence in the place was awakened when Harrison told Gerry: "I shall have a great advantage over you, Mr. Gerry, when we are all hung for what we are now doing. From the size and weight of my body, I shall die in a few minutes, but from the lightness of your body, you will dance in the air an hour or two before you are dead."[45]

The Historic Albemarle County Court House, Charlottesville

Keeping the Dream Alive

*"I'm a great believer in luck, and I find the harder
I work the more I have of it."*
Thomas Jefferson

1776

With the achievements of liberty accomplished, Thomas Jefferson was ready to go home. His present term in Congress would end in mid-August, and he longed to be with his wife, Martha. His only child, Patsy, would be celebrating her fourth birthday in September, and he vowed not to miss it. However, the Virginia Convention in June re-elected Tom to another term, much to his chagrin. Since July 4, he had grown weary of all the quibbling that was going on between delegates, with much ado about nothing.

During that time, Tom received word that Martha was extremely ill. He decided to quit Congress and head to Virginia. First, he had to find a replacement, and that was afforded him with Richard Henry Lee of Virginia chosen as his substitute. By the time Lee arrived to replace him, it was September 3 when he left for his grueling week-long trek to Monticello. Robert Hemings had replaced Jupiter as Tom's personal servant. He was merely 14 and a slave, the son of Tom's wife's half sister, Betty Hemings. (John Wayles, Martha's father, had six children by his slave, Betty, but he never gave them his name. They were in order: Robert, James, Thenia, Critta, Peter and Sally. They all had been inherited by Jefferson when Martha's father died three years earlier. This began an involvement with this Hemings family that would continue with Jefferson for the remainder of his life).

When Tom finally got home, he quickly raced to Martha's bed to comfort her in her illness. Their physician, Dr. George Gilmer, Jr., had paid her several visits. Once Tom made sure she was feeling better, he brought the gifts he bought for her in Philadelphia. One of the house servants brought little Patsy to see her father, and they shared warm embraces and assurances of mutual love. Tom then gave her a new doll and some toys he brought from the big city.

While Thomas Jefferson was home tending his ill wife and keeping his plantation in order, George Washington was heavily engaged in battle with the British in New York with the enemy on the winning side. After defeating the Americans at the Battle of Long Island, the British captured New York City. The next engagement took place in upper Manhattan on September 16, 1776, when George Washington's Army won its first victory at the Battle of Harlem Heights.

Patsy was so happy to have her father home on Sept. 27 for her fourth birthday. Although he was excited for her, he was once again saddened to know that last year at this time was when his second daughter, Jane, died. How he wished she could have been here to celebrate with them. On Sept. 30, Tom was still firmly planted at Monticello, when he declined an appointment to negotiate diplomatic treaties with France. Congress had appointed him to join Benjamin Franklin and Silas Deane in that endeavor. However, Tom felt Martha's continued illness deserved his utmost attention.

When Thomas Jefferson was a young child, he often remembered his father assembling with four other men who were founders of the Loyal Company. His memory would take him back to their plans to one day capture the West, going all the way to the Pacific Ocean. Four of those pioneers were deceased, with only one remaining. As soon as Tom felt it was safe to leave Martha's side, he visited Dr. Thomas Walker at neighboring Castle Hill. He was now 61 and still in good health, the only one of the five who still survived.

Tom had been so consumed with all the conflict between the British and the Americans; he found the dream of his father had been all but erased from his memory. However, spending time with the Walkers brought his father's aspirations back to his remembrance. Although Tom had been sidetracked from the Loyal Company's mission for awhile, he renewed his enthusiasm for it.

While he was at the Walkers, he wanted to get caught up with all the happenings at Castle Hill. He knew that the families of the five Loyal Company members were intermarrying with each other, but until now he hadn't realized how frequent they did this. All lived on plantations at the foot of the Southwest Mountains, all went to the same churches, and all were of the "married well and often" class of planters with large plantations. Therefore, their intermarriage, though confusing, was accepted as the norm.

Dr. Thomas and Mildred Thornton Walker had seventeen children, although some did not survive childhood. Of those who became adults, four daughters married or would marry descendants of the Loyal Company founders. Susanna Walker married Rev. Henry Fry, son of Col. Joshua Fry, on Jan. 16, 1764. By 1776, she had already given him six Fry children. Peachy Walker later would marry Joshua Fry, another son of Colonel Fry. Jane Susanna Walker much later would marry Wesley Thornton Fry, a grandson of Colonel Fry.

Another Walker daughter married into the Maury family on Dec. 17, 1775. Elizabeth Simms Walker had her wedding at Castle Hill amid all the Christmas decorations. She married Rev. Matthew Maury, son of Rev. James Maury and Mary Walker, the niece of Dr. Thomas Walker. Rev. Matthew and Elizabeth Walker Maury would eventually have three of their children marry descendants of Col. Joshua Fry.

While Tom was finishing his visit with Doctor Walker and his dear wife, Mildred, his old buddy, Jack, arrived home from meeting with the overseer of the 15,000-acre plantation of his father. They made plans to ride horses to the top of Tom's Mountain and visit Dabney Carr's grave at Monticello. They also planned to pay their respects to Tom's deceased mother and infant daughter, buried in the same cemetery.

"Jack, there's something that never ceases to amuse me," Tom picked a wildflower from amongst the autumn leaves sprinkled across the mountain grasses.

"What's that, Tom?" Jack was following Tom's lead as they strolled across the field together.

"The object of my amusement is your father."

"I don't blame you. He's always full of surprises. What has he done this time?"

"Jack, remember how he never would buy a coach or carriage for your sisters?" Tom turned to face Jack, who knew what Tom was thinking. "His excuse was that he felt they should learn to walk. You remember that, don't you?"

"Yes," Jack quickly responded, and then the two of them echoed the reason together word for word; "Because he could never afford to marry them to wealthy husbands." Then they laughed together so hilariously they bent over in pain and fell on the grass together, still laughing uncontrollably. Although Walker's daughters did not all marry rich men, they all wed into prestigious planter families that brought the family honor. After they married, they each had their own carriage, which ended their walking days as proposed by their father.

While Thomas Jefferson had relinquished politics so he could spend time with his ailing wife and his oversight of Monticello, he was given another assignment. On Nov. 5, 1776, the House of Delegates in Williamsburg selected him to chair a committee to revise the laws of Virginia. This would serve to replace the archaic laws solemnized by the British parliament. Selected to serve with him was Thomas Ludwell Lee, George Mason, Edmund Pendleton, and his father figure, George Wythe.

In the midst of one of Virginia's severest winters on record, over twenty inches of snow blocked Tom's path to Fredericksburg, where the committee planned their first meeting, held in the middle of January, 1777. Nevertheless, all five men plowed their way through the bitterest elements where they met to decide the process for accomplishing their prodigious task at hand. Both Lee and Mason resigned from the committee, excusing themselves because they were not lawyers. Tom wondered why they even bothered to risk their lives in the storm to make such a preposterous announcement. That left three men to do all the work, with most of it being done by Jefferson.

Because of the *Declaration of Independence* and the Revolutionary War that followed, the Anglican Churches quickly were losing members. During a war against England, it was unpopular and even dangerous to patronize England's church. In Albemarle County, Rev. Matthew Maury, son of Jefferson's former teacher, kept the doors barely open at the Fredericksville Parish. But Rev. Charles Clay was having more difficulty at his St. Anne's Parish church, where Tom served as a member of the vestry.

Jefferson's ardent obsession with religious freedom required the break with a state-sponsored church or religion. If that was accomplished, the clergy would no longer be supported by the government. Therefore, if they were going to be paid, they must receive their financial support from individual contributors or the voluntary offerings taken in their churches. Jefferson proved his desire for religious freedom by starting a new church at the courthouse, called the "Calvinistical Reformed Church." Each Sunday, the parishioners looked forward with amusement and delight when they saw Tom come to church on horseback, carrying a folding chair under his arms, which became his designated seat.

> The courthouse was also a place of worship and Jefferson himself helped organize an independent congregation led by Rev. Clay beginning in 1777 called the Calvinistical Reformed Church. A member of this church, Col John Harvie, introduced Jefferson's famous Bill for Religious Freedom to the Virginia legislature that same year. Many years later Jefferson called the courthouse the "common temple" and proudly spoke of its use each Sunday by four Protestant denominations in turn.

This sign stands in front of the present-day Albemarle County Courthouse, Charlottesville, VA.

Thomas Jefferson recruited twenty-one other men who promised their financial support for Rev. Charles Clay to minister to them on a regular basis. In their formal agreement for the organization of the church, among other items, they wrote that, "we expect that the said Charles Clay shall perform divine service and preach a sermon in the town of Charlottesville on every 4th Saturday till the end of the next session of general Assembly and after that on every 4th Sunday or oftener if a regular rotation with the other churches which shall have put themselves under his care will admit a more frequent attendance."[46]

Jefferson was the first to sign the article for incorporation and offered the greatest amount of support for it. Each one listed how much they would promise to pay Reverend Clay for his services. Tom established the idea of the "common temple" at the courthouse years earlier, where each Sunday a different denomination would hold services. Now, Tom's Calvinistical Reformed Church would have her day on the fourth Sunday.

Because Thomas Jefferson was opposed to state-sponsored churches like the Church of England, he was branded by many as opposed to church or religion of any kind. "How could a man be a Christian and have such negative views toward the church?" was their cry. However, Jefferson showed by his actions that he supported both Christianity and Biblical preaching. After all, his roots were steeped in the passionate teaching of the Bible from his former teacher, Rev. James Maury. During those formative years of the United States as a new nation, Jefferson showed all the evidence of being a true Christian in both belief and practice.

Tom spent the remainder of the winter and the spring of 1777 at Monticello, where he poured over his law books and worked on his Virginia law project. Meanwhile, Martha was pregnant again.

In May, she gave birth to their first son, and Tom couldn't have been happier. That was the ultimate desire of any man, especially those of the planter class. However, no celebration party was planned and no name was given to his son. Doctor Gilmer worked diligently to keep the newborn alive, but he was never strong enough to survive. Within weeks after his birth, the boy died and was buried at Tom's Monticello cemetery.

Meanwhile, Tom returned to his meticulous writing of the new Virginia laws. He had already sent a draft of his proposals to George Wythe and had received Wythe's welcome response. Martha saw little of Tom, as he spent most of his time buried among his library of books and fastened to his writing desk. The citizens of his county kept re-electing him to the House of Delegates, causing him to spend some time in Williamsburg every year attending legislative meetings.

During the winter months of 1777-1778, Thomas Jefferson diligently continued his drafting of Virginia's new laws. Meanwhile, George Washington was stranded with his troops in the bitter snows of Valley Forge. With his men suffering from lack of clothes, food and provisions, they faced potential defeat and disaster for the American cause.

Tom was delighted to hear that in February, the French agreed to join forces with America against the British. By June, Washington's plight had recovered so he and his troops finally left Valley Forge to return to the battlefield.

Jupiter and Suck had married, and she had given birth to a baby girl recently. Sadly to say, their daughter died soon after birth. Tom decided Jupiter should be apprenticed to William Rice. He was a skilled stone mason, who could train Jupiter how to build the columns in the main entrance to Monticello. Once again, Tom needed someone

Thomas Jefferson

he could trust. Jupiter would be more reliable to Tom than anyone else he knew.

As Jupiter began his apprenticeship, he was hired by Rice to chisel a gravestone three foot wide by six feet tall. Taking 18 days to finish, Jupiter's work still remains in the grave yard as a tribute to his beginning days as a stonemason. As he progressed, Jupiter was then given the task originally assigned by Jefferson. He began his work carving the four stone columns that would grace the east portico of Monticello.

On August 1, 1778, Martha gave birth to Mary Jefferson, whose nickname was "Polly". Joy once again returned to the Monticello household, especially since this new daughter had all the appearance of being strong and healthy. After having lost their last two children during infancy, the Jeffersons felt like God's grace favored them once again.

As Martha and her six-year old daughter, Patsy, was consumed with the birth and nurturing of the newborn girl, Tom had his quill in hand as he drafted a bill for establishing religious freedom in America. He believed that the government should provide freedom for its citizens to worship wherever and whenever they choose. Virginia's sanctioned church prior to the Revolution was that of the Church of England. The clergy were ministers of the government, and the citizens were required to support this ministry financially. The people were compelled to go to church and required to have their children baptized.

Jefferson wanted the government forbidden from making any law respecting the establishment of religion. He proposed that there should be no requirement either to attend church or to support it. That should be left to the personal volition of each citizen. The *Statute of Virginia for Religious Freedom* was the name Jefferson gave his prized proposal. (What Jefferson masterfully created was the model for what would become the *First Amendment to the U.S. Constitution* in 1791).

While Thomas Jefferson was involved in writing the new laws of Virginia, he felt it was time to flex his muscle on another burning issue hounding him - the slave trade in America. Ever since he had become a lawyer, he had taken issue with what he called the "abominable crime" of slavery. When he became a burgess, he tried in vain to get it abolished. When he wrote the draft for the *Declaration of Independence* he was adamant in his stand against slavery and was visibly upset when that section regarding it was deleted from his masterful document. Jefferson believed it was a moral depravity and fatal stain on the new nation he had helped to establish.

In October, 1778, Jefferson finally was able to take a major step to negatively affect the practice of slavery in Virginia. He came to the House of Delegates that year with his proposal, "That from and after the passing of that act no slave or slaves shall hereafter be imported into that commonwealth by sea or land."[47] Much to his delight, not only did the House of Delegates approve his proposal, but the entire General Assembly composed of both houses of government passed it, making it the law of Virginia. That gave Virginia the honor of being the first state in the United States to prohibit the further importation of slaves.

James Madison recently had become a new member of the Virginia General Assembly. Like Jefferson, he began his political career at an early age. It didn't take long for the two men to become close friends. Madison lived at Montpelier in Orange County, Virginia, between Monticello and Fredericksburg. Jefferson passed by his plantation many times heading north from his home. (What began in October of 1776 would result in a fifty-year friendship and comradery where they shared the same ideas for the foundation of American government. Jefferson would become known as the Father of the *Declaration of Independence* and Madison, the Father of the Constitution. They worked together to create the Democratic-Republican Party (now known as the Democrats). During the eight years of Jefferson's presidency, Madison would serve in Jefferson's cabinet as his Secretary of State. Madison would follow Jefferson as the fourth President of the United States, garnering strong support from his predecessor).

Marriages of the Dr. Thomas Walker children

1. **Mary "Molly" Walker**, b. July 24, 1742, married Nicholas Meriwether Lewis Nov. 2, 1758, son of Col. Robert Warner Lewis and Jane Crawford Meriwether. (Jane was the aunt of Col. Thomas Meriwether of the Loyal Company).
2. **John "Jack" Walker**, b. Feb. 13, 1744, married Elizabeth "Betsy" Moore June 6, 1764, daughter of Col. Bernard Moore and Anne Catherine Spotswood. (Anne was the daughter of Royal Governor of Virginia Alexander Spotswood and was of the first children born and raised in the Governor's Mansion in Williamsburg.)
3. **Susanna Thornton Walker**, b. Dec. 14, 1746, married Rev. Henry Fry June 16, 1764, son of Col. Joshua Fry and Mary Micou.
4. **Capt. Thomas Walker, Jr.**, b. March 17, 1749, married Margarete Hoops, daughter of Thomas Hoops of Carlisle, Pennsylvania.
5. **Lucy Walker**, b. May 5, 1751, married Dr. George Gilmer, Jr. Aug. 27, 1767, son of Dr. George Gilmer and Mary Peachey Walker. (Lucy's husband was the son of Lucy's aunt, Mary Peachey Walker being the sister of Lucy's father, Dr. Thomas Walker. That made Lucy and her husband, George, first cousins. Dr. George Gilmer, Jr. was the personal physician of Thomas Jefferson.)
6. **Elizabeth Simms Walker**, b. Aug. 1, 1753, married Rev. Matthew Maury Dec. 17, 1775 (son of Rev. James Maury and Mary "Mollie" Walker). (Mary was the niece of Dr. Thomas Walker. Her husband filled his father's shoes as pastor of his Fredericksville church.)
7. **Mildred Walker**, b. June 5, 1755, married Joseph Hornsby in 1770.
8. **Sarah Walker**, b. May 28, 1758, married Col. Reuben Lindsay Oct. 20, 1774.
9. **Martha Walker**, b. May 2, 1760, married George Divers in 1780.
10. **Francis Walker**, b. June 22, 1764, married Jane Byrd Nelson of Yorktown 1798, daughter of Gen. Hugh Nelson and Judith Page.

11. **Peachy Walker**, b. Feb. 6, 1768, married Joshua Fry Sept. 1, 1783, son of Col. John Fry and Sarah Adams, grandson of Col. Joshua Fry.
12. **Jane Susanna Walker**, b. 1778, married Wesley Thornton Fry Jan. 25, 1798, son of Rev. Henry Fry and Susanna Walker, grandson of Col. Joshua Fry.

Governor of Virginia

"When the people fear their government, there is tyranny; when the government fears the people, there is liberty."
Thomas Jefferson

1779

The year of 1779 would prove to be an uneasy year for Tom that would dramatically change his lifestyle. In the midst of winter, he was safely nestled in front of his hearth at Monticello with his wife and two daughters. Patsy was now six, and Polly was trying her best to crawl at five months. Tom thoroughly enjoyed taking his infant daughter to his lap, playing with her and seeing her develop. After Martha lost her last two children, having a baby that would be this healthy at five months was remarkable.

During that time, Tom also was putting the finishing touches on his revision of the new Virginia laws. The British had captured Savannah, Georgia, during the past month. Although he knew before the war was over, the South probably would get involved. He was hoping Virginia would escape the brunt of the Revolution.

1779 began with General George Washington assembling his troops in hibernation for the long bitterly cold winter in Morristown, New Jersey. To Tom, it seemed the war would never end.

In February, Tom petitioned Robert Hemings to saddle up Jefferson's favorite horse, Caractucus, so they could make their way to Williamsburg. The two of them fought the bitter chills of winter as they maneuvered their horses 120 miles to Williamsburg to join Tom's fellow committee members, George Wythe and Edmund Pendleton. As they planned to gather to make their final revisions of Virginia's laws, Tom remembered how two years ago they first met and how he witnessed George Mason and Thomas Ludwell Lee resign from the committee, leaving all the work shouldered by these three.

Tom vividly recalled the meticulous pains the committee took to make sure their 126 proposals were properly worded. "We examined critically our several parts, sentence by sentence," Tom recorded in his daily journal. He wrote that they were "scrutinizing and amending until we had agreed on the whole."[48] When they finally finished, Tom was glad to get home to Martha and the children, though only for a short spell. He was pleased to see Polly had mastered the art of crawling and was now trying to walk. He did not want to miss a moment seeing her daily developments as he and Martha joined Patsy around the open fire in his cozy Monticello.

As Tom readied himself to return to Williamsburg for the next session of the Assembly, he received word that on May 10, 1779, British ships sailed into the Chesapeake. They unloaded 1800 troops along the coastal towns of Virginia. Admiral Sir George Collier's primary goal was to destroy all the storage of tobacco, the cash crop Americans would use to finance the war. In the process of burning some three thousand pounds of the valuable crop, he found it necessary to also burn several towns and capture 130 boats. His men invaded Virginia's shore like termites, as they spent sixteen days raiding every house and village in their wake. Virginia, being without a navy and any way to defend itself, was embarrassingly humbled by the British.

Tom arrived in Williamsburg to take his seat in the House of Delegates in May, 1779. All his thoughts were focused on the proposed revisions of the Virginia laws. George Wythe and he had burned the midnight oil, as they discussed how they would best present these to the Assembly. Pendleton had sent word he could not make it to Williamsburg. That left the entire burden on Wythe, the law professor, and Tom, the fellow he had schooled to be a future president of the new nation. What was to follow was not what Tom had expected.

In the beginning of the new nation, Virginia elected her governor for one year at a time. In 1779, Patrick Henry had just completed his three one-year terms as the first Governor of Virginia. Since that was the maximum allowed by law, another had to be chosen from among the members of the General Assembly. Three men were nominated for Henry's replacement, with Thomas Jefferson winning the vote.

Thus, on June 1, 1779, Thomas Jefferson was elected the second Governor of Virginia. Tom barely beat out his good friend and old college buddy, John Page. It was a friendly contest, and Page was glad for Tom that he won. He wrote a letter of congratulations, part of which he said, "I sincerely wish you all happiness and will do everything in my power to make your administration easy and agreeable to you." Tom returned a response to his dear friend, assuring him he would not allow this political appointment to stand between them. It was not a position Tom really wanted, and he accepted it only out of sense of duty for his beloved Virginia.

As a result, the next three years would be a ghastly nightmare for Tom. The Revolutionary War had already moved to the South, and he knew the inevitable must happen. However, there was no way he could imagine how disastrous it would be for him and Virginia. He was now the governor of the largest state in America, which stretched all the way to the Mississippi River. With one thousand miles of coastline and having no navy to defend it, Virginia was a sitting duck for the British warships. They had already struck once, and it was only a matter of time before they would return.

Tom did not relish politics. He preferred the quietness of his study, where he could put his innovative thoughts on paper. Writing the *Declaration of Independence* was a more satisfying achievement to Tom than all the years he served as a burgess or a delegate to some convention. Tediously pouring over the revisions to the Virginia laws was a greater delight to him than haggling with the politicians who opposed them.

Tom was also a visionary, and his father's dream was still an obsession to him. With all the conflict with England, Tom had little hope he would ever see America stretch all the way to the Pacific. He had just celebrated his 36th birthday, and he was afraid his years might end before his father's dream would become a reality.

On June 18, shortly after becoming governor, Thomas Jefferson submitted the revisions of the 126 laws he had been working on with George Wythe and Edmund Pendleton for the past two years. After lengthy debate, many of them were approved, except bill number 82, which Tom had carefully crafted as the *Statute of Virginia for Religious Freedom*. That bill would continue to be heavily debated in the Assembly until final approval six years later on January 16, 1786. When he witnessed all those who fought his ideas for freedom of religion, Tom's heart was filled with anger toward his foes. The stuffed shirts fought for the Anglican Church and its clergy to continue to be supported and endorsed as the state religion of Virginia.

Jefferson longed for the day when the Baptists, the Presbyterians, the Methodists, the Quakers, his own Calvinistical Reformed church, and all other faiths and denominations could claim the right to worship

God the way they chose without government support or opposition. What Americans take for granted today was heavily debated during the Revolution.

According to John Hood, president of the John Locke Foundation, "No where was the crackdown more evident than in Virginia. The government accused Baptists of child abuse (for not christening their infants) and immorality (for not registering their marriages with the established church). Here are reports from individual Virginia Baptists about how they were treated during the 1760s:

- "Pelted with apples and stone."
- "Ducked and nearly drowned by 20 men."
- "Commanded to take a [a drink of whiskey], or be whipped."
- "Jailed for permitting a man to pray."
- "Meeting broken up by a mob."
- "Arrested as a vagabond and schismatic."
- "Pulled down and hauled about by hair."
- "Tried to suffocate him with smoke."
- "Tried to blow him up with gunpowder."
- "Drunken rowdies put in same cell with him."
- "Horses ridden over his hearers at jail."
- "Dragged off stage, kicked, and cuffed about."
- "Shot with a shotgun."
- "Ruffians armed with bludgeons beat him."
- "Severely beaten with a whip."
- "Whipped severely by the Sheriff."
- "Hands slashed while preaching."[49]

Statute of Virginia for Religious Freedom

"That no man shall be compelled to frequent or support any religious worship, place, or ministry whatsoever, nor shall be enforced, restrained, molested, or burthened{sic} in his body or goods, nor shall otherwise suffer, on account of his religious opinions or belief: but that all men shall be free to profess, and by argument to maintain, their opinions in matters of religion, and that the same shall in no wise diminish, enlarge, or affect their civil capacities."[50]

After Tom became governor, he made plans to move his family to the Governor's Palace at Williamsburg. He was looking forward to the opportunity to live in the spacious mansion he loved to frequent when he was in college. However, he must first of all break the news to his dear wife. Although she was happy for Tom that he won the election, nevertheless she did not much care for the idea of moving. Tom decided to break the news to her as they strolled in their Monticello garden.

"Martha, I need you and the girls with me in Williamsburg. I miss you so much when you are absent."

As she snipped a big scarlet rose off the vine and put it to her nose, Martha said quite thoughtfully, "Thomas, you know how much I love Monticello. I also don't care for the city life. However, to be by your side, I'm willing to make the move."

"You please me greatly, my dear, with your response. There's only one problem."

"What's that, Tom?"

"The Governor's Palace is not quite ready for us to move in. Patrick Henry and his family must first move out. Then there will be alterations to be made to prepare the home for us."

"Where will we live in the mean time?"

"I thought you could stay at The Forest. That was your childhood home, and it is close to Williamsburg."

"That's a good idea, Thomas. I will look forward to spending some time on the James River again."

They immediately gathered their most trusted slaves to help them load their wagons for the move. What Tom failed to tell his wife may have changed her willingness to leave Monticello. He expected the stay at the Governor's Palace would be short lived because he anticipated the Virginia Capital would be moved to Richmond. For years, he had urged the General Assembly to move the Capital further inland for safety and security purposes. He stressed that it was too close to the Chesapeake Bay and the inland rivers, making it an easy target for British ships.

When the Jeffersons finally moved into the Governor's Palace, Tom's daughter, Patsy, was all aglow. She never had seen a home that spacious and marked with splendor. She ran from one room to the other, trying to choose which room would be her very own.

"Oh, Daddy, I love our palace!" shouted Patsy, who would celebrate her seventh birthday here.

"I hope we can live here forever!"

"That would be nice, Patsy, but I'm afraid I can't be governor that long."

"Daddy, I hope you will be the governor for a long time then."

Tom refused to continue that discussion because he couldn't give her any assurances. By this time, he had second thoughts about being governor, and even talked to others about failing to fulfill his present term. Much to the dismay of Martha and Patsy, the Assembly agreed to move to Richmond, holding its final meeting in Williamsburg on Christmas Eve of 1779.

During that time, George Washington had huddled his troops for the second long winter In Morristown, New Jersey, where they suffered in freezing cold weather. Washington had written Governor Jefferson for food, supplies and ammunition. However, Tom found he could do little to help Washington because Virginia's needs were just as great. He was busy writing letters to encourage support, but they all fell on deaf ears.

Meanwhile, as governor, Tom took advantage of his authority to make some major changes to the College of William and Mary. As an alumnus, he had often thought about how his alma mater could be improved. First, to raise the collegiate status of the school, he found it necessary to close the grammar school. Secondly, he elevated the institution to status of a law school and a college of medicine. He added professorships of law and police, of anatomy medicine and of chemistry and modern languages. Furthermore, he appointed his close friend, George Wythe, to be the first Professor of Law in the United States.

By the time the next session of the Assembly convened on May 1, 1780, Jefferson and his family were now living in the spacious estate home of his aunt, Mary Jefferson, and her husband, Lieutenant Colonel Thomas Turpin. (Mary was the sister of Tom's father, Peter Jefferson. Her husband had served as both a magistrate and a sheriff in Goochland County before leading the Cumberland County militia in 1754).

As for Martha, she was getting tired of being uprooted from her home. She dearly missed Monticello, and since leaving there, in less than a year, she had lived in three different homes in three different locales. Now that she was pregnant again, she hoped this would be the end of her moving days for awhile.

Located on Shockoe Hill in Richmond, Tom's new residence conveniently overlooked the temporary site of the General Assembly's makeshift meeting place in two warehouses at the foot of the hill called "Shockoe Bottom". (There the meetings would be held until 1788, when the Capitol Building would be completed on the top of Shockoe Hill according to Jefferson's architectural design.

Thomas Jefferson

As soon as the 1780 General Assembly convened its annual meetings, the delegates were informed that on May 12, the British had captured Charleston, South Carolina. General Charles Cornwallis had landed in February with 8,500 troops. The American patriots led by General Benjamin Lincoln were far outnumbered and were ill-prepared for the British invasion. They fought off the British as long as they could, but three months later Lincoln was forced to surrender Charleston.

Although the capital had moved inland from the Chesapeake, both Governor Jefferson and the General Assembly were getting anxious about how close the British were getting to Virginia. They feared they would march north from Charleston on their way to the seat of government in Richmond.

Tom wanted to find out the progress of the British through North Carolina on their way to Virginia. So he turned to a proven soldier named James Monroe. Coming from Westmoreland County, although only 22, he was already a veteran of the Revolution. Four years earlier, prematurely he left the College of William and Mary to join Washington's army. Being the son of a planter, he was commissioned a lieutenant in the 3rd Virginia Infantry. He was a member of the advanced guard when it crossed the Delaware River, preparing the way for General George Washington. Later he was nearly killed when a musket ball struck his chest at the Battle of Trenton. Before Monroe returned to Virginia, he was promoted by Washington to major after they had survived the bitter winter together at Valley Forge.

On November 3, 1780, the Jeffersons' third daughter, Lucy Elizabeth, was born. Unlike Patsy and Polly, Lucy was frail and sickly from the time of birth. Six months later, Tom would be agonizing with Martha over the death of little Lucy.

That winter would be a disastrous one for Virginia., Thomas Jefferson was in the position to be hardest hit. Led by General Benedict Arnold, British forces returned to Virginia at the end of December That time, Arnold's focus was on Richmond, its governor, and its governing body. When Tom heard of Arnold's scheme, on May 24, 1781, he moved the capital temporarily to Charlottesville. In doing so, Tom dreaded having to tell Martha she would have to move again. This time, he found she was more resistant.

"Thomas, you don't expect me to move again, do you? I have just gone through a difficult pregnancy and have a newborn in bad health."

"I am sorry, dear," Tom responded sympathetically, "but we can't stay in Richmond. The British troops are on their way, and we must head back to Monticello for our safety." Reluctantly, Martha made the move once again, knowing that at least she would be glad it was to Monticello.

Meanwhile, Benedict Arnold led his troops to invade Richmond and with the use of torches, they destroyed homes, public buildings and the legal documents of the Virginia government. After he had his fill of violence, he led his troops back to Portsmouth on the Chesapeake Bay, where they set up defensive positions.

When George Washington heard his home state was being destroyed, he sent his trusted General Marquis de Lafayette to help Jefferson and his government. The native French man aide to General Washington had already become a hero of the Revolution. When he was living in England at only 19 years old, he heard of the *Declaration of Independence* and the colonists' fight for their freedom. He was inspired to join the Revolution. Lafayette was a young man of high social status and was from a wealthy family. Lafayette used his own funds to hire a ship for his trip to America.

Arriving in 1777, he sent a letter to Congress offering to volunteer his services in the Continental army without pay. That got him an audience with George Washington, who commissioned him a major general and made him his close confidante. As a result of the comradeship between the two officers, Lafayette helped persuade the French to join the American cause.

When he arrived in Richmond with his troops on April 29, 1781, he saved the city from further destruction. As Lord Cornwallis moved north from the Carolinas fresh from the victory at Guilford Court House, he chose to bypass Richmond in favor of Williamsburg and Yorktown. However, before he marched to his eastern destinations, he sent his Lieutenant Colonel Banastre Tarleton to seek out and to capture Governor Thomas Jefferson and the Virginia legislature. "Bloody Ban" Tarleton, as he was nicknamed, believed that if he could eradicate the governor, he would deal a fatal blow to Virginia and would give the British an upper hand to win the war. (What Tarleton didn't know was that Jefferson had just resigned his office as governor on June 2 when his term expired. Thomas Nelson, Jr. was now the new Governor of Virginia).

Jack Jouett was the owner of the Swan Tavern in Charlottesville, across the street from the Albemarle Co. Courthouse. His 26-year-old son, Jack Jouett, Jr. was visiting in Louisa County when he overheard

Tarleton and his men planning their scheme to kidnap the governor and his legislature, most of whom were housed at Monticello. About midnight, he mounted his speedy horse and travelled all night for 40 miles to Monticello to warn Jefferson of the dastardly scheme.

By the time Tarleton arrived in Tom's neighborhood, he had traveled all night and was starving. Therefore, he stopped for some rest and breakfast at the home of Dr. Thomas Walker at Castle Hill. Mrs. Walker fixed such a fine breakfast that his attempted capture of Jefferson was greatly delayed. That gave time for Jack Jouett, Jr., to warn Jefferson of the British plans, causing him and his family to escape. That significant event on June 4, 1781, marked a turning point in the Revolution.

"Bloody Ban" and his troops of dragoons refused to leave the area until they had captured seven legislators, ravaged the area, and killed those who got in their way. As soon as Jouett arrived at Monticello, Robert Hemings quickly hitched the horses to the Jefferson carriage, and Martha and the girls raced toward Poplar Forest, some 90 miles south. Tom waited behind until he saw the British dragoons galloping up the mountain toward his place. Meanwhile, Jupiter stayed at Monticello and gathered up all Tom's priceless silver dishes and utensils, hiding them from the British troops. Secretly, Jefferson slipped away from them through the woods, catching up to his family on their way south.

As for Jouett, he was declared a hero and was awarded two pistols and a sword from the General Assembly, which was now meeting as far west as Staunton in the Shenandoah Valley. He would be hailed as "The Paul Revere of the South," but his historic ride to warn the patriots was over twice as long as Paul Revere's ride under more treacherous conditions and terrain. The only difference between the two was there wasn't a Henry Wadsworth Longfellow to write about Jouett's heroic deed.

Once again, Martha was uprooted from her home, except this time she was running for her life. Once they arrived at Poplar Forest, one of their other plantations, they remained there until they believed it was safe to return to Monticello. Although Tom had acquired that 4,800 acre plantation when he took Martha in marriage in 1773, he never had lived there. The Jeffersons barely survived for throughout the hot humid summer in the rustic meager shack, home of the farm's overseer. To make matters worse, on June 30, Tom suffered a horrendous fall from his horse, which left him with a broken arm, handicapping him for six weeks.

Meanwhile, Lord Cornwallis encamped his troops for ten days on another plantation owned by Jefferson called Elkhill. Positioned between Monticello and Richmond, the British General confiscated Tom's house for his headquarters. During that prolonged occupation, the British army destroyed all the corn and tobacco crops, burned all the barns and fences, and slaughtered all the cattle, sheep and hogs, and the young horses. Thirty of Tom's slaves were kidnapped, and Tom heard that most of them later died of small pox and "putrid fever" that spread as a plague through the camp of the British army.

As for the Virginia legislators, they had temporarily removed the seat of government further west over the Blue Ridge Mountains to Staunton. They were fleeing not only for their own safety, but for the protection of legal documents and record books of Virginia.

However, their new governor, Thomas Nelson, Jr., was the Brigadier General of the Lower Virginia Militia. Having held that rank since the spring of 1778, he was more like a warrior than a politician. That was exactly what was needed as the British troops invaded Virginia and threatened to deal the fatal death blow to American freedom. Nelson's home was at Yorktown, where Cornwallis had confiscating for his base of operations. Thus, Governor Nelson had quickly evacuated his wife and family and waited in Williamsburg for George Washington's next orders against Lord Cornwallis and his British troops.

At the beginning of August, 1781, Major General Marquis de Lafayette had arrived in Williamsburg with his 3,000 troops. He was only twelve miles from Cornwallis' encampment at Yorktown. As a result of his wholehearted acceptance by General George Washington, Lafayette lobbied for French General Comte de Rochambeau to bring 7,000 troops from France to help Washington and his 8,500 soldiers.

Rochambeau was able to convince Washington to defeat British General Cornwallis on Virginia soil. On September 14, George Washington and Comte Rochambeau arrived at Williamsburg to meet with Governor Nelson and Marquis de Lafayette. They had just arrived with their troops from a 450-mile march from New York. Only one more piece of the chess board was needed to checkmate Cornwallis. That was the French Navy which had blockaded the Chesapeake Bay.

On October 14, the combined American and French forces stormed Yorktown in a frontal assault. They continued to close in on the 7,500 British troops, forcing them to attempt an escape by way of the York River. Since Nelson was the governor and an established resident of Yorktown, he was designated by Washington to lead the way in that invasion. British commander, Cornwallis, had raided Nelson's mansion and turned it into his headquarters. Having heard that, in an effort to kill Cornwallis, Governor Nelson aimed a cannon at his own home. He also urged his militiamen to fire on it. The Nelson house was so well built that although the cannon balls shook the house, they couldn't destroy it.

By October 19, General Cornwallis agreed to a formal surrender to General Washington. That was through the joint efforts of the American and French armies combined with that of the French navy. Because the Chesapeake was blockaded with 36 armed ships from France, the supply lines from British ships coming from New York forced Cornwallis to surrender, giving America the victory.

While the Patriots were celebrating at Yorktown and throughout America, Thomas Jefferson was still at home nursing his wounds during the past five months. Physically, he was still recovering from his fall from his horse during the summer. Politically, he had been targeted by the Virginia House of Delegates for abandoning his role as the governor in the midst of the British invasion. All the problems during the war were blamed on Tom. He was charged with failure to provide adequate defense of Richmond when he knew the British were preparing for an invasion. Barbs were thrown his way for what the legislatures believed was cowardice for the way he fled Richmond during the crisis. That would continue to haunt him for the rest of his life.

Domestically, Tom's home front was in shambles. When he visited his Elkhill plantation, he was overwhelmed at the destruction and devastation Cornwallis had ravaged across his James River property. He would never be able to forgive the British for carrying off thirty of his slaves, causing most of them to die from disease. Only five of them would survive and willingly return to Monticello to work again for Tom.

As for Martha, Tom could see how all these moves, especially the last one in desperation, was taking a toll on her body. All peace and tranquility that Tom and Martha had enjoyed in their marriage was wounded. They would have a difficult time feeling safe and secure at their mountain home at Monticello. Nevertheless, Tom knew somehow he would recover; knowing that many of his ideas for America still needed his help to see them fulfilled.

During the summer, Tom worked on a detailed response to the charges against him. When the House of Delegates reconvened in December, Tom was there to deliver his reasons for each action taken during 1781. However, much to his surprise, before he got up to speak, he was told the charges against him were groundless, all based on false rumors. Nevertheless, he would not be still until he delivered all he had meticulously prepared.

Both the House of Delegates and the Senate unanimously voted to exonerate Tom of any wrong doing and to acknowledge their appreciation for his conduct. However, Tom had a bitter taste in his mouth for public service. He wrote to his cousin, Edmund Randolph, saying, "I…have retired to my farm, my family and books, from which I think nothing will ever more separate me."[51] As far as he was concerned, Tom had his fill of being in the spotlight of leadership. He returned to his natural desire to drown himself in his books and continue building his beloved Monticello.

The French Connection

"I am savage enough to prefer the woods, the wilds, and the independence of Monticello, to all the brilliant pleasures of that gay capital (Paris) . . . for tho' there is less wealth there, there is more freedom, more ease, and less misery."
Thomas Jefferson

1782

Thomas and Martha Jefferson began their new year snuggled up in front of the warmth of their cozy hearth. As they tuned their ears to the crackling sounds emanating from the fire, Martha took advantage of having Tom's undivided attention.

"Dearest, I have some good news for you."

"What is that, my sweet Martha?"

"I am great with child again." She waited to see his puzzled smile before she continued. "We should have another child that spring."

"What a blessing that will be!" Tom couldn't take his excitement sitting down. He stood up and drew Martha next to him, giving her a warm embrace. "After the dreadful year we have just experienced, we need some cheering up around here. And you have given me promise this will be a splendid year indeed."

The beginning months of Tom's retirement from politics found him busy delegating responsibilities to continue building Monticello. He also enjoyed spending quality time with Martha and his daughters without any interruptions. Polly, at three years old, was into everything. She kept Tom busy moving his papers and his books out of her reach. About the time he sat down to continue his writing, along came Polly to challenge his concentration.

- Nine-year old Patsy also was quite inquisitive. But different from Polly, her mind was focused on learning. She reminded Tom of himself when he was her age. Unlike most other girls, she learned to read and write at an early age. And like her father, she was an avid reader. Whenever Tom was missing a book from his library, he figured Patsy had borrowed it.

On a bitterly cold afternoon in January, Tom was in his study with papers strewn all over his desk. He had a new quill he was trying out as he carefully wrote down his thoughts in his notebook. Patsy quietly entered the room, hoping not to disturb her father. Totally absorbed in thought, Tom didn't notice her until she was sitting next to him. Startled, he looked up to see her peering through the papers on his messy writing table.

"What are you writing, Pa?"

"Patsy, these are what I call my *Notes on the State of Virginia*."

"Well, I can guess they must be things about Virginia, but why are you writing them?"

"Because an important man from France asked me do that."

"What's his name, Pa?"

"Well, if you must know, he is François Barbé-Marbois." Tom finally gave up his writing and put down his quill. He could see that his daughter was full of questions that needed his full attention.

"Why is Fransoys-barbee-marboys so important, Pa?" Tom gave her a broad grin when he saw how well her French sounded when she tackled the foreign man's name.

"He is the Secretary of the French Legation in Philadelphia. Before you continue your line of questioning, let me assure you I want to do everything possible to build a strong relationship with the French."

"Is that why you are so interested in my learning French?" Patsy was on her feet and started strolling back in front of him, just like he often did when he was trying to explain a subject.

"Well, I learned French as a child, and I found it quite helpful in my line of work. I felt it would be important to you, as well."

"Pa, you told me you were interested in going to France. Can you please tell me what that's all about?"

With that, Tom told her how it all started. "After I wrote the *Declaration of Independence* and it was dutifully signed, I was appointed by Congress to travel to France with Ben Franklin as a Commissioner representing America. However, your Ma was quite ill at the time, and it was about the time of your fourth birthday. I had spent too much time in Philadelphia and felt I must leave to come home. Needless to say, Ben Franklin went without me. Then just last year, after I resigned as Virginia's governor, I was appointed by Congress once again to travel to France. There I would join such distinguished men as John Adams, John Jay, Henry Laurens and Ben Franklin, who were already there. Once again, I declined the appointment."

"Wasn't that when we were at Poplar Forest, running for our lives, Pa?"

"That's right, Patsy, and I didn't think it was wise to leave you and Ma and your little sister in a time like that." Tom's daughter now sat back down in her seat, as Tom exchanged positions with her. As he began to stroll, following his father-figure, George Wythe's model, he folded both his hands together behind him.

"I am still planning to travel to France one day after our new nation gets more firmly established and your Ma is able to travel."

Right now, I need to get busy working on my Virginia notes for that important man from France."

"Do you mean François Barbé-Marbois?" Patsy was proud of herself she remembered his name.

"That's the one, daughter." Tom nodded his pleasant approval of her. "I have something to confess. I compiled these notes and sent him to the gentleman already. However, they were done in haste and written during a crisis in our lives. To do justice to them, I believe I need to rewrite them so they would be more complete. Now let's go get washed up for supper." They marched out of the room with their arms wrapped around each other, humming a merry tune.

When Tom wasn't busy with the construction efforts on his plantation or with his family, he was often found in his study working on his *Notes on the State of Virginia*. He had been asked to tell everything he knew about Virginia, including geography, climate, people, animals, laws, history, money and fossil bones.

He began the writing of those notes last summer at Poplar Forest after he had fallen from his horse, breaking his arm. While he was recovering, he refused to be useless. What he lacked in ability to do physically, he more than compensated by pouring over his books and recording everything he felt would help the French know more about America.

Whenever guests arrived at Monticello, they were entertained by Tom and Martha as they played their instruments and sang together. Tom had developed quite a reputation as a good fiddler, and Martha equaled his talent on the harpsichord. Those were some of the happiest days of Tom's life, and he never wanted them to end.

Martha's delivery of another daughter came in May. The proud parents chose to name her "Lucy Elizabeth" after their last child, who never fully recovered from childbirth. They were delighted their newborn appeared healthier than their last. Although Tom was happy to have another child, he was distraught that Martha was so weak. Days after the birth, Martha was so diminished in strength; she couldn't even get out of bed. No matter what Doctor Gilmer did for her didn't seem to work.

Since Tom wouldn't leave her, he moved his writing table next to her bed and brought in his quill and notebook. There he continued to compose his *Notes on the State of Virginia*. However, whenever Martha was awake and responsive, she received all his attention. Tom tried everything to cheer her, using his fiddle and his song and his illustrious accounts of what had been happening at Monticello. He kept her abreast of Patsy's questions about his writings and desire to help him with the research. Polly's shenanigans as a three-year old were sure to bring a forced smile to Martha's lips.

Tom tried to comfort her with Bible readings and prayer. He had her favorite foods prepared for her. Usually she was too weak to eat them or wasn't able to hold them down. After four months of suffering, Martha could not survive another day. On September 6, 1781, Tom's dear wife departed from Monticello to meet her Maker. Although Tom had no doubt she was in Heaven, walking those golden streets, he couldn't stand to live without her. Carved on her tombstone in the Monticello graveyard were Tom's bitter words "torn from him by Death".

Following Martha's departure, Tom was tormented with grief. He wrote in anguish that, I had "lost the cherished companion of my life, in whose affections, unabated on both sides I had lived the last ten years in unchequered happiness."[52] For weeks, Tom refused to leave his room in sorrow. He wouldn't open his thoughts to his daughters or to his sister, Martha, who lived with them at Monticello. Seeing Tom mourn his wife's death reminded his sister how agonizing it was for her to lose her husband, Dabney Carr. Although it had been over nine years since he died, she was still not over it.

During that time of mourning, Tom burned every letter and note he and Martha had written to each other over the years. When he finally came to his senses, he asked Jupiter to get his favorite horse, Caractucus, saddled up for him to ride. The two men galloped off together going nowhere in particular. Jupiter felt like there was no end to their travels. Although he was glad to see Tom come out of his doldrums, he was concerned about whether the horses would survive that lengthy ordeal. After they returned home, Tom began making notes again. Eventually, he wrote to all his concerned friends, telling them lately how he had felt almost as dead as his dear wife. He knew he had neglected Patsy, Polly and newborn Lucy. They depended on him. The nation needed him. During that time of recovery, Tom responded to Marquis de Chastellux, a French friend of his, "Your letter recalled to my memory that there were persons still living of much value to me."[53]

Minister to France

On November 12, 1781, Congress called for Thomas Jefferson once again. Although England lost the war, her king had yet to sign a peace treaty with America, assuring her independence. To assist with writing the treaty, Tom was appointed Commissioner to France once again. There John Adams, Benjamin Franklin and Henry Laurens were waiting to receive him.

Knowing he needed a break from his wife's memories at Monticello, Tom agreed on the appointment. However, the time of the year was all wrong. Since he had to be in Philadelphia on December 27 to board his ship, he must miss Christmas with his daughters. He found it difficult to say good-bye, but he knew they would be safe in the hands of his sister, Martha.

Tom endured the cold, wet journey north only to find upon his arrival that the rivers were frozen, preventing his ship from sailing. Therefore, he spent the bitter winter in Philadelphia stranded. Before he could sail, he received news from England that King George III had officially recognized America's independence. Tom knew his trip to France now would be meaningless, which was verified when the Congress rescinded it on April 1.

Although Tom's opportunity to sail to France was foiled again, he was delighted to return home to see his daughters. Little Lucy was just turning one and learning how to walk. Polly, now four, was one big bundle of love as she cuddled up with her father. At ten years, Patsy reminded Tom so much of himself when he was younger. Always with a book in her hand, she loved learning and exploring. Tom enjoyed the times they walked through the garden and the woods, watching the new blooms of spring. How he wished his dear Martha was still here to enjoy it with them.

Construction at Monticello continued, with Tom taking time to inventory his library. His 2,640 books covered about every subject imaginable. Those Tom categorized by subject. While he was in the record-keeping frame of mind, he wrote down each of his 204 slaves' names and on which of his five plantations they served. Away from politics and the public eye, he was his happiest. Whenever he had time to spare, he continued revising his *Notes on the State of Virginia*.

As summer drew near, and the tree leaves started yielding their autumn brilliance, Tom was torn between Monticello and Philadelphia. He wanted to stay home, but Congress required his service once again. Having been elected as a delegate, he made preparations for another winter up north. This time, Patsy would go with him. After celebrating her eleventh birthday, Tom advised his daughter she would be attending school at Philadelphia. She was delighted, knowing she would be able to travel with her father and to see other parts of her new nation.

After Tom received word that the Peace Treaty had been formally signed in Paris, he was pleased to know a major step had been taken to assure America's independence. However, now there was a race against time. When British King George III signed it on September 3, 1783, he required America to ratify it within six months. Two-thirds of the states were needed to sign their approval. That would require at least nine states to send their delegates to the capital for ratification. Tom found it would be a guessing game where they were to meet.

Congress kept moving the capital city. Whether Philadelphia, Baltimore, Trenton, or Princeton, they each had their time to host the delegation. Finally, Annapolis was decided as the best meeting place. That was fortunate for Tom, as it was much closer to his home. However, before he could take his seat in Congress, he first took Patsy to Philadelphia, where he enrolled her in school.

Thomas Jefferson arrived in Annapolis just in time to greet George Washington, who was there to retire from his commission as General. On December 23, he announced he was looking forward to joining his wife, Martha, at Mount Vernon for Christmas.

What came next was a nightmare of seemingly impossible circumstances. Tom was assigned the arduous task of managing the ratification of the treaty between England and America. That placed on his shoulders the heavy burden of getting at least nine states to the bargaining table to sign the treaty within only six months.

As bitter as the last winter was for Tom, the one to come would be even worse. What he called "severe beyond all memory" deluged the northeastern seaboard with violent snow and ice storms, closing the harbors to ships. Tom thought it would never end. Because the delegates found it difficult to get to Annapolis, there seemed to be no way the treaty could be signed by the six-month deadline on February 3.

Tom was beside himself with anxiety. If the treaty was not ratified, that meant the Revolutionary War was fought in vain. Would Tom be an utter failure once again? He was still licking his wounds from his disappointment as Governor of Virginia. As bad as that was, to fail at the treaty process would be much worse.

Finally, the last of the required delegates made it to Annapolis. On January 14, 1784, all signatures were duly noted. Tom carefully penned the Peace Proclamation to be presented to England and France. America's independence from England appeared finally to become a reality.

While Tom's primary focus had been on the Peace Treaty, he had not forgotten his daughter. He had told Patsy to write to him from Philadelphia often. He wrote regularly, but he let her know he was unhappy she was not answering his letters in a timely fashion. Each time he wrote, he was quick to tell her how to run her life. Among these were instructions on his suggested daily schedule for her and how she was to dress and to behave. Perhaps, he felt she was avoiding him as being too fatherly.

Once the treaty was ratified, Tom was anxious to see his new nation grow by a westward expansion. On March 1, 1784, he submitted to Congress his plan for a government whenever new states were added to America. With Virginia yielding its western lands to the new nation, that seemed to be the ideal time to address that subject. What became known as *"The Ordinance of 1784"* was another futile attempt Tom made to abolish slavery. He proposed that by 1800 all new states should rid themselves of the servitude of those from Africa. Although Congress adopted most of his ordinance, the majority of the delegates refused to approve slavery's end. Sorry to say, it only failed by one vote. Once again, Tom realized they had a "wolf by the ears" mentality that was immovable. That was more so with the southern states than those from the north. He couldn't believe that one man could decide the plight of all the slaves.

While Tom looked at his *"Ordinance of 1784"* as a major disappointment, three years later he realized it would become the foundation for a monumental victory. On July 13, 1787, the Second Continental Congress adopted the *Northwest Ordinance*.[54] That was a document specifying how new states from the Northwest Territory would be admitted to the Union. One of its provisions was a Bill of Rights based on Jefferson's *"Ordinance of 1784"*. That historical manifesto had Tom's fingerprints touching every sentence. All new states would be required to prohibit slavery, to protect religious freedom, to encourage education, to have the benefit of trial by jury, and to provide the right to a writ of habeas corpus.

• Also in March of 1784, Tom came up with a proposal to change the English monetary system of pounds to that of the American dollar. That would include the coinage of pennies and dimes. Jefferson believed to make a clean break with England the United States should have her own unique type of money. Although it would prove to be another brilliant idea Tom proposed, it was surely futuristic, showing once again he was a man before his time. Two years later Congress finally voted to accept Tom's new monetary system for America.

After King George III ratified the peace treaty with America, Congress appointed Thomas Jefferson once again to travel to France. Finally, it became a reality. He was to be a minister plenipotentiary, joining John Adams and Benjamin Franklin as those who would negotiate peace treaties on behalf of America. As a minister plenipotentiary, he would have full authority to settle matters on behalf of America. Tom couldn't wait to join his two long-time friends, patriots who served together in the writing of the *Declaration of Independence.*

Tom decided to take Patsy with him to France. Joining them was Jefferson's personal secretary, William Short. James Hemings, the 19-year old younger brother of Robert, Tom's personal servant, was also a part of his entourage. Tom wanted him to be trained as a French cook. After leaving his two younger daughters in the hands of their aunt Elizabeth Eppes, they left Monticello and traveled to Boston, where their ship was to leave on July 5, 1784. Patsy enjoyed watching the celebration of hoopla at the Boston Harbor the day before, eight years after Congress adopted her father's *Declaration*.

Following 19 days at sea aboard the ship *Ceres*, they received a warm welcome as they arrived in Le Havre, France. Soon Tom found lodging in Paris for himself and a Catholic convent for Patsy. Not only was it the best school available, it was close enough for him to visit her every day. He made sure he brought his completed *Notes on the State of Virginia* with him, where he would have them published.

Shortly after John Adams welcomed Jefferson to France, he awaited his wife, Abigail, and his children, John Quincy and Abigail, who also were sailing from America. When they arrived, they began a life-long relationship between the Jeffersons and the Adams, later to be culminated in the President's House in Washington. John Adams' wife was quite opinionated for a woman, which caused friction with Tom. He was used to a woman being seen, but not heard. Abigail believed just the opposite. To her, a woman should have the same equal rights as a man, and she reminded Tom of that often.

Several months after he arrived in Paris, Tom received word that his two-year old daughter, Lucy, had died of whooping cough. Once again, tragedy had stricken his family. Of his six children, only two were still alive. With Lucy's early death, Tom insisted that his other daughter, Polly, be sent to him. However, she refused to leave her Aunt Elizabeth Eppes in Virginia.

In the spring of 1785, Benjamin Franklin resigned his post as Minister to France, relinquishing that office to Thomas Jefferson. Approaching 80 years of age and having served there throughout the Revolution, Franklin was anxious to finally retire. Tom would miss his dear friend and confidante. At the same time, Tom was told John Adams would be moving to London.

Congress decided to have two ministers plenipotentiary - John Adams in England and Jefferson in France. Although separated by the English Channel, the two men would successfully work together on negotiations involving American interests abroad. A lavish dinner was provided in Versailles in Jefferson's honor. Among all the dignified guests present, Tom was particularly excited to be reunited with his Virginia war hero, the Marquis de Lafayette. Although he appreciated the celebration, none of the extravagance and splendor of the French gatherings ever impressed Tom. He much preferred the quiet, simple life of the American farmers whom he claimed were "the chosen people of God."[55]

While in France, Tom was delighted to shop for many items he would never find in America. Among these was a copying machine, invented in Paris in 1785. That was particularly valuable to him because he had made a practice of meticulously copying by hand everything he had written previously. Now, he was saved that laborious task and the time spent to perform it. He kept writing to Polly for her to come to France, but all was in vain. She continued to resist his passionate pleas.

Although Jefferson was on business in France, he was still needed in America, especially by his home state of Virginia. She needed a new Capitol to be built in Richmond, and who best to design it than Thomas Jefferson? Having no architects in Virginia, the Directors of

Public Buildings called on their former governor for help. They knew he was well versed in designing buildings in that he had studied every known architectural book. Besides, he was in France, where Tom had access to the finest of classic buildings and building designers in the world.

Tom toured many Greek and Roman temples to get some creative ideas. He finally settled on the Maison Carrée, one of the finest Roman temples in France. Employing a draftsman and a sculptor, he presented both the drawings and the scale model of his proposal to Virginia. He was pleased that it was going to be built on Shockoe Hill, where Tom chose to live while in Richmond. This was overlooking the falls of the James River and was near where the legislators had been meeting since coming to Richmond.

On January 16, 1786, the Virginia Assembly finally adopted the *Statute of Virginia for Religious Freedom* written by Jefferson nine years before. As a man ahead of his time, he rejoiced that his new nation had eventually agreed with his revolutionary proposal for freedom of religion. He would have his dear friend, James Madison, to thank for getting it adopted, but only after constant encouragement from Jefferson. This is the way the first part of his new law was worded. (underlined by this author).

Statute of Virginia for Religious Freedom

"(I) Whereas, <u>Almighty God</u> hath <u>created</u> the mind free; that all attempts to influence it by temporal punishments or burthens{sic} or by civil incapacitations tend only to beget habits of hypocrisy and meanness, and are a departure from the plan of <u>the holy author of our religion</u>, who being <u>Lord, both of body and mind</u> yet chose not to propagate it by coercions on either, as was in his <u>Almighty power</u> to do, that the impious presumption of legislators and rulers, civil as well as ecclesiastical, who, being themselves but fallible and uninspired men have assumed dominion over the faith of others, setting up their own opinions and modes of thinking as the only true and infallible, and as such endeavouring to impose them on others, hath established and maintained false religions over the greatest part of the world and through all time; that <u>to compel a man to furnish contributions of money for the propagation of opinions which he disbelieves is sinful</u>

and tyrannical; that even the forcing him to support this or that teacher of his own religious persuasion is depriving him of the comfortable liberty of giving his contributions to the particular pastor, whose morals he would make his pattern, and whose powers he feels most persuasive to righteousness, and is withdrawing from the Ministry those temporary rewards, which, proceeding from an approbation of their personal conduct are an additional incitement to earnest and unremitting labours for the instruction of mankind; that our civil rights have no dependence on our religious opinions any more than our opinions in physics or geometry, that therefore the proscribing any citizen as unworthy the public confidence, by laying upon him an incapacity of being called to offices of trust and emolument, unless he profess or renounce this or that religious opinion, is depriving him injuriously of those privileges and advantages, to which, in common with his fellow citizens, he has a natural right, that it tends only to corrupt the principles of that very Religion it is meant to encourage, by bribing with a monopoly of worldly honours and emoluments those who will externally profess and conform to it; that though indeed, these are criminal who do not withstand such temptation, yet neither are those innocent who lay the bait in their way; that to suffer the civil magistrate to intrude his powers into the field of opinion and to restrain the profession or propagation of principles on supposition of their ill tendency is a dangerous fallacy which at once destroys all religious liberty because he being of course judge of that tendency will make his opinions the rule of judgment and approve or condemn the sentiments of others only as they shall square with or differ from his own; that it is time enough for the rightful purposes of civil government, for its officers to interfere when principles break out into overt acts against peace and good order; and finally, that Truth is great, and will prevail if left to herself, that she is the proper and sufficient antagonist to error, and has nothing to fear from the conflict, unless by human interposition disarmed of her natural weapons free argument and debate, errors ceasing to be dangerous when it is permitted freely to contradict them:

"(II.) Be it enacted by General Assembly that no man shall be compelled to frequent or support any religious worship, place, or ministry whatsoever, nor shall be enforced, restrained, molested, or burthened{sic} in his body or goods, nor shall otherwise suffer on account of his religious opinions or belief, but that <u>all men shall be free to profess</u>, and by argument to maintain, their opinions in matters of Religion, and that the same shall in no wise diminish, enlarge or affect their civil capacities.

. "(III.) And though we well know that this Assembly elected by the people for the ordinary purposes of Legislation only, have no power to restrain the acts of succeeding Assemblies constituted with powers equal to our own, and that therefore to declare this act irrevocable would be of no effect in law; yet <u>we are free to declare, and do declare that the rights hereby asserted, are of the natural rights of mankind</u>, and that if any act shall be hereafter passed to repeal the present or to narrow its operation, such act will be an infringement of natural right."[56]

As a result of the passage of this law for establishing religious freedom, Thomas Jefferson would be branded by many church leaders as an atheist, a deist, a non-Christian, or a Bible-hating thug. Yet, the underlined words in the above document proved that Jefferson believed in God, believed in the ministry of the churches, and believed in the financial support of such ministry. He went a step further calling God "Almighty" and "Creator." And if he hated the Bible so much, then why did he have his family Bible with him when fire consumed all his books and possessions which were at his Shadwell home? Apparently, it had accompanied him to his law office in Williamsburg where he could read it for both research and contentment.

In the spring of that year, Tom made the voyage to England, where he met with John and Abigail Adams in London. During his visit, as Minister to England, Adams took him to a royal gathering, introducing him to King George III. Recalling Tom as the author of the *Declaration of Independence* from England, the king snubbed him by turning his back on him and rudely walking away. That caused Tom to write to George Washington telling him that whereas he had been the enemy of kings before, now I "was ten thousand times more so since I have seen what they are."[57]

While in France, Tom also toured Germany, Italy and Holland. Tom was an explorer and thoroughly enjoying seeing other lands and their cultures. However, the more he saw of other countries, the more his heart pined for Virginia. He wrote that all that he desired was "a very modest cottage with my books, my family, and a few old friends, dining on simple bacon."[58] Those simple necessities would surpass all the splendor of Europe.

After three years in France, finally Tom put his foot down and demanded Polly to be sent to France. She was nine years old, and Tom missed her immensely. He instructed her Aunt Elizabeth to send her with "a careful negro woman, Isabel, for instance, if she has had the small pox."[59] After receiving assurance Polly was on her way, he was anxious until she finally arrived. However, he was shocked when he saw who got off the boat with his young daughter.

Down the gang plank following Polly was a 14-year old slave girl. Polly ran and jumped in Tom's arms, happily greeting each other. Tom recognized that the girl's chauffeur was Sally Hemings, sister of his cook, James, and daughter of his wife's half-sister, Betty Hemings. How could Elizabeth think this teenager was a mature Negro woman? Nevertheless, he was thankful they made the trip safely and that she was there to join her brother. Tom eventually saw her as a blessing to him, being his faithful servant during the rest of his time in France.

Although Polly so adamantly resisted going abroad, quickly she became accustomed to her sister, Patsy's, school. There she was called by her French name, "Maria", which she dearly loved. From thenceforth, her childhood nickname, Polly, would be discarded for her new name.

From May to September of 1787, the Constitutional Convention met in Philadelphia, presided by George Washington. During that time, Tom was disturbed he was absent from those deliberations. However, his best friend, James Madison, kept in touch with Jefferson to get his input.

When Tom received a copy of the Constitution's rough draft, he generally approved it. However, he urged Madison to add a Bill of Rights to it. Without that important addition, Jefferson refused to accept it.

Until the Constitution, the United States had been governed under the Articles of Confederation. However, James Madison for one realized its weaknesses. He had helped write Virginia's Constitution 11 years ago, and that successful document became the skeleton for the U.S. Constitution. On September 17, 1787, the delegates to the Constitutional Convention in Philadelphia signed the Constitution, which then went to each of the states to be ratified. Since there was no Bill of Rights attached to it, Jefferson looked at it as an incomplete legal document. Once again, he was a man ahead of his time. Two years later his recommended idea of a Bill of Rights would be proposed to Congress.

The French Revolution

Although Tom was reappointed to a three-year term as Minister to France in October, 1787, he was not sure he would last that long. He saw "the handwriting on the wall". He was sickened to find the rank disparity between the hungry and homeless in the streets and the raunchy extravagance of the wealthy, the clergy and those in high office. The young French queen, Marie Antoinette, and the King Louis XVI, showed total indifference to the needs of their citizenry.

Tom carefully studied what was wrong with the French government. He noted there was what was called the "Estates-General." That consisted of three classes of people. The clergy of the Roman Catholic Church was the upper class. Then came the nobility. The lowest class was the bourgeois (the businessmen) and the workers (the peasants). Tom never understood that form of chaotic system and had no desire to learn. He saw the excesses of both the church and the king's entourage. The common people making up the third class did all the work and paid all the taxes. Meanwhile, the two upper classes claimed all the rights of the kingdom. That was totally opposite to the revolutionary ideas Tom helped establish in America. He believed that all men were created equal and all had the same inalienable rights provided for them by their Creator.

On April 30, 1789, George Washington was elected the first President of the United States. At his inaugural address he spoke of the need for amendments to the Constitution that would address the individual rights of the U.S. citizens. That had been Jefferson's concept he proposed two years earlier. James Madison followed Washington's suggestion on June 8, in which he introduced his proposed amendments to the Constitution he had authored. On September 25, the Congress recommended the amendments, the Bill of Rights, to each of the states for their ratification.

When Tom wrote his congratulations to George Washington on his recent election, he requested permission to return to Virginia. He had begun to fear for the safety of his daughters. He could see unrest among the citizens of France against the King, and he expected violence in the streets at any moment. Furthermore, while studying at the Roman Catholic convent, 17-year old Patsy wrote to her father for permission to become a nun. His resistance to her passionate request was felt when he abruptly pulled both she and her sister out of the school. Then he was in a dilemma about what to do with them. His heart was set on Virginia, and he wanted to go home.

Before Thomas Jefferson received Washington's response, the French Revolution began. Tom had already met with Lafayette and their patriot friends and was helping to draft a charter of rights in June. Lafayette was setting everything in motion for a change in government. He loved America's *Declaration of Independence*, which he used as his model. Tom was excited they thought his document was so significant to them. He somehow believed that if they used it, they would have the same results. However, Tom was unprepared for the violence they were facing as a result.

The common people organized themselves into a National Assembly. During the summer of 1789, riots and mobs of angry people filled the streets of Paris. On July 14, thousands of armed men stormed the political prison of Bastille, ripping it apart stone by stone. That institution was the epitome of their anger, where so many had been unjustly imprisoned and executed.

Fortunately, Jefferson was still there, as Lafayette and his friends met secretly at Tom's hotel residence. Based on his earlier draft, Tom helped write the *Declaration of the Rights of Man and Citizen*. The Marquis de Lafayette presented that to the National Assembly, which was approved and adopted on August 26, 1789. Under extreme duress, King Louis XVI reluctantly signed into law the French *Declaration*.

Tom's mind recalled how Lafayette and Jefferson's paths had crossed during the American Revolution. It all began with Tom's *Declaration of Independence*. When Lafayette read it, he was inspired to join the Revolution. At only 19 and paying his own expenses, he sailed to America to join General Washington's war for independence. Being commissioned as a Major General, he first served with Washington at Valley Forge. Then when Virginia's government was under attack by the British, Lafayette was sent to defend Richmond on behalf of Jefferson.

Tom realized that Lafayette was instrumental in getting the French to come to America's aid against the British. When Cornwallis was holed up in Yorktown, Lafayette's assistance was needed to force his surrender and end the war against England. Tom and the Marquis had become kindred spirits as a result. They both shared the ideals of revolution and independence against the medieval system that had crippled Europe for a thousand years.

In the fall of 1789 Tom, living in constant fear during the Revolution, gathered his daughters, his two slaves – James and Sally Hemings – and what Tom called "a chienne bergere,"[60] the French version of a shepherd dog. Before this, Tom's only pets were mocking birds. But Maria kept begging for a dog. Before Tom left France, he granted her wish, buying her one that was pregnant, which he called "big with pup." That would be a breed new to America. That helped justify Tom's acquiring a dog. Maria claimed the animal as her special pet, which she called "Buzzy".

Since Tom was only taking a six-month leave of absence from his office, he left most of his belongings in Paris. During the long arduous voyage, Buzzy gave birth to two puppies, which was the highlight of the journey for both Patsy and Maria. James and Sally Hemings likewise shared their joy.

Arriving in Norfolk, Virginia, on November 23, Thomas Jefferson couldn't wait to see the progress on the Capitol he designed for Richmond. When he arrived, he was impressed that it was completed and looked just like the way he designed it. Sitting atop Shockoe Hill made it even more impressive than he imagined it would be.

When the Jeffersons finally returned to Monticello, they found a jubilant celebration awaiting them by their friends, family and slaves. "The Negroes discovered the approach of the carriage….," reported a surprised Patsy. "They collected in crowds around it and almost drew it up the mountain by hand….When the door of the carriage was opened, they received him (her father) in their arms and bore him to the house, crowding round and kissing his hands and feet… It seemed impossible to satisfy their anxiety to touch and kiss the very earth which bore him."[61] Tom was glad to be home, surprised how much he had been missed, especially by his slaves. Although they were still in bondage to him, they made him feel like they were treated better than Negros on other plantations.

The following morning, Tom awoke to find a washtub of ice cold water awaiting his bare feet. As he pulled himself out of bed, he looked around to find the source of the welcome pool of water. Immediately, he thought of Jupiter, whom he found awaiting him in the next room.

"Jupiter, what a pleasant surprise!" Tom rushed to give his black boyhood friend a warm embrace. "I have truly missed my morning footbaths. I suffered some illness while in France, and I knew it must be because I missed your special touch in the morning."

"Mista' Thomas, I've missed ya more than ya'll ever know." Jupiter's face was mixed with smiles and tears of happiness. "Sir, ya mus' get yar feet in de water before its coldness wears off." The two forty-six year old men marched into the bedroom together arms wrapped around each other. Jupiter helped Tom get his feet into the water as he had since Tom's college days.

After Tom soaked his feet, and Jupiter helped him get dressed, they left for an early morning stroll around Tom's plantation. Tom was shocked to see the dismal condition of Monticello, including the buildings and his garden. He asked Jupiter to saddle their horses. After breakfast, Tom would see if the rest of his acreage would be in such disrepair.

As they rode together, Tom let Jupiter know how upset he was about the condition of his property.

"What has been happening around here, Jupiter? This place is a mess."

"I knew ya'd be sad to find it this way, Mista' Thomas. I wish I could've made it better for ya."

"Don't feel bad. You are only one person. It's up to my overseer. He has failed to meet my expectations of him."

When they returned home, Maria was out in the yard throwing a stick to be retrieved by Buzzy. Her young puppies tried to find out what happened to their mommy while she was going after the stick. Tom dismounted from his horse and joined Maria playing with her pets. He was overjoyed to see her so excited about Buzzy and her brood.

Tom was quick to travel to the rest of his plantations, where he found equal dissatisfaction with the way they looked. He felt he needed to personally supervise the continued construction of Monticello and the improvement of his garden and fields. Now that he was home, he refused to leave. He felt Monticello needed him more than all the political aspirations offered him.

First Secretary of State

"The will of the people is the only legitimate foundation of any government, and to protect its free expression should be our first object."
Thomas Jefferson

1790

Before Thomas Jefferson settled into the comforts of Monticello, he was surprised to find President George Washington had appointed him to be the first Secretary of State of the United States of America. Tom had been looking forward to a reprieve from political life. He longed for the quietness and serenity of Monticello. Patsy, now called Martha, was 17, and Maria was 11. Tom wanted to spend some quality time with them, which he had missed during his busy years in France.

For months Tom resisted the request to become Secretary of State. Between the letters of encouragement from George Washington and the personal pleas of James Madison, Tom finally accepted that position on February 17, 1790. However, before he left Monticello, he insisted on hosting his oldest daughter, Martha's wedding to Thomas Mann Randolph, Jr. He had been concerned she might "draw a blockhead." However, with a Randolph-cousin of hers, how could she have gone wrong? He was an alumnus of the College of William and Mary as well as the University of Edinburgh. His father was the cousin Tom grew up with at Tuckahoe. From the time he was two until he was nine, "Mann", as he called him, was his closest friend and schoolmate. Both of them were raised as brothers under the direction of Tom's father, Peter Jefferson. Randolph was his mother's maiden name, and it was quite comforting for Tom to have his daughter presented as Mrs. Martha Randolph. The newly married couple agreed to take care of Monticello in Jefferson's absence.

As Thomas Jefferson made the long journey to join George Washington, he stopped in Philadelphia to visit at the bedside of his ailing close friend and confidante, Benjamin Franklin. At 84, he had served his country well, but was now prepared to leave it in the hands of others. One of his last achievements was three years ago when he was elected president of the Pennsylvania Society for Promoting the Abolition of Slavery. Among all of the old statesman's accomplishments, that was one that made Tom the proudest. He was glad to see such a stalwart of the nation's independence share Tom's conviction that slavery needed to be abolished.

One month later, Dr. Benjamin Franklin died in his sleep on April 17, 1790. Some 20,000 people attended his funeral at Christ Church in Philadelphia, one of the largest ever known at that time. Tom was there when they laid his body to rest in the churchyard next to his wife, Deborah, who predeceased him by sixteen years. Although he was a man of many great accomplishments, the only epitaph he wanted on his grave was: "With his death, America lost one of its most loyal citizens."[62]

When Tom arrived at the United States capital in New York, he was reunited with his old friend, John Adams, who was the first vice president. However, he soon found their friendship quite strained and controversial. They disagreed on almost every subject. Adams was a Federalist, while Jefferson was an Antifederalist. As a Federalist, Adams believed the president should have greater power to rule the people with a heavy hand.

On the other hand, Jefferson believed in a rule by the people. "Why would America have gone through the Revolution if she was going to lean toward empirical rule?" Tom reasoned. Federalists also believed the Constitution was satisfactory without a Bill of Rights. Jefferson believed just the opposite. During the Revolution, New York was a sanctuary city for Loyalists, and during tenuous times, Tom thought he was the only Republican in town with patriot ideals.

Alexander Hamilton, who was Secretary of the Treasury, also was a Federalist. He believed the Constitution was a silly document that was too frail to survive. He believed it would not stand without constant reinforcement. Jefferson feared the federal government would become too powerful with that concept and would have an overreaching centralism as its ultimate object. Hamilton and Adams both believed in the rule of those who were wealthy and wellborn. Jefferson believed all people should have the opportunity to serve in the government. Even in the matter of dress, Hamilton and Jefferson were direct opposites. Whereas Hamilton wore fancy clothes with ruffles, Tom's were rather plain.

The more Tom saw of politics, the more he realized why he would rather be at Monticello. Once he got settled into his secretary's desk, he said that one game was over "and another was on the carpet the moment of my arrival."[63] The new game was the one proposed by Alexander Hamilton, a scheme for the federal government to assume the war debt of the individual states. Tom adamantly opposed the payment of twenty million dollars by the federal government to the states. Virginia had paid her own debts owed for the Revolution. Why couldn't other states do the same?

That game Tom called the "most bitter and angry contest" continued to be played for over two months. He argued that if they could not "milk the cow their own way, they would not suffer her to be milked at all."[64] When Hamilton's proposal finally went before Congress for a vote, it was hopelessly deadlocked in a tie. That is when Hamilton came to Tom, seeking a compromise.

Thomas Jefferson proposed building the nation's capitol on the Potomac River. As par for the course, Alexander Hamilton, a New Yorker, strongly differed with Jefferson. Why not keep the capital in his native New York? However, he agreed to accept Jefferson's plan in exchange for Tom's support of acceptance of the state's war debts. Later, as Tom looked back on that compromise, he felt he had been "duped", causing him to make what he believed was the greatest error of his political life. From thenceforth, every war to be fought by the United States would have to be financed by the federal government. Usually, that would be a heavier load than she would be able to bear.

As Secretary of State, Jefferson's primary responsibility was the diplomatic establishment of his new nation. Tom was at the forefront of negotiations with other countries, especially those which bordered the United States. England and Spain were both involved, as well as the native-American Indians. That was Tom's specialty. However, he also was in charge of the post office, inventions, weights and measures, and the making of money.

With a new quill in hand, Tom made detailed records of every meeting with George Washington and each of his staff. When he wasn't writing in his account books, he was penning letters to his daughters and friends around the world. He and Lafayette were still close friends and allies, and Tom kept abreast of every action taken during the French Revolution. Tom's first official report was about the coinage dilemma. In a concerted effort to break with the English pound and other currency, Tom said, "Coinage is peculiarly an attribute of sovereignty."[65] With that proposition, Tom argued that the United States should make its own currency. His idea was the decimal rule, using the dollar as its basis, and the coins being based on percentages of the dollar. A year later, Congress approved his proposal.

In the fall of 1790, the capital was moved from New York to Philadelphia, where it would be more centrally located. That was the first step closer to the Federal City that Tom proposed both Alexander Hamilton and the president earlier. Although the idea was controversial, George Washington accepted Jefferson's proposal to build the city ten miles square on the Potomac. That would place the Federal City in close proximity to their beloved Virginia, which was supplying half of the nation's real estate.

Major Pierre Charles L'Enfant, an engineer from France, was employed to help Thomas Jefferson plan the city. They worked together to lay out the streets and design the government buildings. Those included the house of Congress and the President's House. There were no architecture schools in Virginia. Tom learned his ideas for buildings from books and from his study of classical structures in Europe. Leaning heavily on *The Four Books of Architecture* by Andrea Palladio, Tom gleaned many of his designs. As a result Tom became recognized as the "Father of our National Architecture."[66]

When the capital was moved from New York to Philadelphia, Tom wrote to Paris. His personal secretary, William Short, had assumed Tom's position as Minister to France until he returned. He also kept in touch with Jefferson on a regular basis. When Tom realized he was staying in America, he arranged for Short to send all Tom's belongings to Philadelphia. That included a boat load of furniture, French heirlooms, books, draperies and other odds and ends he collected during his five years in France. Eighty six cases of furniture included forty four gold leaf lavishly upholstered chairs, six gold leaf sofas, clocks and scientific instruments. When they arrived, Tom clamored to find out where he was going to store all those goods, overcrowding the three-story house he had rented in downtown Philadelphia.

Although he was merely renting the house, he felt he had to redecorate it for his satisfaction. Using his furniture and ornamental objects from France, he felt more at home than he had in months.

When he finished with the restoration of his home, his was the best model of a French-style home in the city of brotherly love.

Tom had a difficult time fitting in with the high social set in Philadelphia. The sophisticated ladies competed for which one might dress the fanciest. Parties were held every week by President and Mrs. Washington, but Tom was not the partying kind. While everyone adorned themselves in their finest, Tom refused to dress the part.

After the beginning of 1791, Tom received word that he had just become a grandfather. In January at Monticello, his daughter, Martha, gave birth to her first child, Anne Cary Randolph. Martha wrote her father often, but Tom very seldom heard from Maria. That troubled Tom and he let her know by sending her bills showing how many letters she owed him. Martha told her Pa that Maria was lazy and stubborn, being difficult for her to handle, especially as she was approaching adolescence.

On February 25, 1791, Alexander Hamilton, Secretary of the Treasury, got his wish, as the National Bank opened for business. He got his idea from that of the Bank of England. Jefferson had fought Hamilton about that, claiming it was unconstitutional. He said the Constitution did not allow the government to have its own bank. President Washington at first saw it Tom's way, but in the end ruled in Hamilton's favor. James Madison, who was on Tom's side, likewise expressed his opposition to the National Bank, but it fell on deaf ears.

A month later, Hamilton proposed the first tax to be levied in the United States. That was a whiskey tax imposed on those who raised corn to be turned into whiskey. Jefferson saw how that would hurt the farmers in his area of the country more than any others. Although Tom opposed that whiskey tax, the president sided with Hamilton once again, signing it into law.

Tom had seen "the handwriting on the wall" after Hamilton got his way, making the federal government accept the states' war debts. The result was that a National Bank was needed, and taxes were needed to be raised to pay for that indebtedness. That was a necessary evil of the beast. One government excess led to yet another.

In September, Tom finally got a break from his political responsibilities to visit his new granddaughter. James Madison and Jefferson traveled together from Philadelphia to central Virginia, where they both lived. While there for a month's visit, Tom insisted that his youngest daughter, Maria, come to live with him in Philadelphia. She was now 13, and Tom felt like it was time for her to learn some of the social graces and literary education of the capital city.

On the way back to Philadelphia, Tom checked on the progress of his new Federal City. Major L'Enfant had laid out the 10-mile square area and designated what part would be reserved for the government buildings and parks. When Tom arrived, he witnessed the first private lots sold to the public. With all the infighting coming from Hamilton, Tom stayed away from Philadelphia as long as he could. If he had it his way, he would have preferred to spend full time helping Major L'Enfant design the future Washington D.C.

When he returned to his government post, another pressing issue faced Jefferson. On September 17, 1787, the delegates to the Constitutional Convention meeting in Philadelphia had signed the Constitution. For all the strengths of that document carved by the hand of James Madison, there were some alarming weaknesses.

As a result, two of the delegates refused to sign it. One was George Mason of Virginia, and the other was Elbridge Gerry of Massachusetts. They were quick to show their concern about the omission of individual liberties in the document. Mason had written the *Virginia Bill of Rights* eleven years earlier and saw the need for that model to be incorporated into the Constitution. Jefferson called Mason, "the wisest man of his generation."[67]

When the Constitution was approved, Tom was in France. When he read the provisions of the new law, he wrote to his good friend and author of the founding document, James Madison, his impressions of the Constitution. After sharing what he liked about Madison's creation, he then highlighted what he felt was its weakness.

"I will now add what I do not like. First the omission of a bill of rights providing clearly and without the aid of sophisms for freedom of religion, freedom of the press, protection against standing armies, restriction against monopolies, the eternal and unremitting force of the habeas corpus laws, and trials by jury in all matters of fact triable by the laws of the land . . . . Let me add that a bill of rights is what the people are entitled to against every government on earth, general or particular, and what no just government should refuse, or rest on inference."[68]

He further instructed Madison that the Constitution would be seriously flawed without a Bill of Rights. According to Thomas Jefferson, "A Bill of Rights is what the people are entitled to against every government on earth."[69]

With a lack of Bill of Rights, some of the states had difficulty voting to ratify the Constitution. The Federalists saw no need for a Bill of Rights and so fought for a quick ratification. However, on December 15, 1791, Jefferson and his fellow Antifederalists got their way. On that date the Bill of Rights was adopted and the Constitution was ratified. That was what Tom was hoping to hear, especially since the first one was modeled after Jefferson's *Statute of Religious Freedom*.

First Amendment to the Constitution

"Congress shall make no law respecting an establishment of religion, or prohibiting the free exercise thereof; or abridging the freedom of speech, or of the press; or the right of the people peaceably to assemble, and to petition the Government for a redress of grievances."[70]

That brought a successful end to a frustrating year for Tom. However, his taste for politics was still bitter, and he longed for his family and farm at Monticello.

Jefferson had enough after three years as Secretary of State and pleaded with Washington to allow him to go home. He had enough of Adams and Hamilton with all their Federalist ideas. But with Washington's urgent prodding, Tom continued to serve. However, he and James Madison, "Father of the Constitution", decided they couldn't agree to the Federalist ideas of Hamilton. Therefore, they began organizing the Antifederalists into what they called the Democratic-Republican Party. Whereas the Federalists believed in a strong national government, the Republicans (as they were nicknamed) stressed states' rights. The Federalists supported the National Bank and Hamilton's big spending program. Madison and Jefferson's Republicans rejected that in favor of a more agrarian-based economy based on farmers and businessmen.

The French Revolution reached its climax in 1793. The New Year was set ablaze in Versailles and Philadelphia as both the French and the Americans celebrated the prospect of independence in France. Although most of the parties in his city bored him, that one was cause for his utmost excitement. He was drawn into the streets where thousands in Philadelphia cheered the prospect of the Frenchmen becoming free like America. *Yankee Doodle* and the *Ca Ira*, liberty songs of both the United States and France were sung enthusiastically by the crowds.

On January 21, 1793, King Louis XVI and Queen Marie Antoinette lost their heads on the guillotine. At the same time, his dear friend and revolutionary hero, the Marquis de Lafayette was imprisoned in Austria for treason. England, Prussia and Austria had aligned themselves in war against France, making Lafayette their bitter enemy.

As Secretary of State and a supporter of the French Revolution, Tom was emotionally distraught about what was happening in France. Furthermore, he strongly disagreed with America's official response. The president issued the Neutrality Proclamation signifying that the United States would remain neutral. As much as Tom didn't like the idea of turning his back on France, he knew he had to bite the bullet and accept it.

On April 13, 1793, Tom celebrated his fiftieth birthday away from his family. But he was determined he would be home for Christmas. Spending a peaceful time with his family and friends in Virginia was such a stark contrast to the violent disagreements he encountered in Philadelphia. It was enough to cause Tom to leave politics once again.

However, before Tom went home voluntarily, he got word that his dear friend and cousin, Thomas Mann Randolph, died on November 19. At only 52, he and Tom were raised together at Tuckahoe and began school together in the building Tom's father had built for them. Recently, "Mann", as Tom called him, was the father-in-law of Tom's oldest daughter, Martha, making this a crisis for Tom's entire family. He dropped all his responsibilities to attend Mann's graveside service at Tuckahoe.

When he returned to the capital city after Christmas, he encountered a historic epidemic of yellow fever that was spreading rapidly throughout Philadelphia. That became the determining factor for Tom to return to Monticello for good. On December 31, 1793, once more Tom tendered his resignation to Washington. Regretfully, it was finally accepted.

As the New Year for 1794 broke on the horizon, Tom felt a new sense of freedom. As he walked down the street, he sensed a heavy burden lifted, making him lighter on his feet. At 50, he was going to be leaving politics for good. Hopefully, he would spend the rest of his days at his beloved Monticello. As soon as he finished his New Year celebration, Tom broke the news to his personal servant, Robert Hemings.

"Boy, I am here to tell you we are going back to Virginia."

"Wha' ya mean, Mista' Thomas? We jus' got here!" The slave man looked at the wide grin on Tom's face and noted the lilt in his voice. He knew that was good news, but he didn't know the reason.

"Robert, my boy, we are through with Philadelphia, with Congress, with Alexander Hamilton, with John Adams, and with George Washington. My resignation was accepted, and we are going back to Monticello."

"Tha' makes me real happy, Mista' Thomas. I jus' wonder how we goin' to ge' all yar things moved."

"Robert, let's start packing, and I will arrange the carriages to get us back home with all my furniture."

On January 5, 1794, Jefferson said his final good-byes to his friends in Philadelphia, as he and his entourage left for Virginia.

Early Retirement

"No occupation is so delightful to me as the culture of the earth, and no culture comparable to that of the garden."
Thomas Jefferson

1794

When Thomas Jefferson returned to Monticello in January, 1794, as far as he was concerned, he was home for good. He had been looking forward to spending time with his family, working on his farms, and building a larger house. He had told his good friend, James Madison, "My health is entirely broken down, and my age requires that I should place my affairs in a clear state." He added that "the motion of my blood…leads me to seek for happiness in the lap and love of my family, in the society of my neighbors and my books, in the wholesome occupation of my farm."[71]

Upon his arrival, his 15-year-old daughter, Maria, was there to welcome him at the door. Her Aunt Martha Carr, Tom's sister, was right behind her. Since her husband, Dabney, died twenty years ago, Martha called Monticello her home. Now that all her children were out of the nest, she was able to give her full attention to the teenager, Maria.

Tom greeted both Martha and Maria with warm embraces. Next, Tom spied his daughter, Martha, coming through the back door. She was wet and shivering from the bitter cold winter weather. When she looked up and saw her father, she rushed to greet him. Although Tom was delighted to see her, he noticed when he embraced her that she was pregnant again.

"Martha, it looks like another's on its way."

"That's right, Pa, I am due to have my third child soon."

John Harding Peach

Martha led her father to the nursery where her youngest child was awaking from his nap. Little Thomas Jefferson Randolph was nearly one year and a half. As she picked up her son to hand him to her father, three-year old Anne Cary Randolph, Martha's oldest child tugged at her grandfather's britches leg, vying for his attention. Tom reached down to wrap Annie with his right arm and little Tommy in his other.

Tom heard hoof prints coming up the road toward the house. He looked out and saw Martha's's husband, Thomas Mann Randolph, Jr. dismounting his horse. Robert Hemings was there to meet the horseman and greeted him warmly. He offered to take his stallion to the stable, making sure he got fed and bedded for the night. Before Mr. Randolph came up the porch, he expressed his appreciation to Robert for his concerns.

Tom welcomed his son-in-law at the front door with open arms. "I congratulate you, Mann, for being elected a state senator."

"I'm just trying to follow in your footsteps, Mr. Jefferson." He took off his hat and gave a simple bow in Tom's honor.

"Stand up, straight, Mann. There's no reason for honoring me. I have officially retired from politics. Besides, you know I always prefer a handshake. No bowing for me."

"So I've heard," Mann looked up at Tom and gave him a broad smile. "You've already paid your dues, Sir. Now it's time for me to pay mine."

"Well said, Mann, we need someone with strong Republican standards to continue the fight at Richmond."

The two men retired to Tom's office, where they shared the latest in political circles. Tom received from his son-in-law an update on the status of Monticello.

The next morning, Robert Hemings awakened his master with a washtub full of ice cold water he had drawn. As Tom was soaking his feet, he said to his servant.

"Why don't you saddle up our horses? After breakfast, we will take a ride together."

While the two men rode around Monticello together, Tom stopped at the cemetery. He was concerned about the graves of his mother and his dear friend, Dabney Carr. They both needed some loving attention. He asked Robert to gather some pine branches and cones to make some grave blankets. The two men worked diligently to cover both the plots for the remaining winter.

While Tom was working at the Monticello cemetery, he then thought about the graveyard at Shadwell. He and Robert traveled to his father's grave and that of his favorite sister, Jane. As they decorated their plots and laid the blankets of pine upon them, Tom thought he could hear Jane's soft, sweet voice singing to him. Although she had long gone to her heavenly home 29 years ago, Jane's songs could never escape Tom. He heard them in his thoughts and dreams, especially when he was in the land of gloom and depression. While standing over his father's grave, he recalled the passionate dream his Pa had to reach all the way to the Pacific Ocean as he and his partners tried to capture the West. Although Tom had never forgotten his father's vision, he now became focused on it more intently. Somehow he hoped and prayed that he would live long enough to see his father's dream come true.

Tom had returned home with grandiose ideas. He decided to replace sections of his former house with a more elegant one. That one must have a dome – like he had seen in Paris. He gathered his slaves, gave them each their specific assignment and recorded their every endeavor. One of his slaves, Isaac, heard Tom singing constantly, evidence to him that Tom was a happy and contented man once again. With tranquility as his focus, he vowed he would never leave Monticello again.

When Tom returned home from the cemeteries, he was met by Sally Hemings and her family. The young slave lady who was now 21 had been the personal servant of Tom's daughter, Maria, since she was a child. When Tom from France sent for his young daughter, then 14-year old Sally was the one who escorted her on the long voyage across the Atlantic. She continued to stay with the Jeffersons until they came home from France over four years ago. Sally's brother, James Hemings, had lived with the Jeffersons in France, where he trained to be a French chef. Another reason Tom was glad to be home was so he could enjoy James' special concoctions from his recipes he learned from abroad. Their mother, Betty, still lived at Monticello, where she now approached sixty years. As the half-sister of Tom's deceased wife, she would continue to be part of Tom's family.

When Tom laid eyes on Sally Hemings, he saw her in a new light. At 21, he could tell she had grown from the girl he knew from the past into a blossoming young lady. She was, in his words, "mighty near white." Her mother was a mulatto when she had children by her white master. That made Sally only one-fourth black. According to Tom, she was "very handsome" and "decidedly good looking." Tom hadn't seemed to notice that before. He also admired her "long straight hair down her back," not found in his other slave women.[72] When he saw her, he reached out his hand, as if to shake hers. She ignored his hand and gave him a simple curtsy instead.

"My, my, my, Miss Sally, how you have grown up overnight."

"Merci, beaucoup, Monsieur." Sally demonstrated to Tom that she hadn't forgotten her French.

Tom smiled at her, and they shared several pleasantries between each other in the French language before others began entering the room.

Dr. Thomas Walker was in failing health when Tom came home in January. He reminisced to Tom about his repeated excursions into the western frontier. As early as 1760, he began making repeat trips to the Tennessee territory and the Kentucky wilderness. After the French and Indian War, he and his friend, Andrew Lewis, led some men to build Fort Loudon on the Tennessee River. He reminded Tom about being called "The Peacemaker" because of the peace treaties he arranged with the Indians. As a result of these, America gained all the lands south of the Ohio River to the reaches of the Tennessee River. That opened the floodgates for settlers to migrate to that new land of opportunity.

Tom brought to Walker's recollection the time when Tom was Governor of Virginia, and he commissioned Dr. Walker to deliver a letter to George Rogers Clark ordering him to build Fort Jefferson on the Ohio River. Both the towns of Clarksville, Indiana, where the fort was built and Clarksville, Tennessee, were named after that same Clark, a hero of the Revolutionary War.

The old saintly doctor told Tom that in 1780 when he was 65 Daniel Smith joined him as they traveled to the falls of the Ohio River. There they met with Clark to journey together to the western boundary of Virginia located on the Mississippi River.

"Walker, I don't know how you've been able to accomplish so much in your lifetime."

"When you live to be 78, you can do a lot of things, Thomas." He paused a moment to get his breath. "Did you remember George Rogers Clark was born here in our neighborhood?"

"I sure do. One of my best moments with him was when Governor Patrick Henry sent him and his troops to capture British outposts north of the Ohio River. It was during the Revolution, and Clark stopped by Monticello to visit with me before he marched to the Kentucky territory."

"My, my, my, Thomas. You've accomplished a lot in your life too."

"I'm just following my example, Doc. That's what you've been teaching me all my life."

As Tom finished his sentence, he saw that Dr. Walker had dozed off, leaving Tom to gingerly tiptoe out of the room.

On the 25th of that month, Walker celebrated his 79th birthday, which brought most of his family and neighbors, including the Jeffersons, to visit by his bedside. They could tell his days were numbered. Within two months, the first white man to discover Kentucky died on March 19, 1794.

Tom knew him as not only his neighbor and former guardian, but even more as the only one of the five remaining dreamers he had known as a child. He remembered Dr. Walker meeting regularly in his father's study, with Peter Jefferson, Rev. James Maury, Col. Joshua Fry and Thomas Meriwether. How well were his memories of the five of them talking about their Loyal Company and their dream of capturing the West. Despondently, the last one of the dreamers just went home to meet their Maker. Tom hoped and prayed once again that, although they were gone, their dream would one day come to pass.

When Thomas Walker died, twelve children survived him. Those at the funeral included the families of the five dreamers, many who had married daughters of Dr. Thomas Walker. That was evident by their married names. Mary Walker was now Mrs. Nicholas Meriwether Lewis; Susanna Walker was now the wife of Rev. Henry Fry. (Elizabeth Simms Walker had also been a minister's wife of Rev. Matthew Maury, but she predeceased her father's death by over a year). Peachy Walker was now Mrs. Joshua Fry (Her husband was a veteran officer in the Revolution).

Tom paid particular attention to one of those at the funeral. He was Meriwether Lewis, the 19-year son of Lieutenant William Lewis and Lucy Thornton Meriwether. As the grandson of Col. Thomas Meriwether, one of the dreamers, that young man had inherited the same vision Tom had acquired - to capture the West. Tom told him of his plan to form what he would call a "Corps of Discovery" to take his father's dream all the way to the Pacific Ocean.

Living at neighboring Locust Hill, Lewis volunteered to lead such an expedition. However, Tom knew he was too young and inexperienced for such an awesome responsibility. However, Tom wouldn't be able to shake the idea of Lewis being able to lead, as he saw a lot of Tom's own sensitivities and aspirations inherent in the youngster.

One of the honored guests at Walker's funeral was John Marshall, a member of the Virginia House of Delegates. Another was James

Madison, a member of the U. S. House of Representatives, who was now engaged to marry Dolley Payne Todd. James Monroe had moved to Albemarle County in 1789 to be near his mentor and law instructor, Thomas Jefferson. He felt honored to be there to pay his respects to Dr. Walker. On many occasions Tom visited Walker's Castle Hill to play the fiddle as Madison and Monroe danced the reel and the minuet with the daughters of Dr. Thomas Walker. The doctor had opened his doors to welcome five men who either were or were going to be United States presidents (George Washington, John Adams, Thomas Jefferson, James Madison, and James Monroe).

When Dr. Walker died, the music came to a screeching halt at Castle Hill. However, in Tom's heart and soul, the old pioneer's dream to capture the West would continue to live, hopefully to be fulfilled in Tom's lifetime.

As soon as the spring blossoms arrived, Tom was rejuvenated. He never saw a flower he didn't like. And they were everywhere he walked. He loved working in his garden, taking notes as to the progress of each of his precious plants. As Robert Hemings brought him his washtub of water each morning and awoke him at dawn, the servant was told to make sure the horses were saddled for their morning ride. Tom and Robert spent many hours on horseback traveling from one plantation to another almost daily. That way Tom could make sure everything was progressing to his satisfaction. "I live on my horse from morning to night," was the way he recorded his day's labor in his account book.

Because he saw so much that needed to be done, he worked diligently. His slaves were commissioned to repair the fences, to use variety in the plowing of the fields, and to plant more fruit and vegetables. Whether it was tobacco, corn or wheat, Tom felt all his crops could show drastic improvement in production. He had purchased 1,157 peach trees that he wanted planted on each side of the road leading up to Monticello.

Tom noticed how poor the soil had become, having been depleted by the growing of tobacco. He therefore introduced a seven-step crop rotation plan to restore the land. To do that, he invented a new kind of plow. To Tom, "The plough is to the farmer what the wand is to the sorcerer. Its effect is really like sorcery."[73] When in France, he observed the Dutch plow used a moldboard in the front of the plow that could use some drastic improvement to make it more effective. By using mathematical formulas, he invented a vastly improved wooden plough that became quite useful for all his farms. It was against Tom's principles to patent something that would help others. So he encouraged others to make use of his new invention. He also planned the building of a saw mill, which produced lumber for his restoration plans.

One of Tom's new additions was that of a nail factory. He gathered his teenage slaves and taught them how to make nails. Monticello became a noisy place as up to ten thousand nails were made each day. Tom used incentives to get the most work from his slaves, giving bonuses to those who were the best workers. Whatever nails were not used to restore and build Monticello would be sold to other builders.

Thomas Jefferson faced a new crisis during the summer of 1794, one that he blamed on his strongest adversary, Alexander Hamilton. Three years ago, as the Secretary of the Treasury, Hamilton imposed a tax on whiskey. That was because he needed more revenue for the federal government to pay off her war debts. Jefferson adamantly opposed the tax, knowing it would hurt western farmers who raised corn and converted their crop to whiskey. He knew they did that out of necessity because the lack of proper roads made it impossible for them to get their raw corn to market. Tom heard that farmers, as a result, were so enraged, they banded together for revenge with their guns loaded.

The Whiskey Rebellion began in July, 1794, and became the first war to break out in America since the Revolution. It threatened to split the new nation to the core. The first test of the power of the U.S Army and the federal government was now tested. In July, federal marshal John Neville was sent to serve summons against those who failed to pay their whiskey tax.

An enraged mob of armed Pennsylvanians reacted violently by burning Neville's house to the ground, while several protesters were killed in the process. President Washington issued a call for federal troops to respond. In August, Meriwether Lewis was quick to respond. Although he had sided with his neighbor, Thomas Jefferson, against the whiskey tax, he was eager to fight on behalf of his nation.

When he arrived at Fort Cumberland, Maryland, he was united with a combined force of militiamen from New Jersey, Pennsylvania, Maryland and Virginia. George Washington once again donned his uniform and chose to lead 13,000 soldiers into battle again the rebellious farmers. However, the proposed conflict failed to take place. When the first troops arrived in Pittsburgh the antagonistic forces had fled the scene. Although the Whiskey Rebellion was over, Tom was upset that it happened in the first place. If President Washington had taken his advice over that of Hamilton's, the whiskey tax wouldn't even exist.

What was more important to Tom at that time was the birth of a new granddaughter. During the events of the Whiskey Rebellion, Martha gave birth to her third child, Ellen Wayles Jefferson. Tom had retired from politics and did his best to keep his mind on his house construction, his garden and his plantations. However, he was constantly reminded how much he was needed to help steer his new nation in the right direction.

James Madison, his close friend, leaned on him regularly for support. Since Tom had left government, Madison's Antifederalists were outnumbered, causing Hamilton's Federalists to be in the majority. One of Hamilton's cronies was John Jay, Washington's appointment for the first Chief Justice of the United States. He had spearheaded a negotiation which became known as "Jay's Treaty." Since the Treaty of Paris of 1783 left some issues unresolved, President Washington addressed these in this new agreement between England and America. He sent Jay to England to reconcile the differences between the two countries. Washington knew a treaty was the only way to avert a war between England and America. However, Jay's Treaty leant favoritism to the British demands, putting the United States at a distinct disadvantage. Nevertheless, Jay's Treaty passed by both houses of Congress and was signed by Washington on November 19, 1794. Since that document favored the Federalists, it stirred James Madison to begin a movement of retaliation.

He stopped at Monticello to share his frustration with Jefferson, who also opposed the treaty's ratification. They were as much in arms about its limitations as they were about the amount of money Americans were going to have to pay to British creditors in war reparations. Once more, Tom blamed it all on Hamilton's insistence on having a National Bank.

As they discussed their plan to help promote the ideas of their Party, Madison saw that Jefferson still retained the passion and commitment for doing what was right for his country. He encouraged him to come out of retirement and think about running for president.

Tom rejected Madison's plea because he was committed to remain firmly glued to his home at Monticello. He wanted to see Washington serve a third term as president. Although he had disappointed Jefferson at times as he sided with Hamilton's Federalist policies, Washington still held Tom's utmost respect.

Both Madison and Jefferson rejoiced when they heard that on January 31, 1795, Alexander Hamilton resigned his post as Secretary of the Treasury. He had been their thorn in the flesh for many years, and hopefully his replacement would be an improvement. However, Tom's world was turned upside down when he heard of George Washington's plans to retire after his second term. He had served as the nation's first president since 1789, and now eight years later it was coming to an end.

In February, 1796, James Madison garnered the support of the Democratic-Republican's party to launch Thomas Jefferson's campaign for president. John Adams had served as Washington's vice president for eight years and was now the candidate of the Federalist Party to run against Jefferson.

On June 1, 1796, Tennessee became the sixteenth state of the young nation. It followed Vermont and Kentucky as being those added to the original thirteen colonies. That was one more state for which Adams and Jefferson were to compete for votes.

Later that year, Tom's daughter, Martha, gave birth to another girl, whom she named Ellen Wayles Randolph, after the daughter she lost in infancy the year before. Hopefully, Tom hoped she would have better success with this one.

Adams-Jefferson Ticket

*"Indeed I tremble for my country when I reflect that God is just:
that his justice cannot sleep forever"*
Thomas Jefferson

1797

When all the dust settled, Tom found himself in a most strenuous situation. By coming in second to John Adams in the presidential campaign, according to present law he was required to serve as his opponent's vice president. The two men, originally good friends, over the years had become bitter enemies. There they were diametrically opposed to each other, being thrust into the compromising situation of having to work together as a team.

There was Adams as a Federalist, who believed in big government, and Jefferson as a Republican, who was committed to a smaller federal government, with more emphasis on the states' rights. In the violent conflict between England and France, Adams took the side of the British, whereas Jefferson was for the French.

While Washington was president, he chose the path of neutrality, refusing to take sides in the matter. When he retired, the two opposing parties took aim at each other and chose sides. With Adams as president, the United States gave her support to England. However, Jefferson as his vice president still sided with France. Jay's Treaty favored England in her war against France. The French were withholding their revolt against the treaty, believing that Jefferson would become the next president. When Adams won, France went on the attack against America, seizing her ships and ordering all Americans captured to be hung.

After the election, Tom moved to Philadelphia to assume the duties of his new office. He was surprised at all the people who were cheering in support of the one they called, "The Friend of the People." On March 4, 1797, at their inauguration Adams and Jefferson stood in stark contrast. Whereas stocky John Adams was dressed in black, bearing a sword, Thomas Jefferson was more plainly dressed, as was his manner. He was adorned with a long blue coat, and his sandy hair now showing gray was tied back into a ponytail. Tom had prefaced the meeting by sending a letter to Adams of best wishes "that your administration may be filled with glory and happiness."[74] However, because Adams was at odds with Tom, he refused his gestures of good will and began regularly ignoring him.

It hadn't begun that way between the two men. Tom recalled how he and John Adams were on a committee of five to write the *Declaration of Independence*. Adams led the group to put all their confidence in one man, Thomas Jefferson, to write the rough draft for the declaration. Once Tom finished his assignment, both Ben Franklin and John Adams helped him edit it, smoothing some of the rough edges. When Tom first went to France, it was to assist Ben Franklin and John Adams to build a positive relationship with their primary ally. When Tom replaced Franklin as the Minister to France, Adams was given the same position in England. Across the English Channel, both Jefferson and Adams worked together to keep a peaceful relationship between America and the two European powers.

John Adams and his dear wife, Abigail, were a great help to Tom when his young daughter, Polly, came to France with her personal servant, Sally Hemings. Their ship first stopped in England, where John and Abigail welcomed them into their home until they could recuperate and continue on their voyage to France. They brought comfort to Tom when they wrote him that his daughter had arrived safely from Virginia and was in good hands at their home. Just as Tom had written documents in Virginia advocating the abolishment of slavery, Adams had done the same in Massachusetts when he wrote his state's constitution in 1780.

When the two men returned to America, their compatible ideas were shattered. As Washington's vice president, Adams became closely aligned with Alexander Hamilton and the Federalists. Tom as the Secretary of State fought against Hamilton's big government and radical spending ideas. He radically opposed Hamilton's National Bank idea, as well as the federal government's acceptance of all the individual states' war debts. Thus, Adams and Jefferson became diametrically opposed on nearly every issue.

When they ran against each other in the election, their relationship had become even more fractured than before. Clearly, they didn't like each other anymore. However, based on the Constitution, they were required to work together. That is when Tom recalled one of his sayings, "When you reach the end of your rope, tie a knot in it and hang on."[75]

Tom's method for tying a knot and hanging on was by becoming more involved with the American Philosophical Society in Philadelphia, which he first joined 17 years earlier. On the day before he was inaugurated as vice president, he was elected to be the president of that prodigious institution. When Tom entered the meeting chambers of the society, he opened a box of fossilized bones he brought from someone's new archeological dig in Virginia. The members were enchanted with what appeared to be a previously undiscovered creature. He also shared with them his recent invention of his iron and mould board plow that revolutionized farming on the plantations.

The society members always looked forward to Tom's new discoveries. They remembered so vividly how he designed a macaroni making machine when he returned from France. That way he could continue eating and serving his favorite pasta dishes.

Started by Dr. Benjamin Franklin in 1743, the year of Tom's birth, the American Philosophical Society was the oldest society of learning in America. Jefferson's love for the flora and fauna and his passion for new explorations and discoveries kept him actively involved through the years. Now, as its president, he would be in the position to further promote his dream to capture the West. Since Adams did not rely on him much, Tom was able to use valuable time working with the A.P.S.

Another way Tom tied a knot and hung on was to continue his efforts in the development of the Federal City on the Potomac. Working closely with Major Pierre Charles L'Enfant, he helped select the architecture of many buildings of the United States government. While serving as Minister to France, Tom was a constant student of European architecture wherever he visited. When he returned to America, his brain was chock full of innovative creative designs for buildings.

After introducing the neoclassical style of architecture into Virginia, Tom used similar inspirations on the new Federal City. "The father of our national architecture" was the honor paid to Jefferson by architectural historian, Fiske Kimball.[76] Because of Tom's influence, many of the federal buildings on the Potomac were designed using the neoclassical style.

Once Robert Hemings helped Tom move into his office in Philadelphia, he awoke Tom one morning with a washtub full of ice cold water for his slumbering feet. Tom had been having headaches and felt rotten. He began sharing his uselessness and frustration to his servant.

"Robert, what do we have on the schedule today?"

"Nudin' I know of, Mista' Thomas."

"That's just like every other day." Tom said disparagingly.

"Wha'd ya' mean, Sir?"

"I mean this is the most meaningless job there is in the whole wide world."

"Why ya say that, Mista' Thomas? Ya's second most powerful man in 'merica. Ya's the big V.P."

"Robert, you know I am a man who loves to be busy. I want to labor to get things accomplished." Tom was taking his feet out of the water as his servant was drying them with a towel.

"Adams doesn't want me doing anything. He really would prefer I was not even around." As he continued his complaints, Tom allowed Robert to help him get dressed.

"Oh, how I wish I could go back to Monticello. It's spring time, and all my flowers are blooming. My garden should be in full color by now, and here I sit idle and miserable." Tom stopped for a moment deep in thought. "Besides, Maria is getting married soon. John Eppes has proposed to her, and their wedding will be in October."

"Eppes, Sir? Ain' tha' last name o' her granma?"

"That's right, Robert. She was Martha Eppes. That's why my dear wife had 'Eppes' as her middle name. Maria will be marrying one of her cousins. But he's a good man, and I am proud for her. She will be 19 by then, and she needs to get on with her life."

Just as Tom had predicted, he was seldom called on for his opinions and became tired of his extreme idleness. His only required duty was serving as president of the Senate. He simply had to be the moderator and vote whenever there was a tie. Since there were never any tie votes for him to break, his job as the moderator of the assembly was rather boring.

Tom was anxious to return home when Congress recessed for the summer. His desire was to continue building his mansion, which seemed like a never-ending project. The next stage was getting the rest of the roof installed. He was tired of having to sleep with the threat of rain or worst, snow, looming overhead.

After his daughter's wedding in October, Tom remained at Monticello until December. The Senate was coming back from recess, and he needed to be there to preside. He dreaded returning to the conflict he found in Philadelphia with John Adams and his Federalist-leaning cabinet. Nevertheless, America was on the brink of war with France, and Tom felt like he might be able to help stop it.

Thomas Jefferson and his Republicans continued to support the French. John Adams and the Federalists were on the side of the British. The French were still enraged at the Jay's Treaty of 1794. Although that had averted war with England because the United States gave into their demands, the French were highly offended. They were the ones who helped America win the Revolutionary War against England. France still had war debts that the United States refused to pay.

Since Adams had become president, France had attacked more than three hundred U.S. ships. The French navy sought to capture and kill each American that was found. Adams sent a peace commission to try to resolve the conflict, but it only made matters worse. Charles de Talleyrand, the French foreign minister, refused the American advances, but he issued a bribe. He sent three agents to demand twelve million dollars for France and $250,000 for himself before he would negotiate with the United States.

President Adams gave labels to the three anonymous agents calling them "X, Y, and Z." As a result the conflict became known as the "XYZ affair." Tom sarcastically referred to it as "the XYZ paroxysms", alluding to the spasms or convulsions that came over him whenever he thought of them.[77]

Rather than provide the money for the bribe, Adams led Congress to triple the American army. He also created the Department of the Navy and sent warships to protect U.S. citizens who were on the sea. The United States was fighting against France, but Adams never declared war. The movement became known as the Quasi-war, which lasted for the next few years.

However, with the French and the U.S. firing shots at each other by waging war on the Atlantic, the worst was yet to come. Congress voided all treaties with France on July 7, 1798. On the following week, Tom was horrified when John Adams led his Federalists to pass the Alien and Sedition Acts. That gave the U.S. government power to infringe upon the liberty of individuals. Anyone who spoke, wrote, or published anything of a "false, scandalous and malicious" nature against the Congress or the president was in violation and could be arrested.[78]

Once more, Thomas Jefferson found himself in a tenuous situation. As the vice president, he was supposed to be working with the president on the same team. However, he could not sit still when he saw freedom of speech and freedom of the press being unashamedly violated. His Republican friends were enraged as well, and they came to Tom for his support. They witnessed a blatant discrimination leveled against them. Some newspaper editors who sided with Jefferson were jailed. When Tom received his mail, he could tell it had been tampered with. He surmised that the Federalists were trying to catch him in violation of one of the controversial sedition acts.

Tom refused to remain silent. He held his peace as long as he could. With a new quill in hand, he composed a lengthy document that passionately attacked the Alien and Sedition Acts. However, he didn't publish them. Somehow the resolves Tom addressed in his creative treatise wound up in the hands of John Breckinridge. He in turn brought it before the Kentucky state legislature, which adopted it as the Kentucky Resolutions on November 10, 1798. "The Resolves", as Tom called them, proposed that states' rights were more powerful than federal rights and that state legislatures could override the ruling of Congress.[79]

When James Madison saw Jefferson's original draft, he asked permission to use it to compose a similar document for Virginia. Thus, the Virginia Resolutions were adopted by its legislature on December 24, 1798. Although they were similar to those of Kentucky, they were a milder version. However, both sets of resolves were the first notable proposals to assert the significance of states' rights. Jefferson was not revealed as the original author. Yet it had his footprints on it everywhere it traveled.

Tom couldn't wait for the winter session of the 1798-1799 Congress to be recessed. In March, he gladly returned to Monticello in time for the planting season on his plantations. His house still needed a roof, and many other improvements needed addressing. He felt like he would never get it fit to be inhabited.

All his family and friends welcomed him home. Even the slaves were glad to see him. They knew as much as they desired their freedom, they were treated with more respect and civility by Jefferson than they were by any other slave owner. Tom was always quick to teach them trades and at times would pay them when they worked overtime.

Jefferson had taken his slave, James Hemings, to France so he could learn how to be a French chef.

Later, the Hemings sister, Sally, escorted Tom's daughter safely across the Atlantic to France. Tom could have sent her back but instead allowed her, as a teenager, to stay in France. During that time, she was taught the French language and many social graces of the gentile ladies who associated with Jefferson. If she had been in America, as a slave, she would have been forbidden to go to school and be educated.

Tom arrived home early enough to witness the birth of his new granddaughter, Cornelia Jefferson Randolph, born on April 26 to Thomas and Martha Randolph at their home in Edgehill, which was in the neighborhood of Monticello. They moved there in 1798 after Martha's husband built a house for his family. Tom looked forward to his visits there because the wooden frame house was one he designed, and he was anxious to inspect his finished creation. He was thankful it was nearby to Monticello so he could be close to his daughter and her family. Tom was a proud grandfather as he spent precious time with their three other children – Anne was eight; Thomas was six; and Ellen was only two. He was sorry he had to be away so much and missed seeing them develop over all the years.

While Tom was home for the summer of 1799, he paid a visit to his daughter, Maria Eppes, at her home in Eppington on the Appomattox River. He found her pregnant with her first child. Although he was excited for her, Tom was despondent to find her baby was expected to arrive while he was in Philadelphia for the next session of Congress.

As winter approached, Thomas Jefferson half-heartedly left Monticello for Philadelphia. That would be his final year as vice president, and with each session, he dreaded it more than the one before. How he wished he could stay home with his family. He longed to be present when his new grandchild was born. He knew Monticello's construction never would be completed unless he was there to see it through.

Jupiter, Tom's childhood friend, trusted servant, and long-time companion, had recently celebrated his 56th birthday, the same age as Tom. They often talked about their early days at Shadwell together, where they both were born.

Tom retraced Jupiter's life after he stayed behind at Monticello and became a stonemason. His former servant had married another slave named "Suck" at Monticello. They now had a son named "Philip Evans", who was nine years old. After being apprenticed to William Rice and carving the majestic columns on the front entrance to

Monticello, Jupiter later became a coachman. Between 1785 and 1789, his reputation was so well established that he was hired by a local stonemason, Thomas Whitlough.

When it came time to leave for Philadelphia, Jupiter had been ill. As they were eating supper together, Tom did all the talking.

"That year I was delighted to hear that New York voted to abolish slavery. Jupiter, I have been trying to accomplish that all my life, and finally, one of our states has done something about it."

As Tom continued talking, he was aware his servant was apparently too weak to respond. Normally, Jupiter would have shown some tears of joy over such an announcement.

"Hopefully, that will help turn the tide and put our nation on the right course. I look for other states to follow suit."

Thomas Jefferson left Monticello the next morning, with no idea this would be the last time he saw his boyhood friend and long-time servant still alive. On his way back to Washington, he stopped to confer with Pierre L'Enfant on the designing of the Federal City and her government buildings. Upon his arrival in Washington, he toured the proposed house for the president. Being under construction for the past seven years, the building should be ready for occupation by next year. Tom took a tour through the majestic mansion, having little idea he would ever be the one living there.

1799 would prove to be a historic year marking the rise and fall of leaders in the world. France installed the leader needed to bring stability to the nation torn by strife and war since the French Revolution began ten years before. In a bold move called the "Coup d'Etat", Napoleon seized control of France on November 9, 1799. Napoleon Bonaparte became the First Consul of France and led in the creation of a new Constitution.[80] America was put at ease because Napoleon brought a message of peace.

France faced new hope, but the United States felt like optimism was dying for her new nation. Regretfully, in 1799, two of the greatest heroes of the Revolution held their final days upon the earth. On June 6, 1799, Patrick Henry, the passionate igniter of the cause for independence from England, died peacefully at his home in Red Hill, Virginia. When Tom paid his respects, he recalled how Henry had set Tom's heart ablaze with the cause of liberty. He also remembered this five time governor of Virginia fueled the movement to add a Bill of Rights to the Constitution. Tom had strongly advocated it, but being in France at the time, he depended on the likes of Henry to fight for Tom's aspirations.

Tom offered the following short eulogy in honor of that staunch reformer. "It is not now easy to say what we should have done without Patrick Henry," said Thomas Jefferson. "He was before us all in maintaining the spirit of the Revolution."[81]

When George Washington breathed his last breath at his Mount Vernon home on December 14, he was considered the greatest hero in America. Having been born in 1732, he lived to be 67 years old. When the old general died, America nearly died with him. There were question marks in the minds of many as to what would be the future of the United States. With their hero gone, who would be able to step into Washington's shoes?

While Tom observed the nation in mourning, he had something closer to home that was riveting. When he received word that Jupiter had died, he was deeply moved to tears. He felt guilty that he wasn't with him in his last days. As he wept in remorse, he was comforted to know the grave of a favorite and faithful servant would be awaiting him at Monticello Tom would later write to his daughter, Maria, saying, "You have, perhaps, heard of the loss of Jupiter. With all his defects, he leaves a void in my domestic arrangements which cannot be filled."[82]

Before the year came to an end, on December 31, Tom's youngest daughter, Maria, gave birth to a new granddaughter for Jefferson. That gave Tom hope for better days to come as he began the nineteenth century.

Several new projects filled Jefferson's idle time during that winter. First, he began writing a guide to help senators with their procedures when in session. *A Manual of Parliamentary Practice* was a compilation of all he had gleaned from the rules and procedures of the Senate for the past three years.[83] (He would be pleased to know it is still in use in Washington).

Secondly, he continued working on another project that had stirred within his soul for the past two decades. What he called "the hobby of my old age" was his proposal of a state university for Virginia.[84] In January, he wrote a letter to Dr. Joseph Priestley about that idea. Tom felt like with his extensive educational background as a scientist, he could garner some support from him.

> "We wish to establish in the upper & healthier country, & more centrally for the state and University on a plan so broad & liberal & *modern*, as to be worth patronizing with the public support, and be a temptation to the youth of

other states to come, and drink of the cup of knowledge & fraternize with us."[85]

Thirdly, Tom took a profound interest in the origin of the Library of Congress which President Adams had recently approved. Having appropriated five thousand dollars, Adams began buying books needed by Congress. No one loved books more than Tom, and so when he thought about a new library, he couldn't resist sharing his ideas for the books that would be needed.

One day, shocking news arrived in a letter from his son-in-law, Jack Eppes announcing the death of Maria's first child, Jefferson's granddaughter. Being frail at birth, her daughter didn't live long enough to make it through one month. Tom sent her his condolences saying, "Mr. Eppes' letters filled me with anxiety for your little one. How deeply I feel...."[86] He tried his best to encourage her.

Tom was increasingly frustrated with all the fighting and bickering in the Senate, causing the session to be needlessly prolonged. On February 11, he shared his abominable feelings in a letter to his oldest daughter, Martha. "Politics are such a torment that I would advise everyone I love not to mix with them. I have changed my circle here according to my wish, abandoning the rich, and declining their dinners and parties, and associating entirely with the class of science, of whom there is a valuable society here."[87] He was referring to his active association with his friends at the American Philosophical Society, who would be the only ones he would miss in Philadelphia.

On April 22, Tom's brother-in-law, John Bolling, died at his home at Chestnut Grove in Chesterfield County, Virginia. He had been married to Tom's sister, Mary, for forty years, with whom they had ten children together. However, Tom knew they had a tumultuous relationship, brought on by Bolling's love for the bottle. Two years before, Tom had warned Mary in a letter, "Mr. B.'s habitual intoxication will destroy himself, his fortune & family. Of all calamities that is the greatest."[88] Tom's feelings of sadness were extended to his daughter on her loss.

When Tom finally left Philadelphia for home, he never expected to return to the city of brotherly love. Soon the Capitol would be opened in the Federal City on the Potomac, making it closer to his beloved Virginia. Although he was still the president of the American Philosophical Society, he made arrangements to conduct his affairs by correspondence.

He took the long way home, stopping to visit his friends and relatives. Tom was anxious to see Maria at her new home, Mont Blanco, overlooking the James River. She was still grieving the loss of her daughter, and Tom felt he needed to personally reassure her of his love. He also paid a visit to his older daughter, Patsy, at her plantation home called Edgehill. In some ways, he was hesitant to return to Monticello because it wouldn't be the same without Jupiter there by his side. However, he wanted to visit his burial site and pay his due respects.

When Tom finally arrived home, he divided his concentration between building a dome onto his Monticello mansion and the coming election. President John Adams had ruffled many feathers over his Alien and Sedition Acts. Although he wanted to be re-elected, the Republicans arose in strong opposition to him. They placed in nomination two of their own, Thomas Jefferson and Aaron Burr. The Federalists countered with President Adams, Charles Pinckney and John Jay.

Tom didn't seek the office. He was looking forward to his retirement with his home, his family and his books. However, those in his party, led by the likes of his good friend, James Madison, compelled him to run for president. Tom finally caved to their wishes because he feared his nation was in major trouble. If he didn't do what he could to replace John Adams, he never would forgive himself. However, during his candidacy, he refused to leave home to fight against his opposition for the nomination. His ardent followers did all the campaigning for him.

However, the Federalists and their newspapers were ablaze with stories, some true, but mostly false, about Jefferson. They claimed if he was elected, there would be civil war and the rich women would be murdered. Because Tom advocated freedom of religion, his enemies rumored he was in favor of freedom FROM religion. Alexander Hamilton called Jefferson "an atheist and a fanatic in politics."[89]

Ministers fanned the flames from their pulpits claiming a vote for Jefferson would be a vote against God and their Bibles. Timothy Dwight, president of Yale University, warned that if Jefferson was elected, "We may see the Bible cast into a bonfire, the vessels of the sacramental supper borne by an ass in public procession, and our children, either wheedled or terrified, uniting in chanting mockeries against God."[90]

Reverend William Linn of New York preached that "the election of any man avowing the principles of Mr. Jefferson would...destroy religion, introduce immorality and loosen all the bonds of society."[91] If Jefferson is elected, a Connecticut newspaper predicted, "Murder, robbery, rape, adultery and incest will be openly taught and practiced."[92]

On June 30, a Baltimore newspaper even reported that Thomas Jefferson was dead.[93] Other newspapers grabbed the story and ran with it. Although it was totally false, by the time it was published, the harm was already done. Tom had hysteria cropping up all around him.

When the electors cast their votes in December, Thomas Jefferson and Aaron Burr, both Republicans, wound up tied for the lead with 73 votes each. John Adams led his Federalist party with 65, barely beating out Charles Pinckney for second, who had 64. Thus, the year of 1800 ended without a clear-cut winner for president. Because of that, the House of Representatives would have to decide between those who tied, Jefferson and Burr.

Surprisingly, one of Tom's bitterest enemies, Alexander Hamilton, broke the tie by campaigning for Tom. Although Hamilton disliked Jefferson, he hated Aaron Burr even more. However, it took 36 ballots before Thomas Jefferson was finally elected the third President of the United States.

However, before he could move into the President's House, he had to move the Adams' family out. John Adams was so confident he would be re-elected that he took up residency as its first occupant on the first of November before the election was ever held.

Jefferson as President

"Agriculture, manufactures, commerce, and navigation, the four pillars of our prosperity, are the most thriving when left most free to individual enterprise."
Thomas Jefferson

1801

By the time Thomas Jefferson finally was elected, he had received little sleep and was physically and mentally drained. For a week in February, 1801, the House of Representatives had gone through 36 separate ballots before they broke the tie in Tom's favor. As a result, the one whom he beat by the narrowest margin, Aaron Burr, was to become his vice president. Tom had as much use for Burr as John Adams had for Tom when he served as his V.P. Regretfully, he would be forced to endure his defeated adversary in the office next to him for the next four years. At least they were from the same party.

Only two weeks remained from the time of his election on February 17 until his inauguration. Tom had been living at the Conrad and McMunn boarding house for the past three months, conveniently located only two blocks from the Capitol. There he was stowed away with thirty of his like-minded Republican supporters awaiting his election and eventual inauguration. They all shared a common dining room, where Tom chose to sit at the coldest end of the table. All the others insisted on him sitting at the head due to his ranking over them. But he politely refused. He planned to stay there until John and Abigail Adams moved their family out of the White House.

March 4, 1801, began for Thomas Jefferson long before daybreak. That was the day of his inauguration, and one of his frequent migraines had been bothering him through the night. Having difficulty sleeping, he finally climbed out of his featherbed and began drawing a washtub of cold water to soak his feet. That was his committed routine since his college days at William and Mary.

Tom's secretary who roomed with him, Henry Woods, was startled out of his sleep. He heard all Tom's rustlings as he was getting his foot washing ceremony ready. As Henry sat up and rubbed his eyes while yawning, he peered over to the source of the dim light from the oil lamp to see what was happening. Then he laid his head down again on his pillow, remembering Tom's early routine.

As he turned on his side where he could see Tom, a bit bewildered he asked in a whispered voice,

"Thomas, what are you doing up so early?"

"Just soaking my feet, Henry."

Now that Tom knew his secretary was awake, he began sharing his troubled soul with him. "I start my day every morning missing my servant. Most of my life, I depended on him to get me out of bed with my water drawn. I needed him to help me get ready to meet the world."

Henry reluctantly pulled himself out of his comfy bed. He knew the heightened significance of this historic day. Knowing his duty was to help Jefferson prepare for his Presidential Inauguration, he hastily jumped into some well-worn breeches.

They heard the blast of the cannon nearby announcing the significance of the moment. Being unprepared for it, as it was barely daybreak, they both turned and looked at each other rather distantly.

"It's so strange," Henry, "This is the day I've spent my life working for. Now that it's finally arrived, I wish it would just go away."

"Why is that, Thomas? Or should I call you Mr. President?"

"Forget any titles. Between the two of us, we can keep our given first names." Tom now had taken his feet from the water and received a towel from Henry. "You know I'm not fond of making speeches. I love writing them, but speaking them is not my cup of tea."

"You'll do just fine, Thomas. Just fine."

"I sure hope you're right." Tom picked out a new pair of red breeches, which he began to pull up on his long bony legs. As soon as Henry saw them, he exclaimed,

"Those don't look presidential. I know you love wearing red, but it's a bit much for that occasion."

As Tom looked down at his legs, he agreed. "Henry, I believe you're right. I think I'll try these emerald-colored ones instead."

After donning his green breeches over his gray stockings, he completed his attire with his gray waistcoat. Then he stood as if to model his outfit.

"Now that looks presidential," Henry assured him with a gregarious smile.

As the two men heard a loud rapping at the door, Henry opened it to a young messenger. The boy was a bit hysterical, having a difficult time catching his breath.

"I have...a message...for Mister...Jefferson." Henry was shocked to see how difficult it was for that poor boy to speak. He took the note from the messenger and took a few coins from his pocket for a tip.

"What was all that about?" Tom now walked to the door and opened the message. As he read it to himself, his knees grew faint as he nearly collapsed. Henry could see Tom's face turn red with what appeared to be rage. He helped Tom to his chair, afraid he may stumble and fall.

"What's the note all about, Thomas? You look like you've seen a ghost."

Tom stood up and marched angrily around the room. "It's about those midnight judges. John Adams has now named 42 federal judges affiliated with his Federalist party. I can't believe he has been so cunning and despicably conniving to do such a thing. These appointments will do everything they can to block our Republican ideas and proposals. They will tie our hands and thus cripple our effectiveness. That Adams scoundrel also appointed John Marshall to be the Chief Justice. He's another one of his cronies. And he's the one who'll be swearing me in today."[94]

Henry put his arm around Tom's shoulder in an effort to settle and to assure him. "Thomas, we can't worry about that now. You have to get ready for your speech."

"I've already sent what I'm going to say to the newspaper. I guess all I have to do now is stand up and read the paper to the assembly, and that should be enough."

"Are you going in such plain clothes? Our presidents have always dressed in their finest suits."

"Henry, you will learn that I am a plain man of plain clothes. Just because I am president doesn't make me any more important than the common man. I want to remind you that 'we are all created equal.'"

"You've got me there, Thomas."

Tom completed his attire with a gray waistcoat and a pair of black shoes. As they heard the parade marching by their boarding house, they knew time would soon arrive for Tom to leave. Henry helped him with his last-minute preparation for their noon departure.

When the moment came to leave, Henry went out to locate Tom's carriage, but Tom stopped him. "Henry, we are walking to the Capitol."

"What do you mean, Thomas? That's not the way it's been done before. It's not befitting for a president to walk to his own inauguration."

"I am going to walk, and you are walking with me. I am equal with everyone else, and if they can go there by foot, then we can too."

The Federal City was still under construction, and the streets were merely paths made in the dirt. Recent rains had made them still soaked with water.

Therefore, Thomas Jefferson arrived with muddy shoes at the Senate chamber in the Capitol to be sworn in as the third President of the United States. That was the first time the Federal City would have such an honor. Washington was sworn in for his first term in New York City and for his second one in Philadelphia. John Adams was also inaugurated in the city of brotherly love. Jefferson's followers swarmed the Senate chamber to hear him speak, with crowds surrounding the exterior. They all wanted to get a glimpse of their hero, as they marched with him to the Capitol, cheering all the way.

Before he was sworn in by newly appointed Chief Justice John Marshall, Tom delivered a masterful speech. Although weak in his delivery, he was brilliant in his composition. He always wrote his own speeches, and he had rewritten that one three times before he got it right. His message was one of unity, reminding the nation they were not Republicans and Federalists, but they were all Americans. His message was so stirring; it was quoted verbatim in newspapers throughout the land. Tom had masterfully combined all his reformation ideas into one concise discourse, setting the stage for his Republican principles. Rather than talk about their differences, he was quick to accentuate the hopes and ideals Americans shared together. Although Tom's delivery was not polished, his message of liberty and unity set the stage for the next twenty four years of Republican leadership in the United States.

When Thomas Jefferson finished his speech that neared perfection, he next faced John Marshall, who would give him the oath of office. Tom found it difficult to face the man he had come to inwardly despise. As he put his hand on the Bible and looked Marshall in the eyes, he was looking at the one who had battled Tom the previous year as

Adams' Secretary of State. Now he would have to deal with him as the newly appointed Chief Justice of the Supreme Court – one selected against Tom's will. Although they had both been trained at the feet of George Wythe, they had become complete opposites in their political philosophies.

Tom remembered first getting to know Marshall at the funeral of his neighbor, Dr. Thomas Walker. Their first meeting was cordial, but they became more estranged after that. Tom felt awkward and uncomfortable standing before Marshall, but he gritted his teeth and tried to make the best of the dreaded occasion. As soon as he gave his oath of allegiance, he was greeted by the marching music of the Marine Corps Band. His day ended as the first president to be sworn in at Washington D.C., as well as the first one serenaded by the music of the Marines.

Afterwards, Tom greeted many of his cheering supporters as he meandered his way back to his boarding house. He took them by surprise because he reached out to shake hands with them, a new practice that Jefferson followed for the rest of his life. (Prior to that, men bowed and women curtsied when they greeted each other).

As he gathered around the dinner table at the hotel that afternoon, his friends all encouraged him to now move to the head of the table. Now that he was their president, they felt like he should have the preferred seat. However, Tom insisted on sitting in his regular seat at the other end, claiming he was now no more important than he was before. His friends genuinely saw in him a true sense of humility and a heartfelt desire to identify with the common man.

As soon as Thomas Jefferson became President of the United States, he enlisted his neighbor, Captain Meriwether Lewis, as his personal secretary. Tom had his eye on that young man since his birth on August 18, 1774, at Locust Hill in Albemarle County, Virginia. As the grandson of Colonel Thomas Meriwether, Tom's young friend shared the passion of Tom's father and the Loyal Company of 1749. Tom often recalled as a little boy the meetings of the five dreamers in Pa's study at Tuckahoe. Colonel Meriwether, Colonel Joshua Fry, Dr. Thomas Walker Rev. James Maury, and Peter Jefferson were now dead. But their dream was still alive!

Thomas Jefferson was determined that his father's dream to capture the West finally would be fulfilled. Who better to help him with that mission than one who had the dreamers' passion flowing through his veins? Just as Thomas Meriwether instilled that vision within his daughter, Lucy, she in turn passed it on to his grandson, Meriwether Lewis.

If that wasn't enough, Lucy Thornton Meriwether sent her son to be tutored by none other than Rev. Matthew Maury. He was the son of Rev. James Maury, Tom's teacher and one of the five dreamers of the Loyal Company. Just as the senior Maury kept the fire ablaze in Tom's bosom to explore the West all the way to the Pacific Ocean, so his son instilled the same in his students.

Meriwether Lewis received another dose of that passion from Thomas Jefferson. When he was only a teenager in 1792, he volunteered to join Jefferson's "Corps of Discovery." That was Tom's name for the embodiment of his father's vision to capture the West. From that point, whenever Tom was at Monticello and Meriwether was at Locust Hill, they gravitated together, keeping their plans alive. Tom took these opportunities to teach Meriwether math and botany. He instilled within the young man a love for the flora and fauna he would discover as he traveled to the Pacific.

Meriwether just barely turned 20 in 1794 when President George Washington called for troops to extinguish the Whiskey Rebellion in western Pennsylvania. Having enlisted in the Virginia militia, Meriwether became one of some 13,000 troops to join Washington. Although he knew that Jefferson was opposed to the federal government getting involved in that fray, he admired Washington and told his mother he passionately wanted "to support the glorious cause of liberty, and my country."[95]

What Meriwether anticipated was going to be an all-out war never materialized. He was disappointed. The rebellious Pennsylvania mobs scattered at the sight of Washington and his troops, eliminating any real conflict.

However, Meriwether Lewis had enough excitement to realize he was addicted to military life. After the Whiskey Rebellion, he remained on duty with some troops near Pittsburgh through the winter of 1794-1795 to assure the rebellion would not reappear. His mother rejoiced to see her son come home safe and sound. However, much to her displeasure, he joined the First United States Infantry, where he served as a sharpshooter. His regiment was led by William Clark, with whom he formed a close friendship and later would choose as his partner in the Corps of Discovery expedition.

On February 23, Tom sent a letter to General James Wilkinson, the U. S. Army's commanding general. He asked him to release Meriwether from active duty, with the stipulation that Captain Lewis would retain his rank and right of promotion. Tom explained his purpose for that request.

On the same day, he penned a letter to Capt. Meriwether Lewis, who was stationed in Pittsburgh. He was serving as the paymaster of the First Infantry Regiment of the Army. Having been discharged to Detroit, he didn't arrive in Pittsburgh to receive his letter until March 5.

Lewis was excited to get correspondence from the president, but he wasn't so sure how to respond. He didn't much care for the title of "personal secretary," as he had no desire to sit at a desk and write letters and make appointments. However, Jefferson assured him Tom would be writing his own letters and had a copy machine to reproduce them. "Your knolege{sic} of the Western country," he wrote, "of the army and of all it's interests and relations have rendered it desirable for public as well as private purposes that you should be engaged in that office."[96]

He noticed that the $500.00 per year salary would mean a cut in pay for him, even with the free room and board at the President's House. However, when he finally realized that the president wanted him to do more military and exploration work, he gladly accepted the position.

After sending a letter to Jefferson, Captain Lewis completed his unfinished business and acquired three horses to make the journey to the Federal City. Riding one horse and pulling two more packed with his supplies, Lewis left shortly after March 10. He found the journey quite challenging, especially since one of his horses went lame. Fighting the cold, wet winter weather, he finally arrived at the President's House by April 2.

As he hobbled up to the president's front door, he was shocked to find Jefferson had returned to Monticello to gather his books, clothes and furnishings. Lewis was greeted by a steward, who introduced him to the housekeeper and three servants. They were Tom's slaves whom he had brought from Monticello and were available to unload Lewis' horses and help him move in. After several days of rest and recuperation, Lewis took the opportunity to return to Virginia where he could spend some time with his dear mother and family and retrieve his other belongings.

By the end of April, the president was seen trotting down Pennsylvania Avenue on his horse, with his entourage of coaches following him. Tom's servants scrambled from the house to accommodate the president's move-in ceremony. Meriwether Lewis followed them and warmly greeted Thomas Jefferson, personally accepting his new position with a joyful heart.

Tom told Lewis he would be his aide-de-camp. He wanted Lewis to weed out the army officers for the purpose of drastically reducing the number of troops. He would be sure none of John Adams' Federalist sympathizers were officers. Tom was at a decided disadvantage because he had not served with them. Therefore, he relied on Lewis to select the officers whom he felt would be loyal to Jefferson and his Republican cause. That was an awesome responsibility to place upon a 26-year old man, but Tom knew he could be trusted for that tedious assignment.

As the President's House (the White House) became the home of only those two men, it was a bit overwhelming. Nothing had been left to chance. It somehow seemed preordained that Thomas Jefferson and Meriwether Lewis would end up as Tom called it, "like two mice in a church."[97] A mansion with over one hundred rooms and many staircases was a bit overwhelming for just the two of them. Although they had an assortment of bathrooms, they only needed one, which they could share. With a fresh coat of whitewash over the sandstone structure, it looked attractive to the outsider. However, when Tom took his first gander at the inside, he was surprised to see how much work still needed to be done.

"Well, Lewis, it looks like I'm going to feel right at home."

"How's that, Mr. President?" Lewis caught himself when he saw Tom leering at him. "I'm sorry, I forgot. How's that, Thomas?"

"Monticello has been under construction for over thirty years and still is unfinished. Thus, I will feel right at home here."

Tom saw the bedrooms were unpainted, and the roof had visible leaks. The lawns were filled with overgrown weeds and needed the split-rail fence Tom would provide to protect them. Rather than allow the house to overwhelm him, Tom chose to use only the portions he needed. As he considered the largest space, the East Room, he noted that the walls were still awaiting their plastering. And Abigail Adams left her clothes line stretched from wall to wall with a few rags hanging on the frazzled rope. Tom was told she was too ashamed to hang her clothes in the back yard and so used the East Room for that purpose.

"This is the perfect room for you," Tom turned to Lewis with a subtle laugh.

"Why is that, Thomas?"

"Because you're an outdoorsman. You like living in the woods more than in the house. This room looks more like the woods than anything I've seen."

"You're right about that, but it's too big for a bedroom."

"Let's divide it in two. You can use half of it for your place to sleep, and the other half can be your office."

"I'll do the best I can with it, Thomas. Where are you going to stay?"

Tom led Lewis from the East Room to the other end of the rustic building. As they entered what would eventually be called the State Dining Room, he exclaimed, "Here's where my office will be."

From that room Tom had a view of the Potomac River, which would lead to his beloved Virginia. He remembered campaigning with President Washington to move the nation's capital to border the Potomac. Every day as he looked out the window, he could visualize the positive impact he had made on America.

Tom methodically planned all the specifics for the expansive room. With his exhaustive assortment of books which would line the walls, he would find himself referring to it often more as a library than as his office. That would be his secret chamber where he would dream great dreams for America.

By the time he was finished with his special room, maps would be pasted on all the empty walls. The window recesses would be adorned with a variety of plants and flowers, featuring his roses and geraniums. His writing desk would accommodate his paper and quills, with a globe of the world at easy reach. He must include his long table where he would work on his maps and research projects. His favorite revolving "whirligig" chair would be placed in front of his desk, and he must have a Windsor bench to elevate his feet when reading.

He brought from Monticello some of his own invented gadgets. That included his revolving book stand, where he could display five open books at a time for ready reference. He also brought his Argand, the best oil lamp of the age, and his perspective glass which would magnify the fine print on the maps and books. And his office wouldn't be complete without his telescopic theodolite, his favorite surveying tool. He would use his candelabrum to reflect the sunlight more directly onto what he was reading. He also had his polygraph copying machine with him.

Tom would be sure to feature some of his French collections. When he left France, he could have filled a boat with his souvenirs. These included some statuettes and figurines to adorn the room. He had a treasured portrait of Maria Cosway, an English artist who lived in Paris. Since he had a passionate relationship with her that developed in France, Tom felt she might best represent the French display in the room. Among all the letters they had written to each other over the years, the one that would be remembered the most was one Tom wrote entitled, "Dialogue between my Head and my Heart."[98] It vividly described the details of his inner struggle to fall in love with one who was a married woman. His head said it was wrong, but his heart shouted just the opposite. Because she belonged to another man, he knew all he could have of her was her lovely picture staring at her from his French table.

And of course, there must be a spot reserved for his pet mockingbird he named "Dick." Tom remembered how he first fell in love with this favorite species nearly thirty years ago. Since he bought his first mockingbird from a slave, he couldn't live without one as his feathered companion, who would serenade him with its vast variety of melodious sounds. Tom would hang Dick's cage in front of one of the windows, knowing that the bird would probably be more out of his cage than in it.

Over 160 years would pass when future President John F. Kennedy met for dinner in Thomas Jefferson's former office, then the State Dining Room. Kennedy had the room filled with Nobel Prize winners who sat around the dining table with him. He opened the ceremony by proclaiming, "I think this is the most extraordinary collection of talent, of human knowledge, that has ever been gathered together at the White House, with the possible exception of when Thomas Jefferson dined alone."[99]

When Lewis saw Tom with his pet mockingbird, he wanted to bring his hunting dogs to stay with him, but Tom refused him.

"A bird in that mansion is one thing, Lewis, but a bunch of coon dogs running around is another."

"Thomas, one of those dogs came from your litter of shepherds you brought home from France."

"That's right, Lewis, but they belong in Virginia, where they can hunt and herd the livestock – not inside the President's House."

_ Once they got settled, Tom was anxious to get started with his elaborate plans to promote Republican ideas and personalities. His first choice for his cabinet was his close friend, James Madison, as his Secretary of State. They were of one heart and soul on matters of importance and had shared the cause for freedom together. With Thomas Jefferson being the father of the *Declaration of Independence* and James Madison as both the father of the Constitution and the Bill of Rights, they would proudly serve together as two of the Founding Fathers of their new nation.

Tom invited Madison and his family to live with him until they could find a house of their own in the Federal City. He received word they would arrive on the first of May. That meant Tom and Lewis would be like "two mice in a church" until Madison's entourage arrived. How delighted Tom was that Dick was now with him. He had desperately missed his melodious singing and whistling. Lewis was always careful to enter Tom's office when the door was shut because he knew Dick would probably be out of his cage. Before he entered, he heard the president and his feathered friend singing and talking to each other. Tom had taught the bird special tunes and whistles known only by the two of them.

Often Lewis would stand outside Tom's door and listen to him playing his violin with the bird majestically singing the tune with him. A frequent visitor of the White House, Margaret Bayard Smith, a society editor wrote, "How he loved the bird! He could not live without something to love, and in the absence of his darling grandchildren, his bird and his flowers became the objects of his tender care."[100]

Smith was the wife of the republican newspaper editor Samuel Harrison Smith. Her husband came to Washington to keep abreast of the current political news. While he was writing the events outside the White House, his resourceful and socially active wife, Margaret, recorded what was going on behind the president's front door.

Shortly after Tom became president, Margaret Smith showed up one day to interview him. Due to all the hateful, negative accusations made against Jefferson during his bitterly-fought election campaign, Mrs. Smith anticipated meeting an obnoxious tyrant. Was she ever surprised? She recorded the following first impression of the president.

"And is that the violent democrat, the vulgar demagogue, the bold atheist and profligate man I have so often heard denounced by the federalists? Can that man so meek and mild, yet dignified in his manners, with a voice so soft and low, with a countenance so benignant and intelligent, can he be that daring leader of a faction, that disturber of the peace, that enemy of all rank and order? . . . I happened to be seated next to him and had the pleasure of his conversation on several subjects."[101]

While Dick kept Tom happy, the women of Washington rebelled against him. They wanted their gala affair at the president's reception, and Tom had nixed it. He made it known there would only be two events per year at the Executive Mansion, on July 4 and at New Year's. Shortly after Tom got moved in, the women stormed the White House. However, Tom was away on his horse when they arrived. Lewis had to bear the brunt of their anger. He was mortified, to say the least. He was battle-tested in the army, but he never received training for the onslaught he would receive from those screaming infuriated women. When Tom finally arrived to find them awaiting him, he used some gentle persuasion to try to see it his way. Whatever he said to them at least got them off his back for awhile.

The following day Tom and Lewis had their morning meeting, where they planned their day.

"What we need in this house is a woman's touch. Wouldn't you agree, Lewis?"

"I agree, Thomas. A woman is always nice to have around."

"What about you? Why haven't you been married?"

"Well, I never had a hankerin' for a woman. I loved my freedom too much to get saddled up with a wife. As a hunter, I liked to come and go as I will. As a soldier, I had no time for a home life either."

"Lewis, the greatest years of my life was when I was married. My dearest Martha only lasted ten years with me before she died. I never have been the same without her."

"Why don't you get another wife, Thomas?"

"No, no, no. That won't do. I promised her on her death bed I would never marry again, and I intend to keep that vow."

"You have two daughters. Why don't you invite them to live here?"

"I have Lewis, but they have lives of their own. Martha is at Edgehill with four children and another one on the way."

"Please tell me about them." Lewis was all ears, as he relished his times listening to Tom's ramblings.

"Anne is the oldest – now ten years old; then there's little Tommy, who's eight. He's my only grandson. Next there's Ellen – now four; Cornelia's the youngest – who will turn two this month. I only wish I could be there for her birthday."

"What about your other daughter, Thomas?"

"Maria is needed at Monticello, where she sees after my farm. She is also due with a child soon. It'll be a contest between my daughters to see which one of my next grandchildren is born next. I've invited the Madisons to stay with us when they come, and I am sure Mrs. Madison will bring some life to the cold house."

"Perhaps she will be able to keep the local women off our backs." Lewis stood to his feet and stretched and yawned. "If they return, I hope you'll be the one to meet them next time."

That evening as Tom climbed the steps to his bedroom, Lewis watched as Dick followed, hopping up the stairs behind him. Whenever Tom would bathe, Dick would mock him whistling, "Wanna bath" and "More 'oap, more oap!" Later, he would remind him of Monticello as he emitted sounds mimicking Tom's horses or his French sheepdogs. Tom wanted Dick by his side even when he slept. He loved falling to sleep listening to his pet bird singing his melodious tunes.

Before James Madison and his family arrived in May, Tom wanted to discuss with Lewis the pressing items that affected America. The Alien and Sedition Acts that made John Adams so unpopular were allowed to expire when Tom took office. He had the opportunity to reinstate them, but he refused, having been adamantly opposed to them from the start. That allowed all those who had been imprisoned for their hostilities against the government to be released.

As they discussed this matter, Lewis said to Tom, "I don't understand why you would allow the likes of James Callender to roam the earth like a roaring lion."

"Lewis, I am for freedom of speech, and all those Adams imprisoned were only exercising their God-given right."

"Didn't Callender have to flee England for his verbal abuse against its government?" Lewis paused before he continued. "Didn't he try to do the same in America? He was always attacking Washington."

"He also tried his best to destroy Alexander Hamilton, claiming he had an affair with Maria Reynolds," added Tom. "But I still defend his right to freedom of speech and of the press."

"You had a meeting with Callender the other day. How did that turn out, Thomas?"

"He had the gall to request the Richmond postmaster's job."

"What did you tell him?"

"I reminded him how I had landed him a job with *The Aurora* newspaper and had loaned him money in the past. But I refused him to honor him with the office of postmaster."

"Why, may I ask, did you do that?"

"He's too radical for my tastes. Although he's a Republican and supports me, he is always digging up dirt on someone. Frankly, I don't care much for men who do that."

Tom politely stood up with Dick on his shoulder and walked over to the birdcage. As he pointed to the wire door, Dick flew onto his perch and began pecking at his seeds. Tom then closed the door of his cage, and Lewis knew it was time for him to leave.

When the carriage of James Madison, Tom's Secretary of State, pulled up in front of the White House, the black coachman opened the vehicle's door, allowing Mr. Madison to be the first to step out of the coach. He in turn reached out his hand for his darling exuberant wife, Dolley. The Washington ladies were pushing and shoving to see who could get the best view of the new first lady in the President's House. A second coach followed, which emptied Dolley's younger sister, Anna Payne, and Dolley's ten-year-old son, Payne Todd, onto the front porch.

Mrs. Madison was born Dolley Payne, the daughter of John Payne and Mary Coles of North Carolina. She was a southern girl of a Quaker family who moved to Philadelphia when she was 15. At 21, she married lawyer John Todd, a fellow Quaker, who gave her two children, William and Payne. In 1793, she lost both her husband and her youngest child to yellow fever. Later, when James Madison came calling, Dolley refused his repeated advances until she finally accepted his proposal for marriage. She knew since he was an Anglican rather than a Quaker, she would be expelled from her church if she married him. However, on September 15, 1794, 43-year old James Madison exchanged vows with 26-year old Dolley Payne Todd.

As soon as Dolley's feet hit the ground in Washington, the Federal City was never the same. Her bright smile and cheerfulness spread throughout the neighborhood. The angry ladies who gave Tom fits now looked at the White House with warm feelings. Before long, she had them all on her side. Remembering each of the ladies by their first names, her outgoing and sparkling personality quickly led to the dinner parties upon which they thrived.

Although that blue-eyed beauty with black hair was only in the Executive Mansion a short time before the Madisons found their own house on "F" Street, she didn't need long to make her mark in society. She had the unique gift of offering constructive criticism to the president on his dress, his furnishings and his etiquette without giving offense. She tried her best to add a womanly touch to the White House. It bothered her that Tom insisted on greeting his guests in his rather plain clothes and house slippers. Many who came to see him for the first time were confused because they thought he was one of the household staff rather than the President of the United States.

Thomas Jefferson

James Madison entered the White House as Thomas Jefferson's closest friend. The two of them worked hand in hand to try to handle the relationship between America and the other nations. Their first mutual problem was with the nation of Tripoli on the southern shore of the Mediterranean Sea.

In 1796, President John Adams signed the Treaty of Tripoli, which authorized the United States to pay tribute money to that Muslim nation and its Barbary Pirates. That was something the northern Africa Barbary States of Morocco, Tunis, Tripoli and Algiers had demanded for centuries. They had state-sponsored pirates who seized and plundered foreign ships. They not only imprisoned all the occupants of the ship but also demanded exorbitant ransoms from the passenger's family and government.

Wealthy European nations were in the habit of paying a hefty annual ransom to the Barbary Pirates to exempt their ships from piracy. When the United States signed the Treaty of Paris in 1783 and became an independent nation, President Washington felt compelled to pay the annual ransom as well. When John Adams became president, he continued the same irrational policy.

Thomas Jefferson and James Madison, the founders of the Democratic-Republican Party, believed there should be no negotiation with terrorists and refused to pay any more ransom money to the Barbary nations, including Tripoli and its hundreds of pirate ships. They would band together to establish a new policy for America that would be followed for the next two hundred years.[102]

"Can you believe Tripoli is demanding $225,000 for ransom to keep the pirates from raiding our ships?" Tom asked as he paced the room in his meeting with his Secretary of State.

"That's beside the $25,000 we've been giving to them as an annual fee." James Madison offered his total support for Tom's adamant stand against the ransom. Whenever the two men were together, Tom had tried, but failed, to remain seated because he towered over the much shorter "Jemmie", as his friends called him. With Tom being over six foot two and Madison only five foot four, he was careful to keep from dwarfing his good friend, especially since he hardly weighed a hundred pounds. To Tom, size meant nothing because Madison was a giant of a man in his eyes.

"Jimmie, I believe it's time to shut down the flow of money to our enemies."

"I agree, Tom. But that will mean war." Madison's bright blue eyes stared directly into those of Tom's, and his voice lowered to that of a whisper.

"If that's what it takes, then so be it," said Tom. "We both agree we shouldn't continue giving in to their demands."

"I think you are so angry about this that I could beat you in a game of chess." Madison suggested as a way to change the subject.

When their decision was known across the Atlantic, Tripoli wasted no time declaring war against the United States. Jefferson's retaliation was to send naval vessels to the Mediterranean. Tom was inherently an isolationist and hoped America would only need a navy to defend her own territories at home. However, now he saw that in order to protect the interests and citizens of the United States abroad, he must organize a navy and build more ships.

U.S. Representative Albert Gallatin had been tapped by Jefferson to be his Treasury Secretary. Within five years, that 40-year old Swiss immigrant had risen to the status of House Majority Leader. Gallatin gained Tom's favor because he had been a leading spokesman opposing Alexander Hamilton and his Federalist policies. Both men shared the vision of cutting taxes and paying off the national debt. They began by repealing the unpopular whiskey tax and ended all internal taxes. Jefferson had campaigned on the promise that "ordinary Americans would never see a federal tax collector in their whole lives."

They took the axe to the $83 million national debt, pledging to eventually eliminate that heavy burden on the U. S. citizens. Gallatin helped Jefferson trim the staff of the executive branch and make drastic cuts to the military. By the time he ended his career, that Swiss immigrant would go down in history as the longest serving Treasury Secretary in U. S. history.

Although Tripoli had declared war with America, Congress wouldn't officially retaliate with a formal declaration of war until the following year on February 6, 1802. However, Captain Andrew Sterret of the American ship, *Enterprise*, captured Tripoli's 14-gun corsair ship, *Tripoli*, on August 1, 1801, the first American naval victory of the Barbary Wars.[103]

Before 1801 came to an end, the new-baby contest between Tom's two daughters was settled. Martha came in first, with her daughter, Virginia Randolph, being born in August, while Maria gave birth in September to a new grandson for Tom named "Francis Wayles Eppes." That was her second attempt at being a mother, having lost her first one before she was one month old. Tom kept his hopes up this child would be the fulfillment of Maria's passionate desire to be a good mother. He was particularly excited he was his second grandson.

Baby boys were rare in the Jefferson family, and Tom was glad to see Martha and Maria each have a son of their own to keep their family name alive. The year ended with Tom giving his State of the Union address, but because he was a better writer than a speaker, he sent the address to the House clerk, who read it publicly. To him, delivering it publicly would make him appear too proud. That set a precedent that would last over one hundred years until President Woodrow Wilson changed it in 1913.

Thomas Jefferson received so much opposition from religious leaders during his campaign for president that a preacher from the north came to Tom's defense. John Leland, pastor of a Baptist church in Cheshire, Massachusetts, chose to use an unusual object lesson to illustrate his support for Jefferson. He encouraged the ladies of his church to create the largest block of cheese the world had ever seen. Dubbed "the mammoth cheese," Leland and his Cheshire Baptist ladies planned to personally present this to Jefferson at the White House. This was to show their unwavering support for the religious liberty he had provided for America. They knew that without their hero, they might be imprisoned or banned for their uncompromising convictions.

The newspaper reporters had a field day with the proposal of the giant block of cheese. Most were critical of it to the point of outright ridicule and hilarity. However, some supported the unique ladies' project. A Rhode Island newspaper reported that the round block of cheese was formed in a cider press, with a diameter of six feet. 900 cows used their milk for its creation. All this was marked with an engraving with the motto, "Rebellion to tyrants is obedience to God."[104] One of the newspapers opposed to the efforts of the Baptists, called it the "mammoth cheese" because it was ludicrous beyond imagination, absolutely disgusting.

The next-to-impossible project began in the summer of 1801 but wasn't completed until the latter part of November. While the cheese was being made, Leland, the Baptist pastor, planned a way for it to get to Washington. Loading it on a wagon, he sluggishly transported it to the Hudson River, where it was transferred to a sloop. From there it sailed to Baltimore. A wagon finalized the trip to the White House.

On New Year's Day of 1802, Thomas Jefferson opened his door to welcome Elder John Leland and "the mammoth cheese." As the two men shook hands, news reporters shoved each other to get the best view of the president and to see his response to his heavily-publicized unique gift.

"This is unbelievable, Reverend Leland, I kept hearing about all this cheese coming to my house. But I couldn't believe it until I saw it."

"Mr. Jefferson, please accept this as a token for the singular blessings that have been derived from the numerous services you have rendered to mankind in general."[105]

"This means so much to me because it is coming from Massachusetts, where my Republican ideas are shunned." As Tom walked out to the wagon, he was overwhelmed that such a block of cheese could have been made. How was this accomplished, Leland?"

"I am proud to say this was produced by the personal labor of freeborn farmers with the voluntary and cheerful aid of their wives and daughters, without the assistance of a single slave."

"I am truly pleased by that, Leland. That proves slavery is not needed in America. I believe it is the curse of our nation, and I can't wait to see the day it is abolished." Tom was walking around the wagon carefully examining its contents as he talked. "How big is this cheese, Leland?"

"I weighed it in August at 1230 pounds. It is 15 inches thick and has a diameter of four and half feet."

"I want to thank the people of Cheshire, who showed the extraordinary proof of the skill with which those domestic arts which contribute so much to our daily comfort are practiced by them.".

"I will be honored to share your sentiments to them, Mr. President."

"You must have heard about my macaroni machine. Always having macaroni at the White House, I need lots of cheese to go with it. I have enough now to satisfy our needs for years to come."

"Mr. President, I heard about the church services held at the Capitol each Sunday. Is that correct?"

"That's right. I was attending them while I was vice president, but I must confess being lax after getting in the White House. However, if you will preach there this Sunday, I will promise to be there. We have a different church denomination that meets there each week. This gives each their opportunity to share their convictions."

"At your request, I would count it an honor to present the sermon this Lord's day."

On Sunday morning, Elder John Leland arrived at the Capitol with his Bible in hand. He expected to see Thomas Jefferson come to church in a royal carriage. Instead, he spied him riding his horse to the meeting. The preacher's sermon on January 3, 1802 was on the text, Luke 11:31: "Behold a greater than Solomon is here."[106] As a result of that message, Jefferson began the practice on Sunday of regular church attendance in the Capitol, always arriving by horseback. He began referring to this as "the common temple" just as he had with the Albemarle County Courthouse as early as 1777.

The Danbury Baptists and the Wall of Separation

While the Baptists from Massachusetts were making cheese for Jefferson, Baptists from Connecticut found another way to get the president's attention. On October 7, 1801, they wrote the following letter to the White House. (Significant words are underlined by this author for emphasis).

> The address of the Danbury Baptist Association in the State of Connecticut, assembled October 7, 1801.
> "To Thomas Jefferson, Esq., President of the United States of America
>
> > "Sir, Among the many millions in America and Europe who rejoice in your election to office, we embrace the first opportunity which we have enjoyed in our collective capacity, since your inauguration, to express our great satisfaction in your appointment to the Chief Magistracy in the United States. And though the mode of expression may be less courtly and pompous than what many others clothe their addresses with, we beg you, sir, to believe, that none is more sincere.
> > "Our sentiments are uniformly on the side of religious liberty: that Religion is at all times and places a matter between God and individuals, that no man ought to suffer in name, person, or effects on account of his religious opinions, [and] that the legitimate power of civil government extends no further than to punish the man who works ill to his neighbor. But sir, <u>our constitution of government is not specific</u>. Our ancient charter, together with the laws made coincident therewith, were adapted as the basis of our

government at the time of our revolution. And such has been our laws and usages, and such still are, [so] that Religion is considered as the first object of Legislation, and therefore what religious privileges we enjoy (as a minor part of the State) we enjoy as favors granted, and not as inalienable rights. And these favors we receive at the expense of such degrading acknowledgments, as are inconsistent with the rights of freemen. It is not to be wondered at therefore, if those who seek after power and gain, under the pretense of government and Religion, should reproach their fellow men, [or] should reproach their Chief Magistrate, as an enemy of religion, law, and good order, because he will not, dares not, assume the prerogative of Jehovah and make laws to govern the Kingdom of Christ.

"Sir, we are sensible that the President of the United States is not the National Legislator and also sensible that the national government cannot destroy the laws of each State, but our hopes are strong that the sentiment of our beloved President, which have had such genial effect already, like the radiant beams of the sun, will shine and prevail through all these States--and all the world--until hierarchy and tyranny be destroyed from the earth. Sir, when we reflect on your past services, and see a glow of philanthropy and goodwill shining forth in a course of more than thirty years, <u>we have reason to believe that America's God has raised you up to fill the Chair of State out of that goodwill which he bears to the millions which you preside over</u>. May God strengthen you for the arduous task which providence and the voice of the people have called you--to sustain and support you and your Administration against all the predetermined opposition of those who wish to rise to wealth and importance on the poverty and subjection of the people.

"And may the Lord preserve you safe from every evil and bring you at last to his Heavenly Kingdom through Jesus Christ our Glorious Mediator."

Signed in behalf of the Association,

Neh,h Dodge }
Eph'm Robbins } The Committee
Stephen S. Nelson }[107]

Although the president received this letter long before his mammoth block of cheese arrived at his front door, he waited until the Baptist pastor from Massachusetts came before he gave his written response. The cheese was what made the headlines, but on that New Year's Day, but Thomas Jefferson was more concerned about the Danbury Baptists than he was about the surprised gift being unloaded from the wagon.

Tom asked Pastor Leland to discuss the letter from his Baptist neighbors in New England. Before he sent a response, he wanted to see if Leland had the same concerns. The main concern of the Danbury Baptists was that "our constitution of government is not specific." After his meeting with Leland, he penned the following letter.

> Messrs. Nehemiah Dodge, Ephraim Robbins, and Stephen Nelson
> A Committee of the Danbury Baptist Association, in the State of Connecticut.
>
> Washington, January 1, 1802
>
> "Gentlemen,--The affectionate sentiment of esteem and approbation which you are so good as to express towards me, on behalf of the Danbury Baptist Association, give me the highest satisfaction. My duties dictate a faithful and zealous pursuit of the interests of my constituents, and in proportion as they are persuaded of my fidelity to those duties, the discharge of them becomes more and more pleasing.
>
> "Believing with you that religion is a matter which lies solely between man and his God, that he owes account to none other for his faith or his worship, that the legislative powers of government reach actions only, and not opinions, I contemplate with sovereign reverence that act of the whole American people which declared that their legislature would "make no law respecting an establishment of religion, or prohibiting the free exercise thereof," thus <u>building a wall of separation between Church and State</u>. Adhering to this expression of the supreme will of the nation in behalf of the rights of conscience, <u>I shall see with sincere satisfaction the progress of those sentiments</u> which tend to restore to man all his natural rights, convinced he has no natural right in opposition to his social duties.

"I reciprocate your kind prayers for the protection and blessing of the common Father and Creator of man, and tender you for yourselves and your religious association, assurances of my high respect and esteem." [108]

Th Jefferson
Jan. 1. 1802

If Tom had only known how controversial his letter would become for the next two centuries, he probably would have written more to explain in detail what he meant about "the wall of separation between Church and State". Did he mean to say that the church should not interfere in the affairs of the state? Or was he more concerned about the government's interference with religion? The intents of this letter would be argued in the courts and in the political arena for the ages to come.

Thomas Jefferson proved by his actions what he meant was for the government not to interfere with one's religious beliefs or practice. The first Sunday after he wrote the letter, he went to church, and he did so in the nation's Capitol. Furthermore, he continued his attendance there throughout the remainder of his presidency. By doing that, he proved his belief that the church could be involved in government, but the government was not to interfere with the church. That would be an infringement on Jefferson's documents regarding religious liberty.

Because of Jefferson's policy not to accept gifts while he was in office, three days later he sent $200 to Leland to pay for the cheese. The only room large enough to house it was the East Room, where his personal secretary lived. There, Lewis could keep a watchful eye on it. Hopefully, he would be able to keep any stray mouse from attacking it. (According to eye witnesses, the cheese was last served at Jefferson's presidential reception in 1805, three years later).

After Tom accepted the mammoth cheese into the White House, the reporters continued their derision of it. The *Norwich Packet* newspaper erroneously reported that bakers in New York were "now preparing an oven of a magnitude sufficient to make a loaf of bread proportionate to the cheese."[109] Another mocked the gift by writing that a glassmaker had blown the largest bottle ever to be filled with American Porter beer to go with the cheese. One thing was for certain. As long as Jefferson was in the White House, the news reporters were kept busy. Most of them were Federalists and enjoyed writing anything that would discredit him or mock whatever he did or wrote. Usually, they didn't have to make up a story. Jefferson's life was an open book of uncanny situations and unique ideas.

Meriwether Lewis

"Captain Lewis and myself are like two mice in a church."
Thomas Jefferson

1802

What was it that attracted Thomas Jefferson to Meriwether Lewis? Could it have been his physical features? After all he was over six feet tall like Tom. He was lean and slim like Tom. He shared Tom's disciplined lifestyle, arising early, getting plenty of exercise, and eating healthy. Coming fresh out of the army, he was in superb condition to fight any obstacle that stood in his way.

Could it be that Tom saw in Lewis his intellectual prowess? He knew he was a quick learner and soaked up everything he was taught like a thirsty sponge. As a child Tom had begun teaching Lewis when the boy visited his neighboring Monticello and recognized him as an ideal student. He challenged him with homework assignments, and he always completed them promptly and thoroughly. Tom shared what he learned from Maury's School to take thorough notes about everything he saw and learned. He taught those things to Lewis and saw the young boy take to it like a fish in the water.

Tom loved teaching Lewis about the flowers, the trees, and the varieties of plants he had discovered in America, as well as in France. They enjoyed talking about all the wild animal adventures they experienced. Lewis got Tom to take him hunting, fishing, horseback riding and surveying. When the two would go canoeing together, Tom taught Lewis what he knew about navigating rapids and mapping out the waterways. Lewis was like the son Tom never had. Since Meriwether's Pa died when he was only five, he looked to Tom as his father figure.

Could Lewis have been attracted to Tom because of the president's inherent ability to befriend the Indians? Tom's father always welcomed the native-Americans into his home, and Tom grew up with the same hospitality. He treated Indians with dignity and respect and taught Lewis to do the same. Tom and Lewis both were taught by Maury's instruction to keep the golden rule as taught by Jesus in the Beatitudes. They knew that if they respected the Indians, they would get respect in return. Reverend James Maury tutored Tom with the teachings of Jesus, and later the preacher's son, Rev. Matthew Maury taught the same to Lewis.

Perhaps Tom saw within Meriwether Lewis the drive and determination needed to risk life and limb to accomplish anything he set his mind to. He remembered so well the time Tom discovered Lewis as a child hunting in his bare feet in the snow. Although he chastised him for it, he also realized Meriwether's willingness to endure the roughest situations he faced.

Tom put all his trust in Lewis because he was a man of impeccable character. The young man had proven himself to be honest, reliable, prompt and trustworthy. He was a man of his word. Tom knew if he got a handshake from Lewis, he had a firm commitment that was set in stone, absolutely unbreakable. And it didn't hurt that Lewis shared Tom's Republican convictions.

Tom possibly chose Lewis to be his future discoverer because of his significant family heritage. He descended from what Tom claimed was one of the distinguished families of Virginia. Meriwether Lewis was the grandson of one of the five dreamers who showed up regularly at Tom's house when he was a young lad both at Tuckahoe and Shadwell. Tom remembered Colonel Thomas Meriwether as the largest property owner in his neck of the woods and probably the richest of all. His money was needed to make sure the dream to capture the West was properly funded.

Thomas Meriwether married Elizabeth Thornton, who gave him ten children including Lucy Thornton Meriwether. Lucy then married Lieutenant William Lewis, son of Colonel Robert Warner Lewis and Jane Crawford Meriwether. (The Lewis and Meriwether clan intermarried with one another eleven times). William Lewis' grandfather, Colonel Nicholas Meriwether II, owned a 1020-acre tract of land called the "Roundabout" which later would become part of the city of Charlottesville.

William Lewis served as commander of one of the first regiments of the Revolution raised in Virginia. In 1775, he became 1st Lieutenant of the Albemarle County militia. Like George Washington, he served his country without pay. Regretfully, only four years later he died of pneumonia, only two days after he nearly drowned as he tried to cross a river on his horse. His mount was swept away in the swift current as he was returning home from a battle site. He was laid to rest at Cloverfields, the 3,000 acre plantation which had been in the Meriwether family since 1729 and was the birthplace of his wife.

Lucy was left as a widow with three children – Jane at 9 years, Meriwether at 5, and Reuben as only two. They were all born at Locust Hill in the small community of Ivy, west of Charlottesville. Lucy's life was dedicated to loving her neighbors and serving them anyway she could. Whenever someone was sick, he called on Lucy for help. Her herbal remedies and medical knowledge was shared wherever she traveled. Through her desire to help others get healed from their maladies, she inspired both a son and a grandson to choose to become physicians. Besides, her sons, Meriwether and Reuben, were diligent as herbal doctors wherever they traveled.

Meriwether's mom was also praised for her cooking skills. Tom said she "made very nice hams - better than even Monticello could produce."[110] When Meriwether was a lad, he remembered occasionally saddling a few hams on his horse to deliver to his distant neighbor, Thomas Jefferson.

Although the women of her day didn't go to school and weren't encouraged to read and write, Lucy Meriwether Lewis was unique. As best she could, she collected many books she herself enjoyed and likewise shared with her children. When she wrote her last will and testament, she thoughtfully considered which books would best suit each of her children's needs.

Lucy also was quick on the trigger when it came to guns. Once, some British soldiers came to Locust Hill, looking to stir up trouble. They got all the trouble they could bargain for from Meriwether's mom, when she scared them away with her trusty rifle.

That was the same gun she used to kill her dinner earlier that afternoon. The men folk had left her house with their hunting dogs going after deer. When they found the deer, the dogs cornered it near Lucy's house, and she politely took her rifle and shot it. When the men returned home, they found she had gutted and dressed the deer and had cooked it in some venison stew when they arrived from their night in the woods.

While all these factors influenced Thomas Jefferson's choice for Meriwether Lewis to be his personal secretary and to lead his Corps of Discovery, Tom himself summarized his qualifications this way. "It was impossible to find a character who to a compleat (sic) science in botany, natural history, mineralogy & astronomy, joined the firmness of constitution & character, prudence, habits adapted to the woods, & a familiarity with the Indian manners & character, requisite for that undertaking. All the latter qualifications Capt. Lewis has."[111]

At five years old, Meriwether inherited his father's estate. That included the Locust Hill plantation of nearly 2,000 acres, 520 pounds in cash, 24 slaves, and 147 gallons of whiskey. That was quite an awesome responsibility for a preschooler. Therefore, his uncle, Col. Nicholas Meriwether of Belvoir, became his guardian until he reached the age to inherit.

Six months after Meriwether's father died, at Locust Hill, his mother married Captain John Marks, another Revolutionary War soldier. After Lucy married John, she gave birth to two more children: John Hastings and Mary Garland Marks. Since John Marks felt he needed property of his own, he moved his wife, Lucy, and her children to Georgia. Meriwether was eight years old when his family settled along the Broad River in the Goose Pond Community of Wilkes County.

Five years later his mother decided Meriwether should return to Virginia for formal schooling to prepare him for the oversight of his plantation. There, he began attending Maury's School for Boys, then taught by Rev. Matthew Maury. (He was the son of James Maury, who had taught three future presidents, Thomas Jefferson, James Madison and James Monroe).

John Marks died in 1791 in Georgia, which led Meriwether's mother to move back to Virginia. After she moved from Georgia, her son, Meriwether, at 18 began to settle down as the planter at his Locust Hill plantation. However, in 1792 when he heard that Thomas Jefferson was beginning the Corps of Discovery, he volunteered to lead the expedition, following his grandfather's dream to capture the West. Although Tom admired the young man, he believed at 18, he was much too young for the assignment. Although he chose an older man to go instead, his Corps of Discovery was put on hold for ten years. For two years Meriwether farmed Locust Hill, growing corn, wheat and tobacco. All the while, he yearned for something more challenging. He was not the kind of man to settle down.

When the Whiskey Rebellion broke out in 1794, as soon as President Washington called for federal troops to volunteer, Meredith Lewis left all and followed. He knew in his heart that those who were rebelling about taxation without representation were doing what was right. However, he had such admiration for George Washington that he chose to follow him in opposition to those who rebelled against the whiskey tax. As he joined the Virginia Volunteer Corps, he shared with his mother that he wanted "to support the glorious cause of liberty, and my country."[112]

- After that rebellion fizzled, he got a taste of soldiering that he loved. On May 1, 1795, Meriwether Lewis joined the regular U.S. Army, beginning with the rank of Ensign. There he became close friends with a fellow Virginian from his native Albemarle County. Captain William Clark was in charge of the Chosen Rifle Company composed of specialized sharpshooters. After six months, the two men parted company because Clark resigned due to health and family problems. However, Lewis and Clark remained close friends, and Lewis always regarded Clark as being the best soldier he had known.

In 1799, Lewis was promoted to Lieutenant, becoming a recruiting officer in his local Charlottesville, Virginia station. Later, the army moved him to Detroit, where he became the regimental paymaster. That position required him to travel to different posts, where he was able to see the good and the bad among the military officers. On December 30, 1800, he was promoted to the office of Captain.

As soon as Thomas Jefferson was elected third President of the United States, he knew he needed Meriwether Lewis as his right hand man. He had watched him grow and develop from the time he was born and was the ideal man for the job. What he was looking for was not so much a personal secretary, but one who would eventually lead his Corps of Discovery. Meriwether already had volunteered for that assignment nine years ago. Tom knew where Lewis' heart was and that they were kindred spirits.

After Lewis set up shop at the President's House, he dined with all those who visited Thomas Jefferson, including world leaders and educators. To prepare Lewis for his Corps of Discovery expedition, Tom brought to the White House such significant personalities as Dr. Benjamin Smith Barton, a noteworthy botanist; Dr. David Rittenhouse, famed mathematician and astronomer; Dr. Caspar Wistar, foremost authority on fossils; and Dr. Benjamin Rush, a noted physician from Philadelphia.

Thomas Jefferson remained as president of the American Philosophical Society, where he had access to the finest astronomers and cartographers in Philadelphia. Lewis had regular training from Jefferson on botany, astronomy, geography and navigational practices. But Tom left no stone unturned to give Lewis the finest training he needed to prepare him to chase their ancestor's dream, going all the way to the Pacific.

Tom had friends visit him on a daily basis, all of whom also befriended Lewis. His dinner parties were rather small, giving more opportunity for each one present to share freely with one another. Although Tom's clothes were plain, his sumptuous meals soon became the talk of the town. Tom always had a French chef to fix his meals. That way he would offer his guests a combination of menus from France as well as from Virginia.

Tom had three Frenchmen in his employ at the White House. Jean Pierre Sioussat served as the master of ceremonies. Although he was only twenty when Tom hired him, he came highly recommended. Since he was a native from Paris and well-versed in all the customs and etiquette of the Europeans, he greeted each guest with grace and dignity. Tom called him simply "French John, the doorkeeper."

Étienne Lemaire was in charge of all the selection and purchase of the meal's delicacies. He was the first to rise each morning to organize his staff to start fires in the hearths. Then he would make sure Jefferson's slaves did all the dusting, cleaning, silver polishing and other preparations for their guests. One would be sent to the livery to take care of the animals, while another would prepare the washtub for the president's early footbath.

Honoré Julien was his 42-year old French master chef par excellence. His reliable helper and apprentice was Edith Hern, a 15-year old slave girl from Monticello. Tom chose her to join his White House staff, due to her strong sense of loyalty and the desire to learn and improve on her skills. While Julien cooked his French specialties, Edith added her Virginia down-home tastes.

Jefferson's guests noted: "never before had such dinners been given in the President's House. The meals were cooked in the French style and the dessert was extremely elegant."[113] Guests at the White House were treated to such delicacies as boeuf à la mode, nouilly à macaroni, and blanc mange. Tom possessed his own macaroni maker, which he had acquired in France. He developed the habit of ending his dinners with the French delicacy of ice cream, often as pie à la mode. Perhaps, no one in America popularized that dessert more than did Thomas Jefferson while he was in the White House.

Tom upset many of his guests because he sat people around the table at random or "pell-mell" rather than by their rank. That treated everyone, including himself as the president, as being equal.

To encourage open conversation, he insisted on having an oval table where ideas could flow freely. Any subject was fair game. Whether it was geography, Indian affairs, botany, philosophy, mathematics, architecture or politics, Meriwether Lewis sat there and soaked it up like a sponge.

Regular guests included all the members of Tom's chosen cabinet and their wives. Author Thomas Paine, artist Charles Wilson Peale, journalist Joel Barlow, and lawyer Mahlon Dickerson were all served at the table of Thomas Jefferson.

Margaret Bayard Smith summarized Jefferson's unique gregarious hospitality when she wrote the following about one of Tom's dinners at Monticello. His White House meals followed the same protocol.

"We sat at table, until near sun down, where we enjoyed agreeable and instructive conversation, in which everyone seemed to expect and wish Mr. J should take the chief part. That is the part of the day, in which he gives most time to his guests and seems himself most to enjoy society; and I found during the few days we passed..., these were the most social hours. The dessert is not removed; the wine freely, but not rapidly circulated round the table, and the ladies do not withdraw, until the hospitable master leads the way. Everyone who has known has acknowledged the colloquial powers of that excellent man. He is frank and communicative in his manner, various and delightful in his conversation.

"With a mind stored by much reading, long experience, accurate observation, deep research, an intimate acquaintance with the great and good men of Europe and America; with the events, and scenes and customs of both countries; he possesses a store of intellectual wealth, which falls to the lot of few; and of those, how many possess the treasure, have not the faculty of imparting it to others. But, Mr. J, has not only the sterling gold, but has the baser coins, which afford an easy currency of thought, and are so important in social intercourse. No subject could be started, which he did not illustrate by luminous observations, or enliven by sprightly anecdotes.

"One quality he has, which I never knew equaled in any other man: a quick and intuitive perception of the character, taste and feelings of his guests, and with a benevolence, equaling in warmth, the greatness of his perception; he always turned the conversation, so as to draw forth the powers and talents of each guest, bestowing on all, the same gracious attention: he, above all men, has the art of pleasing, by making each pleased with himself. Why can I not recollect every word which fell from his lips, during these charming conversations, for every word deserved to be remembered?"[114]

A year after Tripoli declared war against the United States, the U.S. Congress on February 6, 1802, returned the favor. That would escalate the war with Tripoli and would last throughout the presidency of Thomas Jefferson and his successor, ending in 1815. Meanwhile, another Barbary nation, Morocco, declared war against America on June 17. Fortunately, Jefferson was able to negotiate a peace agreement with that northern African nation within a few months. That action helped restore some stability to the region for the remainder of the year.

After the first year of Meriwether Lewis' career as Tom's personal secretary, Tom called his sidekick in for his annual evaluation. When Lewis saw Dick in his cage, he knew whatever Tom had on his mind was quite serious.

"Lewis, I know you didn't take kindly to the idea of leaving your military post and joining me indoors for a spell." Tom was sitting in his revolving "whirligig" chair with his feet propped up on his Windsor stool.

"It's been difficult at times, but by living in that cold, drafty unfinished East Room with the leaky roof, including a giant piece of cheese, I may as well have been outside anyway." Lewis was sitting across his desk from him where they could communicate more directly.

"Do you remember the main assignment I gave you as my aide-de-camp?"

"Yes, I do, Thomas. I was to cut the size of the army troops down to their 1796 level and weed out the officers who were Federalist sympathizers."

"Let's see how you've done?" Tom began looking through an assortment of documents spread freely over his desk. Several papers had fallen to the floor, and Lewis reached down to retrieve them. He was feeling anxious, but yet he didn't know how Tom could find fault with his performance.

"First, did you meet your goal of shrinking the size of the army?"

"Yes, sir, in 1796 the army had 3,359 total enlistments, including officers. Then it ballooned to over 14,000 two years later."

"There is no way, Lewis, that we ever needed an army that large. It just meant too much unnecessary taxation on our people."

"I agree, sir. I believe you'll be pleased that I not only am recommending the 1796 level. I am taking it a step further. I have trimmed so much that I now recommend we have only 3,287 men, which is 72 less than in 1796. That will give us one regiment of infantry, one of artillery, and a skeleton crew on the U.S. Army Corps of Engineers."

"That's what I like to hear. Now what did you do about all those meddling Federalists?"

"They're all gone, as well, sir. I believe the only officers left are each loyal to you."

"Very well, Lewis. You have done well, and I am proud of you. There was no one I would have trusted this job more than to you, and you didn't let me down. I remember when you were a child, even then I could always count on you to keep your word and complete your assignments faithfully and thoroughly. That will prepare you for what's coming ahead."

"What's that, sir?"

"That remains to be seen, Lewis." Tom lowered his head and stared at the papers on his messy desk, "What do you think about helping me establish a military academy for the training of army officers?"

"I like that idea, sir. I know when I got rid of the Federalist officers; the pickings are lean for any replacements for them."

"With a corps of engineers, we need to train officers in mechanical engineering. I've already got a spot for such a school."

"Where's that, sir?"

"Up the Hudson River in New York is one of the oldest forts in the nation, built in 1788. Washington began using it as his headquarters the following year."

"You're talking about West Point, sir."

"Right you are, Lewis. Why don't we name it the West Point Military Academy? During the March session, I will recommend that to Congress." Lewis heard Dick whistling, which signified to Tom that he was giving his wholehearted approval of his challenging idea.[115]

Jefferson was thankful he had a Congress that would approve almost any of his suggestions. On March 16, 1802, they accepted his recommendations for the reduction of the army and the founding of West Point. The next month they repealed the whiskey tax and other excise taxes. Tom had recommended shortening the naturalization laws so that one could become a U.S. citizen in only five years rather than the established 14-year rule. Once again, Congress voted to approve it. On May 3, the legislature officially incorporated Washington as a city. That gave Jefferson the authority to hire a mayor.

One man Jefferson kept away from his dinner table was James T. Callender. He had the reputation as a journalist of being a snake in the grass. Possessing a poisonous quill, he was always seeking the next scandal he could expose, whether true or untrue.

When John Adams was president, he had Callender imprisoned for his violation of the Alien and Sedition Acts. That was because he tried to dishonor the Treasury Secretary, Alexander Hamilton, saying he, as a married man, was involved sexually with another woman.

Thomas Jefferson freed all those in prison who violated Adams' unpopular Sedition Acts. That was because he believed in freedom of speech and of the press, even if it dishonored or destroyed those in political office. When Callender was released, he insisted that Tom would award him with the position of postmaster in Richmond.

Lewis had warned Tom that Callender probably would seek revenge, and during the summer of 1802, he had all his guns loaded. He published a scandalous article in the *Richmond Recorder* intending to ruin Jefferson's political career. Whether his claims were true or false could not be proven at the time. But he was determined to share his feelings no matter what. Here's the way the newspaper reported Callender's scathing remarks.

The President Again

"It is well known that the man, *whom it delighteth the people to honor*, keeps, and for many years past has kept, as his concubine, one of his own slaves. Her name is SALLY. The name of her eldest son is TOM. His features are said to bear a striking although sable resemblance to those of the president himself. The boy is ten or twelve years of age. His mother went to France in the same vessel with Mr. Jefferson and his two daughters. The delicacy of that arrangement must strike every person of common sensibility. What a sublime pattern for an American ambassador to place before the eyes of two young ladies!

"If the reader does not feel himself *disposed to pause* we beg leave to proceed. Some years ago, that story had once or twice been hinted at in *Rind's Federalist*. At that time, we believed the surmise to be an absolute calumny. One reason for thinking so was that: A vast body of people wished to debar Mr. Jefferson from the presidency. *The establishment of that* SINGLE FACT would have rendered his election impossible. We reasoned thus; that if the allegation had been true, it was sure to have been ascertained and advertised by his enemies, in every corner of the continent. The suppression of so decisive an enquiry serves to show that the common sense of the federal party was overruled by divine providence. It was the predestination of the Supreme Being that they should be turned out; that they should be expelled from office by the *popularity* of character...."[116]

That was only the beginning of a series of articles Callender published which painted Thomas Jefferson as a grossly immoral and crooked person. He accused him of having an affair with his "Black Sally," of having another affair with another man's wife, and cheating on a debt he owed. Callender's poisoned words only came to an abrupt end when he died the following year by drowning in a pool of water after being totally consumed with alcohol. Although Tom's nemesis had now departed, Tom's reputation would be tainted during the rest of his lifetime and forevermore. Jefferson wrote in response, "I am really mortified at the base ingratitude of Callender. It presents human nature in a hideous form."[117]

Although James and Dolley Madison had been in a home of their own since last summer, Dolley still was called on to be the hostess at the White House whenever lady guests were invited. Tom felt like that would eliminate any false rumor of a scandalous affair at the Executive Mansion. Dolley had a cheerful, magnetic personality that made all women feel right at home meeting with the president. Although she was raised with the rigidness of a Quaker, her brilliant smile and sparkling personality warmed the most frigid minds when they came calling at the President's House.

Tom and Lewis took a break from Washington long enough for the president to return to Monticello for the first birthdays of Tom's two youngest grandchildren, one at Martha's and the other at Maria's. He enjoyed being on his horse again, riding around his plantation checking on his crops and becoming reacquainted with his slaves. He was always anxious to see how his Monticello construction had progressed, as it was still unfinished. Whenever Tom was away, it seemed all the work on the house ceased. The workers seemed to wait for him to motivate them to continue.

As for Lewis, he was happy to be with his family again at nearby Locust Hill. His mother had just celebrated her fiftieth birthday and was overjoyed to see her oldest son once again. After burying two husbands, she had remained a single widow for the past eleven years. She was still just as busy as ever. Whenever someone was sick in the surrounding neighborhoods, they were quick to call on her to bring her favorite poultice for their cure. However, she did her best to try to make Lewis her priority while he was home.

Lewis' sister, Jane, had married her cousin, Edmund Anderson, son of David and Elizabeth Anderson of Hanover Co., Virginia, where they now lived. Lewis was saddened to hear that her husband was a drunk and loose with his money, bringing their family to poverty. Having a house full of children didn't help matters.

Reuben, Lewis' brother, was just as wild as Meriwether remembered him. Rather than get an education, he chose to be an outdoorsman and a fur trader. Reuben learned from his mother how to doctor the sick with herbal remedies and enjoyed helping those in need just as she had done. He had built a unique friendship with the Indians, which served him well when he negotiated treaties with them. Fortunately, he was home long enough for the two brothers to talk about old times and to find out what had been happening with each of them lately.

Lewis' half brother, Hastings, was now 16 and preparing to become a doctor like his mother, except he was planning to go to college and make it his life's profession. Hastings' sister, Mary, was now 14 and was looking forward to marriage and raising a family of her own.

During the summer of 1802, Thomas Jefferson and Meriwether Lewis continued their working relationship, Lewis always being available when called on. Tom had a cabin for Lewis on the Monticello property where they could be within shouting distance of each other. During the sultry, humid Virginia days in August, Tom and Lewis set in motion their plans to finally fulfill their ancestor's dream.

Tom had just acquired the book, *Voyages from Montreal, on the River St. Lawrence, Through the Continent of North America, to the Frozen and Pacific Ocean*. The book recently had been published in London in 1801, written by Alexander Mackenzie. As the two men read it aloud together, they were so excited they couldn't sit still. They took turns marching around the room shouting their glee with what they were reading. That book opened the door for their plan to capture the West, going all the way to the Pacific.

In the book, Mackenzie told about expeditions he had led through Canada in 1792 and 1793. He and his North West Company had as its goal to find the best way to transport furs across the nation. His writings shared his dismal failure at finding a navigable river or waterway that ran from central to western Canada. What Tom and Lewis found so intriguing was that what he looked on as failure, they would see as victory.

First, they realized that someone had made it all the way to the Pacific, although part of it had to be by land. Secondly, they believed that if a man could make it to the Pacific in the frozen tundra of the north, surely someone could do the same in a warmer climate south of there. Thirdly, in their studies of the Missouri River going west from the Mississippi, they believed it was possible it could somehow connect to the Columbia River already discovered traveling east from the mighty Pacific. If their theory was right, then they would be able to transport furs and other goods all the way from New Orleans to the Pacific Ocean. What alarmed them both is that if they didn't act soon, the British would get there first. If they did, they would have full control of all the lucrative fur trade.

"When I was just a little boy, Lewis, I listened through the door of my father's study when he met with your grandfather, Thomas Meriwether, and the other men in the Loyal Company." Tom stopped talking long enough to put whistling Dick into his cage for the night. Then he continued.

"Those men got together often and kept sharing their dream of capturing the West, going all the way to the Pacific. All five of them have passed on without experiencing what they had wished. Now you and I have the opportunity to accomplish what they only dreamed about."

"It's hard to believe that might finally become a reality." Lewis shared as he sipped on his tankard of peach cider.

"Ten years ago you, as an 18-year old kid, wet behind the ears, you volunteered to lead my Corps of Discovery. That was my last effort to attempt to carry out my father's dream."

"It really upset me, Thomas. I didn't go hunting for weeks after that."

"You are known for being moody. I imagined you were in the doldrums for awhile."

"Whatever happened to the fellow you chose instead of me?"

"He only made it as far as Kentucky, and when I found out he was doing that secretly as an agent of France, I pulled the plug on him. That's as far as he went, and the expedition was a failure."

"I know I was too young and inexperienced at that time, but I can assure you that if I had been chosen, I never would let you down."

"Lewis, I hope you'll give me another chance to choose you." Tom got up from his chair and reached out his hand to Lewis for a handshake.

Meriwether jumped to his feet and threw out his hand to firmly clutch the outstretched fingers of the president. "I'm your man, Sir. When do I start?" Lewis was excited that he was at a loss for words. Tom could tell by his facial expressions that his young personal secretary was overjoyed.

"Let's sit down and talk it over. We have some obstacles to overcome before we can move forward, Lewis." As the men reclaimed their chairs, they toasted their proposed journey with the tapping of their tankards together.

"First, we have to determine how much this will cost. Second, I have to figure a way to get Congress to approve such an endeavor. How many men do you think you will need?"

"I think a dozen will do, Thomas. If we have too many, I think we will scare the Indians. That might make them hostile to us."

"I believe you're right, Captain Lewis. Your vast experience in the army gave you a lot of common sense."

"Remember how I used to give you homework assignments when you visited Monticello as a boy?"

"How could I ever forget, Sir?"

"Well, your next assignment is to make a list of all the equipment and supplies you will need for your expedition. You've got to have enough to last you both ways. I want to make sure you get back home all right."

"I'll get right to it, Thomas. You can count on me."

"I am fully confident of that, my son. I have put my trust in you since you were born, and you've never failed me."

When Tom returned to Washington, his oldest daughter, Martha, followed him. He had been trying ever since he had been there for her to live with him, but she always had declined. Although Dolley Madison came whenever she was needed, she couldn't provide the daily female presence that Tom so desperately needed. Her timing now was impeccable because of the scandal Tom faced from the Callender onslaught.

However, this problem was minor compared to the one he saw on the horizon. Jefferson was angry when he heard that on October 15, 1802, King Carlos IV of Spain had given Napoleon the Louisiana Territory in exchange for a political favor. The following day, Spain withdrew free access for the United States to the Mississippi River through the port of New Orleans. That came as part of the treaty in which Spain ceded Louisiana to France. Consequently, Thomas Jefferson knew he must do whatever he could to rectify the alarming situation. He figured if he could arrange to buy New Orleans from France, he could solve the problem. Tom worked steadily in his office to devise a plan that might work. Knowing that the nation which owned the capital of Louisiana would have access to all shipping on both the Mississippi and Missouri Rivers, Tom decided to go to Congress to seek approval to purchase New Orleans from France.

Meanwhile, Lewis had completed his homework and now had a firm proposal to offer the president. All supplies and salaries for the round-trip journey came to $2500, which included $696 for gifts to offer the Indians they would meet along the way.

During the winter of 1802/1803, Martha, was always present at the White House as Tom's hostess and overseer of the household staff. She brought two of her children with her, 10-year-old Thomas Jefferson Randolph and 6-year-old Ellen. They called the boy "Jeffy" to differentiate between both his father and grandfather, both named "Thomas". They were the first children to live in the White House, and Tom was excited to have them around.

Ellen loved sitting on her grandpa's lap as he read her one of his story books. She enjoyed playing with Dick whenever he was out of his cage. Tom often found Jeffy in his office trying to learn what he could from his grandpa. He also listed to Tom when he taught Lewis ways to improve his grammar and his choice of words when writing. He liked inspecting the gardening and drafting tools in Tom's office, especially when Tom would teach them how to use them.

Tom loved gardening, and he had a drawer full of tools he had been longing to use. Before winter settled in, he gathered some tulip and daffodil bulbs to plant them around the White House. His two grandchildren were eager to help and to learn his planting methods.

"When you see these shoot out of the ground and bloom next year, you will know that spring is around the corner." Tom told the children as he picked up his tools. "Now before we go in the house, I want to see the two of you race around the house and see who can come in first." As he saw them take off, he was glad to see them get the exercise they needed. Tom knew that was one of the elements of a long and healthy life.

Martha and Maria and the grandchildren being in the Executive Mansion helped to diffuse the rumors that escalated from Callender's series of scandalous articles. People began to see Tom as a family man with grandchildren who loved and admired him. Tom had backslidden from his church attendance. Finally, he changed his ways once again, taking his daughter and grandchildren to the Capitol for church. He was hoping that would help to dispel the damaging rumors spread by Callender.

Tom ended 1802 with a delightful Christmas, as his daughters and his grandchildren gathered around the tree and sang their favorite carols together. They were accompanied by Tom on his fiddle and Martha on her pianoforte, while Dick was whistling up a storm.

As Thomas Jefferson faced the new year of 1803, he knew he had some steep mountains to climb. One of these was the case before the Supreme Court billed as "Marbury v. Madison". The suit brought by William Marbury against Secretary of State James Madison began with the 42 "midnight judges" appointed by out-going President John Adams the day before Jefferson was sworn in office. Then Secretary of State John Marshall under Adams left the 42 commissions for these appointments on the desk of his replacement, James Madison.

The new Secretary of State had to deliver those commissions to their recipients before they could be sworn in as judges. Before Madison moved to Washington to assume his office, President Jefferson, still angry over the way Adams administered this sneaky maneuver, removed twelve of the commissions from Madison's desk. Five more he reassigned to members of his Democratic-Republican party. When Madison found the remaining 25 mandates on his desk, he delivered them per his job requirement.

William Marbury, who was appointed by Adams as judge in Washington D.C., was one of those whose commission failed to be delivered. Therefore, he and three others who were slighted filed a lawsuit against James Madison. As 1803 began, the battle had been brewing over a year since Marbury filed the suit on December of 1801. During this time Tom had many meetings with his Secretary of State, in which this topic was at the top of their agenda. The date on the docket for this case was February 11, 1803. Both Jefferson and Madison were readying themselves for what would prove to be one of the most significant cases ever tried by the United States Supreme Court.[118]

Louisiana Purchase

*"The Louisiana Purchase is considered
the greatest real estate deal in history."*
Library of Congress-

1803

As Tom ended his long day in the office at the beginning of a new year, he looked over to the French side of the room where Maria Cosway's portrait was prominently displayed. With Dick whistling on his shoulder, Tom gingerly picked up her image and kissed her goodnight. His head told him that was wrong, as she belonged to another. But his heart couldn't resist. Oh, how he had loved her!

Tom was in tears as he realized once more how much the French meant to him. He owed them everything. From the time he was Governor of Virginia during the Revolution until he became President of the United States, the French people were always a vital part of his life.

His loyal ties to France began with General Marquis de Lafayette. When Tom was the frightened, runaway Governor of Virginia in the spring of 1781, Lafayette brought his revolutionary troops to Richmond to repel the British army, which had targeted both the governor and the Capitol of Virginia.

If it was not for French General Comte de Rochambeau, Tom knew America more than likely would still be under British rule. When Lafayette read Tom's *Declaration of Independence,* he was inspired as a 19-year old French officer to pay his own passage and expenses to join the Revolution in America. As a result of his wholehearted acceptance by General George Washington, he influenced General Rochambeau to bring 7,000 troops from France to help Washington. The French were there when America needed them the most.

Rochambeau was able to convince Washington to defeat British General Cornwallis on Virginia soil. The French and the Patriots marched 450 miles to Williamsburg, where they were joined by Lafayette and his 3,000 soldiers. But they still would not have been able to ambush Cornwallis at Yorktown if the French Navy had not blockaded the Chesapeake Bay with her ships.

When Jefferson was in France for five years, he built on his strong ties to Lafayette. The eventual outcome was that Lafayette leaned on Tom to help him write the declaration that led to the French Revolution. Although Tom was saddened to see the end results of that historic event, he was thankful that Lafayette and the French people saw the need for freedom from the tyrannical rule of a dictator and all the excesses that accompanied the reign of King Louis XVI and his Queen Marie de Antoinette.

Tom realized that practically everything he did or thought had something related to land of the Parisians. He remembered the years he spent preparing to go to France as her ambassador. Of course, Tom knew if he hadn't been in France, he would have never fallen in love with Maria Cosway. What blissful days they experienced together, now only left for the memories.

How vividly he recalled the five years when he was introduced to all the French dignitaries. During that time, he spent many days with his mentor, Dr. Benjamin Franklin, whom he was going to replace as France's Minister. His mind was focused for a moment on how alert the old man was as he was approaching eighty upon returning to America.

The furniture in his house, much of his equipment, and all his architectural ideas came from his stay in France. Then his mind traveled back to his childhood over 50 years ago, when he learned French at Tuckahoe and even more under Rev. William Douglas and Rev. James Maury. If he hadn't been proficient in French, he would have been at a striking disadvantage when he served as Minister to France.

When he became Secretary of State, he was tenacious in his loyalty to the French government, leading him to be visibly upset with President Washington's philosophy of neutrality. Tom felt strongly that since France was responsible for America winning the war, she should be her close ally against England. When he became vice president, he adamantly opposed John Adams because he, as president, was pro-British, whereas Jefferson was pro-French. Now that Tom was president, he made sure France was once again America's close friend and ally.

Jefferson also reflected on how the French had dramatically changed his life, even in America. His butler, his baker and his chef were all from France. He depended on the French to manage his household and to be the first to greet his visitors. They were necessary to advise him of proper protocol and etiquette, as well as delight his guests with their scrumptious French meals and exquisite service. He had the French to thank for his macaroni maker and the import of ice cream to America.

Then his mind returned to the nation of France, where Napoleon Bonaparte was now in charge. As thankful as he was for the French Revolution, he was greatly disturbed at the misguided direction new leader was taking his nation. In a bold move called the "Coup d'Etat", Napoleon seized control of France on November 9, 1799. Washington had died, and Napoleon had become ruler of the Parisian nation, all within a month of each other. He quickly became the First Consul of France and led in the creation of a new constitution.

Tom could remember how he first respected the new French leader because he had brought a message of peace. Napoleon had a passionate admiration for the United States and stressed the need to restore friendship between the two nations. Later, however, the leopard changed his spots and became a despot set on trying to rule the world, thereby becoming a threat to America. By 1802 he had been elected First Consul for life, giving him full authority over France. Later, in 1804 he would proclaim himself to be "Emperor Napoleon I". Napoleon's armies extended French rule, institutions and influence throughout all of Europe, making him a formidable foe.

By the time 1803 arrived, Tom had been meeting with Secretary of State James Madison and Treasury Secretary Albert Gallatin about the desire he had to buy New Orleans and to authorize an expedition up the Missouri River to seek a route to the Pacific Coast. Once they all agreed on the proposal and the money that would be involved, Tom sent two requisitions to Congress in January, 1803. His first request was for permission to purchase New Orleans and west Florida from France for as much as ten million dollars. After he received approval for that purchase, he asked for another $2500.00 for his Corps of Discovery expedition. It was not a hard sell because it was a paltry portion compared to the ten million Congress had just approved for New Orleans. He presented his plea for funds by requesting 10 or 12 men with, "Their arms & accouterments, some instruments of observation, & light & cheap presents for the Indians would be all the apparatus they could carry, and with an expectation of a soldier's portion of land on their return would constitute the whole expense."[119]

In order to sell the idea to Congress, he couched each of these requests with commerce as the main issue. He made sure the senators and representatives knew how important it was to build a passageway for the fur trade from coast of coast. The United States must beat England in the race to control the valuable western trapping for animal furs. If Tom had given his primary motive for the requests – the desire to fulfill his father's dream, he knew Congress would balk. Fortunately for Tom, his additional request was granted as well. Next, Tom must arrange for the New Orleans offer to be negotiated with Napoleon.

Jefferson had been working on such an expedition to capture the West for the past twenty years. In 1783 it was with George Rogers Clark (brother of Captain William Clark). In 1787-88 he made the attempt with John Ledyard and in 1793 with Andre Michaux. All those efforts resulted in failure. Tom was bound and determined to give Meriwether Lewis the best opportunity to finally reach Tom's targeted goal – the Pacific Ocean.

While Thomas Jefferson was working on a deal to buy New Orleans, he was deeply involved with the Marbury v. Madison trial before the Supreme Court. Both he and James Madison were present on February 24, 1803, when Chief Justice John Marshall ruled on the case. Although Marshall reprimanded Jefferson and Madison for the part they played in the undelivered commissions, he ruled in their favor by denying William Marbury and the other judges their appointments by then President John Adams.

What made this one of the most significant cases for the Supreme Court was that it established the power of judicial review. As a result, from henceforth the highest court would be authorized to review all laws passed by Congress and the president.[120] If any were found in violation of the Constitution, they could be invalidated by the U.S. Supreme Court. This gave the court the power it needed to be equal to the other two branches of government.

Robert R. Livingston was Jefferson's Ambassador to France. He was an older man like Tom with a wealth of experience. The two men went back a long way, having begun their relationship when they were asked to serve together for composing the *Declaration of Independence*. For the next 25 years, Livingston was the Chancellor of New York the highest judge in the state. He held the honor of swearing in George Washington as the first President of the United States. Tom then selected him to be his Ambassador to France, the same position Jefferson held for five years from 1784 to 1789.

Jefferson notified Livingston about the decision of Congress to purchase New Orleans. Although he fully trusted him to persuade Napoleon to sell, he decided on a backup plan. He must have James Monroe, who was then the Governor of Virginia, in France when the deal was made. Tom wasn't leaving anything to chance.

James Monroe was one of Tom's favorite students. When Jefferson was Governor of Virginia during the war, Monroe was his right-hand man. During that time, he was being schooled by Tom on the elements of law and its corresponding philosophy. Most everything he knew about law, he had learned at the feet of Jefferson. In 1799, he moved into Tom's neighborhood at Ash Lawn in Albemarle County, near enough where Tom could keep in close touch with him.

Tom knew Monroe would be an asset in France because he had served there as Minister Plenipotentiary from 1794 to 1796. With that title, he had been given full authority to negotiate treaties and represent America on behalf of the president. He had established solid credentials with the authorities in France and was well respected there. In 1799, he was elected to a four-year term as Governor of Virginia. Tom knew whenever he needed help from his home state; he could depend on Monroe to come through. Monroe had the same assurances from Jefferson regarding the needs of Virginia.

Tom made certain that Governor James Monroe would be on the next ship leaving Virginia in the month of March, 1803. Monroe was sent as Minister Plenipotentiary with full authorization to seal the deal on behalf of the United States. Arriving in France on April 12, Monroe and Livingston got their heads together on the offer proposed by the president and Congress. To begin the negotiations, they would offer to buy New Orleans for two million dollars, being prepared with a counter offer of up to ten million for the combination of New Orleans and west Florida. If Napoleon wouldn't sell, then they would at least obtain permission for the United States to have free passage through New Orleans to their ports on the Mississippi.

What they didn't know was that two days before Monroe arrived from Virginia, Napoleon had told Decrès, his Minister of Marine, "I know the value of Louisiana. Nevertheless, I will cede it to the United States."[121] By that time he was concentrating all his efforts on European expansion and was desperate for money to fund it. He had tried in desperation to become a dominate force in North America by first conquering Hispaniola (the Caribbean island occupied by Haiti). His plan was to use that as his base of operations to help conquer the western hemisphere. However, due to a violent slave insurrection and a yellow fever plague, Napoleon found that mission was futile. The best thing he could do was to put his full concentration on the building of his kingdom in Europe. By that time, if America wanted Louisiana, he would sell it to her.

Known as the Louisiana Territory, in 1803 that land mass was larger than the entire United States. Named after King Louis XIV of France, it was discovered by French explorer La Salle and claimed for his mother country in 1682. Eighty years later, in 1762, France ceded all the Louisiana Territory west of the Mississippi, including New Orleans, to Spain. The following year all of the same territory east of the Mississippi River was ceded to England. When the Revolutionary War ended, the United States gained control of all British properties in America, including all lands east of the Mississippi. On October 1, 1800, after the battle of Marengo, Napoleon obtained its return to France by the Treaty of San Ildefonso.

When the emissaries of France and the United States gathered on April 30, 1803, James Monroe had only one proposal in mind. He offered two million dollars for the city of New Orleans. Napoleon's calm reply sent chills up Monroe and Livingston's spines. Plainly he said,

"I don't want to cede only New Orleans to you, but all of Louisiana, your price will be mine."[122]

The two American ambassadors turned to look at one another in utter amazement. Monroe asked to be excused so he and Livingston could discuss the unbelievable offer.

They came to the conclusion that since Congress authorized ten million for New Orleans and west Florida, it should be safe to think that fifteen million for all the Louisiana Territory (including New Orleans) should be approved by the president and Congress. After all, with that land mass of 827,000 square miles, that would double the size of the United States. (That was about four cents an acre).

What a deal! While they discussed a lower figure, they believed that if the offer was lower than Napoleon expected, then the deal might be dead on arrival. They had no way of contacting President Jefferson. But they must make the decision on his behalf. What would he do in that situation? Having been taught and trained by Jefferson, and having a close friendship with him, James Monroe decided he had Tom's best interest in mind.

While the Monroe/Livingston meeting was taking place, Napoleon had one of his own, in which he was quoted as saying to two of his ministers: "I renounce Louisiana. It is not only New Orleans that I will cede; it is the whole colony, without reservation. I renounce it with the greatest regret. To attempt obstinately to retain it would be folly. I direct you to negotiate that affair with the envoys of the United States."[123]

Later, when the two sides sat down together, Monroe made the offer of fifteen million and was pleasantly surprised when Napoleon said, rather bluntly: "Perfect! Let us close the deal." Napoleon added the following to the terms of the agreement: "Let them know that we separate ourselves from them with regret. Let them always remember that they have been French. May the common origin, language, and customs perpetuate friendship."[124] On May 2, 1803, the treaty was signed by both parties with a note of glorious victory for the United States.

When James Monroe returned to America, he couldn't wait to share with the president the amazing results of his congenial meeting with the Emperor of France. Jefferson had recently celebrated his sixtieth birthday on April 13, but the birthday present Monroe brought him was the best one of all. However, it was belated because he didn't receive the startling news until July 3, when Monroe returned to Washington. As the nation celebrated its 27th anniversary the following day, Thomas Jefferson, James Monroe, James Madison, Albert Gallatin and Meriwether Lewis had their own victory party in the White House.

As they dined together on the Fourth of July, in the midst of their festive celebration, they weighed some heavy obstacles standing in their way. First of all, there was a deadline attached to the purchase agreement. This must be ratified by Congress by October 30 or it was dead.

Secondly, when Spain heard about the Louisiana Purchase, she expressed strong opposition to the transaction. France and Spain had made a secret treaty where France pledged not to sell New Orleans to another country. Although Napoleon broke their agreement, he knew Spain didn't have the military power to nullify his deal with America.

Thirdly, Tom questioned the constitutionality of the transaction. He knew the Constitution did not grant the federal government the right to acquire more territory. That bothered Tom greatly. James Madison, who had penned the Constitution, sat in the room with him and discussed that at length with Jefferson. The two of them had formed the Democratic-Republican party to accentuate the absolute principles of the Constitution. They knew that the Federalists who opposed them would have a field day with this.

Tom's plan to justify the purchase as legal was to suggest a constitutional amendment. However, he realized that would take too much time. He heard that Napoleon was having second thoughts about his decision to sell Louisiana, and Tom knew that he must meet the October 30 deadline or lose the deal.

Although as Jefferson predicted, the Federalists in Congress fought tenaciously against the transaction with France, Tom's Republican majority came through with the Senate's ratification of the treaty on October 20, 1803. The next day a signed copy of the Louisiana Purchase agreement was on its way to Napoleon. Only then could Thomas Jefferson and his trusted cabinet breathe a sigh of relief. By November 3, both houses of Congress authorized Jefferson to take possession of the Louisiana Territory.

With that one real estate deal thirteen future states would come into existence. Montana, North Dakota, South Dakota, Minnesota, Wyoming, Nebraska, Iowa, Colorado, Kansas, Missouri, Oklahoma, Arkansas and Louisiana eventually will be carved out of the Louisiana Purchase.

During the first part of 1803, while Jefferson and his cabinet members were making decisions about the Louisiana Purchase, Meriwether Lewis was on special assignment. As soon as Congress approved Jefferson's request of $2,500 for his western expedition, Tom sent his personal secretary into intensive training school. Jefferson had a passionate thirst for the mysteries of life in the West. Not only did he want to find a navigable route to the Pacific, but he wanted Lewis to find every plant, animal and Indian along the way. Tom taught him how to make extensive notes on each of his findings and send some samples back home to the President's House. That even included Indian chiefs and savage children. Those would be object lessons to the Congress and to visitors at Washington about the progress made on the expedition. He should look for dinosaur bones, volcanoes and salt mountains.

From January through June, Meriwether Lewis was getting his hands-on training in various locales among many prominent learned men. Tom first sent him to Harper's Ferry, arriving there on March 15, where he obtained guns, ammunition and other equipment from the U.S. Army arsenal. That included an iron boat frame. From the skeleton of that vessel Lewis spent a month creating a new kind of keelboat that could be used in high altitudes.

During that time, he had artisans make knives, fishing tackle and pipe tomahawks. He also wrote letters to army commanders who had their posts along the Ohio River, asking them for their recommendation for some men who wanted to join Jefferson's Corps of Discovery.

Then Lewis was off to Philadelphia, where he received intensive instruction from Tom's friends in his American Philosophical Society, of which Jefferson was still her president. Lewis received tutoring from Dr. Benjamin Rush, a prominent physician. He learned all about the details of plants from botanist, Dr. Benjamin Smith Barton, and about the amazing discoveries of the universe from astronomer, Dr. Benjamin Smith Martin. Dr. Caspar Wistar taught Lewis as an anatomist. Most in this elite group of scholars had dined with Jefferson and Lewis at the White House. While in Philadelphia, he shopped for supplies and equipment for his journey. Those included uniforms for his men and whatever was needed for his doctoring of his men and others he encountered along the way.

Meriwether Lewis left Philadelphia on June 1 to return to his home base at the White House. Tom was anxious to see him again and to learn of all his experiences in his crash course with the astute men of academia. Lewis couldn't wait to show Tom the supplies and equipment he had purchased for the adventure.

When Lewis arrived, Tom was still awaiting word from James Monroe about the outcome of his meeting with Napoleon and hopefully, the purchase of New Orleans. While they awaited Monroe's return ship from France, the two men worked diligently to make final preparations. Tom didn't want to leave one stone unturned in his perfectionist tendencies. Nothing would be left to chance. He wanted to know everything Lewis had learned. Whatever was lacking in his training, Tom made sure he acquired it before he left.

Captain Lewis knew he needed a qualified man who could help lead the expedition. He could think of no one better qualified than his old army buddy, Captain William Clark. On June 19, he sat down to write him a rather lengthy letter requesting his desire for him to assist him with his proposed journey to the Pacific Coast. While detailing the specifics of the Corps of Discovery, he asked Clark to help recruit some men to accompany them. To do his best to convince Captain Clark to join him in this endeavor, he clearly identified his purpose, his plan and his plea for Clark to help lead this historic, most challenging endeavor. In his letter, he said among other things:

"From the long and uninterupted friendship and confidence which has subsisted between us I feel no hesitation in making to you the following communication.... My plan is to descend the Ohio in a keeled boat thence up the Mississippi to the mouth of the Missourie, sic) and up that river as far as is practicable with a keeled boat, there to prepare canoes of bark or raw-hides, and proceed to it's source, and if practicable pass over to the waters of the Columbia or Oregon River and by descending it reach the Western Ocean....

"If therefore there is anything under those circumstances, in that enterprise, which would induce you to participate with me in it's fatiegues, it's dangers and it's honors, believe me there is no man on earth with whom I should feel equal pleasure in sharing them as with yourself."[125]

While Lewis was writing his letter to Clark, Tom was penning one of his own. On the following day, June 20, 1803, he wrote a lengthy document that detailed what the Corps of Discovery was to entail. When Lewis met with Tom in his office, he received all he needed to know about the requirements and expectations for his journey. After Tom had made a copy for himself, he gave the manuscript to Lewis to review regularly.

Thomas Jefferson was anxious to hear from Monroe, and when his ship finally arrived, Tom rejoiced that he had a safe journey. He was even more excited when he heard about Napoleon's historic offer. Rather than just getting New Orleans, the United States had received all the Louisiana Territory. By this becoming U.S. territory, he knew it would make the expedition through that land mass much smoother. As Lewis went on his journey, he would now be exploring for the first time the other half of America.

After hearing the formal public announcement about the Louisiana Purchase on July 4, the 27th anniversary of the signing of the *Declaration of Independence*, Lewis said his goodbyes at the White House as he headed for the West. As soon as he saw Lewis ride off at the beginning of sunrise, Tom collapsed in his favorite whirligig chair, and Dick whistled him one of his favorite tunes. What was happening to Tom was that his dream was coming to pass, the same dream his father and four other men had since the time Tom was born. Now sixty years later, Tom believed it was finally happening. His lengthy letter regarding

Meriwether's job description while leading the expedition is quoted in part as follows:

> "To Meriwether Lewis esq. Capt. of the 1st regimt. of infantry of the U. S. of A.
>
> "Your situation as Secretary of the President of the U. S. has made you acquainted with the objects of my confidential message of Jan. 18, 1803 to the legislature; you have seen the act they passed, which, tho' expressed in general terms, was meant to sanction those objects, and you are appointed to carry them into execution.
>
> "Instruments for ascertaining, by celestial observations, the geography of the country through which you will pass, have been already provided. Light articles for barter and presents among the Indians, arms for your attendants, say for from 10. to 12. men, boats, tents, & other travelling apparatus, with ammunition, medicine, surgical instruments and provisions you will have prepared with such aids as the Secretary at War can yield in his department; & from him also you will recieve authority to engage among our troops, by voluntary agreement, the number of attendants above mentioned, over whom you, as their commanding officer, are invested with all the powers the laws give in such a case.
>
> "As your movements while within the limits of the U.S. will be better directed by occasional communications, adapted to circumstances as they arise, they will not be noticed here. What follows will respect your proceedings after your departure from the United states.
>
> "Your mission has been communicated to the ministers here from France, Spain & Great Britain, and through them to their governments; & such assurances given them as to its objects, as we trust will satisfy them. The country [of Louisiana] having been ceded by Spain to France, the passport you have from the minister of France, the representative of the present sovereign of the country, will be a protection with all its subjects; & that from the minister of England will entitle you to the friendly aid of any traders of that allegiance with whom you may happen to meet.

"The object of your mission is to explore the Missouri river, & such principal stream of it, as, by it's course & communication with the waters of the Pacific Ocean, whether the Columbia, Oregan, Colorado or and other river may offer the most direct & practicable water communication across that continent, for the purposes of commerce..." "Given under my hand at the city of Washington that 20th day of June 1803.

Th. Jefferson Pr. U.S. of America"[126]

Beginning of the Expedition

"The object of your mission is to explore the Missouri river, and such principal stream of it, as, by its course and communication with the waters of the Pacific Ocean."
Thomas Jefferson

1803

Meriwether Lewis was in a race against time. He had planned to leave Washington much sooner, but he had been delayed. His goal was to get as far as he could before winter enveloped him with its bitter northern snows and frozen tundra. He also knew he had to make it down the Ohio River before the water level began falling as the summer wore down.

As he pushed his horse steadily from Washington to Harper's Ferry, he had anxious thoughts about his plans. All the "what ifs" were troubling him. What if the wagon load of supplies he ordered from Philadelphia did not arrive in Pittsburgh, his place of departure on the Ohio River heading west? What if the arsenal in Harper's Ferry forgot to send the fifteen rifles he needed? What if the 55-foot keelboat he ordered to be built was not finished? What if his letter to William Clark didn't make it to its destination? And if it did, what if he rejected Meriwether's plea to join him? Pressure was intense, but he was determined that nothing would defeat him.

By the end of the day, he had reached Frederick, Maryland. He heard good news and then bad. The supply wagon had passed through town ten days ago on its way to Pittsburgh. That was good! But when he was told the driver left the rifles and other weapons at Harper's Ferry because it was too heavy for his wagon - that was bad. Lewis was forced to hire another teamster from Frederick to make sure all the arms made it to Pittsburgh. However, he also failed to come through. Finally, the third wagon driver completed what seemed to be an impossible task, bringing the supplies to the banks of the Ohio.

Lewis arrived in Pittsburgh on July 15, and his boat was to be completed within five more days. The builder was just getting started and told Lewis he could not have it finished until July 30. He was glad to see his arms arrive from Harper's Ferry on July 22. However, since that was one week after he arrived in Pittsburgh, he worried himself sick about that until he saw them delivered. The wagon also brought with it seven recruits needed to make it down the Ohio River. More good news was that he received a letter from William Clark on July 29, telling him he would be honored to co-lead the expedition. He concluded his welcome letter with these refreshing words:

> "This is an undertaking fraited with many difeculties, but My friend I do assure you that no man lives with whome I wold perfur to undertake Such a Trip &c. As yourself, My friend, I join you with hand & Heart."[127]

Lewis rejoiced to know Clark had accepted his offer so willingly. However, coupled with all the good news, there was bad that seemed to outweigh the good. His boat was not completed by the 30th, and he didn't know if the task would ever be done. The builder happened to be a drunk and only worked when he was somewhat sober. With alcohol being his priority, he didn't care much when the boat would be finished. While Lewis charged him with "unpardonable negligence", he constantly nagged him to get the job done. He was the only boat builder within a hundred miles, and he was all that Lewis had. However, the leader of the Corps fumed and raged because he wrote to Jefferson that "the river is lower than it has ever been known by the oldest settler in that country."[128]

Lewis kept wondering if he would ever make it to the Pacific. He was finding it impossible just to leave Pittsburgh, now being two months behind schedule. During his long wait, he had someone come to his rescue. He had been dreading celebrating his 29th birthday on August 18 all alone. On that special day, a traveler came by with a black dog of the Newfoundland breed. Meriwether played with the animal a bit and fell in love with him. He gave the man $20 for the friendly pet, feeling he needed him when he was out in the wild wooly west. Naming his big web-footed friend "Seaman", he felt he was finally getting even with the president. Tom wouldn't let him have all his hunting dogs, or even one of them, at the White House. Without Tom saying so, Lewis felt it was because he would be in competition with his precious mockingbird, Dick. Now, however, Lewis would finally have a furry friend he could have by his side day and night. Wouldn't Tom like to see him now? One thing about it – Lewis refused to say anything about the dog whenever he wrote to Jefferson.

Finally, his 55-foot keelboat was finished. It was a sturdy structure, large enough to carry 2 captains and as many as 20 oarsmen to maneuver it. With a proud sail waving in the air, it could be sailed, rowed, pulled or towed, either way. Lewis was thrilled to see the finished product.

However, now it was the end of August, and the water was so low in the Ohio that Lewis needed to get an additional smaller boat called a "pirogue". The flat bottom design of that vessel would help it to maneuver easily over the rocks, and with paddles and a sail, Lewis felt like it was ideal to navigate. Having the additional vessel shifted part of the heavy load off the keelboat to help keep it from dragging the bottom of the river. In a letter to the president on September 8, 1803, from Wheeling, Virginia, Lewis wrote to justify his acquisition,

> "I have been compelled to purchase a pirogue at that place in order to transport the baggage which was sent by land from Pittsburgh, and also to lighten the boat as much as possible. On many bars the water in the deepest part does not exceed six inches. I have the honour to be with the most perfect regard and sincere attachment."
>
> You're Obt. Servt.
> MERIWETHER LEWIS. Capt.
> 1st U.S. Regt. Infty.[129]

Lewis had requested William Clark to recruit some crew members for their expedition team. His requirements were they must be young, unmarried, rugged woodsmen with certain skills that would facilitate their journey. He couldn't wait to see whom he had chosen. He wouldn't know until he met up with him at Clarksville, Indiana, after Cincinnati. Being the co-leader of the journey, Lewis knew they would both need to approve each of the men. Although he realized he couldn't appoint crew members himself, he needed to have at least some volunteers to get the two boats down the challenging shallow Ohio River.

One of these was an 18-year-old Irishman named George Shannon. Lewis thought he was too young and tried to discourage him from coming. But the teenage boy was tenacious. He had been watching the trying problems Lewis had with the boat building, along with how upset this was making the captain. Shannon had shared Seaman's attempt to keep Lewis encouraged. At the same time, the young man kept badgering Lewis to let him go on the trip. What he wanted was to become a permanent member of the crew, but he would settle for the first leg of the trip to meet William Clark. Lewis finally decided to give him a try.

Finally, Captain Lewis, had persuaded eleven men to join him. They, along with Seaman, the dog, launched the boats for their Corps of Discovery mission to capture the West, going all the way to the Pacific Ocean. Although Lewis was excited to leave Pittsburgh, his anxiety was heightened when he and his men fought the obstacles of the lowering water and challenging rocks and shoals in the troubling river.

Soon Seaman was standing on the front edge of the boat barking in excitement, his tail wagging wildly in the wind. Lewis turned to see what all the commotion was about. Then he looked ahead of them in the water and saw tree squirrels swimming from one side of the river to the other. He could tell Seaman wanted to chase them. However, the trained dog waited for Lewis to give the command before he dove off the boat. As soon as he said, "Go git 'em, Seaman," the big black canine was off the keelboat and into the water, and before Lewis knew what was happening, he saw his faithful hunting dog standing before him with a dead squirrel in his jaws. Lewis reached down to pat him on the head and give him a scratch between his ears. When he did so, he saw the limp squirrel released in his other hand. "Good boy. You're such a good doggie," Lewis praised him repeatedly, and then gave him some jerky for a reward. From that moment on, whenever Seaman wanted to go squirrel hunting in the water, he got the go-ahead from Lewis. The Newfoundland dog with web feet provided the squirrel dinner for the crew on many nights during the journey.

Lewis and his men on September 28 embarked for some rest and relaxation in Cincinnati. Here Meriwether ran into a physician who was excavating fossils in Kentucky. He claimed he found the bones of the extinct mastodon at the Big Bone Lick. Lewis was excited to find what that animal was all about. His training from the American Philosophical Society told him about that creature who roamed the earth millions of years ago, quite similar to the wooly mammoth further north. However, he had never seen any fossils to prove it.

Although Lewis was way behind schedule and knew Clark was waiting for him, he couldn't resist traveling with Dr. William Goforth to examine his findings. He knew Jefferson would be even more excited to hear about his discovery, as he knew he had never seen anything like that before. Knowing the president's wishes for all things new to be communicated to him, Lewis boxed up some of the specimens and sent them to the White House.

On their way from Cincinnati to Clarksville, Indiana, they stopped at the village of Limestone (now Maysville), Kentucky. They met a fellow there named John Colter, who, having heard about the expedition asked if he could join. When Lewis inquired about his background, he said he was born near Staunton, Virginia in the Appalachian Mountains, not far from Meriwether's home at Locust Hill. He and Lewis also shared that they were both outdoorsmen and avid hunters. Lewis knew that was the kind of man he needed and invited him to come aboard.

While still in Limestone four days later, the persistent teenage boy, George Shannon, was relentless about going all the way to the Pacific with Lewis. Once he found that Colter had been approved, he pleaded to be included among the chosen. He assured Lewis that like Colter, he was also a Kentuckian, having moved from his native Pennsylvania to the blue grass state in 1800. Lewis gave him temporary approval, letting him know it would be up to Will Clark to make the final decision.

After getting back on course, they traveled further down the Ohio River. Lewis, his dog "Seaman" and his twelve men then docked at Clarksville, Indiana, on October 14, where they would join their co-leader, Captain William Clark. As soon as Clark saw that rag-tag team of sailors coming, he rushed to greet Lewis and his crew. Before he could get to Lewis, Seaman intercepted him by running to greet Clark so passionately that he almost knocked him off his feet.

"Well, now look what we have here." Clark said to Lewis as he was reaching down to stroke the big black dog.

"What have you done? Gone and got yourself a dog, did ya?"

"You know me, Will." Lewis tried to calm down Seaman and separate him from the two men. "I can't live outdoors without having me a dog."

"Didn't you tell me that Mister President didn't want you to have a dog?"

"That's right. But what he don't know won't hurt him. Besides, I'm not in the White House anymore. I've been set free!"

"Knowing you like I do, Merry, I can understand. You weren't much of one for settling down. You've moved from Virginia to Georgia and back to Virginia. Then you joined the army and travelled everywhere. Having a desk job in some stuffy ol' mansion is not your cup o' tea."

Lewis then introduced Clark to all the crew, who thanked them for getting the boats on the first leg of their journey. Next, Lewis took him aboard the keelboat and introduced him to the craft especially built for their journey.

"Merry, why don't you and your crew come to my cabin, and we'll cook you up some possum stew."

"Will, I haven't had that specialty for many moons. Oh, how I miss Ma's possum stew!"

"Don't you get any of that at the White House?"

"Shucks no! I've been trying to live on French food for the past two years, and I don't think I'll ever get used to it." The men put their arms around each other and laughed as they walked up the pathway together.

When Clark got to his cabin, his servant, York, came to the door to greet them.

"Merry, I want you to meet York."

"Pleased to meet you," Lewis said, as he paused for a moment of reflection. He looked into the dark brown eyes of the tall young black man, quite muscular, standing before him. "Will, is that the servant you told me about when we served together years ago?"

"He's the one. He's been with me all my life, having been given to me as a servant when he was only eleven." As Clark was talking, Lewis sized up the two men together. Both stood around six foot, appearing to be the same height as he. He could also tell that York was well built, showing he was used to hard work.

"Merry, I hope you'll let me take York with me. He's been with me so long; I don't think I could make it without him."

"If he'll help you, then he'll be an asset to me. There's room on the boat for him. Bring him on."

When they went in the cabin, they smelled the possum stew already prepared and waiting for them to wash up and sit around the table where they ate, drank and were merry for the rest of the evening. They were told the story about how Will had acquired the roomy, well equipped cabin. He said his older brother, General George Rogers Clark, built that structure after founding the town of Louisville,

Kentucky, across the river. Will proudly shared many of the amazing stories about his famed brother and how he fought off both the British and the Indians to tame the wild Kentucky wilderness. He shared about his sister, Lucy, who lived with her husband, William Croghan on the 694-acre plantation, Locust Grove, near Louisville.

The next morning, they were awakened from their sleep by Seaman, as he was hysterically barking outside their window. Slipping on their shirts and breeches, they went to the door to find the men whom Clark had carefully chosen as the crew for the expedition.

Lewis saw seven men standing before him. Clark introduced them to his partner and invited them to join them for a hearty breakfast. York had been up hours before preparing the fire in the hearth and getting the meal together. York and Seaman had become great friends already, as the dog got fed before the men ever awoke. Seaman was a natural at retrieving things, and York was amazed at how the mutt would bring him items he thought he would need to get the house ready for company.

* Lewis and Clark, as co-leaders of the Corps, both had to agree on any recruits as crewmen. Clark had his seven for Lewis to approve, and Lewis had two. All men were from Kentucky and would be known through the trip as "the nine young men from Kentucky."[130] As the men were selected for the crew, Lewis wished he could see how each of these men would help or hurt their cause. Would they be loyal to both men? Would they be honest and trustworthy? Would they be skilled enough to make the trip successful? Would they be hard working and healthy?

Lewis knew he had President Jefferson to satisfy. He could not underestimate the importance of placing his mark of approval on each of Clark's men. As he considered each one, all young woodsmen from Kentucky, he wholeheartedly gave his consent. Clark had already approved Lewis' two recruits, John Colter and George Shannon. Once all the choices were made, Captain Clark swore all the men into the U.S. Army in a formal induction ceremony.

1. JOHN COLTER. A muscular blue-eyed Virginian came as an experienced frontiersman. What Lewis knew about Colter was he had remarkable hunting skills, making him a viable asset. What he didn't know was that Colter would eventually do something that would warrant a court martial.
2. GEORGE SHANNON. A young blue-eyed Pennsylvania native. He was both handsome and intelligent. What he knew was that

he was a persistent, courageous Irish teen, who appeared to be intensely loyal and dedicated to the task. If Lewis had only known how foolish Shannon would be at times, having the habit of getting lost when sent scouting new areas, he might have sent him back to Pittsburgh, where he found him.

3. SGT. CHARLES FLOYD. He was the first of Clark's recruits and would be the commanding officer under William and Clark. Lewis knew the success or failure of the trip would fall on the shoulders of that one man. Clark boasted his resume when he told Lewis at age 18, Floyd had been appointed the constable of Clarksville Township, where they were now sitting. He was also the son of Charles Floyd, who had soldiered with Clark's brother, George Rogers Clark and Daniel Boone. When he enlisted in the U.S. Army two months ago on August 1, he was assigned immediately as a commissioned officer. Clark pointed out that Floyd was an expert at sampling soils, which would be a valuable asset. Lewis knew the president wanted the details of the soils and terrain accurately documented throughout the journey. Since Clark spoke so highly of Sergeant Floyd, Lewis knew he must be the man to lead the other men, and he gave his wholehearted stamp of approval.

4. NATHANIEL PRYOR. Next to consider for approval would be that cousin of Sergeant Floyd. Being born in Amherst County, Virginia, just 40 miles from Lewis' home, made him almost a sure shot for acceptance. However, he was married, which went against Lewis' rules. For him alone Lewis made an exception. Since joining the army on October 20, Clark could speak of his impeccable character. He was also impressed with how well he accomplished whatever he set his hands to do. Lewis gave his approval, assigning him to be in charge of the men when they were on the keel boat.

5. WILLIAM BRATTON. He also enlisted in the army on October 20. During his short stint under Capt. William Clark, he had proven himself to be an excellent hunter and woodsman. What he brought to the team was his craft as a blacksmith and gunsmith, which would prove to be invaluable for the expedition. Approved by Lewis.

6. GEORGE GIBSON. Lewis was already impressed with this new army enlistment of October 26. The first night they were in Clarksville, Gibson retrieved his fiddle and brought the room to life playing his reels and merry songs. That got all

the men trying their best to carry a tune in their inebriated condition. Lewis knew if that was Gibson's only asset, it was a plus. However, Clark sold Lewis as being an experienced woodsman and skilled hunter. And he also knew sign language, most helpful in dealing with the Indians. Lewis thought he was a good choice.
7. JOHN SHIELDS. Clark claimed he was one of the best gunsmiths and blacksmiths in the country. Keeping all their guns in working order would be of utmost importance. Although Lewis knew of his skills, he only wished he knew about his character flaws that would later lead to a court martial.
8. JOSEPH FIELD. He was one of two brothers who stood before Lewis for approval. Being from Lewis' neighboring Culpeper County, Virginia, helped his credentials. He had already heard of the Field brothers' reputation for being skilled hunters and woodsmen. Clark assured them they both appeared loyal and faithful in all their assignments.
9. REUBIN FIELD – Lewis approved of both he and his brother. He was impressed with how well they got along with each other. He saw no sibling rivalry or jealously between them. He was especially impressed that Reubin had the credentials of being an excellent marksman and was quick on his feet. Those would all be needed for a successful expedition.

The Lewis and Clark expedition began when they shook hands on that site. Both of them were broad shouldered, six feet tall and rugged woodsmen. What distinguished them was Clark's red hair contrasted with Lewis' light brown hair.

Later, a statue of that historic handshake would be installed at the Falls of the Ohio State Park, marking the spot where it supposedly took place. On October 26, 1803, both the keelboat and the pirogue set sail, headed for the Mississippi River. All the men who left Pittsburgh with Lewis, except for young George Shannon, were left behind to find their way home.

Aboard the boats were Lewis and Clark, "the nine young men from Kentucky," York, Clark's black servant, and Seaman, the black Newfoundland dog.

The twelve men labored rigorously as they rowed and maneuvered the two boats going west on the Ohio. With the water level being unusually low, they were challenged to keep the vessels off the rocks and into the primary current of the river. Their next point of interest was where the Cumberland River connected to the Kentucky side of the Ohio, and then later where the Tennessee River made an identical confluence.

Their next stop was made on November 11 at Fort Massac, a U.S. Army base on the Ohio. Two men had been selected from Daniel Bissell's 1st Infantry Regiment to join the Lewis and Clark expedition. They were Pvt. John Newman and Pvt. Joseph Whitehouse. Newman would become Lewis' worst nightmare; Whitehouse would prove to be dependable, although quite passive. They were the first active-duty military to be recruited. Lewis also was introduced to George Drouillard, who would serve as their interpreter with the Indians and would become one of the most reliable assets to both Lewis and Clark.

10. JOHN NEWMAN. Hindsight's better than foresight in this case. The problems and headaches this army private would create caused Lewis to repeatedly regret he ever chose him. Newman was a scheming conniver who would do anything to destroy loyalty and comradery among the team members. Eventually, he would have the most serious charge of mutiny leveled against him in a court martial. As a result, he received 75 lashes and was discharged from the permanent party on Oct. 13, 1804.
11. JOSEPH WHITEHOUSE. He was also an army private, but he was just the opposite of Newman. He would prove to be loyal and a hard-working corpsman. His talent for making and repairing buckskin clothing was a viable asset. His willingness and faithfulness to carry out the most meaningless task proved to be invaluable to the success of the journey.
12. GEORGE DROUILLARD. A welcome addition to the Corps of Discovery as their interpreter. Lewis had trouble spelling his name. So in his journals he usually referred to him as "Drewyer". Being half French and half Indian from the Shawnee tribe, he possessed skills the rest didn't have. That went beyond his ability to speak the language of the Indians, even using sign language. That black-haired, brown-eyed giant of a man proved to be the best hunter of the team, being a woodsman from the most remote regions above Detroit. He was second only to Reubin Field as a speedy runner.

Captain Lewis had expected eight army recruits from South West Point fort in Tennessee to meet him there. Since they were nowhere to be found, he sent Drouillard to the Volunteer State to retrieve them. Three days later they launched their boats back into the descending current of the Ohio going west. Seaman seemed to love the idea of more recruits added at each stop. All the men made him their pet and mascot. Seaman relished every moment of it, showing his appreciation by bringing them many of their meals.

Meriwether Lewis was jubilant when he finally spied the glorious Mississippi River ahead. He had so worried himself that they wouldn't make it down the much-too-shallow Ohio without either wrecking their boats or becoming unable to move them through the rocky shoals. On November 14, they landed at the northeast juncture of the two rivers. Although there was not a fort or a sign of humanity at the place later to be named Cairo, Illinois, the two captains couldn't proceed up the Mississippi River until they completed their first geological survey of the expedition.

Lewis knew that the president would have a vital interest in the results of such a study. That survey would be an important part of their expedition. As he used his sextant and other surveying tools, Lewis remembered so well all that Thomas Jefferson taught him. Those skills had been passed down from Jefferson's father, Peter, who worked with Col. Joshua Fry to make the famous Fry-Jefferson map of 1755. Lewis had no doubt he had received training from the finest and most able of men. William Clark was equally qualified for that assignment. He added to his surveying qualifications that of cartography. As a result, he worked tirelessly making a detailed map of that significant intersection of the Ohio and Mississippi Rivers.

Lewis and Clark and their half-Shawnee interpreter, George, traveled inland across the Missouri River to begin their peaceful negotiations with the Indians in that area. Seaman, who never left his master's side, had jumped in the boat with them. They had successful meetings with both the Delaware and Shawnee Indian chiefs, spelling out to them why they were making their expedition through their lands. Lewis brought some of his gifts to present them from President Jefferson. He told them their land had now been purchased by the United States, and Jefferson was now their great father. One of the Shawnees took a liking to Seaman and offered to buy him from Lewis with three beaver skins. As much as Lewis wanted to make friends with the Indians, there was no way he would part with his pet dog. Of course, Seaman was greatly encouraged his master thought that much of him. Lewis and Clark ended their ceremony with the Indians around a campfire smoking the peace pipe together.

Returning to their boats and ending their survey, they left Cairo on November 20, traveling then upstream on the might, where they faced the new challenge of struggling against the current. As they fought against the raging waters coming toward them, they realized how they were undermanned. Eight days later on the 28th, they arrived at Fort Kaskaskia, Illinois, the U.S. Army post located the furthest west from Washington. That would be the last contact Lewis and Clark would have with military bases.

While at Fort Kaskaskia, they were introduced to some more army personnel, who were commissioned to join Jefferson's Corps of Discovery. Those were Sgt. John Ordway and privates Peter Weiser, Richard Windsor, Patrick Gass, John Boley, and John Collins. These all came from Russell Bissell's Company of the 1st U.S. Infantry Regiment. That would bring their team to 20 men plus York, Clark's servant, and Seaman. In addition, John Dame, John Robertson, Ebenezer Tuttle, Isaac White, and Alexander Willard of Capt. Amos Stoddard's company, U.S. Corps of Artillery, also enlisted for the journey. (All but Willard were assigned for their return trip and thus were not included as permanent members of the expedition). Willard brought the total number to 21. Others were selected, but they were assigned to the return trip from the Mandan villages (in present-day North Dakota) the next winter, from where he would send the keelboat back with them to St. Louis.

13. SGT. JOHN ORDWAY. That native of New Hampshire was well-educated, giving him an advantage over most of the others. He was also an expert on Indians. He would be responsible for analyzing Native American life and culture and making a detailed account of his findings. He would be most reliable as second in command under Sgt. Charles Floyd, always available and able to lead the group whenever he was needed. He was given the responsibility of keeping daily records of the journey, delegating guard duties, and issuing the daily provisions for the men

14. PETER WEISER, Pvt. A native of Pennsylvania, he was invaluable to the group as a hunter and fur trapper, fulfilling his assignments without any reason for him to be reprimanded in any of the journals written during the expedition.

15. RICHARD WINDSOR, Pvt. He was an experienced and most able hunter, who once had to depend on Capt. Lewis to save his life from a fatal fall.
16. PATRICK GASS, Pvt. He was another native Pennsylvanian, who was Scotch Irish. With his barrel chest and ruddy face peeking through his scraggly beard, he was such an excellent woodworker he was nicknamed, "Beaver." That experience Indian fighter would serve as the Corps' main carpenter. Lewis saw in him such leadership qualities that he would later promote him to the rank of sergeant.
17. JOHN BOLEY, Pvt. He proved to be an asset to the team. He was disciplined once with three other men for bad behavior, being restricted to camp for ten days. Therefore, he was removed from the permanent party and assigned to the return team.
18. JOHN COLLINS, Pvt. When that Canadian joined the Corps, he would become one of the greatest problems for Lewis and Clark. If Lewis could have looked into the future, he would have been able to see a rebelliously uncontrolled demon of a man, who would be court martialed on two separate occasions, with a total of five charges in which he was found guilty. He would prove to be one of the bad apples in the barrel.
19. ALEXANDER WILLARD, Pvt. He showed himself to be the strongest of the men, except for Clark's servant, York. Although he would be useful as a blacksmith, he would later be court martialed for sleeping on duty. That was such a serious violation; he could have suffered punishment by death. Instead, he received a total of four hundred lashes.

With the extra men coming aboard, Lewis saw the necessity of adding another boat he called the "White Pirogue" to his fleet, making a total of three vessels. Captain Clark left Kaskaskia with the crew and the boats on December 3, heading north on the Mississippi toward St. Louis. Winter was quickly approaching, and they knew they must reach their winter camp soon. Lewis stayed behind with Seaman. Taking care of some unfinished business, he then took the land route, where he reunited with Clark and the men in Cahokia, Illinois, on December 7.

On December 12, 1803, Captain William Clark led his expedition team to what would become their winter headquarters on the Wood River, just northeast of St. Louis. Clark knew they must camp on the east side of the Mississippi River until the Louisiana Territory on the west side was officially transferred to the United States. Meanwhile, Meriwether Lewis was spending his time meeting with foreign dignitaries to try to iron out grievances and to state the purpose of their mission. The Spanish still had rights to the Louisiana Territory they hadn't yet relinquished. Jefferson warned Lewis to try to appease them as much as possible, not inciting any hostility or violence while on the expedition. He also spent time in St. Louis gathering additional supplies for their winter campground.

On December 22, 1803, George Drouillard obediently returned from Tennessee with the eight army recruits Lewis sought to enlist for the expedition. They were from Captain John Campbell's company of the 2nd U.S. Infantry Regiment, stationed at South West Point near present-day Kingston, Tennessee. Captain William Clark looked them over and promptly dismissed half of them as being not worth their salt. The other four whom he approved were Corporal Richard Warfington, and Privates Hugh Hall, Thomas Howard and John Potts.

20. CPL. RICHARD WARFINGTON. That North Carolina native had gained the rank of corporal before he was recruited by Lewis. He had proven leadership skills at South West Point. When Captain Clark accepted his assignment into the Corps of Discovery, he chose him to be the leader of the return team. That put him in charge of the white pirogue (dugout canoe) with the six French fur traders and guides assigned to his crew. They would travel from their Camp Dubois up the Missouri River to the Mandan villages (in present day North Dakota). With that being his destination, he would not be a part of the permanent party. He would then lead his French Canadians back to St. Louis, never being able to see the fulfillment of the expedition.

21. HUGH HALL, Pvt. After he was chosen among the recruits from Tennessee, Captain Clark came to realize he was a bad apple in the barrel. Before they even left Camp Dubois heading up the Missouri, on May 17, 1804, Hall was court martialed for AWOL, to be given twenty lashes on his bare back. On the next month, June 29, he received his second court martial, that time for stealing whiskey from the keg while it was being guarded. His punishment was increased that time to fifty lashes on the bare back.

22. THOMAS P. HOWARD, Pvt. Born in Brimfield, Massachusetts, he was entrusted to be one of Capt. Clark's couriers, who delivered his mail and other messages. Howard appeared to be a faithful soldier with the exception of his court martial on Feb. 10, 1805. He deeply disappointed Lewis, who recorded the details of his crime.

> *"that evening a man by the name of Howard whom I had given permission to go the Mandane village returned after the gate was shut and rather than call to the guard to have it opened scaled the works an Indian who was looking on shortly after followed his example. I . . . convinced the Indian of the impropriety of his conduct, and explained to him the risk he had run of being severely treated, the fellow appeared much alarmed, I gave him a small piece of tobacco and sent him away Howard I had committed to the care of the guard with a determination to have him tried by a Court-martial for that offence."*[131]

23. JOHN POTTS, Pvt. The only German immigrant of the crew proved to be a worthy soldier. A miller by trade, he was faithful to his task and was awarded more pay at the end of the expedition than the other enlisted men. Afterwards, he returned to the Missouri River country as a fur trader and was killed by the Blackfeet Indians.

The men worked diligently to prepare their winter camp and build shacks for sleeping, having them ready by Christmas Eve. Captain Lewis came in plenty of time with the supplies they needed to carry them through the winter. Christmas was an eventful day for the weary men of the Corps of Discovery. Captain Clark wrote about it in his journal:

> *"Christmas 25th Decr: . . . found that Some of the party had got Drunk (2 fought) the men frolicked and hunted all day, Snow that morning, Ice run all day, Several Turkey Killed . . . Three Indians Come to day to take Christmas with us . . ."*[132]

By the time the year of 1803 came to an end, Lewis and Clark sat around a campfire reflecting on all their most meaningful moments of their expedition. Seaman was lying by the fire, all snuggled up next to Lewis, being stroked lovingly and wagging his tail in the process.

The next five months would find the Lewis and Clark regiment firmly established at what they called "Camp River Dubois." It was there that Clark drilled the men to prepare them for their historic expedition. Choosing and preparing the right men to form the Corps of Discovery took an entire winter. Sometime during those months, the permanent party to make the Lewis and Clark Expedition had increased by the following:

24. GEORGE FRAZER, Pvt. His main contribution to the Corps was as a writer. He was the only one who Lewis and Clark gave permission to write a journal about the expedition. He was first chosen for the return team, but was later transferred to the permanent party.
25. SILAS GOODRICH, Pvt. – When he found out about the expedition and Captain Clark being in charge, he was quick to volunteer. He and Clark had served together in the army in Ohio. He would be a welcome addition with his knowledge of map making. He proved himself to be the best fisherman of the team, pulling in huge catfish that weighed over one hundred pounds.
26. JOHN B. THOMPSON, Pvt. – That native of Northampton, Massachusetts was another transfer from Capt. Amos Stoddard's regiment at Fort Kaskaskia. Although he was a four-year veteran with the army and good with a gun, he added his value to the party by serving as a cook.
27. MOSES REED., Pvt. – That soldier was bad news from the start. On August 8, 1804, he deserted the expedition and headed back to St. Louis, from whence he came. Captain Clark sent four privates to retrieve him, and if he didn't surrender peacefully to *"put him to death." When they found him, they returned him to the camp, where his punishment was to "Run the gantlet four times through (sic) the Party & that each man with 9 switches (sic) should punish him and for him not to be considered in future as one of the Party."*[133] He was then sent back to St. Louis.

28. HUGH MCNEAL, Pvt. – That native of Pennsylvania proved to be a dedicated member of the permanent party, found throughout the Lewis and Clark record books.

On May 16, William Clark enlisted two French Canadians as permanent members. In October, he added another one of their ilk to the team.

29. PIERRE CRUZATTE, Pvt. – He would prove to be a valuable addition to the team. He was half-French Canadian and half Omaha Indian. Thus, he spoke both languages, as well as English, making him an asset as an interpreter. He was also a skilled river pilot, with the innate ability to read rivers and know the best current to steer the boat. Where he really made the difference with the men was when he entertained them with his talented fiddle, causing them to dance and forget all about their troublesome problems. That became almost a nightly routine for him. Clark found him at St. Charles, Missouri two days after they left their base camp on the Mississippi.
30. FRANCOIS LABICHE, Pvt. – He also enlisted with Clark at St. Charles as the other French Canadian on the permanent team. He became the second boatman behind Cruzatte and also served as second behind Drouillard as a tracker. He was second interpreter behind Drouillard because he knew English, French and several Indian dialects. His greatest value came in his ability to converse with the Shoshones in the following year.
31. JEAN BAPTISTE LEPAGE, Pvt. When the Corps of Discovery reached the Hidatsa and Mandan Indians in October, 1804, another French Canadian chose to join the expedition. He was needed to replace Pvt. John Newman, who had been discharged from the permanent team and sent back to St. Louis. LePage was a fur trader who was living among the local Indian tribes.

The Corps of Discovery membership was now complete, which included York and those to be added in 1805. (Due to their rebellion, both John Newman and Moses Reed were sent back to St. Louis with the return party).

Seaman had already become a viable asset to the Lewis and Clark Expedition. On July 4, William Clark listed Seaman in his journal as one of the explorers. The next day, Lewis' big black pet helped save some injuries by driving an aggressive beaver out of the men's lodging. On July 14, Sgt. Ordway was amazed at Seaman's passionate pursuit of an elk swimming down the river.

Seaman quickly became recognized as the sensitive ears and nose of the party. The night watchmen learned to count on Seaman to keep them alert of danger and help keep them awake. If they appeared to be sleeping, one lick of the dog's long slimy tongue was all it took to bring them to attention. The men knew that Seaman could hear and distinguish sounds more acutely than all them put together. They learned what each of his sounds meant, and at times his shrilling barks would warm them of rattlesnakes or grizzly bears.

While Seaman functioned well in and around water, he was not as adept when he wandered away from it. On August 25, Lewis and Clark took Seaman for a hike to visit a sacred spot of the Indians called the "Mountain of Spirits." The day was hot and sultry, and Lewis' dog was becoming overheated. His heavy black winter coat was not suitable for that kind of exercise. After two miles into the hike, Lewis dismissed Seaman, sending him back to the creek. As soon as the overwrought dog spied the running water, he took a leap and splashed into the creek. With the cold current rushing all around, his tongue quickly lapped up the water like there would be no tomorrows.

Back at the White House

"Peace and friendship with all mankind is our wisest policy, and I wish we may be permitted to pursue it."
Thomas Jefferson

1804

The President's House wasn't the same without Meriwether Lewis. Thomas Jefferson and he had a father-son type of relationship for over two years. And Tom really missed him. He longed to be doing what his personal secretary was doing in St. Louis. He wished he could have been on that challenging journey down the Ohio River, especially where it flowed into the Mississippi. When he opened the crate full of bones from the mastodon at Big Bone Lick, he was envious of Lewis, wishing he would have been there with him.

Tom anxiously awaited hearing from Lewis, and as far as he was concerned, his letters were too far in between. Whenever the post man would arrive at the White House door, Tom was there to joyfully greet him, usually in his rag-tag clothes and house slippers. When correspondence arrived from Lewis, that was the first on the list for Tom to open.

As the new year of 1804 began, Tom felt depressed because of the loneliness he had been experiencing the last four months. He missed Martha and Maria, his own flesh and blood, more than anyone. Next, he longed to be with his grandchildren. However, there was a special place in his heart for Meriwether Lewis, the son he never had. Now that he was gone, at times it was like cutting his heart out. If his beloved bird, Dick, wasn't with him, survival in the White House would have been difficult. He was all alone. Both his son-in-laws ran for the office of U.S. Representative from Virginia that past year, and both won.

For four months out of the year, they must reside in Washington D.C. while Congress was in session. Thomas Mann Randolph, Jr., the husband of Martha, was the older of the two. Jack Eppes, Maria's husband, had just turned 30, quite young for a congressman. Tom, of course, invited them to stay with him in the White House during those winter months. Although they dined with him and met with him in his study, neither one of them could fill the shoes of Lewis. Although Tom was hospitable with them and respected them highly as part of his family, still he was never able to have that father-son relationship with them that he had with Lewis.

As Tom sat down to plan out his new year, he was overwhelmed at how much was on his plate. First and foremost, Maria was due any day with her next baby. How he wished he could be by her side rather than here with her husband. Neither Tom nor Jack could leave Washington because Congress was in session. She would be all alone. Tom was particularly concerned because she lost her first child following birth. Her son, Francis, survived and was now two years old. This would be her third attempt at childbirth, and Tom knew how difficult each one was for her. It brought back bitter memories of how he lost his dear wife, Martha, in childbirth. Pity the thought that it could happen again to Maria.

The second priority on Tom's list was his presidency. He would be entering his fourth year, and he must decide if he would run for re-election. He had already retired from public office once, and his disgust with the politics of Washington suggested strongly to him that Monticello would be a better choice than the White House. However, by stepping down, he would be surrendering to the slander and negatives hailed against him. No, he determined he would run for another four years to help him vindicate his ideas and policies and hopefully even the false rumors thrown his way.

In his own words, Jefferson wrote, "The abominable slanders of my political enemies have obliged me to call for that verdict from my country in the only way it can be obtained." If he won another election it would be "my sufficient voucher to the rest of the world and to posterity, and leave me free to seek, at a definite time, the repose I sincerely wished to have retired to now."[134]

One of the main reasons Jefferson felt motivated to seek another term was because of his father's dream. Ever since he was a little boy eavesdropping outside his father's office door, he inherited the vision to capture the West, going all the way to the Pacific. As an old man of 60, he was finally on the threshold of accomplishing his life-long goal.

At the beginning of 1804, the Louisiana Territory still had not been transferred into the hands of the United States. Would he dare leave office before that was all finalized? He wanted to reach out to the native-American Indians to bring them into his nation's fold. Now that much of their hunting grounds belonged to the United States, Jefferson would invite Indian chiefs to powwow with him, having them dine with him in the White House. He felt he was now their great white father. He was hoping for their respect and cooperation with him in the new era of westward expansion.

Another reason for seeking another term was because of Meriwether Lewis and the Corps of Discovery. What would the American Philosophical Society say if Jefferson abandoned ship in the middle of that historic journey? He was still the Society's president, and he felt deeply indebted to all those involved in that organization. That dream of Tom's father was now their dream as well. There is no way he would want to dash their hopes and trust they had in him as their leader.

And what about Lewis? Was he going to send him to the Pacific Ocean and then leave him abandoned in the midst of his expedition? He was not only an army captain leading an army regiment to forge a trail for others to follow to the other side of North America. He was not only his personal secretary who had spent over two years with him in the White House. He was much more than that to Tom. Meriwether Lewis was like the son he never had. As his neighbor, he had seen him grow from a helpless little lad to a giant of a man. Tom spent years training him, educating him, and preparing him for that journey he was on. If Lewis and his expedition was the only reason for Jefferson to run for re-election, then that was cause enough.

On January 13, Tom wrote to Lewis that the transfer of Louisiana to the United States had been scheduled for December 20. However, he had not received word yet to verify that. What made the transfer of ownership so cumbersome was because Spain and France both had past issues with which to deal. The two nations had agreed to what was called the Third Treaty of San Ildefonso on October 1, 1800. In that agreement, Spain gave France the Louisiana Territory. However, they did that secretly, with the understanding that Napoleon of France would never sell or cede that land mass to a foreign nation. Because it was secret, those who ruled and lived in the Louisiana Territory thought in 1803 that it belonged to Spain. They flew the Spanish flag there proudly.

When Napoleon transacted the Louisiana Purchase, he did so in violation of the agreement in the treaty. Thus, Spain was infuriated that the sale of the Louisiana Territory happened without her consent. However, she finally realized she was too weak compared to Napoleon's power to go to war over it.

From October 20, 1803, when the U.S. Senate ratified the treaty until December 20, two months later, the whole transaction stood in limbo. Spain had to first resolve its anger against France and then eventually transfer legal title of the Louisiana Territory to Napoleon's regime. That was necessary before France could give the United States a clear deed to what would double the size of the America. On November 30, New Orleans hosted a ceremony to make the transfer from Spain to France, replacing the proud flag of Spain with the powerful flag of France. Three weeks later on December 20, 1803, another New Orleans celebration occurred as the United States flag of 15 stars and 15 stripes was raised after the French flag came down.

One month later, the president finally got the official word that the U.S. flag was waving proudly over New Orleans, the capital of the Louisiana Territory. Immediately, Tom sat down to write Lewis about the good news. That message from Thomas Jefferson gave Lewis the full authority of the United States to venture into the Indian lands of the West. Tom said he wanted Lewis to tell the Indians they have a new father in President Jefferson, as their lands now belonged to the United States. In conciliation, Tom instructed Lewis to offer the chief of the Osage tribe a free trip to Washington. That would enable him to meet his new father and hopefully be impressed by the White House and the power and numbers of the Americans. At the same time, Tom sent more good news. Lewis had been accepted as a member of the American Philosophical Society.

The month of February was a busy one for Thomas Jefferson. During that month, he was re-nominated to represent his Democratic-Republican Party in the new election for president. However, for vice president, the party replaced Aaron Burr with George Clinton, the governor of New York. The party leaders realized how utterly useless and contrary Burr had been to Jefferson. Tom wholeheartedly agreed on the need for a replacement. Of course, Aaron Burr vehemently disagreed. He was fighting mad and was out for the worst kind of revenge.

On February 15, Tom's daughter, Maria, gave birth to a baby girl named Maria Jefferson Eppes. As much as Tom longed to be with her and to see his new granddaughter, he was bound to stay in Washington. He was pleased that her sister, Martha, would be with her.

Jefferson's focus returned to his conflict with the Barbary state of Tripoli. On October 31, 1803, Captain William Bainbridge's warship, the *Philadelphia*, ran aground in the Tripoli harbor on the Mediterranean. Tripoli captured and plundered it, threatening to convert it into a ship of its own. All 307 crew members, including the captain, were imprisoned. Commodore Edward Preble was in charge of the six-ship squadron from the United States, one of which was the captured *Philadelphia*.

Commodore Preble was determined to do whatever was necessary to keep the *Philadelphia* from becoming a pirate ship. That would be a disgrace to the U.S. Navy, as well as to all the United States of America. To carry out his plan of revenge, he captured an enemy ship of the Ottoman Empire. Then he had her converted into a frigate of his own, calling her the *Intrepid*. 25-year old Lieutenant Stephen Decatur was then commissioned to sail the *Intrepid* into the Tripoli harbor and destroy the *Philadelphia* to keep it out of enemy hands.

On the evening of February 16, 1804, the mission was rendered a success as the American sailors on the *Intrepid* set fire to the captured ship. They safely escaped the enemy firepower coming from the Tripoli harbor, as they victoriously watched the *Philadelphia* sink into the sea in blazing glory. When Decatur returned to America, he was given a hero's welcome and promoted to captain, the youngest ever to receive such a high office. Sixteen months later, the entire crew of the *Philadelphia* was released when Jefferson offered Tripoli a $60,000 ransom.

March 9, 1804, was another significant date on Jefferson's calendar. He had appointed Captain Amos Stoddard of the U.S. Artillery as commissioner to meet at St. Louis for the official transfer of Upper Louisiana to the United States. He came from the nearby Fort Kaskaskia. Stoddard in turn asked Captain Meriwether Lewis to be his official witness. Just as had been done in New Orleans last year, the same procedure would be followed in St. Louis.

As the Spanish flag came down, the French tri-colored flag was raised. Most of the residents of St. Louis were French and thus shouted enthusiastic cheers when that happened. They loved the sight of it so much that they asked Capt. Stoddard to leave their beloved flag wave one more day, which he gladly authorized. The next day the guns saluted the raising of the Stars and Stripes after the Tricolor came down. While most of the St. Louis residents were saddened, the

U.S. soldiers proudly cheered and spent the rest of the day in joyful celebration.

Tom had been fuming at the delay of Congress to adjourn. Every day when his son-in-laws returned from the House of Representatives, Tom would drill them about what was accomplished that day. Day after day, all they could say was "nothing." Oh how he hated politics! Delay, delay, delay! Why couldn't matters be resolved quickly and forthrightly? He had received word that Maria had not yet recovered from her delivery and was quite ill and weak. He wrote that she needed some of his aged Sherry wine at Monticello. He also hoped she would be at his home when he returned so he could be with her. It was four miles from where she was staying in Eppington to Monticello, and she was unable to get out of bed. Thus, her slaves carried her on a stretcher up the mountain to her father's house. After receiving the Sherry per her father's instructions, she laid in wait for his arrival.

Due to the delay in Congress, Tom and her husband weren't able to leave Washington until April 4. By the time he arrived at Monticello, he could tell she was on her death bed. How could that happen to his precious 25-year old daughter, still in her youth? On April 17, 1804, there was no more life in Maria's body, as she lay limp in her father's arms. All the life seemed to be drained from Tom's body as well, as he bitterly wept for her. Maria was buried at the Monticello cemetery next to the grave planned for her father, with her mother laid to rest on the other side of him.

Martha was once more summoned to help her father with his prolonged grieving spell. That reminded her how she did the same for him when her mother died. However, then she was just a child, who was inexperienced with that sort of thing. Now she knew how to handle her father in his misery. She knew time would be the best medicine, and she afforded him that.

Tom was still in mourning when Captain William Clark and his merry band of forty-two men were leaving from St. Louis. On May 14, 1804, they launched their keelboat and two pirogues into the Missouri River and officially began their Lewis and Clark Expedition. They would use a combination of oars, poles, tow-ropes and sails in order to propel the boats against the upstream current. Captain Meriwether Lewis would join the party further upstream at St. Charles a week later. He had been detained in St. Louis, making arrangements for the free trips to Washington offered by Jefferson to the Indians. It didn't take long for 14 Osage Indians, including their two chiefs, to jump at the opportunity to travel to the Federal City and meet with their Great White Father.

After Aaron Burr was discarded as Jefferson's vice president in favor of New York's Governor George Clinton, Burr went after Clinton's job. By obtaining one of the most powerful offices of the land, Burr felt that would be the revenge he needed against Jefferson. However, the prominent former Treasury Secretary from New York, Alexander Hamilton, had a lot to say about his problems with Burr. Hamilton was the one primarily responsible for Burr losing the presidency to Jefferson in 1801. Now, Hamilton led a crusade to keep Aaron Burr from being governor of his state. When Burr lost the election to Morgan Lewis, he turned his wrath on Hamilton for revenge.

Aaron Burr challenged Alexander Hamilton to a duel. Although that was the old way for men to settle grievances, times had changed. New York had declared dueling as illegal. Therefore, Burr circumvented the New York law by staging the duel in Weehawken, New Jersey, immediately across the New York state line. With their .56 caliber dueling pistols in hand on July 11, 1804, Burr fatally shot and killed Hamilton.

When Thomas Jefferson heard what happened, his angry heart stirred within him, for Aaron Burr was his sitting vice president. How would he handle this new problem facing his candidacy for re-election? How would he face Burr when he saw him again? He heard that he was being scorned by people in Washington, Philadelphia, Boston and New York, all points in between. Although dueling was legal in New Jersey, both New York and New Jersey wanted him tried for murder. Meanwhile, Burr returned to Washington to continue his office of vice president, which would not expire until March, 1805.

While his vice president was away from Washington instigating a duel, which killed the former Treasury Secretary, Tom was in the White House entertaining 14 Osage Indians. The recipients of a free trip to Washington by Jefferson had arrived from the Louisiana Territory on July 11. According to Tom, they were "certainly the most gigantic men we have ever seen."[135] Although Tom stood at six foot two, those Native Americans stood taller than he, some as much as seven feet in height.

Their aboriginal dress and features quickly became the talk of the town. Tom was proud to showcase them to all who came to the White House. He even had them entertain the public with the Osage dances on the north lawn of the Executive Mansion. The observers gawked at their shaved heads, their enlarged ears and their gigantic appearance. The Indians proudly displayed the variety of paint spread all over their body, including red, vermillion, verdigris and yellow. President Jefferson, who considered he was their Great White Father, graciously received products made by their own hands. Those included tomahawks, blankets and jewelry, which he proudly displayed in the White House, along with all the relics and artifacts Captain Lewis sent him from his travels.

Tom reciprocated their offer of gifts by giving them friendship medals made of silver or pewter. He believed those Indian chiefs were among the finest people he had ever met. "We are all now of one family," he told the Indians, "born in the same land, and bound to live as brothers....You have furs and peltries which we want, and we have clothes and other useful things which you want. Let us employ ourselves then in mutually accommodating each other."[136] After lodging his Osage guests for three months at the White House, he had them tour Baltimore, Philadelphia and New York before the returned to their land at the Place-of-the-Many-Swans in the valley of the Osage River.

When Aaron Burr returned from his duel with Alexander Hamilton, he had nothing to do with the president and his Indian friends. Tom likewise had little to do with Burr. Although he was still grieving from his daughter's death, he lost himself with the excitement of his first guests from the Louisiana Territory.

Thomas Jefferson delighted himself in the spectacular off-the-wall events that raised eyebrows from among the highbrows of Washington society and the Federalist sympathizers. If they thought Indians dancing around the White House was unusual, they would be more alarmed later to see two bears in cages prominently displayed in the front yard. Whenever anyone visited the Executive Mansion, they were given the presidential tour. Plastered on the walls would be an assortment of unusual relics and animal skins sent from Lewis to Jefferson or received from the Indians.

Tom received a package from Lewis during the late summer of 1804. Whenever that would occur, the president would stop everything he was doing to quickly open it. How surprised he was to receive his first stuffed animal sent from his secretary. As he looked it over, he couldn't quite figure out what it was. Then he recognized the odd-looking creature as a badger. Although he had never seen one, he remembered a specimen of one that was sent from Canada to Europe in 1788.

That was all recorded by Tom's American Philosophical Society in Philadelphia.

What amazed Tom so much about his cherished gift from Lewis was that it demonstrated Tom's taxidermy skills he had taught his secretary years ago. He was pleased to see Lewis knew how to use them. As a result, Tom could display his stuffed animals in the White House.

Meriwether Lewis wrote the president often, keeping him abreast of their progress and the new things they were discovering. He had found two animals unknown to scientists – the plains horned toad and the eastern wood rat. Since William Clark was an accomplished cartographer, he was carefully drawing maps of every place the Corps of Discovery ventured. The sextant and other surveying tools enabled him to make accurate calculations for the maps. While Jefferson had a White House full of Indians, he heard that Lewis hadn't seen one for the first 640 miles up the Missouri River. Apparently, they were all either hunting buffalo on the prairie or hanging out with the president.

Later that summer, Tom received a disappointing letter from Lewis informing him that a leading member of their corps died of "bilious colic" (ruptured appendix) on August 20, 1804. The victim was Sergeant Charles Floyd, one of the original nine men from Kentucky, the only one who would die on the Lewis and Clark Expedition. Lewis explained how difficult it would be to replace such a faithful leader of his men. Since he was also the expert of different kinds of soils and land quality, his detailed journals recording these would be equally missed. Sergeant Floyd was buried in Sioux City, Iowa, near the place of his death.

Two days later, the first election was held west of the Mississippi in which the majority of the crew chose Patrick Gass to replace their fallen leader. They affectionately called their ruddy-faced Irishman "Beaver" because he was their best woodworker and lead carpenter. That rough and tumble jovial fellow from Pennsylvania would be promoted to Sergeant Patrick Gass.

President Jefferson was pleased that on June 15, Congress ratified the 12th Amendment to the Constitution, changing the way the vice president was to be decided beginning with the upcoming election. That would eliminate the endless frustrations Tom had endured during his first election. Never again would the vice presidential candidate be in open competition against that of president. Tom received notification that on August 3, Commodore Edward Preble had launched an attack on Tripoli that was still in progress. Regretfully for Jefferson, America's war with the Barbary States seemed like it would never end.

While the president was entertaining the Osage Indians and dealing with Congress and the Barbary War, he also anxiously awaited hearing any news on the progress of Meriwether Lewis. While he was waiting, he later found that a united effort of the Corps was needed to drive a prairie dog from his hole. Lewis insisted on keeping it alive and sending it later to Jefferson. Lewis also reported seeing many antelope, mule deer and coyotes. He and Clark would describe in their account books 122 animals they saw that were previously unknown to science. They also discovered 178 plants new to the botanical records.

November was another busy month for Jefferson as he won re-election for president, handily defeating Charles Pinckney of South Carolina. On November 8, he submitted his State of the Union address to Congress. The president outlined for the first time how the United States could now lay claim to territory that would eventually become the state of Indiana. That was accomplished through the *Treaty of Vincennes* of August 18, 1804 and the *Treaty of St. Louis* of November 3, 1804. The first treaty was made with the Delaware tribe of Indians, who thereby ceded, within the limits of the present state of Indiana, 1,910,717 acres of land. That was ratified by the Piankeshaw Indian tribe, at Vincennes, on the 27th of August, 1804.

In the *Treaty of St. Louis*, the tribes of the Sauks and Fox ceded to the United States 14,000,000 acres of land, situated principally within the limits of the present state of Illinois, including part of Missouri lying west of the Mississippi.

Thus, Tom looked back on his past year as quite significant. Those two treaties added substantially to the land acquisition of the Louisiana Purchase and was gradually fulfilling Jefferson's father's dream of capturing the West.

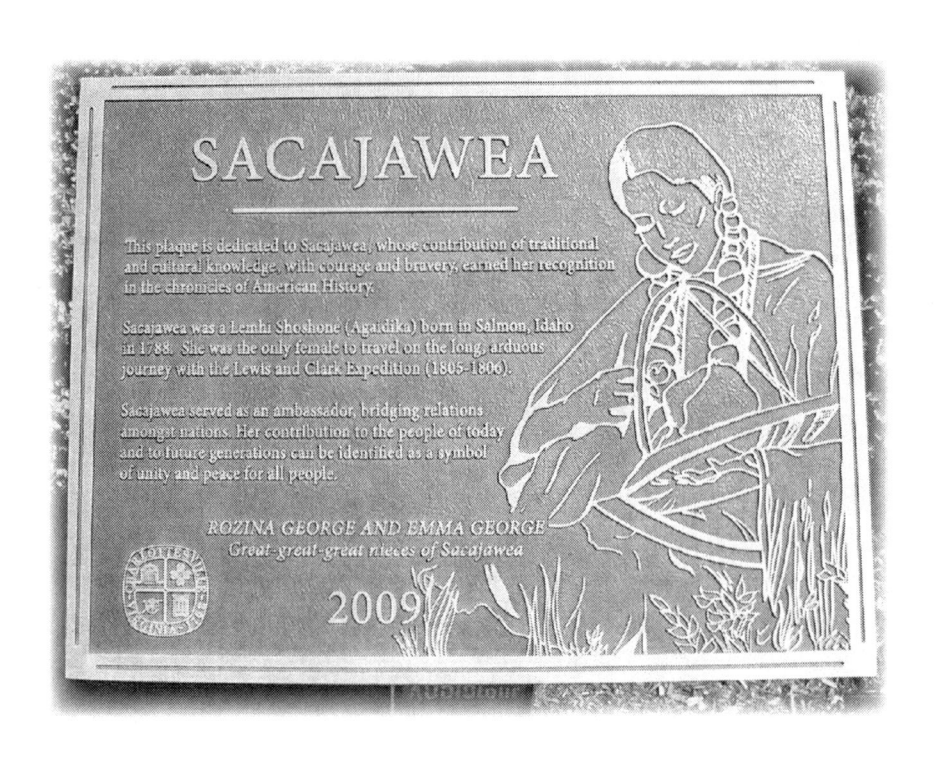

SACAJAWEA

This plaque is dedicated to Sacajawea, whose contribution of traditional and cultural knowledge, with courage and bravery, earned her recognition in the chronicles of American History.

Sacajawea was a Lemhi Shoshone (Agaidika) born in Salmon, Idaho in 1788. She was the only female to travel on the long, arduous journey with the Lewis and Clark Expedition (1805-1806).

Sacajawea served as an ambassador, bridging relations amongst nations. Her contribution to the people of today and to future generations can be identified as a symbol of unity and peace for all people.

ROZINA GEORGE AND EMMA GEORGE
Great-great-great nieces of Sacajawea

2009

Sacajawea

President Bill Clinton honored Sacajawea as Honorary Sergeant of the Regular Army. A newly minted dollar coin commemorated her unique place in history.

1805

When Meriwether Lewis befriended Sacajawea and enlisted her help, it was one of the wisest decisions he ever made. He came to realize that without her, more than likely; they never would have made it to the Pacific Ocean. Thus, the life-long ambition of Thomas Jefferson to fulfill his father's dream would have been lost to antiquity.

When he first met her, she was only seventeen and visibly pregnant. He was amazed at her beauty with her long black hair and piercing brown eyes. Having met with the chiefs and other leaders of the Indians, Lewis hadn't been that close to a Native American woman. As he came to know her better, he saw her beauty was much deeper than her tanned skin. It extended deep into her heart and soul.

It all started on Sunday, November 11, 1804, as his men were building Fort Mandan for their winter quarters. Lewis heard Seaman barking wildly and tried to find the source of his excitement. When he heard the musical honking sounds of a flock of Canadian geese flying south, he figured that's what had stirred Seaman's attention. However, all of a sudden, his big black dog quickly charged toward some visitors, greeting them with friendly moans and a wagging tail.

Recognizing from Seaman's instincts these folk came in peace, Lewis reached out to welcome a French fur trader and two Indian squaws. His name was Toussaint Charbonneau, and the two women were his wives. He appeared to be a much older man, but the girls were mere teenagers. Much to his delight, Lewis received four Buffalo robes from the French Canadian as gifts.

As his visitors joined Lewis and Clark for dinner around the campfire, they were properly introduced to them. Charbonneau told about himself and how he came to meet his wives, both of whom were from the Shoshones, (or Snake tribe, as he called it).

Of particular interest to Lewis was the pregnant girl, wondering how soon her baby would come. He found she was kidnapped by Hidatsa warriors when she was only twelve. That capture took place at the Three Forks of the Missouri in the Rocky Mountains. As she entered her teens, she found she was at Metaharta, a Hidatsa village where the Knife River begins, near present-day Bismarck, North Dakota. Later, she and another Shoshone female teen were sold to Charbonneau as slaves. He made them both his wives and was the father of Sacajawea's expectant baby.

Lewis and Clark asked these strangers to join their expedition team for the remainder of their journey. They were needed as interpreters. Sacajawea spoke both Shoshone and Hidatsa Indian languages, although no English. Her husband spoke French and Hidatsa. Lewis was informed he would be crossing the Bitterroot Mountains in Shoshone territory and would need to trade the Shoshone tribe for excess horses the Indians had corralled.

William Clark explained in his journal that Charbonneau was hired "as an interpreter through his wife." Although Charbonneau spoke no English, Pvt. Francois Labiche spoke both English and French. To translate from Shoshone would take Sacajawea. She in turn would translate to her husband. Then he would give the interpretation to Labiche, thus completing the cycle.

By October 24, 1804, the Corps of Discovery had traveled for five months up the Missouri River to arrive at the Hidatsa-Mandan villages, which had a population larger than St. Louis or Washington D.C. at the time. Finding the natives friendly and Lewis and Clark needing a secure place to build their winter quarters, they chose to settle there. They began the construction of what they called Fort Mandan, living as neighbors to the Hidatsa tribe during that bitter winter of 1804/1805. Lewis knew that Jefferson would delight in this because one of his goals for this trip was to become friends with the Indians.

Their first encounter with the Native Americans once they left St. Louis for their expedition happened on May 31, 1804, when William Clark met with Big Track, one of the leaders of the Osage tribe. By

Thomas Jefferson

that time, Meriwether Lewis already had formed a binding relationship with chiefs of the same tribe, providing free trips for them to see the president in the White House.

During their five-month journey up the Missouri, the second clans of Indians the Corps of Discovery encountered were the Otoe and Missouri tribes. August 3, 1804, was the first time Lewis and Clark held a council with any of the red nations. Jefferson encouraged Lewis to take plenty of gifts on his journey to share with the Indians along the way. The chiefs of both the Otoe and Missouri tribes were given Jefferson's peace medals and Stars-and-Stripes flags.

Lewis and Clark demonstrated their compasses, telescopes, magnets and surveying tools. The Indians stood in amazement at all these new-fangled inventions. Lewis was proud of his air gun and was quick to discharge it to their hearts' content. They did everything they knew to show the Indians that their new Great White Father came offering peace and prosperity for all those who sided with him and his efforts to journey all the way to the Pacific Ocean.

On August 30, 1804, Lewis held a friendly council with the Yankton Sioux Indians near present-day Yankton, South Dakota. While the Corps was encamped there, a Sioux baby was born, and Lewis wrapped him in the 15-star U.S. flag and declared him to be "an American." Each tribe that Lewis encountered, he offered its chief a free trip to Washington to meet the Great White Father.

The next month was not so fortunate for the expedition. On September 24, there was a confrontation with the Lakota or "Teton" Sioux tribe. Instead of having a peaceful council as Lewis and Clark had planned, the Lakota leaders played like they were drunk and threatened to imprison the members of the Corps if they didn't get more presents from Lewis and Clark. One of the chiefs threatened Clark, who pulled out his sword and commissioned his men to arms. Fortunately, the Lakota backed down rather than fight, eliminating any further problems.

On December 17, as they were finishing up their winter facilities at Fort Mandan, the temperature dropped to minus 45 degrees fahrenheit, which was the coldest most of the men had ever experienced. By the time Christmas arrived, all the Corps members were safely protected, as the fort was completed.

Christmas was a day of joyful celebration as the men all relaxed from their labors. According to Sgt. Patrick Gass, *"Flour, dried apples, pepper, and other articles were distributed in the different messes to enable them to celebrate Christmas in a proper and social manner."*[137]

The brandy and rum flowed freely, and the men danced merrily to the fiddle tunes of Pierre Cruzatte and George Gibson. Gass continued,

"*I was awakened before Day by a discharge of 3 platoons from the Party and the french, the men merrily Disposed, I give them all a little Taffia (type of cheap rum) and permited 3 cannon fired, at raising Our flag, Some Men Went out to huntr and the others to Danceing and Continued untill 9 oClock P.M. when the frolick ended &c.*"[138]

As the freezing, blustery, snow-bound winter engulfed them at Fort Mandan, on February 11, Sacajawea gave birth to her son, Jean-Baptiste Charbonneau. Having no midwife to help her, she depended on Meriwether Lewis to guide the baby into the new world.

He was reminded of his mother's volunteer efforts to doctor anyone she knew that needed help. She taught Lewis everything he knew about herbs, medicines, doctoring and even delivering babies. He learned from her that the extraction from the rattles of the rattlesnake helps ease the birth pangs. Whenever he had the opportunity to help someone, it made him feel closer to her mother. He missed her so much, and he knows the feeling was mutual. He wrote to his younger brother, Reuben, often, who kept Lewis in touch with his mother and all his family in Virginia.

Her new bundle of joy, she named Jean-Baptiste, the French spelling for John the Baptist. Being the forerunner of Jesus, she believed her little son would be the forerunner of many others to follow after they blazed the trail to the Pacific.

At first, Seaman would bark at the mysterious coos and cries coming from little Jean, but he finally settled down as he got used to them. He took it on himself to become the baby's personal bodyguard and hearkened to every sound he made. William Clark, who had no children of his own, was magically drawn to Sacajawea's son, affectionately calling him "Little Pomp" or "Pomp", which meant "leader." When Lewis and Clark prepared to leave Fort Mandan for the Pacific, they saw Sacajawea strap her baby on her back with a cradleboard, as she always did throughout the expedition.

Thomas Jefferson found he was hearing less and less from his personal secretary. As the expedition moved further west, it became more difficult to get letters and materials sent to the president. Unless a reliable party was traveling toward Washington D.C., it was impossible to make the necessary connections. Jefferson became quite concerned and impatient about what was happening to Lewis and Clark. He looked to Lewis' younger brother, Reuben, for help. Writing often to

Thomas Jefferson

him in Tom's native Albemarle County, Virginia, he would find that Reuben and his mother somehow received contacts or information about Lewis that was new to the president.

Before Meriwether Lewis left his winter camp at Fort Mandan, he made sure to gather all samples, relics and papers Jefferson would enjoy. He would send them with the return party who left Mandan for St. Louis on April 7, 1805. With the help of the other men, Lewis inventoried his shipment to the president. It would take four months before that arrived at the White House, with all the animals surviving the trip safely, except the grouse. There would be no stuffed animals this time. Lewis wanted Jefferson to see them alive. All the cages and boxes were listed as follows:

1. A prairie dog in a cage. (Something totally new to Jefferson and the American Philosophical Society).
2. A sharp-tailed grouse in another cage.
3. Four magpies, all in a single cage. (As much as Tom enjoyed his mockingbirds, Lewis felt he would be pleased to add these to his bird collection).
4. Four boxes and a trunk. Inside were specimens from various animals, such as horns, pelts and skeletons. Lewis included samples of soils, minerals, plants and insects, all unique to the West. Also, he included Indian artifacts and Ariaka tobacco and its seed. Each item was properly labeled listing the date it was found, its location, its name and a brief description. This was the way Jefferson had trained him for years how to do an inventory.

After suffering through the harsh bitter winter that literally froze the skin off the faces of some of the Indians, Lewis and Clark led their Corps of Discovery out of Fort Mandan at 4 p.m. on April 7, 1805. After discharging those who would make the return trip to St. Louis, Lewis and Clark headed west up the Missouri River with their army regiment, Clark's slave, York; Sacajawea and her new-born baby; and a Mandan Indian who would help them find the Shoshone nation.

Lewis and others kept regular records of their daily activities. Seaman had been overlooked in his journal for the past eight months. However, on April 18, 1805, when one of the men shot a goose that landed in the river, Seaman dove in after it, bringing it back for the evening meal.

The next week Lewis was worried because Seaman was missing throughout the night. He wrote in his journal that *"my dog had been absent during the last night, and I was fearful we had lost him altogether, however, much to my satisfaction he joined us at 8 O'clock that morning."*[139] Later that morning, Lewis took Seaman with him hunting for a river called the Yellowstone. There he shot a buffalo calf, giving him and all the men a hearty dinner that afternoon.

On the following day, one of the best riflemen of the team, Joseph Field, was sent by Lewis to hunt again in the same area. Seaman went with him, where they spied several pronghorn antelope swimming in the river. Without giving Field a chance to shoot, Seaman leaped into the water to swim after them. Sgt. Ordway recorded in his journal saying Seaman captured one of the pronghorns and *"Drowned & killed it and Swam to Shore with it."*[140] Once again, the men had Lewis' talented Newfoundland canine friend to thank for dinner. Several days later, Lewis himself would provide the evening meal, when he killed a grizzly bear that had chased him for seventy or eighty yards after being shot.

On May 5, it was Seaman's turn again to get dinner. When he spied another pronghorn, he didn't wait for him to head for water. He was able to chase him down on land, where he tackled him and put the death blow to his jugular vein.

One date worthy of note was on May 14. *"The Corps noted huge herds of buffalo, elk, deer, wolves and antelope. Six of the men attacked a grizzly with their rifles. Although the bear was hit many times, it continued to pursue them. It took eight balls to kill it."*[141]

May 19 came and Seaman was once again the star of the day, except this time in a disastrous sort of a way. One of the crew shot a beaver in the river, and Seaman wasted no time diving after him. When Lewis' dog grabbed the beaver by its hind leg, the wounded animal retaliated by chomping onto one of Seaman's rear legs. The dog instinctively released the beaver's leg and clamped his powerful jaws around the neck of his prey. Lewis quickly dove into the river to rescue Seaman when he saw his dog swimming out of the water with the dead beaver in his mouth. However, Lewis was devastated when he saw blood pouring out of Seaman's leg. The beaver's teeth had severed a main artery.

Thanks to Lewis' mother, he knew exactly what to do in making a tourniquet and saving his dog from bleeding to death. Then he sewed up his leg with a needle and thread. During the night, the men were uncertain if Seaman would survive the episode. However, the next morning they saw him lift up his head, although weekly, and wag his tail. New hope was the focus of the days ahead for Seaman.

Ten days had passed since the dog's gamble with death, and he was back to old form. That was proven as a bull buffalo stormed through the camp in the middle of the night. All the men except those on guard duty were tucked into their bedrolls. The confused, wayward buffalo awakened Seaman, who with his loud yelps and quick-footedness drove the shocking intruder out of the camp. Fortunately, no one was hurt, although none could continue their night's slumber. Occasionally, that would happen again when a wayward buffalo needed to be chased from the camp by Seaman.

It became a regular occurrence that Lewis' furry friend would bark wildly all night long at the grizzlies surrounding their sleeping quarters. Although the noise he made was a nuisance, without it the men would be attacked in the night by bears. For that, they were grateful for Seaman keeping them alive. Whether it was retrieving a wounded deer for dinner from the river or catching wild geese, Seaman was a valuable member of the Corps of Discovery.

On June 30, in what was to become Great Falls, Montana, William Clark said he saw 10,000 buffalo grazing on the plain beneath his view through his looking glass. On the 4th of July, it was party time in the Lewis and Clark camp. With Cruzatte and Gibson fiddling up a storm, the men drank and danced and then drank some more until the last of their supply of alcohol went dry.

Meriwether Lewis spoke to his men about the significance of that day, it being the 29th birthday of the *Declaration of Independence*. He was only a boy of two when Jefferson, the one who was responsible for that trip to the Pacific, penned those powerful, historic words. That was merely the beginning of our nation's freedom, as it took seven years of war with England for the United States to establish her independence. That was the first time the Americans in the crew heard that vital history lesson. The Frenchmen and Indians present were equally enlightened, with the French proud their country helped win the Revolution.

The following month, the Corps of Discovery reached its next major destination – the Shoshone nation. As he viewed the snow-capped Rocky Mountains looming ahead of them, Lewis knew the waterways were growing narrower. To get through or over the challenging precipices, he would need to find many horses. Sacajawea assured him the Shoshones had an ample supply of wild horses that might be available. One of the main reasons that Sacajawea and the

Mandan Indian journeyed with them was to locate the Shoshones and create a friendship with them.

On August 8, Sacajawea became visibly excited when she spied what she called "Beaverhead Rock." When the men saw her exuberant joy, they saw something they hadn't seen since the birth of her son, they all called "Pomp." She told Lewis the rock she saw that looked like the head of a beaver marked the beginning of the territory of her people. The Shoshones, she assured them, would be found either on that river or the next one proceeding from it to the west.

Meriwether Lewis gathered a small party of men, and they set out ahead of the rest of the expedition in search of the Shoshones. On August 12, Lewis became the first U.S. citizen to cross the Continental Divide as he stood atop Lemhi Pass in the Rockies at an elevation greater than 7300 feet above sea level. As he now had come to the end of the Louisiana Territory, he had also reached the western edge of the United States. (One day that spot would mark the state line between Idaho and Montana).

Lewis gave this account of his historic moment. *"We proceeded to the top of the dividing ridge from which I discovered immense ranges of high mountains still to the West of us with their tops partially covered in snow."*[142] Although he was awestruck by their beauty, he was overwhelmed at how difficult it would be to cross all those treacherous mountains. He must get horses, and get them now. He also must be the bearer of bad news to the president because he failed to find a waterway connection from the Pacific Ocean to New Orleans. That had been one of Thomas Jefferson's hopes and aspirations. One of the main reasons Congress approved this expedition was to locate such a waterway.

As Lewis was overwrought with depression over his apparent failure, he quickly overcame it when the following day he came face to face with Cameahwait, the chief of the Shoshones. Fortunately, as they and their parties encountered each other, they were mutually friendly. He was pleased to know they would follow him back over the pass to meet with the rest of the Lewis and Clark Expedition.

When Sacajawea met Chief Cameahwait, she was overjoyed to find he was her brother. They hadn't seen each other since she was kidnapped five years ago. At that time, her brother had not arisen to the status of leader of his people. Never in her wildest dreams did she imagine him in such a noble position. The chief was equally jubilant to be introduced to his new nephew, Jean Baptiste, now six months old.

There was a day of rejoicing at the reunion of Sacajawea with her brother. The following day, August 18, belonged to Lewis, being his 31st birthday. He felt especially blessed that it was on his birthday that he received all the horses he needed from the Shoshones. Rather than his men giving Lewis birthday presents, they opened up their supply bags to retrieve gifts for Chief Cameahwait and his Shoshone people. They found this was the first time that Indian tribe had ever laid eyes on a white man. When they parted company, they did so with congenial spirits for each other. The Shoshones had come to admire Seaman's faithfulness to Lewis, sticking like glue to him. They also were amazed at how Seaman had become the protector and playmate of Chief Cameahwait's six-month old nephew, Jean Baptiste. They wondered whether he was more the child's pet than that of the Meriwether Lewis.

In September, Lewis and Clark had friendly encounters with two other Indian tribes, the Flatheads and the Nez Percé. The Flatheads, or "Salish", as they preferred to be called, gave them more horses and directions and the only thing the Indians had to eat, which were berries. Having left the grazing lands of the buffalo, the men found their rations were quickly diminishing. While they hungered for meat, they had to satisfy themselves with berries. The Nez Percé were the most likeable and hospitable of any of the Indians. They helped Lewis and Clark build some canoes for their trip on the Columbia River to the west of them.

In October, the expedition forged further west into the Oregon Territory, entering into the present state of Washington. During that time, William Clark noted in his journal that Sacajawea had been such a help to them as a token of peace for all the Indians they encountered along the way. On October 6, they finally found their waterway to the Columbia River and onto the Pacific Ocean. As they launched their canoes into the raging waters of the Clearwater River, they were excited to become waterborne once again.

Another month went by when on November 7, 1805, they first set their sights on their ultimate destination, the Pacific Ocean. Shouts rang out among all the party when William Clark exclaimed, "Ocean in view! O! the joy." He later recorded that historic event in his journal. *"Great joy in camp we are in view of the Ocian that great Pacific Ocean which we been so long anxious to See. and the roreing or noise made by the waves braking on the rockey shores (as I Suppose) may be heard distinctly."*[143] What they heard was only wishful thinking because the crashing waves of the Pacific were still another eight days away.

On November 15, 1805, the great day of their expectations finally arrived when they reached the Pacific Ocean. Over 4,000 miles of travel had been experienced by Meriwether Lewis before he reached his Pacific destination. Eleven days of constant downpours did their best to rain on their parade and dampen their exuberant spirits and joyful celebration. Even in the midst of the storms, Meriwether Lewis rejoiced to know that his beloved father figure, President Thomas Jefferson, had finally fulfilled his father's dream. Although it had taken over sixty years, one of the major goals of Jefferson was now a reality. Lewis was pleased that he was the one who helped bring it to pass.

Their next Christmas would be spent at Fort Clatsop on the Oregon side of the Columbia River. They chose this site with a Democratic process. For the first time in American history, each person had a vote to decide where they would settle for the winter. That included a woman, a black man, and the French Canadians. Even Seaman offered his vote with some emotional barks and the wagging of his tail. Having arrived at their desired site, they first had to build the fort before they could settle there. In the midst of the driving rain, within two weeks they worked with precisioned teamwork to get their winter quarters ready, calling it "Fort Clatsop." Their name was chosen to honor the friendly local Clatsop Indian tribe. Here they would spend the next three months before they made their return trip home. While at Fort Clatsop, the men found plenty of elk to hunt and salt to process from the ocean water of the Pacific.

When it came time for Christmas day of 1805, everyone was safe in their newly built fort. The Clatsop Indians joined in their holiday festivities. William Clark recorded their celebration together in his journal. *"At day light that morning we we[re] awoke by the discharge of the fire arms of all our party and a Solute, Shouts and a Song which the whole party joined in under our windows. after which they retired to their rooms were cheerful all the morning. after breakfast we divided our Tobacco which amounted to 2 carrots one half of which we gave to the men of the party who used tobacco, and to those who doe not use it we make a present of a handkerchief, The Indians leave us in the evening all the party Snugly fixed in their huts. I received a present of Capt. L. of a fleece hosiery Shirts Draws and Socks, a pair Mocker sons of Whitehouse a Small Indian basket of Gutherick, two Dozen white weasels' tails of the Indian woman, and some black root of the Indians before their departure."*[144]

On March 23, 1806, Lewis and Clark broke up camp on the Pacific and headed for home, which was four thousand miles away. Since no messages could be sent from there to the president, Jefferson had no idea they had fulfilled his father's dream. Lewis knew he must get to St. Louis as quickly as possible to properly notify his commander-in-chief. Little Jean Baptiste had celebrated his first birthday at Fort Clatsop. Seaman was looking forward to leaving the damp, dreary Pacific because it was infested with fleas that kept him agitated all the time.

After canoeing up the Columbia and Snake Rivers, they retrieved their horses from the friendly Nez Percé Indians, who had held them safely for Lewis and Clark. They needed them to cross the Bitterroot Mountains.

The Blackfeet Indians were one of the two hostile tribes that plagued the expedition. While Lewis and his men were sleeping one night, two of their warriors snuck up and tried to steal their guns. The men quickly awoke and struggled with the warriors, both of whom got shot and killed. Knowing the rest of the Blackfeet would be heavy on their trail, they broke camp immediately and hurried their trip home. They were now men on the run. Lewis was disturbed that all the friendship and good will he had established with the Indians would possibly be vanished by that one unfortunate incident.

On August 11, Lewis and Pierre Cruzatte went elk hunting. After each shooting once, they reloaded. As Lewis aimed to shoot again, he was struck with a bullet from Cruzatte's gun that hit him in the buttocks. As his hunting partner ran to his aide, Lewis, writhing in pain, cried out angrily to Cruzatte, "Damn you. You shot me." However, the French Canadian flatly denied it, saying the bullet must have come from an Indian.

Cruzatte helped Lewis get back to camp, where his men dressed the wound but could not ease his pain. They knew that Cruzatte, being nearsighted, honestly believed he did not shoot his captain. Lewis refused to press charges against him, but he found it difficult to sit comfortably for several weeks. The only way he could have some relief was to lay flat on his stomach in the boat. By the time they got to St. Louis, he was so excited that he forgot all about his injury.

Jefferson's Dream Come True

*"I like the dreams of the future better than
the history of the past."*
Thomas Jefferson

1806

As soon as Thomas Jefferson heard the good news from his personal secretary, whatever he was doing at the time came to an abrupt end. All time stood still. He went to his study and closed the door, instructing his doorman not to accept visitors. He nestled himself into his favorite whirligig chair, propping his feet upon his Windsor stool.

His mind was carried back to those curious times as a passionate little boy, when he would eavesdrop outside his father's office door. Whenever he saw Thomas Meriwether, Joshua Fry, Dr. Thomas Walker and Rev. James Maury gather at Tuckahoe, he knew they must be there to discuss their dream. They had received authorization from King George III of England to form the Loyal Company.

As the charter members of the organization, they began their dream by sending their own Dr. Thomas Walker on an expedition to find what was on the other side of the Appalachian Mountains. In 1750 he became the first white man to cross the Cumberland Gap into what was later called Kentucky. Upon his return, the Loyal Company met again to plan a longer expedition – one that would carry them further west. Where would it all end? Why not try to go all the way to the western edge of North America to the Pacific Ocean? Tom's father, Peter Jefferson, had become obsessed with that dream. Sixty years ago as a lad of only two, Tom began feeling the heartbeat of his father for such an unbelievable venture.

Tom never told his Pa about his listening to the five men's conversation behind closed doors. But he found that his father carried no secrets about what his Loyal Company was planning. Quite often Tom remembered his Pa taking him on his knee in the quietness of the evening and passionately telling his son about his dream. He, as merely a preschooler, was serenaded to sleep many a night by his father talking about new things he was discovering about the western frontier. His goal was that before he died, he would know of someone who had heard the breaking of the waves of the Pacific thousands of miles from Tuckahoe.

Sorry to say, Peter Jefferson passed away when Tom was only 14. But Tom would make sure that although his Pa died, his dream wouldn't die with him. With his father's absence, the Loyal Company was now down to three, Col. Joshua Fry dying years before that. But eventually, they had all died without ever having achieved their goal.

Tom became the passionate burden bearer of the dream of the Loyal Company, but more personally "his father's dream." His goal was like his Pa, that before he died he would be able to know someone who could witness the crashing of the waves of the Pacific Ocean four thousand miles around the globe. Although he was now an old man of 62, he finally accomplished what his father never had. However, if his Pa hadn't instilled his passion to go west into his son, the Corps of Discovery (or Lewis and Clark Expedition) would never have become a reality. Oh, for the joy and satisfaction to know that his personal secretary had witnessed the crashing of the waves on the Pacific Ocean at the mouth of Columbia River.

As Tom lay back in his chair from sure exhaustion and weakness, he heard Dick, his faithful mockingbird, whistling "Yankee Doodle" so eloquently that Tom almost fell asleep. Besides Dick, there were other birds in Tom's office. Ever since Meriwether Lewis left years ago, Tom experienced many hours of loneliness. He always tried to get his daughters to move in with him at the White House, but they had their own homes and plantations to care for in Virginia.

After Maria died, Tom only had Martha left whom he would encourage to accompany him at the Executive Mansion. Finally, she consented to join her father for the winter of 1805/1806, bringing her six children with her. She was heavy with child when she came, giving birth to James Madison Randolph, on January 17, 1806, becoming the first child born in the White House. She had built such a close relationship with Tom's Secretary of State and his charming wife,

Dolley, that she named her son after him. One wonders if her baby was a daughter if she would have been named Dolley Madison Randolph.

Tom had new life instilled within his soul. He was young all over again, as he played and sang with his grandchildren. It was just like old days when he drug out his fiddle, and Martha sat down at the pianoforte, harmonizing together on their instruments.

Anne, his oldest grandchild, was now 15 and had her mind on the social life of Washington. Jeff, his oldest grandson, was now 13 and needed his grandpa's introduction into the facts of life. Although he was born "Thomas Jefferson Randolph", he was nicknamed "Jeff" to distinguish him from both his father, Thomas, and his grandfather, Thomas. Ellen was 9; Cornelia was 6; Virginia was 4; Mary was 2; and then little "James Madison," Tom's newborn bundle of joy. That all reminded Thomas Jefferson how much he detested politics and the public life. Where he would rather be was with his family, and he couldn't wait to retire to Monticello. No matter how much he was coerced, he would refuse to serve another four years.

After Dick finished whistling "Yankee Doodle", the other mockingbirds tried their hand at testing their talents. Because of Tom's past loneliness, he kept adding more birds to his study. He now had one he called "New Orleans"; another one was "St. Louis"; and yet another was "Pacific." All three were named in commemoration of the Louisiana Purchase and the Corps of Discovery.

All three birds learned from Dick how to whistle and sing, as well as mock the sounds of those they frequently heard. New Orleans was the first to join Dick in making musical sounds. Next was St. Louis. Pacific was the hardest one to get with the music, which Tom attributed to him being too old to learn new tricks. One thing the old bird did well was to mimic the incessant crying sounds of the newest Jefferson in the household. Whenever the newborn "Jimmy" would let out a wail, he would hear an echo coming from Pacific's cage, wailing right along with him. New Orleans chose to mimic Tom's granddaughters' voices. St. Louis was more inclined to mock the voice of Jeff. Dick continued to mock the barking of the dogs at Monticello and the creaking sounds of the ship at it rumbled across the Atlantic.

Whenever Tom would go upstairs to bed, he left the other birds caged in his study. As was their custom, Tom would lead the way as Dick hopped up the stairs behind him to his bedroom. There in peace and solitude, Dick would serenade Tom into the deepest and most sublime sleep.

During the first months of 1806, all Tom could think about was his daughter, his grandchildren, and Meriwether Lewis, who was like the son he never had. He was so anxious to see him again and hear firsthand all his exciting adventures. Hopefully, there won't be anything that will prevent him from returning safely and in a timely manner.

With all the excitement Tom had been experiencing, he was hoping it would never end. However, sorry to say, it was short lived, as trouble was looming on the horizon. Aaron Burr, his former vice president, was at it again. It wasn't enough that Tom had to live with the shameful memories of Burr's killing of Alexander Hamilton. Now, he would be faced with a much more serious dilemma. This one would require a dramatic decision by Jefferson that would adversely affect his presidency.

Aaron Burr was a vengeful man. Whenever someone did him wrong, they could expect Burr to get even with them. Alexander Hamilton was at the top of his list for vengeance, and he lost his life at the end of dueling pistol as a result.

When Thomas Jefferson preferred a new vice president over Burr, the president climbed to the top of Burr's hit list. Although Burr acted like he had done nothing wrong and was cordial to Jefferson, he was in the act of planning a conspiracy that would undermine, if not destroy, all that Tom had worked to accomplish during his illustrious presidency.

Although Jefferson knew feelings were strained between him and Burr, he didn't know how deep-seated Burr's revenge was until a year after he left office. As early as February, 1806, Tom began receiving letters from Joseph H. Daveiss of Kentucky. Each letter gave more hints of Aaron Burr's conspiratorial activities. What puzzled Tom was that Daveiss was a Federalist, on the opposite aisle from Tom's Republican party. Thus, Tom at first didn't take the letters seriously. However, on July 14, Daveiss wrote to give the president the details of Burr's intended actions.

According to Daveiss, Burr was planning a rebellion within the Louisiana Territory with the intention of becoming its sole ruler. He had conspired with other American leaders to take over both the Louisiana Territory and even Mexico. Tom still refused to believe these letters, feeling they were issued for political reasons, being that Burr himself was a Republican. After all, Tom reasoned, what did Daveiss have to gain by sending such accusations against Burr?

Tom was more preoccupied during that time with his family. He knew that after springtime began, Martha would be taking his seven grandchildren back to Edgehill in Albemarle County. His only consolation would be that he would return to Monticello about the same time, or soon thereafter. He was pleased how Anne, his oldest granddaughter, was quickly growing up to be a young lady. He had observed she was strong willed and motivated to get what she wanted in life. She reminded him so much of her mother, who had borne the awesome responsibility of caring for her father when his dear wife died. Although his daughter, Martha, was only a ten-year-old child, she became the glue to hold her father together from that moment on.

Although Tom admired Anne and loved her personality, he showed more preference to Jeff, who was just beginning puberty. Jeff was a country boy, who was finding it difficult to deal with city life. He couldn't understand why his grandpa forbade him to go out in the yard and shoot squirrels, rabbits and birds. Why couldn't he have a hound dog that could help him tree possums? He reminded Tom of Meriwether Lewis, who was like the son he never had. He was all country, and no amount of training from Tom would ever take that passion from his soul.

Tom had other activities in mind that would draw him and Jeff together. Rather than killing birds, Tom got his grandson to help him with the mockingbirds. They needed more time spent with them to help them sing, whistle or break bad habits they had acquired. As soon as it was warm enough to fill the flowerbeds with seeds and cuttings, Tom took Jeff along to share in his favorite spring hobby. Hopefully, the young teen would learn to love gardens as much as Tom did. Jeff bathed himself also in Tom's extensive library. Like Tom, he was a quick learner and highly motivated to improve his mind and soul. Tom would use his mockingbirds and his books to capture the attention of his younger grandchildren as well. They thoroughly enjoyed planting new flowers around the White House.

Margaret Bayard Smith gave the following observation at the executive mansion.

> "Mrs. Randolph and Madison called and I promised to take tea with Mrs. R(Randolph) in the evening. While I sat looking at him (the president) playing with these infants, one standing on the sofa with its arms around his neck, the other two youngest on his knees, playing with him. I could

scarcely realize that he was one of the most celebrated men now living."[145]

Once Martha and the children headed for Virginia, Tom once again worked from sunup to sundown on the matters concerning his presidency. On April 19, he sent James Monroe and William Pinckney as joint commissioners to England. Hopefully, they would be able to convince King George III to stop his warships from boarding and searching American ships, including taking some Americans as prisoners.

While Jefferson had major concerns abroad, he was unaware he had more devious ones on the home front. He and Captain Meriwether Lewis had screened their army officers thoroughly, trying to weed out all those who would stand in opposition to Jefferson. However, one of them was about to turn against the president, and it so happened it would be his highest ranking officer. James Wilkinson was the commanding general of the U.S. Army, while at the same time being a secret agent for Spain. When Aaron Burr began his conspiracy against the United States, he found a friend in General Wilkinson.

Spain was still upset about losing the Louisiana Territory and was willing to help whoever would help her retrieve it. The Spanish authorities found Aaron Burr had the political connections to serve their purpose. He traveled extensively through many states to drum up support for his treasonous cause, including time with Andrew Jackson at the Hermitage, his home near Nashville, Tennessee. At the time, Jackson was the Major General of the Tennessee militia and refused to become a part of any of Burr's antics. That didn't stop Burr.

General James Wilkinson decided to compete with the president in exploration of the Louisiana Territory. While Lewis and Clark were headed west to the Pacific, Wilkinson sent Captain Zebulon Pike, Jr. up the Mississippi River from St. Louis in search of the headwaters for that major body of water. When he returned, Pike was sent up the Missouri and Red Rivers to find their headwaters. One of the highest mountains in Colorado would be named "Pike's Peak" because of Zebulon Pike's discovery of it and his attempt to climb it. (All these endeavors were without the knowledge or authority of the president. While that was being done behind Tom's back, he was intensely wondering what was happening with his personal secretary.

On June 12, 1806, Thomas Jefferson received shockingly belated news that his old friend and early father-figure George Wythe's funeral was held in Richmond, Virginia, the day before. Tom was speechless, as he fell limply into his chair, feeling totally helpless. He was angry at first that he had not been informed about the funeral – the largest in Virginia's history and the president didn't know about it. However, his anger was mixed with sadness that his close friend, the one who tutored him in law wasn't available to him anymore. While he believed his soul was in heaven, his body laid six foot under in St. John's Church Cemetery.

Tom grew increasingly disturbed about Wythe's death when he found that Wythe's 18-year-old grandnephew, George Wythe Sweeney, was charged with poisoning him. Tom was told Wythe's last words were breathed in exasperation crying out, "I am murdered!"[146]

Tom's mind reflected on his close ties with the old judge. He remembered as it was yesterday how George Wythe took him under his wings at the College of William and Mary and infused within Tom's veins all he knew about law. Tom had told others that Wythe made him "the honest advocate of my country's rights." Jefferson affectionately recalled how Wythe took him to live in his majestic home when he was still a student in Williamsburg.

Tom's introspective mind recalled his introduction of the *Declaration of Independence*, and Wythe was the first of the seven Virginians who signed it. In 1779, when Tom was governor of Virginia, he named his old friend, George Wythe, as the first professor of law in the entire United States. With Wythe in Richmond and Jefferson in Washington, they were not as close as they once were. But Tom knew whenever he needed help or just a shoulder to cry on, his good friend, George Wythe, was always available. He knew with his death, there never would be another "father of American jurisprudence" like him.

Several weeks later Tom answered the door to a post man with a letter from Richmond Mayor William DuVal. Tom was moved by the mayor's kind words saying, "*I believe that the great and good Mr. Wythe loved you as sincerely as if you had been his son; his attachment was founded on his thorough knowledge of you, personally. Some years ago, he mentioned that if there was an honest man in America, Thomas Jefferson was that person; everything he said has been verified.*"[147]

Tom remembered the abundance of books in Wythe's inexhaustible library, each of which he allowed Tom free rein to read at will. In Wythe's will, he bequeathed his entire library to Thomas Jefferson. They became a part of Jefferson's library that would become the basic collections of the Library of Congress after a fire destroyed all its valuable collections during the War of 1812.

Later, Tom received a report showing Wythe's epitaph.

>This tablet is dedicated to mark the site
>Where lies the mortal remains of
>GEORGE WYTHE
>Born 1726 – Died 1806
>Jurist and Statesman
>Teacher of Randolph, Jefferson and Marshall
>First Professor of Law in the United States
>First Virginia Signer of the Declaration of Independence
>Erected by
>Patriotic Citizens of Virginia[148]

Lewis and Clark returned with their men to St. Louis on September 23, 1806, to the roars of the crowds of people on the riverbank, haling them as heroes. The men of the Corps of Discovery in their canoes fired their guns in the air in response. That was the first time they received any public recognition from Americans, and they didn't know what to expect. More than expected were all the parties held in their honor.

In the midst of all the excitement and celebration, Lewis priority was to notify the president that their expedition was completed. Jefferson thought it would only take them a year, but the journey lasted over two years. Lewis quickly wrote Thomas Jefferson a letter and sent it to the White House. He was grateful to have a post man once again. Two years without mail delivery had rattled Lewis' nerves. He had wished he knew what was happening with the president and how he would handle troublesome decisions.

He began his letter to Thomas Jefferson as follows:

>"It is with pleasure that I announce (sic) to you the safe arrival of myself and party at 12 OClk. Today at that place [St. Louis] with our papers and baggage. In obedience to your orders we have penetrated (sic) the Continent of North America to the Pacific Ocean, and sufficiently explored the interior of the country to affirm with confidence that we have discovered the most practicable rout which dose exist across the continent by means of the navigable branches of the Missouri and Columbia Rivers . . ."

In the letter he gave the following credit to Clark.

> "With respect to the exertions and services rendered by that esteem able man Capt. William Clark in the course of late voyage I cannot say too much; if sir any credit be due for the success of that arduous enterprise in which we have been mutually engaged, he is equally with myself entitled to your consideration and that of our common country . . ."[149]

Lewis knew how much he depended on William Clark to make that trip successful. Clark was the field general who trained, drilled and disciplined the troops. He was always with the men to deal with daily problems and procedures. Meriwether Lewis was away from the crew many times, especially in the days of preparation in St. Louis. During that time, he found it necessary to spend much of his valuable time organizing the Indians for their free trip to Washington.

When William Clark was first recruited, he was designated as an army lieutenant for the Corps. However, Lewis promised him the promotion to captain if he would agree to join the Corps. Thus, he and his men always referred to him as "Captain Clark". Both Lewis and Clark were disturbed that Clark's promotion was delayed. After repeated efforts by Lewis to expedite the matter, he finally gave up trying. When they returned to St. Louis, they were distraught that Clark's promotion had not been authorized.

It was a month later before the president received the letter from Lewis. Meanwhile, he received more disturbing details about Aaron Burr's treasonous activities. Not only had he recruited General James Wilkinson, but now he had added General William Eaton to his dastardly entourage. Since Jefferson had no secretary with whom to share his troubled feelings, he spent a lot of time with Dick and his other mockingbirds. They offered him plenty of opportunity to unload his heavy burdens without any political repercussions.

Lewis wrote to Jefferson that he would have some welcome visitors coming with him to Washington. One was Chief Big White of the Mandan tribe. He first met him two years ago on October 24, 1804. Big White and his 25-member hunting party were the first to welcome him to the Mandan villages. Lewis and Clark found them so hospitable; they built a fort nearby and spent the winter with them. When they were returning from the Pacific, Big White and all his people gave them a rousing reunion party, welcoming them home.

Big White agreed to come to Washington if he could bring his wife, his son, Jessaume, Jessaume's wife and their two sons. Although that would overload the canoes, Lewis gladly welcomed them aboard. He knew the president would be pleased to have some more Indian visitors at the White House.

Charbonneau and his wife, Sacajawea, chose to stay at the Mandan villages when Lewis left for St. Louis. As they said their goodbyes, Lewis settled with Charbonneau giving him $500.33 for his horse, his tepee and his services.

Sacajawea, who was more valuable to the expedition than her husband, received nothing. Perhaps, Lewis felt like the $500 would be shared with her. Nonetheless, it made her feel worthless, like she was not as important as the men, both white and Indian. Was not she the one who carried her child on her back over the Rocky Mountains, trekking the most treacherous territory she could experience? Was not she the one who opened the way for them to befriend her people, the Shoshones, and receive all the horses they needed from them? Was not she the one who provided encouragement and assurance they would reach their destination successfully? Although she received nothing in the way of money or gifts, she at least received hugs and thanks from both Captain Lewis and Captain Clark.

On October 26, 1806, Thomas Jefferson sat down to respond to Lewis' letter.

> "I received, my dear sir, with unspeakable joy your letter of Sep. 23 announcing the return of yourself, Captain Clarke, & your party in good health to St. Louis. The unknown scenes in which you were engaged & the length of time without hearing of you had begun to be felt awfully. Your letter having been 31 days coming, that cannot find you at Louisville & I therefore think it safe to lodge it at Charlottesville. Its only object is to assure you of what you already know my constant affection for you & the joy with which all your friends here will receive you.
>
> "Tell my friend of Mandane also that I have already opened my arms to receive him. Perhaps, while in our neighborhood, it may be gratifying to him, & not otherwise to yourself to take a ride to Monticello and see in what manner I have arranged the tokens of friendship I have received from his country particularly, as well as from other Indian friends: that I am in fact preparing a kind of

Indian Hall. Mr. Dinsmore, my principal workman, will show you everything there. Had you not better bring him by Richmond, Fredericksburg & Alexandria? He will thus see what none of the others have visited & the conveniences of the public stages will facilitate your taking that route. I salute you with sincere affection. Th. Jefferson"[150]

In early November Lewis and Clark left St. Louis. Big White and his family accompanied them, along with some Osage Indians led by Pierre Chouteau of St. Louis, Sergeants Gass and Ordway, Pvt. Labiche and Pvt. Frazier, and Clark's servant, York.

When they arrived in Louisville, Kentucky, on November 9, George Rogers Clark celebrated the arrival of his brother, William, like the prodigal son in his return home. A banquet fit for a king was enjoyed by all the starving men. Afterwards, bonfires were blazing throughout the evening to show appreciation for their unrivaled accomplishment. Four days later, when they later arrived in Frankfort, Kentucky, their return party divided.

Pierre Chouteau and the Osage Indians went directly to Washington. Captain Clark went to Fincastle, Virginia, to see his childhood sweetheart, Julia Hancock. Although he hadn't seen her since she was twelve, his love for her was so strong that he named a river in her honor. Captain Lewis took Big White and his family to Charlottesville, where he introduced them to his mother and family at Locust Hill.

Meanwhile back in Washington, on November 27, the president issued a public warning that "sundry persons, citizens of the U.S. or resident within the same, are conspiring & confederating . . . against the dominions of Spain."[151] With that warning, Jefferson mandated that all military and civil officials in America do what they could to prevent "the carrying on such expedition or enterprise by all lawful means within their power."[152]

One week later, on December 2, 1806, the president delivered his state of the union message to Congress. As he reported about the Corps of Discovery, he wrote,

> "The expedition of Messrs. Lewis and Clarke for exploring the river Missouri, & the best communication from that to the Pacific ocean, has had all the success which could have been expected....In the course of their journey they acquired a knowledge of numerous tribes of Indians hitherto

unknown; they informed themselves of the trade which may be carried on with them, the best channels & positions for it, & they are enabled to give with accuracy the geography of the line they pursued....it is but justice to say that Messrs. Lewis & Clarke, & their brave companions, have, by that arduous service, deserved well of their country."[153]

 Everywhere Lewis went when he returned to Virginia, he was greeted with open arms. Many celebratory dinners and balls honored him and his Indian friends. When he finally arrived in Washington, it was late in the day on December 28. The city was anxiously awaiting his arrival, and gave him and Big White and his family a glorious reception. The next evening Lewis took his Indian friends to the theatre, and during intermission some of them danced on the stage for the amazed audience.

 The Osage Indians arrived with Pierre Chouteau on December 30, when Thomas Jefferson gave them a rousing welcome into the White House. The following day, Chief Big White and his Mandan Indians arrived and were treated royally by the president.

 New Year's Day was reserved especially for Meriwether Lewis. One year ago on this very day, while sitting on the Oregon beach on the Pacific Ocean, Lewis predicted this is the way it would happen. His goal, he recorded in his journal, was to set foot in the White House on January 1, 1807. Mission was accomplished as planned. Tom rejoiced that his long lost son had returned home, and they both shed tears of delight as they melted in each other's arms.

The First Dog in the White House

*"Do you want to know who you are? Don't ask.
Act! Action will delineate and define you."*
Thomas Jefferson

1807

As Thomas Jefferson and Meriwether Lewis sat at the breakfast table on New Year's Day at the White House, they had a joyous reunion. Lewis was overwhelmed with all the delicious items spread before him. The Virginia ham and plum pudding was graced with muffins and corn bread. As they sipped their coffee together, Lewis commented,

"Mister President, what a pleasure it is to have all these fine foods to eat. Many times on our journey, we either went without, or if we had food, it was mighty scarce."

"Lewis, my son, how many times have I asked you not to call me by my title?"

"Please forgive me, Thomas. Having been separated from you for such a long time caused me to forget."

"Yes, Lewis, it seemed much longer than it actually was. I never will have words enough to tell you how much you were missed."

"I share the same sentiment, but I must say I didn't have much idle time to dwell on it." Lewis turned his head to see who or what was whistling at him. Coming from one of the cages hanging in Jefferson's office were the sounds of Dick, the president's prized mockingbird. Lewis quickly recognized the tune as that of "Yankee Doodle". He turned back to look at Jefferson, who sat back rather relaxed with a sheepish look on his face.

"It sounds like you still have your pet bird, Thomas."

"Wrong you are, my dear friend. I have four mockingbirds in my treasury now."

Tom led Lewis into his office, which overlooked the majestic Potomac River. There he revealed to him a cage hanging from each of four windows. He introduced Lewis to three mocking birds he had acquired while he had been on his expedition. They each were named to remind Tom of the dream of his father. One he named "New Orleans"; another he called "St. Louis"; and the last one he named "Pacific." Lewis felt honored that two of the birds made him think of the journey he had recently completed.

As Tom was showing Lewis his mockingbirds, his attention was drawn out the window to a big black ball of fur laying out in his yard. He hadn't seen anything like that since Lewis sent him the bear cubs he displayed on the White House lawn.

"Lewis, what in the name of heaven have you brought with you?"

"What do you mean, Thomas? Are you talking about Seaman?"

"What kind of varmint is that?"

"Nothing but a dog, Sir."

"I've never seen one like that? What breed is it?"

"He's is a Newfoundland. I call him "Seaman" because he thrives in the water. You should see him go after ducks, squirrels and otters as they swim in the rivers. Why, he even goes after deer…"

Jefferson quickly interrupted him. "Lewis, you sound like that dog has been with you a long while."

"That's right, Thomas. He went all the way from Pittsburgh to the Pacific and back with us. He has been my constant companion and faithful sidekick."

"Why didn't you ever tell me about your friend before?"

"I felt like I had more important things to share when I wrote."

"Well, Lewis, you're not going to leave your furry friend outside, are you?"

"You said you don't ever want a dog in the White House."

"Lewis, that's true with most dogs. However, when you have one that travels all the way to the Pacific and back, an exception can be made. Now go fetch Seaman."

As soon as Lewis opened the door, he saw his faithful pet slouched down on the doorstep with his tail wagging wildly and his big brown eyes begging to come in.

Thomas Jefferson

"Come, Seaman," invited Lewis. The dog appeared hesitant, as his eyes were fixed on the president. Appearing to wait for Jefferson's permission, he heard Tom beckon,

"Come on in, Seaman. You're more than welcome here."

As Seaman strode up the steps into the White House, he nudged against his master, beckoning for him to scratch between his ears.

As Tom closed the front door, he reached down and stroked Seaman lovingly until the dog's eyes fastened on his, showing his delight.

"Lewis, let me show you to your room."

"Don't I have the same one?"

"Yes, you do, but I've made some changes." As Tom opened the door to the East Room to show him his quarters, he kept his eyes glued on Lewis to see his reaction.

"Thomas, look at all the decorations in my room!" He was ecstatic. "That will make me feel right at home!" The walls were filled with souvenirs Lewis sent from his western expedition. What Tom couldn't hang on the walls, he displayed on tables strewn throughout the cluttered room.

"Thomas, you can tell there's no first lady in this White House. If there was, there would be no way you could keep all these things stored in that room."

"That's right, Lewis, but since we are like two mice in a church once again, we can keep the place the way it suits two backwoods bachelors."

"I like that, Thomas. No matter what it looks like, it surely beats living out in the bitter cold outdoors or being swarmed by pesky mosquitoes."

"Don't forget about the buffaloes you said invaded your camp at night, as well?"

"I will try to put all that behind me now, Thomas. What a relief to be able to sleep without living in danger."

Seaman made his self right at home in the East Room, finding a corner where a bearskin rug was laying. He claimed that as his bed, as he sniffed it thoroughly with his tail wagging his approval. Lewis and Tom smiled at each other as they saw Seaman making his nest on the bear he helped capture on the journey.

"Lewis, tomorrow Congress will meet to settle with your men what we owe them." Tom said as he cleared one of the wing chairs for a place to sit. "I need you to give me your recommendations." As he paused to give Lewis time for him to find a seat, he asked,

"May I ask you a personal question?"

"What's that, Thomas?"

"Why are you so anxious about sitting? I notice you have been limping around here as if you were in pain. And now, you seem to have a problem wanting to sit down."

"Well, I was hoping you didn't notice. I really didn't want to bring it up. You won't believe me if I tell you."

"I can hardly wait. You can't hold me in such utter suspense."

"Thomas, while on the journey, one of my men shot me."

"I'm glad to see you are still alive. Where were you wounded?"

"In the buttocks, Sir."

"You're surely making that up, Lewis," Tom suggested as he smiled and fought back a guttural laugh.

"I wish I was, Thomas."

Tom couldn't restrain himself any longer. He broke into open hilarity to the point he felt his stomach ache. Lewis found himself laughing along with the president, although he didn't believe his painful experience was a bit funny.

"Lewis, last year was a dismal year for me. Today is the first day of 1807, and I needed a good story to lighten my mood. Please tell me the details."

With all their laughter, Seaman was awakened from his slumber and waddled over to join the men. Lewis, realizing his dog must be thirsty, beckoned one of Tom's slaves to bring a large bucket of water. He emphasized "large" because he knew how Seaman loved his water.

As Tom was stroking the Newfoundland's large furry ears, he asked Seaman in a friendly tone of voice,

"Why are you slobbering so much, boy? Your drool is getting all over my breeches. That's alright, though. I don't mind a bit."

"Thomas, he'll sure keep you wet with his slobber. And wait 'til you see how much he sheds."

"I can testify to that, Lewis. Look at all the hair I have in my hand by just stroking his back and ears."

When Seaman saw the bucket full of water, he was quick to consume it, slopping it noisily until it was empty.

Lewis returned to the subject at hand, telling Jefferson how Pierre Cruzatte accidentally shot him while they were hunting elk together. A bullet from Cruzatte's gun was found lodged in Lewis' buttocks, having penetrated from one side out the other. It was all an accident, but I was upset when Cruzatte denied he did it, blaming it on the Indians. He revealed to Jefferson how painful his return back to St. Louis was. He was forced to lie on his stomach in extreme discomfort and open humiliation all the way down the Missouri River. After the two men settled down from their amusement over the situation, Tom asked,

"Lewis, when you make your recommendation for the compensation of your men, what will you say about Cruzatte?"

"I will ask the same for him as I do for the others. He was a faithful member of the team. What he did was an accident. I won't hold that against him."

"I commend you for that response, Lewis. Please let me know what you believe your men's awards should be."

Lewis paused for a moment to gain his composure. "I promised the men they would receive an equal compensation of lands as that of a Revolutionary War soldier."

"I believe that would be 320 acres. Is that what you figure, Lewis?"

"I agree. I also have some monetary awards to recommend. I am still working on those figures. I hope Private Labiche can receive extra compensation. Besides his regular duties, he served as our translator from French to English."

"Anyone else, Lewis?"

"John Shields needs more, because he kept our guns in working order. The Fields brothers should get more because they did more work than the others."

"Can you think of anyone else?"

"Oh, yes, I mustn't forget George Drouillard, who was a man of much merit. He helped us a lot with his sign language and was an excellent hunter and woodsman. I signed him on for $25 a month, but I want to recommend $30 instead."

"What about the Indian woman who helped you get to the Pacific?"

"That was Sacajawea, Sir. No award was promised her. She only went with us because we hired her worthless husband, Charbonneau. I promised him $25 a month as an interpreter, but I don't think he earned it. Nevertheless, I paid him $500.33 for his horse, his tepee and his services. Since he's a French Canadian and not an enlisted man, he hopes to get his payment in cash."

"What about William Clark's slave?"

"York was his name. He wasn't hired to go with us. He only agreed to go because Captain Clark required that of him."

"Did he do anything to help you get to the Pacific?"

"Thomas, when we went over the Rockies, we might not have made it without him. He could lift twice his weight and pull more than any white man on our expedition."

"What did he get as a reward?"

"He received nothing. Apparently he thought Clark would give him his freedom as compensation. He asked that of him, but Clark refused."

"Lewis, this truly disturbs me. Regarding slavery, I have said repeatedly, 'This abomination must have an end, and there is a superior bench reserved in heaven for those who hasten it.' Life just hasn't been fair to those of African descent. Why shouldn't York, although a mere slave, be justly rewarded?"

"I agree wholeheartedly, Thomas. But that was all in the hands of Clark, being his master."

"That's true. What's done is done, but it sure doesn't make it right."

On the following day, January 2, 1807, the House of Representatives named Willis Alston, Jr., of North Carolina as the chairman of the committee to recommend compensations for members of the Corps of Discovery. Meriwether Lewis brought his recommendations to the committee. William Clark could not be present because he was detained by his beloved Julia Hancock in Virginia, whom he hoped to marry.

Alston carefully considered Lewis' suggestions, but he discarded some of them. He agreed with each man receiving 320 acres each, but he didn't accept anything additional for Labiche, Shields, Drouillard or the Field brothers. He was generous, however, in offering double pay for all. That would provide $5 per month for privates; $7 for corporals; $8 for sergeants; $30 for Lieutenant Clark; and $40 for Captain Lewis. The total compensation for the expedition to the Pacific would be $11,000. Alston also recommended giving Lewis and Clark 1600 acres of property each. Although Alston's bill was hotly debated by the House, on February 28, it passed by a 62 to 23 margin and was quickly approved by the Senate.

Washington was bitterly cold in January, but Seaman didn't mind. Lewis knew his pet couldn't stay cooped up inside the house, no matter how big it was. He loved the outdoors, and the colder it was, the better he liked it. He thrived in ice and snow especially. With all the wide open spaces in Washington at that time and the nearby Potomac River, Seaman felt right at home. His only problem was he couldn't find any grizzlies, buffalo or elk grazing on the grounds. Perhaps, he could find him a squirrel or a rabbit to chase.

One of the first items on Lewis' agenda when he returned from the Pacific was to attend a ball held in his and Clark's honor. It would be held on January 14, hopefully when William Clark could pull himself away from Julia Hancock long enough to attend. Pierre Chouteau of St. Louis and Chief Big White of the Mandan tribe accompanied Lewis to the celebration. Clark was absent, still being detained by his fiancée, and most of the accolades were directed toward Lewis, even proposing to change the name of the Columbia to the Lewis River.

Meriwether felt uncomfortable with all this fanfare about himself because he believed that William Clark deserved equal treatment and recognition for his efforts. He continued to press for Clark to be promoted to "Captain", the title Lewis insisted on calling him. However, Secretary of War Henry Dearborn continued to block such a promotion.

Meanwhile, at the White House, Lewis learned that the president's son-in-law, Thomas Mann Randolph, Jr., was living in an upstairs bedroom. Serving in Congress as a U. S. Representative from Virginia, he lived with Jefferson whenever he was in Washington. His wife, Martha, spent the last winter with her father in the White House, but this year she felt she was best needed in Virginia to take care of her home at Edgehill as well as her father's at Monticello. She also had to care for a house full of children, including Jimmy, who celebrated his first birthday on January 17. Tom remembered him being born in the White House the year before and wished he could have been in Virginia to congratulate him personally.

Martha's husband, Mann, kept the president and Lewis briefed each day as to the deliberations of Congress. Around the supper table each evening, the three of them found it difficult to ignore political discussions. The major issue of the day did not involve Lewis and Clark, but rather Aaron Burr. For the past year, he had been conspiring against the president to wage war against the United States.

"Wait a minute," said Lewis, raising his voice in utter amazement, "Was that the same Burr who was your vice president?"

"That's right," offered Mann.

"Wasn't he also the one who killed Alexander Hamilton in a duel?"

"Yes, he's the one," Tom slowly admitted.

"He's always been a thorn in the side of our president," Mann was getting more agitated by the minute.

Thomas Jefferson then shared with Lewis his account of how Aaron Burr had been tormenting him the past year. He tried to believe the conspiracy had been crushed by the beginning of 1807. What he didn't know was that Burr was still plotting his treasonous activities. General Wilkinson had abandoned Burr's list of supporters last October, sending a post to Jefferson regarding Burr's evil intentions. During January, in the midst of their discussions about this odorous scoundrel, Aaron Burr was arrested near New Orleans for treason.

That prompted Jefferson to deliver a special message to Congress on January 22. At the heart of that document was the reference to the letter of General Wilkinson, which was revealed in one of the paragraphs presented to Congress.

> "The General's letter, which came to hand on the 25th of November, as has been mentioned, and some other information received a few days earlier, when brought together developed Burr's general designs, different parts of which only had been revealed to different informants. It appeared that he contemplated two distinct objects, which might be carried on either jointly or separately, and either the one or the other first, as circumstances should direct. One of these was the severance of the Union of these States by the Alleghany Mountains; the other an attack on Mexico. A third object was provided, merely ostensible, to wit, the settlement of a pretended purchase of a tract of country on the Washita claimed by a Baron Bastrop. That was to serve as the pretext for all his preparations, an allurement for such followers as really wished to acquire settlements in that country and a cover under which to retreat in the event of a final discomfiture of both branches of his real design."[154]

While Jefferson was confident that Burr was imprisoned until he stood trial for treason, he flew into a rage when it was revealed that the grand jury had released him. After receiving notification of that, he called Lewis into his office to release his emotions.

"Lewis, would you help me understand what I've just read?"

Lewis read the post silently, trying his best to digest it. "Thomas, it says the jury declared Burr 'not guilty of any crime or misdemeanor against the United States.'"

"How in the name of God could the grand jury determine his innocence without all the evidence? I wasn't asked to testify! What kind of trial could they have had?"

"Thomas, what makes it even worse is that the jury condemned the arrest. It called those responsible for capturing him 'the enemies of our glorious Constitution.'"

"Enemies of the Constitution! I should call James Madison in here to see what he thinks of me being an enemy of the Constitution!"

The more Jefferson talked about this, the more riled he became. Lewis witnessed him prancing the room like a lion with one arm held behind him. He knew whenever Tom walked like that; he was in a somber frame of mind and quite determined to make some changes.

"Burr is on the loose again, having demanded his release. Lewis, I will do whatever I can to find him and bring him to trial, if I have to go after him myself."

"Hopefully, that won't me necessary. You have notified Congress about Burr's treasonous activities. I would suggest we wait on further developments."

"Speaking of Congress, Mann didn't attend the meetings today because he is too weak to move. He has come down with a dreadful cold that is emitting a fever."

"Thanks for informing me of that, Thomas. You must remember that I doctored our men while we were on our expedition. I learned most of what I know from my mother."

"That's right, Lewis. How well I remember her going from one house to another in our neighborhood helping sick folks with her amazing remedies. I always admired her."

"You don't know how much I have missed her and long to be with her in the near future, Thomas."

"Hopefully, it won't be long. We just have to wait for Congress to recess. Usually, that will be about springtime."

After Congress received official word from Jefferson, another warrant was issued for Burr's arrest. He was recaptured in mid-February in present-day Alabama. After being in Fort Stoddert for two weeks, he was escorted to Richmond, Virginia, to stand trial for treason. Heavily guarded by nine men, his thousand-mile trip to Richmond was conducted on horseback arriving on March 26.

While Aaron Burr was on his way to stand trial, on March 3, Jefferson signed a bill abolishing the slave trade, making it illegal in the United States. He knew it wouldn't take effect until the next January 1. That would be the earliest date the Constitution would allow it. Article 1 Section 9 of the Constitution read in part:

"The Migration or Importation of such Persons as any of the States now existing shall think proper to admit shall not be prohibited by the Congress prior to the Year one thousand eight hundred and eight..."[155]

When Thomas Jefferson signed the bill on March 3, he couldn't wait for it to take effect. By 1808, he finally would see the abolishment of the abominable practice he had been fighting since he first entered office as a young burgess in Virginia. That was nearly forty years ago when he was only 25. Although it took all these years of strenuous deliberations to accomplish that, Tom was pleased to see if finally coming to an end. Although he knew that would not end slavery, at least it was the first step in the right direction. If no more slaves could legally be transported from abroad, then the abominable institution may eventually disintegrate. Hopefully, he hoped to live long enough to see slavery in the United States abolished forever.

While Burr was on his long arduous trek to stand trial in Richmond, Jefferson appointed Meriwether Lewis governor of the Territory of Upper Louisiana (Congress recently had divided the Louisiana Territory. The Territory of Orleans would be to the south of the northern boundary line of present Louisiana. The Territory of Upper Louisiana included everything north of that, St. Louis being its principal city. Although he was honored by that gesture from the president, Lewis didn't assume his duties in St. Louis until a year later).

On March 2, the Senate approved Lewis as a new governor. Therefore, he resigned his commission with the army. Mann, Jr. had taken a turn for the worse, with his fever rising and falling. The president's physician kept coming to the White House to bleed the infection from his veins. Nothing seemed to be working for him. Lewis stayed with Mann constantly, applying the herbal remedies his mother taught him. In the process, Mann's virus spread to Lewis, with both of them suffering. Next, it spread to the president. Tom had kept his daughter, Martha, informed about her husband's demise. Once he wrote that "the quantity of blood taken from him occasions him to recover strength slowly."[156] After all three became ill together, he notified her that "we are but a collection of invalids."[157]

William Clark finally pried himself free of Julia Hancock long enough to return to Washington in early March. He came to gather the land warrants and money for his men. From there, he would take them to St. Louis to distribute them. When he arrived, he was shocked to see his partner in the Corps stricken with illness and incapacitated.

"Lewis, you traveled all across the country and suffered the worst conditions any man could endure. You went through all that as a virile man who could withstand any disease that came your way. Now that you live in the splendor of the White House, you become sicker than a dog."

"Clark, don't be comparing me to my dog. He's in a lot better shape than I am." Lewis whispered these words weakly from his sick bed.

"Where is Seaman? Whatever happened to him?"

"The president said he could stay in the house, but he preferred the outdoors. You should see him romping through the woods and chasing whatever varmint he can find. You will find him often swimming in the Potomac."

Clark saw Lewis' voice getting weaker every word he uttered. He decided to take care of his business at hand while Lewis was still alive. Lewis gave him the land warrants and $6,896 in cash as payment for the enlisted men. Clark had to get Big White back home. After he and his family got to St. Louis, perhaps Nathaniel Pryor would take him up the Missouri to the Mandan village.

Dr. Benjamin Rush of Philadelphia had sent Lewis some pills for his illness. Sharing them with Tom and Mann, all three men gradually recovered and were back on their feet. Lewis recalled all the blood the doctor had extracted from Mann, all with no results. He was amazed at how those pills had accomplished much more than the doctor's bleeding a patient nearly to death.

Spring had sprung in Washington, and Congress was taking her recess. Jefferson knew he must travel to Richmond for the Burr treason trial. Lewis, as governor of Upper Louisiana, needed to be in St. Louis, the capital city of his new government. However, before he left the eastern seaboard, he planned to go north to Philadelphia.

"Lewis, when do you think you will arrive in St. Louis?" Tom was busy packing Dick and his three other mockingbirds in his carriage.

"I don't rightly know, Sir."

"Well, I can't emphasize the importance of you being there to govern. I hear the natives are restless there, and people tend to take the law into their own hands whenever they don't have a leader at the helm."

"I understand that, Thomas. However, I must take care of my business in Philadelphia before I return."

"Please refresh my mind as to why you must go there."

"First, and foremost, I must try to get my journal and maps published. You have emphasized to me how important it is to get these into print. I am getting pressure on all sides to make sure these are distributed into the hands of the people."

"That's right, Lewis. You must give due diligence to that. I almost forgot. I guess I just have Burr's trial overwhelming me now. What else must you do in the city of brotherly love?"

"The American Philosophical Society has some meetings planned for me." While Lewis continued the conversation, he was gathering his belongings for his trip north, tossing them helter-skelter into his coach.

"I am pleased you want to meet with their members. Your trip to the Pacific was as much their dream as it was mine. They trained you for the journey and then supported you and Clark every step of the way." Tom's slaves had put everything on his carriage that he would need at Monticello for the next season. His four bay horses were snorting, indicating they were anxious to get going. His black coachman was sitting in place; patiently waiting for the president's parting gestures at the White House.

Seaman just returned from his morning jaunt down to the Potomac and back. He was panting heavily and slobber was dripping freely on his feet. He had no idea where he was going, but as long as it was with his master, it was alright with him. Tom reached down and stroked his final goodbyes on Seaman's big ball of fur and gave him some parting adieus.

"Lewis, I want to leave you with some advice I have found helpful."

"What's that, Thomas?"

"A mind always employed is always happy. Although we are parting once again for another unknown time, we can be happy if we stay busy. I want to advise you as a father to a son. Watch that alcohol doesn't take you down the path of destruction. You will have many occasions to celebrate your accomplishments in Philadelphia. Just be careful that your parties don't distract you from your real purpose in life."

"I will do my best to follow your wise counsel, Thomas."

"Don't forget to write and let me know when you arrive in St. Louis. I know you are needed there as soon as you can make it."

"You have my word. I will arrive there as soon as possible." The two men gave their parting hugs and handshakes as they climbed into their separate coaches and headed toward their respective destinations

Aaron Burr's trial began at the end of March. Jefferson was delighted the trial would be held in Richmond. How fitting it would be held in the building he designed and in the city where he had chosen to remove the capital from Williamsburg. He had every reason to believe that all the odds against Burr were in his favor.

His only obstacle was the judge who would rule in the trial. John Marshall, the Chief Justice of the U.S. Supreme Court, came from his office in Richmond to preside over one of the most significant trials in American history. Jefferson was enraged when he heard this was happening to him. Marshall had proven to be his enemy. The president still carried bitter feelings for former President John Adams' midnight appointment of Marshall just prior to Jefferson's first day in office six years ago.

Although the trial would go down as one of the most significant in history, within days, a verdict was rendered on April 1, 1807. District Attorney George Hay brought the government's case before the court calling for Aaron Burr to be charged with treason and high misdemeanor. He brought evidence against Burr for treason, showing how he planned to capture New Orleans and make it the capital of his proposed empire. He was also charged with high misdemeanor for sending a military expedition against territories belonging to Spain.

To represent Burr's defense was Edmund Randolph, a former Attorney General and the Secretary of State under George Washington. He argued that no act of treason was committed by his client. Burr chose to take the stand in his defense, pleading his innocence to the charges against him. He emphasized that the grand jury of the Mississippi Territory already had exonerated him. He then stirred the emotions of the judge when he complained about how cruelly he had been treated in the Richmond jail. While he was being held over for trial, he claimed he suffered mental anguish when he had been denied the use of any writing supplies which were needed to write his daughter, Theodosia.

Chief Justice Marshall was quick to render his opinion on the treason charge, claiming that the government didn't have sufficient evidence against Burr. Therefore, he declared him "not guilty". Thomas Jefferson was furious over such a determination. He felt like he had been played the fool, right there in front of all his high-level colleagues and political cronies.

Having dismissed the treason charge did not end Burr's trial. He still had to answer the accusations of high misdemeanor against him, and Marshall set his bail at $10,000. That would involve a jury trial and would be strung out through the summer of 1807.

Thomas Jefferson worked diligently to gather any and all evidence against Burr. He leaned on the assistance of James Madison and

Andrew Jackson. George Hay, the prosecuting U.S. Attorney, compiled a list of over 140 witnesses. General James Wilkinson, who had been personally involved with Burr, sought to uncover other witnesses for the prosecution.

On May 22, Jefferson was back in the court room, as the trial of Aaron Burr continued in Richmond. Joining Chief Justice Marshall was U.S. District Judge Cyrus Griffin of Virginia. The president was pleased to see a friendly face sitting next to Marshall. Cyrus Griffin had served with Jefferson in the Continental Congress and was the sixteenth and last president of that political body. When George Washington was elected first President of the United States, Griffin willingly stepped down from his office in favor of the new regime. He began serving as U.S. District Court Judge while Jefferson was governor of Virginia in 1779. Now, eighteen years later, they would face each other again. Hopefully, the president hoped this would tilt the scale in his favor.

George Hay led a team of four lawyers representing the prosecution. Edmund Randolph's defense team included five attorneys. He may as well have added another because Aaron Burr insisted on cross examining most of the prosecution's witnesses himself. On June 15, General James Wilkinson finally arrived in Richmond to stand before the grand jury as the key witness on behalf of the prosecution. Washington Irving, always looking for a good story, watched as the General "strutted into court" and "stood for a moment swelling like a turkey-cock."[158]

When Wilkinson concluded his testimony, the grand jury concluded that Burr was guilty of both treason and high misdemeanor. However, as the trial continued Justice Marshall turned the tables on the prosecution. On September 1, he ruled some key evidence as inadmissible. With instructions that favored the defense, Marshall sent the case to the jury. With the limitations the judge gave to the jury, the members felt they had no other choice than to declare Burr "not guilty". Some of its members felt like the decision would have gone the other way if different directions were given by Justice Marshall.

Thomas Jefferson had high hopes the grand jury would turn that case against Burr. But as he feared, Chief Justice Marshall found a way to oppose the president. Jefferson couldn't hide his emotions, infuriated over the outcome. He complained about the bias of the judge and how he could arbitrarily sway a jury. "It now appears we have no law but the will of the judge."[159] He continued his assertions when he wrote to General Wilkinson, "The scenes which have been acted at Richmond are such as have never been exhibited in any country, where all regard to public character has not yet been thrown off. They are equivalent to a proclamation of impunity to every traitorous combination which may be formed to destroy the Union."[160]

As for Aaron Burr, although he was acquitted, he had been disgraced. He felt he had no other choice but to flee the country and sail to England and then later to France. Wherever he went, he continued to conjure up some treasonous plans against America.

Thomas Jefferson returned to Monticello defeated. Filled with anger and vengeance, he also suffered shame and disgrace. How would he now face his family and his neighbors? Would he ever have the confidence of his nation to follow his leadership any longer? Those were all perplexing questions that bombarded Tom on his way home.

Contrary to Jefferson's pessimistic appraisal of what public opinion would be of him, he was amazed to find just the opposite. When he returned to Monticello, everyone was there to give him a welcome home celebration. His family, friends and neighbors all congratulated him for what he thought was a dismal failure. When he returned to Washington in November for the next session of Congress, he found the majority of congressmen honored him as a hero. They felt that Jefferson's exposure of Burr's conspiracy saved the nation from war. Some felt so enraged at Chief Justice Marshall they tried to amend the Constitution to limit the power of the judicial branch.

Although members of Jefferson's majority Republican party urged him to serve a third term, they couldn't convince him to stay. Long before the Burr trial, Tom felt he had enough of politics and longed to retire to Monticello. After the disturbing result in Richmond, Jefferson was more convinced than ever that he wanted no more of Washington. At the beginning of 1809, he passed his torch to James Madison, the next President of the United States.

As for William Clark, he failed to receive the promotion to captain that Lewis promised him. Secretary of War Henry Dearborn blocked all efforts that both Lewis and Jefferson recommended for such a promotion. What the president couldn't do with the U.S. Army, he knew he had authority to do with the state militias. Therefore, in March of 1807, he appointed Clark to a much higher office than "captain". He made him a Brigadier General of the Upper Louisiana Militia and the Superintendent of Indian Affairs over the same jurisdiction. After having received his 1600 acres from the government, in January, 1808,

Clark married his childhood sweetheart, Julia Hancock, in Fincastle, Virginia.

Sacajawea still lived at the Mandan village with her husband, Charbonneau. While Clark was traveling with them, he was disturbed to see how her husband abused her both verbally and physically. From the time of her son's birth, Sacajawea noticed how Clark took a liking to him, nicknaming him "Pomp". When the expedition was completed, Clark encouraged the Indian guide to send Pomp to St. Louis, where he would put him in boarding school. He even offered to take care of Sacajawea also. He wrote a letter to her saying this:

> "As to your little Son (my boy Pomp) you well know my fondness for him and my anxiety to take and raise him as my own child. I once more tell you if you will bring your son Baptists to me I will educate him and treat him as my own child--I do not forget the promise (sic) which I made to you and Shall now repeat (sic) them that you may be certain-- Charbono, if you wish to live with the white people, and will come to me, I will give you a piece of land and furnish you with horses, cows, & hogs . . . Wishing you and your family great success (sic) & with anxious expectations of seeing my little dancing boy Baptists I shall remain your friend."[161]

At first she refused, but after he married, she changed her mind. William Clark was thankful that Pomp would now be separated from all the abuse given by his father. In 1811, Sacajawea would give birth to a daughter named "Lizette". However, due to her death in her mid-twenties from typhoid fever the following year, she wouldn't be able to raise her. According to the Orphan's Court Records in St. Louis, on August 11, 1813, William Clark was listed as the legal guardian of both Jean Baptiste and Lizette Charbonneau, only possible legally at that time if both parents were dead.

As for York, in 1811 William Clark finally granted his request to be freed. York asked for that favor when he returned from the expedition to the Pacific. His expectations were inexcusably squelched when he didn't receive his freedom as a reward for his faithful service to the Corps of Discovery. All the other men were amply rewarded with land and money, but he got nothing. When Clark later released him, he gave him a wagon with six horses. That he used to establish a freighting enterprise going from Richmond, Kentucky to Nashville, Tennessee. He died of cholera in 1832.

The remaining career of Meriwether Lewis would be short-lived. Rather than take Jefferson's pungent advice to get to St. Louis as soon as possible to assume his position of governor, Lewis did just the opposite. He went to Philadelphia to get his journal of the expedition published and to give a dutiful report to the American Philosophical Society. From the time of his arrival, he was celebrated as a gallant hero. He went from one gala affair to another, all of which had liquor flowing freely. Lewis was still single and lonely, bothered that his friend, Clark, was getting married, and why not him? In the midst of his parties in his honor, he courted several ladies whom he hoped to wed, but none of them worked out. Meanwhile, Lewis became addicted to alcohol as the splendor of his achievements was diminishing.

Sometime after the first of 1808, Lewis finally made it to St. Louis, where he began his new career as governor. However, he failed miserably in that endeavor. There was nothing that could compare to his heroics and the euphoria he experienced leading the Corps of Discovery to the Pacific and back. He ran up a $4,000 debt as governor that he couldn't pay. He continued his drinking problem and suffered from what some called a bout of malaria. During the early hours of October 11, 1809, at the young age of 35, Lewis was found dead at a cabin on the Natchez Trace in Tennessee. Bullets had entered both his head and his chest. Whether he died by suicide of self-inflicted wounds or by murder is still inconclusive. Nevertheless, when Jefferson received that shocking news, he went into a self-imposed isolation. He followed the same routine of remorse and depression as when he lost his wife and then later his daughter, Maria.

Meriwether Lewis was the son he never had. He was the one who fulfilled his father's dream. Tom's thoughts returned to his childhood days when he listened outside his father's study. Five men had created the Loyal Company for the ultimate purpose of capturing the West and going all the way to the Pacific. Tom had to wait over fifty years and become President of the United States before his father's dream could be fulfilled. However, one added ingredient was needed to achieve Jefferson's life's ambition. That was Meriwether Lewis. Thomas Jefferson knew without his faithful dedication and dogged determination and strong leadership abilities, his father's dream may never have been fulfilled. Jefferson retired from public office in 1809 and spent his retirement years building the University of Virginia and continuing to build his beloved Monticello. Tom boldly asserted, "All my wishes end where I hope my days will end, at Monticello."[162]

His wishes were fulfilled during his seventeen years of retirement. Thomas Jefferson's Monticello has provided this fitting tribute to the Father of Independence. "On June 24, 1826, Jefferson's physician was called to his bedside because of an illness, and his condition worsened until he lost consciousness on July 2. From then on, Jefferson slept fitfully, waking only to inquire whether it were yet the Fourth of July. Around noon on the fourth -- the Jubilee of Independence -- Jefferson died in bed at the age of eighty-three. Coincidentally, his friend, colleague, and co-signer of the Declaration of Independence, John Adams, died just hours later that day."[163]

Thomas Jefferson personally designed his own tombstone to memorialize only his three most cherished accomplishments. Those were as: "Author of the Declaration of American Independence, of the Statute of Virginia for Religious Freedom, and Father of the University of Virginia".[164] Although those were the most significant to Jefferson, yet they only represented a small sampling of that which portrayed him as a man ahead of his time.

As a young boy, Tom had begun dreaming of this future nation. Listening through the door of his father's study, he was inspired by five men who were passionate about their vision. They planned how they would one day capture the West, going all the way to the Pacific. As Thomas Jefferson came to the end of his life, he was laid to rest with the full assurance he had fulfilled his father's dream. Furthermore, he died with the satisfaction that his ideas of religious liberty had become the framework of America.

In a letter of reply to a Baptist Address in 1807, Thomas Jefferson gave the following summation of his belief about religious liberty. "Among the most inestimable of our blessings is that ... of liberty to worship our Creator in the way we think most agreeable to His will; a liberty deemed in other countries incompatible with good government and yet proved by our experience to be its best support."

An Addendum:
The Thornton Legacy

The foundation of Fredericksburg, Virginia

The intermarriage of the Thorntons into the members of the Loyal Company and the family of George Washington

Although adventurous men ran the Loyal Company, they had the unwavering support of two notable tenacious women. They were the daughters of Colonel Francis Thornton, Jr. and Mary Taliaferro (pronounced "Toliver"). As their mother's name implied, they had Italian blood flowing through their predominant English veins. Mary was the daughter of Colonel John "The Ranger" Taliaferro, a burgess and justice in Essex County, Virginia. He settled on the Powhatan Plantation in that county, the birthplace of his daughter.

William Thornton was the immigrant ancestor of his family who came from Yorkshire, England, to Virginia sometime before 1651. The Thorntons were a prominent family of planters in Essex County near Fredericksburg, Virginia. Their home called "Snow Creek" was on a land grant of some 700 acres. Eventually, an 8,000 acre land grant became their home, much of which became Fredericksburg. By 1780, Francis Thornton III was living in his new home called "Fall Hill." (That home is still in existence - listed on the Virginia Landmarks Register and the National Register of Historic Places).

Francis Thornton, Jr., grandson of his immigrant ancestor, was justice of Essex County and a burgess for Spotsylvania County between 1723 and 1726, after it was divided from Essex County.

Among the many children of Francis and Mary (Taliaferro) Thornton, Jr. was a son and two daughters, Elizabeth and Mildred. They appeared to be the youngest of their siblings but were among the most influential. Their brother, Lieutenant Colonel Francis Thornton II was a leader of the militia, a justice and a member of the powerful House of Burgesses, all representing Spotsylvania County, Virginia. He and two of his brothers married three daughters of Roger Gregory and Mildred Washington, the aunt of George Washington. Thus, by the Thornton brothers marrying the Gregory Sisters, they became part of the future first president's family.

Elizabeth Thornton was born ca. 1717, and her sister, Mildred, followed her in 1721, both born in Snow Creek in what was then Spotsylvania County. They became key players in the Loyal Company because of their marriages to two of the primary partners.

Elizabeth Thornton was the older of the two, and in 1735, she married Col. Thomas Meriwether, one of the wealthiest men of Virginia. He had descended from Nicholas Meriwether, who came from Wales to Jamestown, Virginia, around 1652. He was a friend of King George II, who gave him thousands of acres of valuable land. Just prior to his marriage to Elizabeth, the king granted her husband 17,952 acres in Albemarle County, where the Thorntons built their Cloverfields estate.

Col. Thomas Meriwether was one of the five men in the Loyal Company. One of the other visionaries in that project was Dr. Thomas Walker, who found Elizabeth Thornton's younger sister, Mildred, much to his liking. She previously had married Nicholas Meriwether, the cousin of the husband of her sister, Elizabeth. Since Nicholas died shortly after their marriage, he left Mildred who was an attractive widow who still had not reached adulthood. Now she was wealthy, having inherited his Meriwether properties. Therefore, she brought with her in marriage the 15,000 acre estate on which Dr. Thomas Walker would build his impressive Castle Hill mansion. That would help to establish Dr. Thomas and Mildred Walker as one of the most prominent families of Albemarle County.

Descendants of Mildred Thornton

1. MILDRED[1] THORNTON *(COL. FRANCIS[A], FRANCIS[B], WILLIAM[C], WILLIAM[D])* was born 21 Mar 1721 in Snow Creek, Spotsylvania Co., VA, and died 16 Nov 1778 in Castle Hill, Albemarle Co., VA. She married (1) NICHOLAS MERIWETHER Abt. 1738 in Virginia, son of Col. NICHOLAS MERIWETHER and ELIZABETH CRAWFORD. He was born July 11, 1699 in New Kent Co., Virginia, and died in 1739 in Virginia. She married (2) DR. THOMAS WALKER 22 Jun 1741, son of THOMAS WALKER and SUSANNA PEACHEY. He was born 25 Jan 1715 in Rye Field, Walkerton, King & Queen Co., VA, and died 19 Mar 1794 in Castle Hill, Albemarle Co., VA.

Child of MILDRED THORNTON and NICHOLAS MERIWETHER is:

    i.   MILDRED THORNTON[2] MERIWETHER, b. 19 May 1739, Snow Creek, Spotsylvania Co., VA; d. 16 Nov 1779, Castle Hill, Albemarle Co., VA; m. JOHN SYME, Abt. 1753, VA; b. Abt. Dec 1727, Hanover Co., VA.

Children of MILDRED THORNTON and DR. WALKER are:

    ii.   MARY "MOLLY"[2] WALKER, b. 24 Jul 1742, Castle Hill, Albemarle Co., VA; d. 09 Feb 1824 Albemarle Co., VA; m. COL. NICHOLAS MERIWETHER LEWIS, 02 Nov 1758, Castle Hill, Albemarle Co., VA; b. 19 Jan 1728, "Belvoir", Louisa Co., VA or Albemarle Co., VA; d. 08 Dec 1808, "The Farm", Albemarle Co., VA.

    iii.   COL. JOHN** "JACK" WALKER, b. 13 Feb 1744, Castle Hill, Albemarle Co., VA; d. 02 Dec 1809, near Madison Mills, Orange Co., VA; m. ELIZABETH "BETSY" MOORE, 06 Jun 1764, Chelsea, King William Co., VA; b. 21 Oct 1746, "Chelsea", King William Co., VA; d. 10 Sep 1809, Belvoir, Albemarle Co., VA.

    iv.   SUSANNA "SUSAN" THORNTON "SUKEY" WALKER, b. 25 Dec 1747, Castle Hill, Albemarle Co., VA; d. Bet. 19 - 26 Feb 1808, Elim (Meander) Plantation, Madison Co., VA; m. REV. HENRY "HARRY" FRY, 16 Jun 1764, Albermarle Co., VA; b. 19 Oct 1738, Alberene, Albemarle, Virginia; d. 07 Aug 1823, Elim (Meander) Plantation, Madison Co., VA.

    v.   CAPT. THOMAS** WALKER, JR., b. 17 Mar 1749, Castle Hill, Albemarle Co., VA; d. 1798, Albemarle Co., VA; m. MARGARETE HOOPS, 1772, Albermarle Co., VA; b. 1754, Carlisle, Pennsylvania; d. 1811, Albemarle Co., VA.

    vi.   LUCY WALKER, b. 05 May 1751, Castle Hill, Albemarle Co., VA or Pen Parke, Albemarle Co.; d. 22 Apr 1825, Pen Park, Albemarle

Co., VA; m. LIEUT. DR. GEORGE** GILMER, JR., 27 Aug 1767, The Glebe, Albemarle Co., VA; b. 19 Jan 1741, Williamsburg, VA; d. 29 Nov 1795, Pen Park, Albemarle Co., VA.

vii. ELIZABETH SIMMS WALKER, b. 01 Aug 1753, Castle Hill, Albemarle Co., VA; d. 25 Dec 1792, Albemarle Co., VA; m. REV. MATTHEW** MAURY, 17 Dec 1775, Albermarle Co., VA; b. 10 Sep 1744, Prince William Co., VA; d. 16 May 1808, Cismont, Albemarle Co., VA.

viii. CHARLES SAMUEL WALKER, b. 1754, Castle Hill, Albemarle Co., VA; d. early death possibility.

ix. MILDRED "MILLY" WALKER, b. 05 Jun 1755, Castle Hill, Albemarle Co., VA; d. Shelby Co., KY; m. JOSEPH HORNSBY; d. Shelby Co., KY.

x. SARAH WALKER, b. 28 May 1758, Castle Hill, Albemarle Co., VA; m. COL. REUBEN LINDSAY.

xi. MARTHA WALKER, b. 02 May 1760, Castle Hill, Albemarle Co., VA; m. GEORGE DIVERS; b. Framington plantation, Albemarle Co., VA.

xii. REUBEN WALKER, b. 1762, Castle Hill, Albemarle Co., VA; d. infancy; m. MARY RANDOLPH LEWIS.

xiii. WILLIS (WILLIAM) HENRY WALKER, b. 1761, Castle Hill, Albemarle Co., VA; d. early death possibility.

xiv. HON. FRANCIS** WALKER, b. 22 Jun 1764, Castle Hill, Albemarle Co., VA; d. Mar 1806, Castle Hill, Albemarle Co., VA; m. JANE BYRD NELSON, 1798, Nelson House, Yorktown, VA; b. 1775, Nelson House, Yorktown, VA; d. 1808, Castle Hill, Albemarle Co., VA.

xv. PEACHY WALKER, b. 06 Feb 1767, Castle Hill, Albemarle Co., VA; d. 28 Oct 1811, Danville, Kentucky; m. LT. JOSHUA** FRY, 01 Sep 1783, Castle Hill, Albemarle Co., VA; b. 01 Sep 1763, Albemarle Co., VA; d. Abt. 1839, Danville, Kentucky.

xvi. JAMES WALKER, b. 1771, Castle Hill, Albemarle Co., VA.

xvii. JUDITH MILDRED WALKER, b. 1776, Castle Hill, Albemarle Co., VA.

xviii. JANE SUSANNA WALKER, b. 1778, Castle Hill, Albemarle Co., VA; d. 30 Aug 1815, Madison, VA; m. WESLEY THORNTON FRY, 25 Jan 1798, Madison, Virginia; b. 25 Mar 1779, Spotsylvania Co., VA; d. 15 Mar 1863, Virginia.

** *Revolutionary patriots – soldier or supplier*

References Consulted

1. Jefferson's Religious Beliefs, Thomas Jefferson's Monticello, accessed July 23, 2012, http://www.monticello.org/site/research-and-collections/jeffersons-religious-beliefs
2. Shadwell, Thomas Jefferson's Monticello, accessed July 23, 2012, http://www.monticello.org/site/research-and-collections/shadwell
3. Bo Perrin, Black Robe Regiment, @AHCWatch, Posted Friday 1st July 2011 from Twitlonger, accessed July 23, 2012, http://www.twitlonger.com/show/bfnmu5
4. Quotations on the Jefferson Memorial, Thomas Jefferson's Monticello, last accessed July 23, 2012, http://www.monticello.org/site/jefferson/quotations-jefferson_memorial
5. The Revocation of the Edict of Nantes, October 22, 1685, The History Guide, by Steven Kreis, last revised May 12, 2004, accessed July 23, 2012, http://www.historyguide.org/earlymod/revo_nantes.html
6. Autobiography of Thomas Jefferson, 1743-1790, Together with a Summary of the Chief Events in Jefferson's Life – Thomas Jefferson, accessed July 23, 2012, http://books.google.com/ebooks/reader?id=5lG7ISgjvr0C&printsec=frontcover&output=reader
7. Argument In The Case Of Howell Vs. Netherland 2 - Thomas Jefferson, The Works, Vol. 1 (Autobiography, Anas, 1760-1770) [1905], The Online Library of Liberty, accessed July 23, 2012, http://oll.libertyfund.org/?option=com_staticxt&staticfile=show.php%3Ftitle=800&chapter=85803&layout=html&Itemid=27
8. The Declaration of Independence, accessed July 23, 2012, http://www.ushistory.org/declaration/document/index.htm

9. Tuckahoe, Thomas Jefferson's Monticello, accessed July 23, 2012, http://www.monticello.org/site/research-and-collections/tuckahoe
10. Tuckahoe Plantation, accessed July 23, 2012, http://www.tuckahoeplantation.com/Tuckahoe_Plantation/Welcome.html
11. Historical Marker Society of America, last modified July 12, 2012, accessed July 23, 2012, www.hmsoa.org/va/albemarle/item/99702-site-of-viewmont
12. Autobiography of Thomas Jefferson, 1743-1790, Together with a Summary of the Chief Events in Jefferson's Life – Thomas Jefferson, accessed July 23, 2012, http://books.google.com/ebooks/reader?id=5lG7ISgjvr0C&printsec=frontcover&output=reader
13. Parson's Cause Speech, Patrick Henry, December 1763, Red Hill Patrick Henry National Memorial, accessed July 23, 2012, http://www.redhill.org/speeches/parsonscause.htm
14. Patrick Henry's Treason Speech, United States History, accessed July 23, 2012, www.u-s-history.com/pages/h1266.html
15. The Athenaeum, Issues 271-322, edited by James Silk Buckingham, etc., p. 543, accessed July 23, 2012, http://books.google.com/books
16. Ibid
17. Biography of Patrick Henry, Red Hill Patrick Henry National Memorial, accessed July 23, 2012, www.redhill.org/biography.html
18. Autobiography of Thomas Jefferson, 1743-1790, Together with a Summary of the Chief Events in Jefferson's Life – Thomas Jefferson, accessed July 23, 2012, http://books.google.com/ebooks/reader?id=5lG7ISgjvr0C&printsec=frontcover&output=reader
19. Patrick Henry's Resolutions Against the Stamp Act, May 29-30, 1765, Red Hill Patrick Henry National Memorial accessed July 23, 2012, http://www.redhill.org/speeches/stampact.htm
20. Autobiography of Thomas Jefferson, 1743-1790, Together with a Summary of the Chief Events in Jefferson's Life – Thomas Jefferson, last accessed July 23, 2012, http://books.google.com/ebooks/reader?id=5lG7ISgjvr0C&printsec=frontcover&output=reader
21. Quotations on Slavery and Emancipation, Thomas Jefferson's Monticello, accessed July 23, 2012, http://www.monticello.org/site/jefferson/quotations-slavery-and-emancipation
22. Virginia Historical Society, by R.A. Brock, p.15, accessed July 23, 2012, http://books.google.com/books

23. History of the United States, from their first settlement as English . . .by David Ramsay, etc., p.359, accessed July 23, 2012, http://books.google.com/books
24. Thomas Jefferson: The Apostle of Americanism By Gilbert Chinard, accessed July 23, 2012, http://books.google.com/books
25. Autobiography of Thomas Jefferson, 1743-1790, Together with a Summary of the Chief Events in Jefferson's Life – Thomas Jefferson, last accessed July 23, 2012, http://books.google.com/ebooks/reader?id=5lG7ISgjvr0C&printsec=frontcover&output=reader
26. Argument In The Case Of Howell Vs. Netherland 2 - Thomas Jefferson, The Works, Vol. 1 (Autobiography, Anas, 1760-1770) [1905], The Online Library of Liberty, accessed July 23, 2012, http://oll.libertyfund.org/?option=com_staticxt&staticfile=show.php%3Ftitle=800&chapter=85803&layout=html&Itemid=27
27. Wolf by the Ears, Thomas Jefferson's Monticello, accessed July 23, 2012, http://www.monticello.org/site/jefferson/wolf-ears
28. Thomas Jefferson Family Cemetery, accessed July 23, 2012 www.http://carolshouse.com/cemeteryrecords/monticello/
29. Autobiography of Thomas Jefferson, 1743-1790, Together with a Summary of the Chief Events in Jefferson's Life – Thomas Jefferson, last accessed July 23, 2012, http://books.google.com/ebooks/reader?id=5lG7ISgjvr0C&printsec=frontcover&output=reader
30. Thomas Jefferson on earthquakes & Congress, accessed July 23, 2012, www.thomasjeffersonleadership.com/ . . ./thomas-jefferson-on-earthquakes
31. Andrew Tribble, Thomas Jefferson's Monticello, accessed July 23, 2012 http://www.monticello.org/site/jefferson/andrew-tribble
32. Autobiography of Thomas Jefferson, 1743-1790, Together with a Summary of the Chief Events in Jefferson's Life – Thomas Jefferson, last accessed July 23, 2012, http://books.google.com/ebooks/reader?id=5lG7ISgjvr0C&printsec=frontcover&output=reader
33. Day of Fasting, Humiliation and Prayer for Boston (June 1, 1774), Principles of Freedom, accessed July 23, 2012, http://research.history.org/pf/declaring/dayOfFasting.cfm
34. The Writings of Thomas Jefferson, Vol. I by Thomas Jefferson, c. 1896, accessed July 23, 2012, www.http://books.google.com/books

35. Autobiography of Thomas Jefferson, 1743-1790, Together with a Summary of the Chief Events in Jefferson's Life – Thomas Jefferson, last accessed July 23, 2012, http://books.google.com/ebooks/reader?id=5lG7ISgjvr0C&printsec=frontcover&output=reader
36. The Thomas Jefferson Papers, The Library of Congress, accessed July 24, 2012, http://memory.loc.gov/ammem/collections/jefferson_papers/mtjtime2a.html
37. Autobiography of Thomas Jefferson, 1743-1790, Together with a Summary of the Chief Events in Jefferson's Life – Thomas Jefferson, accessed July 23, 2012, http://books.google.com/ebooks/reader?id=5lG7ISgjvr0C&printsec=frontcover&output=reader
38. Documents from the Continental Congress and the Constitutional Convention, 1774-1789, The Library of Congress, accessed July 24, 2012, http://memory.loc.gov/ammem/collections/continental/jeffer.html
39. Public Speaking, Thomas Jefferson's Monticello, accessed July 24, 2012, http://www.monticello.org/site/research-and-collections/public-speaking
40. Documents from the Continental Congress and the Constitutional Convention, 1774-1789, The Library of Congress, accessed July 24, 2012, http://memory.loc.gov/ammem/collections/continental/jeffer.html
41. The War Inevitable by Patrick Henry, March 23, 1775, accessed July 24, 2012, http://www.constitution.org/col/war_inevitable.txt
42. The Declaration of Independence, accessed July 23, 2012, http://www.ushistory.org/declaration/document/index.htm
43. Autobiography of Thomas Jefferson, 1743-1790, Together with a Summary of the Chief Events in Jefferson's Life – Thomas Jefferson, accessed July 23, 2012, http://books.google.com/ebooks/reader?id=5lG7ISgjvr0C&printsec=*frontcover&output=reader
44. Jefferson's "original Rough draught" of the Declaration of Independence, The Library of Congress, accessed July 24, 2012, http://www.loc.gov/exhibits/declara/ruffdrft.html
45. Benjamin Harrison, Principles of Freedom, accessed July 24, 2012, http://research.history.org/pf/signers/bio_harrison.cfm
46. Proceedings of the Massachusetts Historical Society, Vol. 42, by Massachusetts Historical Society, p. 342, accessed July 24, 2012, http://books.google.com/books

47. October 1778 -- 3rd Of Commonwealth - General Assembly, Begun And Held, accessed July 24, 2012, http://www.virginia1774.org/Slave%20Nonimportation%20Act.html
48. Memoirs, Correspondence, and Private Papers of Thomas Jefferson, Volume 1, by Thomas Jefferson Randolph, c.1829, accessed July 24, 2012, http://books.google.com/books
49. Thomas Jefferson's Baptist Neighbors by John Hood, Carolina Journal Online, Aug. 24th, 2011, accessed July 24, 2012, http://www.carolinajournal.com/daily_journal/display.html?id=8156
50. Virginia Statute for Religious Freedom, Virginia Historical Society, accessed July 24, 2012, http://www.vahistorical.org/sva2003/vsrf.htm
51. The Domestic Life of Thomas Jefferson, by Sarah N. Randolph, accessed July 24, 2012, http://books.google.com/book
52. The Life of Thomas Jefferson: In 3 Volumes, Volume 1 By Henry Stephens Randall, accessed July 24, 2012, http://books.google.com/book
53. The Thomas Jefferson Timeline: 1743 – 1827, The Thomas Jefferson Papers, The Library of Congress, accessed July 24, 2012, http://memory.loc.gov/ammem/collections/jefferson_papers/mtjtime2a.html
54. The Northwest Ordinance, The Library of Congress, accessed July 24, 2012, http://www.loc.gov/rr/program/bib/ourdocs/northwest.html
55. Notes on the State of Virginia, by Thomas Jefferson, accessed July 24, 2012, http://xroads.virginia.edu/~hyper/hns/yoeman/qxix.html
56. Virginia Statute of Religious Freedom, Virginia Historical Society, accessed July 24, 2012, http://www.vahistorical.org/sva2003/vsrf.htm
57. King Quotes, by Notable Quotes, accessed July 24, 2012, http://www.notable-quotes.com/k/kings_quotes.html
58. Selected Quotations from the Thomas Jefferson Papers, The Library of Congress, accessed July 24, 2012, http://memory.loc.gov/ammem/collections/jefferson_papers/mtjquote.html
59. 59 Life of Thomas Jefferson: third president of the United States By James Parton, p.331, accessed July 24, 2012 http://books.google.com/book
60. Dogs, Thomas Jefferson's Monticello, accessed July 24, 2012 http://www.monticello.org/site/house-and-gardens/dogs

61. The Planter's Northern Bride, by Caroline Hentz, c.1854, Academic Affairs Library, University of North Carolina at Chapel Hill, Date written -1997, accessed July 24, 2012 http://utc.iath.virginia.edu/proslav/prficlha1t.html
62. The Adolescent Nation Mourns the Loss of a Founding Father, The Franklin Institute, accessed July 24, 2012 http://sln.fi.edu/franklin/timeline/death.html
63. Memoir, Correspondence, and Miscellanies: From the Papers of . . . , Volume 4 by Thomas Jefferson Randolph, c. 1829, accessed July 24, 2012, http://books.google.com/books
64. Thomas Jefferson Letters, Tool for SEO, accessed July 24, 2012, http://website-tools.net/google_keyword/word/thomas+jefferson+letters
65. Coinage, Library of Economics and Liberty, accessed July 25, 2012, http://www.econlib.org/library/YPDBooks/Lalor/llCy243.html
66. "Architecture is my delight," Thomas Jefferson's Monticello, accessed July 25, 2012, http://www.monticello.org/site/jefferson/architecture-my-delight
67. The Virginia Declaration of Rights, National Center, accessed July 25, 2012, http://www.nationalcenter.org/VirginiaDeclaration.html
68. Jefferson's Service to the New Nation, The Thomas Jefferson Papers at the Library of Congress, accessed July 25, 2012, http://www.loc.gov/teachers/classroommaterials/connections/thomas-jefferson/history4.html
69. Rights, Thomas Jefferson to James Madison, The Founder's Constitution, accessed July 25, 2012, http://press-pubs.uchicago.edu/founders/documents/v1ch14s30.html
70. Ibid
71. Thomas Jefferson Quotes III, Notable Quotes, accessed July 25, 2012, http://www.notable-quotes.com/j/jefferson_thomas_iii.html
72. Sally Hemings, Thomas Jefferson's Monticello, accessed July 25, 2012, http://www.monticello.org/site/plantation-and-slavery/sally-hemings
73. Plowing, Thomas Jefferson's Monticello, accessed July 25, 2012, http://www.monticello.org/site/plantation-and-slavery/plowing
74. Enclosure to John Adams, The Letters of Thomas Jefferson: 1743-1826, accessed July 25, 2012, http://www.let.rug.nl/usa/P/tj3/writings/brf/jefl118.htm

75. Thomas Jefferson, Quoteworld.org, accessed July 25, 2012, http://www.quoteworld.org/quotes/7183
76. The Universal Significance of Jefferson's Architecture By Travis McDonald, Thomas Jefferson's Poplar Forest, accessed July 25, 2012, http://www.poplarforest.org/sites/default/files/architecture-universal-significance.pdf
77. The life of Thomas Jefferson, Volume 2, p. 537, by Henry Stephens Randall, c. 1871, accessed July 25, 2012, http://books.google.com/books
78. Foreign and Domestic Crises in the Adams Administration, encyclopedia.com, accessed July 25, 2012, http://www.encyclopedia.com/doc/1G2-2536600778.html
79. The Kentucky Resolutions of 1798, Government Transformers, accessed July 25, 2012, http://www.constitution.org/cons/kent1798.htm
80. Napoleon: Director, Consul, and Emperor, 1799-1815, Anjou History, accessed July 25, 2012, http://webpub.allegheny.edu/employee/a/acarr/anjouhistory/napoleon.html
81. Biography of Patrick Henry, Red Hill National Memorial, accessed July 25, 2012, http://www.redhill.org/biography.html
82. The life of Thomas Jefferson, Volume 2, by Henry Stephens Randall, c. 1871, accessed July 25, 2012, http://books.google.com/books
83. Manual of Parliamentary Practice, Thomas Jefferson's Monticello, accessed July 25, 2012, http://www.monticello.org/site/research-and-collections/manual-parliamentary-practice
84. Quotations on the University of Virginia, Thomas Jefferson's Monticello, accessed July 25, 2012, http://www.monticello.org/site/jefferson/quotations-university-virginia
85. Ibid
86. Thomas Jefferson's Garden Book, By Thomas Jefferson, University of North Carolina, accessed July 25, 2012, http://books.google.com/books
87. The life of Thomas Jefferson, Volume 2, by Henry Stephens Randall, c. 1871, p. 535, accessed July 25, 2012, http://books.google.com/books
88. Mary Jefferson Bolling, Thomas Jefferson's Monticello, accessed July 25, 2012, http://www.monticello.org/site/jefferson/mary-jefferson-bolling

89. Alexander Hamilton to Harrison Gray Otis, Digital History, accessed July 25, 2012, http://www.digitalhistory.uh.edu/documents/
90. God And Man At Monticello: How Jefferson Beat The Religious Right, By Tim Hackler, The Washington Post March 28, 1993, accessed July 26, 2012, http://www.timhackler.com/god_monticello.html
91. Ibid
92. Ibid
93. Ibid
94. The Midnight Appointments by Richard A. Samuelson, White House History, accessed July 26, 2012, http://www.whitehousehistory.org/whha_publications/publications_documents/whitehousehistory_07.pdf
95. Meriwether Lewis, Claude Moore Health Sciences Library, accessed July 26, 2012, http://www.hsl.virginia.edu/historical/medical_history/lewis_clark/corps.cfm
96. The Way of the Western Sea by David Lavender, The Journals of the Lewis and Clark Expedition, accessed July 26, 2012, http://lewisandclarkjournals.unl.edu/read/?_xmlsrc=lc.lavender.01.xml&_xslsrc=LCstyles.xsl
97. **Exploring Lewis and Clark's Charlottesville-Albemarle County, Virginia – Transcript, accessed July 26, 2012,** http://www2.vcdh.virginia.edu/lewisandclark/video/archive2.html
98. Dialogue Between My Head and My Heart, Thomas Jefferson's Letter to Maria Cosway, Paris, October 12, 1786, accessed July 26, 2012, http://www.uncp.edu/home/berrys/pdfs/jefferson_head_heart.pdf
99. Remarks at a Dinner Honoring Nobel Prize Winners of the Western Hemisphere, April 29, 1962, The American Presidency Project, accessed July 26, 2012, http://www.presidency.ucsb.edu/ws/?pid=8623
100. Jefferson's Bird, p. 385, The first forty years of Washington society: portrayed by the family letters . . . by Margaret Bayard Smith, c. 1906, http://books.google.com/books
101. Quotations on Jefferson in Conversation, Thomas Jefferson's Monticello, accessed July 26, 2012, http://www.monticello.org/site/jefferson/quotations-jefferson-conversation
102. America and the Barbary Pirates: An International Battle Against an Unconventional Foe, by Gerard W. Gawalt, The Thomas

Jefferson Papers, accessed July 26, 2012, http://memory.loc.gov/ammem/collections/jefferson_papers/mtjprece.html

103. Lifting the Yoke, Discovering Lewis & Clark, accessed July 26, 2012, http://lewis-clark.org/content/content-article.asp?ArticleID=3170
104. Mammoth Cheese, Thomas Jefferson's Monticello, accessed July 26, 2012, http://www.monticello.org/site/research-and collections/mammoth-cheese
105. Ibid
106. Church in the U.S. Capitol, by David Barton, The Wall Builders, written 2005, accessed July 27, 2012, http://www.thewordmp3.com/church_at_the_capitol.html
107. From the Danbury Baptist Association
The Papers of Thomas Jefferson, Volume 35: 1 August to 30 November 1801, accessed July 27, 2012, http://www.princeton.edu/~tjpapers/volumes/documents/DanburyBaptists.pdf
108. Jefferson's Letter to the Danbury Baptists, The Library of Congress, accessed July 27, 2012, http://www.loc.gov/loc/lcib/9806/danpre.html
109. Mammoth Cheese, Thomas Jefferson's Monticello, accessed July 27, 2012, http://www.monticello.org/site/research-and-collections/mammoth-cheese
110. Lucy Meriwether Lewis Marks, VCDH – University of Virginia, accessed July 27, 2012, http://www2.vcdh.virginia.edu/encounter/projects/homesteads/map/graveyards/lucymarks.html
111. Meriwether Lewis: Intrepid Explorer, National Park Service, accessed July 27, 2012,
112. Ibid
113. Jeffersonian Dinners, Thomas Jefferson's Monticello, accessed July 27, 2012, http://www.monticello.org/site/research-and-collections/jeffersonian-dinners
114. Quotations on Jefferson in Conversation, Thomas Jefferson's Monticello, accessed July 27, 2012, http://www.monticello.org/site/jefferson/quotations-jefferson-conversation
115. West Point, Thomas Jefferson's Monticello, accessed July 27, 2012, http://www.monticello.org/site/research-and-collections/united-states-military-academy-west-point
116. Sally Hemings Accusation, Sept. 1, 1802, PBS archives, accessed July 27, 2012, http://www.pbs.org/jefferson/archives/documents/ih195822.htm

117. James Callender, Thomas Jefferson's Monticello, accessed July 27, 2012, http://www.monticello.org/site/research-and-collections/james-callender
118. Marbury v. Madison (1803), Milestone Documents in the National Archives, accessed July 27, 2012, http://www.ourdocuments.gov/doc.php?doc=19
119. Preparing for the Journey, Lewis & Clark Expedition, accessed July 27, 2012, http://www.nps.gov/nr/travel/lewisandclark/preparing.htm
120. Marbury v. Madison (1803), Milestone Documents in the National Archives, accessed July 27, 2012, http://www.ourdocuments.gov/doc.php?doc=19
121. Napoleon Bonaparte, First Consul and Emperor, By: Ben Weider, CM, CQ, SBSjT, Ph.D, Napoleonic Society, accessed July 27, 2012, http://www.napoleonicsociety.com/english/Mortefontaine
122. Ibid
123. Louisiana Purchase, by Ripley Hitchcock, 1903, accessed July 27, 2012, http://www.usgennet.org/usa/topic/preservation/history/louis/
124. Napoleon Bonaparte, First Consul and Emperor, By: Ben Weider, CM, CQ, SBSjT, Ph.D, Napoleonic Society, accessed July 27, 2012, http://www.napoleonicsociety.com/english/Mortefontaine
125. The Lewis and Clark Bicentennial Sourcebook, Lewis and Clark Bicentennial Council, accessed July 27, 2012, http://atfiles.org/files/pdf/bicentennialsourcebook.pdf
126. Transcript: Jefferson's Instructions for Meriwether Lewis, The Library of Congress, accessed July 27, 2012, http://www.loc.gov/exhibits/lewisandclark/transcript57.html
127. The Lewis and Clark Bicentennial Sourcebook, Lewis and Clark Bicentennial Council, accessed July 27, 2012, http://atfiles.org/files/pdf/bicentennialsourcebook.pdf
128. Lewis and Clark Expedition, West Virginia Archives and History, accessed July 27, 2012, www.wvculture.org/history/settlement/lewisandclark01.html
129. Ibid
130. Nine Young Men From Kentucky, Lewis And Clark Trail, Accessed July 27, 2012, www.lewisandclarktrail.com/legacy/louisclark/kentuckyboys.htm
131. Meriwether Lewis Journal, Feb. 9, 1805, Lewis and Clark Journals, accessed July 27, 2012, http://lewisandclarkjournals.unl.edu/read/?_xmlsrc=1805-02-09.xml&_xslsrc=LCstyles.xsl

132. National Trail Site One, Lewis & Clark Interpretive Center & Camp Dubois, accessed July 27, 2012, shttp://lewisandclarktrail.com/section1/illinoiscities/Woodriver/interpretivecenter.htm
133. Captain Clark's Journal, Lewis and Clark journals, extract of, accessed July 27, 2012, http://www.ic.unicamp.br/~stolfi/PUB/misc/misc/realwork/EXPORT/projects/voynich/00-06-07-wordgrammar/Notes/054/texts/engl.lac.txt
134. Election of 1804, Thomas Jefferson's Monticello, accessed July 27, 2012, www.monticello.org/site/research-and-collections/election-1804
135. Osage Indians, Discovering Lewis & Clark, accessed July 27, 2012, http://lewis-clark.org/content/content-article.asp?ArticleID=2535
136. Ibid
137. December 24, 1804, Gass' Journal, accessed July 27, 2012, http://lewisandclarkjournals.unl.edu/read/?_xmlsrc=1804-12-24.xml&_xslsrc=LCstyles.xsl
138. Photo Mural 9, Lewis and Clark, National Park Service, accessed July 27, 2012, http://www.nps.gov/jeff/planyourvisit/photo-mural-9.htm
139. Seaman, Inside the Corps, PBS, accessed July 27, 2012, http://www.pbs.org/lewisandclark/inside/seaman.html
140. Seaman, Jefferson National Expansion Memorial, accessed July 27, 2012, http://www.nps.gov/jeff/historyculture/seaman.htm
141. Ibid
142. Lewis and Clark Timeline, Jefferson National Expansion Memorial, accessed July 27, 2012, http://www.nps.gov/jeff/historyculture/lewis-and-clark-timeline-1805.htm
143. Ibid
144. Journals, PBS Louis and Clark site, accessed July 27, 2012, http://www.lewisclark.net/journals/index7.html
145. Our Breakfast Table, Thomas Jefferson's Monticello, accessed July 27, 2012, http://www.monticello.org/site/jefferson/our-breakfast-table
146. The Mysterious Death of Judge George Wythe, by Bruce Chadwick, Historynet.com, accessed July 27, 2012, http://www.historynet.com/the-mysterious-death-of-judge-george-wythe.htm
147. Ibid
148. George Wythe, Find A Grave, accessed July 27, 2012, http://www.findagrave.com/cgi-bin/fg.cgi?page=gr&GRid=2792

149. Clark's Commission, Discovering Lewis and Clark, accessed July 27, 2012, http://lewis-clark.org/content/
150. Return of Lewis and Clark, Thomas Jefferson's Monticello, accessed July 27, 2012, http://www.monticello.org/site/return-lewis-and-clark
151. The Early Republic, 1800-1809, The Library of Congress, accessed July 27, 2012, http://memory.loc.gov/ammem/collections/jefferson_papers/mtjtime3c.html
152. Ibid
153. Thomas Jefferson - To The Senate And House Of Representatives Of The United States In Congress Assembled:, Miller Center, UVA, accessed July 27, 2012, http://millercenter.org/president/speeches/detail/3495
154. Jefferson Administration Documents Concerning the Burr Conspiracy and Trial, University of Missouri-Kansas City School of Law, accessed July 27, 2012 http://law2.umkc.edu/faculty/projects/ftrials/burr/burrjeffproclamation.html
155. Prohibition of the Slave Trade (1807), by Kevin Outterson, Enotes, accessed July 27, 2012, http://www.enotes.com/prohibition-slave-trade-1807
156. Isaac Coles, Thomas Jefferson's Monticello, accessed July 27, 2012, http://www.monticello.org/site/research-and-collections/isaac-coles
157. Ibid
158. The Treason Trial of Aaron Burr by Doug Linder, University of Missouri-Kansas City School of Law, accessed July 27, 2012 http://law2.umkc.edu/faculty/projects/ftrials/burr/burraccount.html
159. Ibid
160. Ibid
161. Jean Baptiste Charbonneau, Inside the Corps, PBS, accessed July 27, 2012 http://www.pbs.org/lewisandclark/inside/jchar.html
162. All My Wishes End, Thomas Jefferson's Monticello, accessed July 27, 2012, http://www.monticello.org/site/jefferson/all-my-wishes-end-monticello
163. Ibid
164. Ibid
165. http://cleverquips.blogspot.com/2012/03/faith-of-our-fathers.html

Index

A Manual of Parliamentary Practice, 191
Adams, Abigail, 152, 153, 156, 184, 195, 202
Adams, James, 229
Adams, John, 113, 115, 117, 120, 147, 149, 152, 153, 156, 164, 171, 178, 181, 183, 184, 187, 193, 194, 195, 197, 198, 202, 207, 209, 228, 234, 236, 238, 313
Adams, John Quincy, 152
Adams, Samuel, 120
Alabama, 309
Albemarle County, 6, 11, 28, 31, 33, 45, 49, 50, 70, 76, 85, 94, 96, 97, 99, 102, 106, 107, 126, 199, 221, 239, 281, 293, 320, 321, 322
Albemarle County, VA, 45, 178, 223
Alexandria, VA, 299
Alien and Sedition Acts, 187, 188, 193, 207, 228
Alleghany Mountains, 308
Alston, Willis, Jr., 306
American army, 113, 187
American Philosophical Society, 185, 192, 223, 243, 250, 267, 268, 273, 281, 312, 317
Anderson, Edmund, 230
Annapolis, MD, 84, 150, 151
Antifederalists, 164, 169, 180
Apollo room, 87
Appalachian Mountains, 70, 251, 289
Appomattox River, 189
Armistead, Judith, 64
Arnold, Gen. Benedict, 139, 140
Bainbridge, William, 269
Ball, Mary, 53
Baltimore, MD, 150, 194, 211, 272
Barbary Pirates, 209
Barbary States, 209, 274

Barbary War, 274
Barbary Wars, 210
Barbé-Marbois, François, 146, 147
Barlow, Joel, 225
Barton, Benjamin Smith, 223, 243
Bastille, France, 159
Bastrop, Baron, 308
Beatitudes, 14, 220
Belvoir, Albemarle Co., 45, 222, 321
Big Bone Lick, 250, 265
Big Sall, 17, 19, 41, 44
Bill of Rights, 152, 157, 158, 164, 168, 169, 190, 205
Bismarck, ND, 278
Bissell, Daniel, 256
Bissell, Russell, 258
Bitterroot Mountains, 278, 287
Blackfeet tribe, 261, 287
Blue Ridge mountains, 17, 50, 142
Boley, John, 258, 259
Bolling, John, 31, 75, 192
Boone, Daniel, 254
Boston, MA, 97, 103, 105, 106, 107, 110, 152, 271
Botetourt, Gov. Lord, 87, 91
Bratton, William, 254
Braxton, Carter, 120
Breckinridge, John, 188
Broad River, 222
Bruton Parish Church, 64, 69, 71
Burr, Aaron, 193, 194, 195, 268, 271, 272, 292, 294, 297, 307, 308, 309, 312, 313, 314, 315
Burr, Theodosia, 313
Burwell, Rebecca, 67, 77
Cahokia, IL, 259
Cairo, IL, 257
Callender, James, 207, 228, 229, 232, 234
Cameahwait - Shoshone chief, 284, 285

335

Camp Dubois, 260, 262
Campbell, John, 260
Canada, 231, 272
Carr, Dabney, 2, 3, 5, 6, 11, 12, 13, 14, 15, 31, 66, 67, 75, 76, 94, 95, 96, 103, 125, 148, 173, 174
Carter, Judith Harrison, 64
Carter, Landon, 77
Carter, Robert "King", 64, 77
Cary, Anne, 70
Castle Hill, 11, 35, 37, 38, 45, 52, 54, 58, 65, 76, 77, 124, 125, 178, 320, 321, 322
Charbonneau, "Pomp", 280, 284
Charbonneau, Jean Baptiste "Pomp", 280, 284, 285, 287
Charbonneau, Lizette, 316
Charbonneau, Toussaint, 277, 278, 298, 305, 316
Charles City County, VA, 31, 92
Charleston, 139
Charlottesville, VA, 31, 70, 84, 96, 102, 127, 139, 140, 220, 221, 223, 298, 299
Chesapeake Bay, 114, 134, 137, 139, 140, 142, 143, 236
Cheshire, MA, 211, 212
Chesterfield County, VA, 31, 192
Chief Big White, 297, 298, 299, 300, 307, 311
Chouteau, Pierre, 299, 300, 307
Church of England, *11, 73, 101, 102, 128, 129*
Cincinnati, OH, 249, 250, 251
Clark, Capt. William, 21, 22, 176, 223, 243, 244, 248, 251, 252, 253, 254, 255, 256, 257, 258, 259, 260, 261, 262, 263, 264, 273, 274, 278, 279, 280, 281, 283, 284, 285, 287, 290, 294, 296, 297, 298, 299, 305, 306, 307, 311, 312, 315, 316, 317
Clark, George Rogers, 176, 238, 252, 254, 299
Clark, Lucy, 28, 39, 75, 83, 84, 96, 114, 131, 139, 148, 149, 153, 177, 200, 220, 221, 222, 253
Clark, William, 21, 200, 223, 238, 243, 247, 248, 249, 250, 251, 254, 257, 259, 260, 263, 270, 273, 278, 280, 283, 285, 286, 297, 305, 306, 307, 310, 315, 316
Clarksville, IN, 176, 249, 251, 254
Clarksville, TN, 176
Clatsop tribe, 286
Clay, Rev. Charles, 96, 100, 107, 126, 127
Clearwater River, 285
Clinton, Bill, 277
Clinton, George, 268, 271
Cloverfields, VA, 37, 221, 320
Coles, Mary, 208
College of William and Mary, 11, 34, 45, 49, 61, 64, 67, 138, 139, 163, 295
Collins, John, 258, 259
Colorado, 242, 246, 294
Colter, John, 251, 253
Columbia River, 231, 244, 246, 285, 286, 287, 290, 296, 307
Connecticut, 105, 115, 213, 215
Conrad and McMunn boarding house, 195
Constitution, 129, 130, 157, 158, 164, 167, 168, 169, 185, 190, 204, 238, 241, 273, 309, 315
Continental Congress, *45, 95, 106, 110, 111, 113, 114, 151, 314*
Continental Divide, 284
Cornwallis, 143
Cornwallis, Gen. Charles, 139, 140, 142, 143, 159, 236
Corps of Discovery, 177, 199, 200, 222, 223, 227, 231, 237, 243, 244, 248, 250, 253, 256, 258, 259, 260, 261, 262, 263, 267, 273, 278, 279, 281, 282, 283, 290, 291, 296, 297, 299, 306, 316, 317
Cosway, Maria, 203, 235, 236
Coup d'Etat, 190, 237
Croghan, William, 253
Cruzatte, Pierre, 263, 280, 283, 287, 304, 305
Culpeper County, VA, 255
Cumberland County, VA, 138
Cumberland Gap, 36, 289
Cumberland River, 256
Dame, John, 258
Danbury Baptist Association, 213, 215
Danbury Baptists, 213, 215

336

Daveiss, Joseph H., 292
Davies, Rev. Samuel, 77, 80
Day of Fasting, Humiliation & Prayer, 105
Deane, Silas, 124
Dearborn, Henry, 307, 315
Decatur, Stephen, 269
Declaration of Independence, 20, 31, 84, 102, 113, 115, 117, 118, 119, 120, 126, 129, 130, 135, 140, 146, 152, 156, 159, 184, 204, 236, 238, 244, 283, 296, 318
Declaration of the Causes and Necessity of Taking up Arms, 113
Delaware River, 84, 139
Delaware tribe, 84, 139, 257, 274
Democratic-Republican Party, 130, 169, 180, 209, 268
Detroit, MI, 201, 223, 256
Dick, the mockingbird, 204, 205, 207, 226, 227, 231, 233, 234, 235, 244, 249, 265, 290, 291, 297, 301, 311
Dickerson, Mahlon, 225
Dickinson, John, 113, 120
Dinsmore, Mr., 299
Dinwiddie, Governor, 50, 54
Divers, George, 131
Dodge, Nehemiah, 215
Douglas, Rev. William, 28, 35, 42, 45, 47, 50, 236
Drouillard, George, 256, 257, 260, 263, 305, 306
Dunmore, Gov. Lord, 85, 95, 106, 111, 114
DuVal, William, 295
Eaton, William, 297
Edgehill, VA, 189, 193, 206, 293, 307
Edict of Nantes, 7, 8
Elizabeth (Thornton) Walker, 141
Emerson, Ralph Waldo, 111
Entail, *244*
Eppes, Elizabeth, 152, 153
Eppes, Jack, 192, 266
Eppes, Maria Jefferson, 268
Eppington, VA, 189, 270
Essex County, VA, 319
Evans, Philip - slave, 189
Fairfax, Lord, 53
Falls of the Ohio State Park, 255
Fauquier, Gov. Francis, 66

Federal City, 166, 168, 185, 190, 192, 198, 201, 205, 208, 271
Federalist, 164, 169, 180, 181, 183, 187, 194, 197, 202, 210, 226, 227, 229, 272, 292
Federalists, 164, 169, 180, 184, 187, 188, 193, 198, 217, 227, 242
Field, Joseph, 255, 282
Field, Mary, *18*
Field, Reubin, 255, 256
Flatheads tribe, 285
Florida, 237, 239, 240
Floyd, Charles, 254, 258, 273
Fontaine, Jacques, 10
Fontaine, Mary Anne, 7, 10, 37
Fontaine, Rev. Francis, 10
Fort Clatsop, 286, 287
Fort Cumberland, 15, 49, 55, 179
Fort Duquesne, 48, 49, 54
Fort Kaskaskia, IL, 258, 259, 262, 269
Fort Le Boeuf, 48, 53
Fort Loudon, 176
Fort Mandan, 277, 278, 279, 280, 281
Fort Massac, IL, 256
Fort Pitt, 45
Fort Stoddert, AL, 309
Fox tribe, 274
France, Minister of, *149, 158, 166, 184, 185, 236*
Francis Wayles Eppes, 210
Frankfort, KY, 299
Franklin, Benjamin, 113, 115, 117, 120, 124, 146, 147, 149, 152, 153, 164, 184, 185, 236
Frazier, George, 262, 299
Frederick, MD, 247
Fredericksburg, 126, 130, 299, 319
Fredericksville Parish, 11, 88, 126
French and Indian War, 55, 70, 176
French Canadian, 263, 278, 287, 305
French Revolution, 158, 159, 166, 169, 170, 190, 236, 237
Fry, Col. Joshua, 7, 11, 28, 34, 37, 48, 49, 50, 51, 53, 55, 56, 57, 60, 63, 69, 76, 77, 125, 131, 177, 199, 257, 289, 290
Fry, Henry, 49, 76, 77, 125, 131, 177
Fry, Joshua, Jr., 177
Fry, Wesley Thornton, 125, 131
Fry-Jefferson Map, 34, 37, 49

Gallatin, Albert, 210, 237, 241
Gass, Patrick, 258, 259, 273, 279, 280, 299
George III, King, 20, 50, 66, 70, 74, 78, 85, 87, 95, 107, 109, 113, 119, 149, 150, 152, 156, 294
Georgia, 21, 119, 133, 222, 252
Gerry, Elbridge, 84, 120, 168
Gibson, George, 254, 255, 280, 283
Gilmer, Dr. George, 55, 70, 84, 131
Gilmer, Dr. George, Jr., 96, 123, 128, 131, 148
Gilmer, George, Jr., 84
Gilmer, Peachy Ridgway, 70
Glascock, Million, 53, 54, 58, 69, 88
Glascock, Thomas, 54, 88
Gloucester County, VA, 64
Goforth, William, 251
Goochland County, VA, 28, 31, 35, 49, 138
Goodrich, Silas, 262
Governor of Virginia, 87, 95, 130, 133, 134, 140, 151, 176, 235, 239, 314
Great Awakening, 77, 80
Great Falls, MT, 283
Gregory, Roger, 320
Griffin, Cyrus, 314
Haiti, 240
Hall, Hugh, 260
Hamilton, Alexander, 164, 165, 167, 171, 179, 180, 184, 194, 207, 210, 228, 271, 272, 292, 307
Hancock, John, 120
Hancock, Julia, 299, 306, 307, 310, 316
Hanover County, VA, 230, 321
Harper's Ferry, 242, 247, 248
Harrison, Benjamin, 120
Harvie, John, 58, 62
Hay, George, 313, 314
Hemings, Betty, 123, 157
Hemings, James, 152, 175, 189
Hemings, Robert, 110, 141, 170, 174, 178, 186
Hemings, Sally, 157, 160, 175, 184, 228
Henrico Co., VA, 18, 31
Henry, Justice John, 72
Henry, Patrick, 61, 71, 73, 74, 77, 78, 79, 80, 85, 87, 89, 95, 102, 103, 108, 111, 114, 117, 134, 137, 176, 190, 191
Hern, Edith - slave, 224

Hidatsa tribe, 263, 278
Hispaniola, 240
Hoops, Margarete, 131
Hornsby, Joseph, 131
House of Delegates, 126, 128, 130, 134, 143, 144, 177
Howard, Thomas, 260, 261
Howell, Samuel, 94, 95
Hudson River, 211, 227
Huguenots, 7, 10, 37, 38, 49, 89
Ice cream, 224, 237
Idaho, 284
Illinois, 258, 259, 274
Indian Banks, Richmond Co., VA, 54, 88
Indiana, 274
Indians, 11, 20, 21, 42, 45, 48, 50, 165, 176, 220, 230, 232, 233, 238, 245, 253, 255, 256, 257, 258, 261, 263, 264, 267, 268, 270, 271, 272, 273, 274, 277, 278, 279, 281, 283, 285, 286, 287, 297, 299, 300
Intolerable Acts, 105
Intrepid - frigate, 269
Iowa, 242, 273
Irving, Washington, 314
Isham, Mary, 18
Ivy, VA, 221
Jackson, Andrew, 294, 314
James River, 25, 26, 92, 137, 143, 193
Jamestown, VA, 320
Jay, John, 147, 180, 193
Jay's Treaty, 180, 183, 187
Jefferson, Anna, 31, 55
Jefferson, Elizabeth "Bet", 31, 40, 83
Jefferson, Ellen Wayles, 180
Jefferson, Jane, 31, 39, 83
Jefferson, Lucy, 31, 89
Jefferson, Maria, 25, 65, 157, 160, 161, 163, 167, 173, 175, 186, 189, 191, 192, 193, 206, 210, 211, 229, 234, 265, 266, 268, 270, 290, 317
Jefferson, Martha, 28, 39, 75, 92, 94, 96, 97, 99, 100, 101, 111, 114, 123, 124, 128, 129, 131, 133, 134, 137, 138, 139, 140, 141, 143, 145, 146, 147, 148, 149, 150, 151, 152, 157, 159, 160, 163, 164, 167, 170, 173, 174, 180, 181, 186, 189, 192, 193, 206, 210, 211, 229, 232, 233, 234,

265, 266, 268, 270, 290, 291, 293, 294, 307, 310
Jefferson, Martha "Patsy", 31
Jefferson, Mary, 138
Jefferson, Mary "Polly", 27, 31, 35, 129, 133, 134, 139, 145, 146, 148, 149, 153, 157, 184
Jefferson, Peter, *1, 2, 7, 17, 18, 19, 25, 27, 28,* 31, 34, *40, 42, 49, 50, 51, 52, 53, 56, 57, 60, 76, 77, 92, 138, 163, 177, 199, 289, 290*
Jefferson, Peter Field, 31
Jefferson, Randolph, 31, 55
Jesus, 4, 14, 63, 89, 102, 220, 280
John the Baptist, 280
Jouett, Jack, 140, 141
Jouett, Jack, Jr., 141
Julien, Honoré, 224
Jupiter, *17, 18, 19, 20, 41, 42, 43, 44, 51, 58, 64, 66, 67, 84, 85, 86, 90, 91, 94, 99, 100, 109, 110, 123, 128, 129, 141, 148, 160, 161, 189, 190, 191, 193*
Kennedy, John F., 204
Kentucky, 31, 45, 50, 70, 176, 177, 181, 188, 232, 250, 251, 252, 253, 255, 256, 273, 289, 292, 299, 316, 322
Kentucky Resolutions, 188
Kimball, Fiske, 186
King Carlos IV of Spain, 233
King George III, 73
King William County, VA, 10, 77
Kingston, TN, 260
Knife River, 278
L'Enfant, Pierre Charles, 168, 190
La Salle, 240
Labiche, Francois, 263, 278, 299, 305, 306
Lafayette, Gen. Marquis de, 140, 142, 153, 159, 165, 170, 235, 236
Lakota Sioux tribe, 279
Laurens, Henry, 147, 149
Le Havre, France, 152
Ledyard, John, 238
Lee, Francis Lightfoot, 77, 95, 103, 120
Lee, Richard Henry, 77, 87, 95, 103, 114, 120, 123
Lee, Thomas Ludwell, 77, 126, 134
Leland, Rev. John, 211, 212
Lemaire, Étienne, 224

Lemhi Pass, 284
L'Enfant, Pierre Charles, 166, 185
Lepage, Jean Baptiste, 263
Lewis and Clark Expedition, 21, 255, 262, 263, 270, 273, 284, 290
Lewis Mountain Baptist Church, 101
Lewis, Andrew, 176
Lewis, Anne Jefferson, 31
Lewis, Charles, 31, 89
Lewis, Jane Meriwether, 18, 25, 27, 28, 35, 39, 40, 53, 56, 57, 58, 59, 75, 76, 83, 84, 92, 96, 99, 111, 114, 124, 125, 130, 131, 175, 220, 221, 230
Lewis, John, 38, 73
Lewis, Lucy Meriwether, 221
Lewis, Meriwether, 21, 38, 101, 114, 130, 177, 179, 199, 200, 201, 202, 203, 204, 205, 206, 207, 208, 216, 219, 220, 221, 222, 223, 224, 225, 226, 227, 228, 229, 230, 231, 232, 233, 238, 241, 242, 243, 244, 245, 247, 248, 249, 250, 251, 252, 253, 254, 255, 256, 257, 258, 259, 260, 261, 262, 263, 264, 265, 266, 267, 268, 269, 270, 272, 273, 274, 277, 278, 279, 280, 281, 282, 283, 284, 285, 286, 287, 290, 292, 293, 294, 296, 297, 298, 299, 300, 301, 302, 303, 304, 305, 306, 307, 308, 309, 310, 311, 312, 315, 317
Lewis, Morgan, 271
Lewis, Nicholas Meriwether, 77, 177
Lewis, Reuben, 131, 221, 230, 280, 281
Lewis, Robert Warner, 220
Lewis, William, 177, 220
Library of Congress, *192, 235*
Lincoln, Gen. Benjamin, 139
Lindsay, Reuben, 131
Little Sall - slave, 100
Livingston, Robert R., 115, 120, 238
Locust Grove, KY, 253
Locust Hill, 177, 199, 200, 221, 222, 230, 251, 299
Locust Hill,, 222
Logstown, 50
London, 11, 18, 31, 107, 153, 156, 230
Longfellow, Henry Wadsworth, 141
Louis XIV, King, 7, 240
Louis XVI, King, 158, 159, 170, 236

Louisa County, 2, 6, 31, 77, 94, 96, 140, 321
Louisiana, 21, 233, 235, 239, 240, 241, 242, 245, 260, 267, 268, 269, 284, 311, 315
Louisiana Purchase, 235, 241, 242, 244, 267, 274, 291
Louisiana Territory, 233, 240, 242, 244, 260, 267, 268, 271, 272, 292, 294, 310
Louisiana, Territory of Upper, 310
Louisville, KY, 252, 253, 298, 299
Loyal Company, 13, 28, 35, 38, 48, 50, 56, 63, 70, 124, 125, 130, 177, 199, 200, 231, 289, 290, 317, 319, 320
Lyons, Peter, 72, 73, 74
Macaroni maker, 212, 224, 237
Mackenzie, Alexander, 230
Madison, Bishop James, 2, 5
Madison, Dolley, 178, 208, 229, 232, 291
Madison, James, 2, 89, 130, 154, 157, 158, 163, 167, 168, 169, 173, 178, 180, 181, 188, 193, 204, 207, 208, 209, 222, 234, 237, 238, 241, 309, 313, 315
Mandan tribe, 258, 260, 263, 278, 281, 284, 297, 298, 300, 307, 311
Mandan village, 258, 311, 316
Mandan villages, 260, 278, 297, 298
Manly, George, 95
Marblehead, MA, 84, 120
Marbury v. Madison, 234, 238
Marbury, William, 234, 238
Marie Antoinette, 158, 170
Marks, Capt. John, 222
Marks, Dr. John Hastings, 230
Marks, Hastings, 31
Marks, John Hastings, 222
Marks, Mary Garland, 222, 230
Marshall, John, 177, 197, 198, 234, 238, 313
Martin, Benjamin Smith, 243
Maryland, 15, 49, 55, 84, 179, 247
Mason, George, 126, 134, 168
Massachusetts, 84, 105, 111, 115, 120, 168, 184, 211, 212, 213, 215, 261, 262
Maury, James, Jr., 2, 89

Maury, Matthew, 2, 3, 4, 5, 6, 7, 10, 14, 37, 65, 89, 125, 126, 131, 177, 200, 220, 222
Maury, Rev. James, 2, 3, 4, 5, 6, 7, 10, 11, 13, 14, 15, 28, 37, 43, 50, 56, 57, 59, 60, 62, 63, 64, 71, 72, 73, 74, 78, 88, 89, 101, 102, 125, 128, 131, 177, 199, 200, 220, 222, 236, 289
Maury's School, 12, 62, 89, 219, 222
Maysville, KY, 251
McNeal, Hugh, 263
Mediterranean Sea, 209, 210, 269
Meriwether, Col. Thomas, 7, 28, 56, 130, 177, 320
Meriwether, Jane Crawford, 130, 220
Meriwether, Lucy Thornton, 177, 200, 220
Meriwether, Nicholas, 55, 130, 220, 222, 320
Meriwether, Thomas, 37, 50, 60, 63, 77, 177, 199, 220, 231, 289
Mexico, 292, 308
Michaux, Andre, 238
Micou, Mary, 49, 131
Milden Hall, 55
Milden Hall, Richmond Co., VA, 54
Mildenhall, Suffolk, 54
Mississippi River, 70, 135, 176, 231, 233, 239, 240, 244, 255, 257, 258, 259, 260, 263, 265, 273, 274, 294
Mississippi Territory, 313
Missouri, 263, 274
Missouri River, 6, 56, 70, 231, 233, 237, 242, 246, 247, 257, 260, 261, 270, 273, 278, 279, 281, 294, 296, 299, 305, 311
Missouri tribe, 279
Mockingbird, 204, 249, 290, 301
Monroe, James, 89, 139, 178, 222, 239, 240, 241, 243, 244, 294
Mont Blanco, VA, 193
Montana, 242, 283, 284
Monticello, 31, 76, 89, 91, 92, 93, 96, 99, 107, 109, 110, 111, 114, 123, 124, 125, 126, 128, 129, 130, 133, 134, 137, 138, 140, 141, 142, 143, 144, 145, 147, 148, 149, 150, 152, 160, 161, 163, 165, 167, 169, 170, 171, 173, 174, 175, 178, 179, 180, 186, 187, 188, 189, 190, 191, 193, 200,

340

201, 202, 203, 206, 207, 219, 221, 224, 229, 230, 232, 266, 270, 291, 293, 298, 307, 312, 315, 317
Montpelier, 130
Moore, Elizabeth "Betsy", 45, 76, 130
Morgan, Dr. John, 84
Morocco, 209, 226
Mount Vernon, VA, 150, 191
Napoleon Bonaparte, 190, 233, 237, 238, 239, 240, 241, 242, 243, 244, 267, 268
Nashville, TN, 294, 316
Natchez Trace, 317
National Bank, 167, 169, 180, 184
Natural Bridge, 99
Nelson, Stephen, 215
Nelson, Thomas, 77, 87, 120, 140, 142
Neutrality Proclamation, 170
Neville, John, 179
New Hampshire, 258
New Jersey, 133, 138, 179, 271
New Orleans, LA, 231, 233, 237, 238, 239, 240, 241, 243, 244, 268, 269, 284, 302, 308, 313
New York, 115, 120, 124, 165, 166, 190, 216, 227, 238, 268, 271, 272
New York City, 124
New York, NY, 84, 142, 143, 164, 198
Newfoundland, 248, 250, 255, 282, 302, 304
Newman, John, 256, 263
Nez Percé tribe, 285, 287
North Carolina, 21, 34, 139, 208, 260, 306
North Dakota, 242, 258, 260, 278
Northern Neck, 52, 64
Northwest Ordinance, 151
Notes on the State of Virginia, 146, 147, 148, 150, 152
Ohio, 176, 255, 262
Ohio River, 48, 50, 54, 176, 243, 244, 247, 248, 249, 251, 255, 256, 257, 265
Omaha tribe, 263
Orange County, VA, 130
Ordinance of 1784, 151
Ordway, John, 258, 264, 282, 299
Oregon, 244, 285, 286, 300
Oregon Territory, 285
Orleans, Territory of, 310

Osage tribe, 268, 271, 272, 274, 278, 299, 300
Otoe tribe, 279
Ottoman Empire, 269
Pacific Ocean, 6, 7, *11*, *13*, *21*, *28*, *36*, *50*, *54*, *63*, *70*, *77*, *124*, *135*, *175*, *200*, *224*, *230*, *231*, *237*, *238*, *242*, *243*, *246*, *247*, *248*, *250*, *251*, *266*, *267*, *277*, *279*, *280*, *283*, *284*, *285*, *286*, *287*, *289*, *290*, *294*, *296*, *297*, *299*, *302*, *305*, *306*, *312*, *316*, *317*
Page, John, 64, 65, 66, 77, 94, 134
Page, Mann, 64, 65, 77
Page, Maria Judith, 25, 65
Page, Matthew, 64
Paine, Thomas, 225
Paris, France, 70, 145, 150, 152, 153, 159, 160, 166, 175, 203, 224
Parson's Cause, 78, 89
Payne, Anna, 208
Payne, John, 208
Peace medals, 279
Peace Treaty, 150, 151
Peachey, Roy, 53
Peachey, Samuel, 54
Peachey, Susanna, 52
Peachey, Tom, 55
Peachey, William, 15, 52, 54, 55, 58, 69, 88
Peachy, Capt. William, 55
Peale, Charles Wilson, 225
Pen Park, VA, 84, 321, 322
Pendleton, Edmund, 126, 133, 135
Pennsylvania, 113, 114, 115, 120, 131, 164, 179, 200, 201, 251, 253, 258, 263, 273, 321
Philadelphia - warship, 157, 269
Philadelphia, PA, 84, 110, 111, 113, 114, 120, 124, 146, 149, 150, 151, 157, 164, 166, 167, 168, 169, 170, 171, 184, 185, 186, 187, 189, 190, 192, 198, 208, 223, 243, 247, 271, 272, 273, 311, 312, 317
Piankeshaw tribe, 274
Pike, Zebulon, Jr., 294
Pinckney, Charles, 193, 194, 274
Pinckney, William, 294
Pirogue, 249, 255, 260
Pittsburgh, PA, 50, 179, 200, 201, 247, 248, 249, 250, 254, 255, 302

341

Poplar Forest, VA, 141, 147
Potomac River, 165, 166, 185, 186, 192, 203, 302, 306, 311, 312
Potts, John, 260, 261
Powhatan Plantation, 319
Preble, Edward, 269, 273
President's House, 153, 166, 194, 201, 202, 204, 208, 223, 224, 229, 242, 265
Price, Rev., 106
Priestley, Dr. Joseph, 191
Primogeniture, *18, 21, 26*
Pryor, Mitchie, 31
Pryor, Nathaniel, 254, 311
Quaker, 208, 229
Quartering Act, 78
Quasi-war, 187
Queen Marie de Antoinette, 236
Raleigh tavern, 87, 95, 106
Randolph, Peyton, 77
Randolph, Anne Cary, 7, 10, 37, 70, 96, 106, 107, 126, 130, 167, 174, 189, 206, 291, 293
Randolph, Cornelia Jefferson, 189, 206, 291
Randolph, Edmund, 144, 313, 314
Randolph, Ellen Wayles, 180, 181, 189, 206, 233, 291
Randolph, Isham, 31
Randolph, James Madison, 290
Randolph, Jane, 18, 25, 27, 31, 40, 53, 99
Randolph, John, 87
Randolph, Mary Jefferson, 291
Randolph, Peter, 58, 61
Randolph, Peyton, 77, 78, 79, 87, 108, 111, 114
Randolph, Thomas Jefferson, 174, 233, 291
Randolph, Thomas Mann, 25, 26, 65, 69, 94, 170
Randolph, Thomas Mann, Jr., 163, 174, 266, 307
Randolph, Virginia, 210
Randolph, Virginia Jefferson, 291
Randolph, William, 18, 25, 26
Rappahannock River, 54, 55
Red Hill, VA, 190
Red River, 294
Reed, Moses, 262

Republican, 130, 164, 169, 174, 183, 188, 195, 197, 198, 202, 204, 207, 209, 220, 242, 268, 292, 315
Republicans, 169, 187, 193, 194, 198
Revere, Paul, 141
Reynolds, Maria, 207
Rhode Island, 21, 211
Rice, William, 128, 189
Richmond County, VA, 52, 54, 55, 59, 88
Richmond, KY, 316
Richmond, VA, 52, 54, 55, 58, 88, 111, 114, 117, 137, 138, 139, 140, 142, 143, 153, 154, 159, 160, 174, 207, 228, 235, 295, 299, 309, 310, 311, 312, 313, 314, 315
Rittenhouse, David, 223
Rivanna River, 6, 38, 40, 76, 100
Robbins, Ephraim, 215
Robertson, John, 258
Robinson, John, 78
Rochambeau, Gen. Comte de, 142, 235
Rocky Mountains, 21, 278, 283, 284, 298, 305
Rogers, Jane, 31
Rosewell, Gloucester Co., VA, 65
Rush, Dr. Benjamin, 223, 243, 311
Sacajawea, 21, 22, 277, 278, 280, 281, 283, 284, 285, 298, 305, 316
Saint Anne's Parish, Albemarle Co., 96
Sal, little - slave, 100
Salish tribe, 285
Sally Hemings, 123
Sauk tribe, 274
Sawney - slave, 19, 25, 50, 51, 58, 59, 76
Seaman, the Newfoundland dog, 248, 250, 251, 253, 255, 257, 258, 259, 262, 263, 264, 277, 280, 281, 282, 283, 285, 286, 287, 302, 303, 304, 306, 311, 312
Secretary of State, 130, 163, 165, 169, 170, 184, 199, 204, 208, 209, 236, 237, 313
Shadwell, 12, 17, 18, 19, 25, 28, 31, 33, 38, 41, 42, 43, 44, 50, 52, 53, 56, 57, 58, 59, 61, 62, 75, 76, 89, 90, 96, 100, 101, 114, 156, 175, 189, 220
Shannon, George, 250, 251, 253, 255
Shawnee tribe, 45, 256, 257

Shenandoah Valley, 38, 50, 99, 141
Sherman, Roger, 115
Shields, John, 255, 305, 306
Shockoe Hill, Richmond, VA, 138, 154, 160
Short, William, 152, 166
Shoshone tribe, 278, 281, 283, 285
Shoshones, 263, 283, 284, 298
Sioussat, Jean Pierre, 224
Sioux City, IA, 273
Sioux tribe, 273, 279
Skelton, Bathurst, 92
Skelton, John, 94
Slavery, Abolition of, *164*
Small, Dr. William, 66, 67, 68
Smith, Daniel, 176
Smith, Margaret Bayard, 205, 225, 293
Smith, Samuel Harrison, 205
Snake River, 287
South Carolina, 119, 139, 274
South Dakota, 242, 279
South West Point, TN, 257, 260
Southwest Mountains, 5, 124
Spain, 70, 165, 233, 240, 241, 245, 267, 268, 294, 299, 313
Spotswood, Alexander, 130
Spotsylvania County, VA, 49, 319, 320
St. Anne's Parish, 106, 107, 126
St. Charles, MO, 263, 270
St. John's Church, 111, 114, 295
St. Louis, MO, 258, 259, 260, 262, 263, 265, 269, 270, 274, 278, 281, 287, 294, 296, 297, 298, 299, 302, 304, 307, 310, 311, 312, 317
Staffordshire, England, 55
Stamp Act, 78, 80, 84
Statute of Religious Freedom, 169
Statute of Virginia for Religious Freedom, 129, 135, 136, 154, 318
Staunton, VA, 2, 141, 142, 251
Sterret, Andrew, 210
Stoddard, Amos, 258, 262, 269
Suck - slave, 110, 128, 189
Summary View of the Rights, 108, 113
Swan Tavern, 140
Sweeney, George Wythe, 295
Taliaferro, John "The Ranger", 319
Taliaferro, Mary, 319
Taliaferro, Richard, 69
Talleyrand, Charles de, 187

Tarleton, Col. Banastre, 140, 141
Tennessee, 36, 45, 176, 181, 257, 260, 294, 316
Tennessee River, 176, 256
The Ordinance of 1784, 151
The Parson's Cause, 71, 72, 89
Thompson, John B., 262
Thornton, Elizabeth, 56, 220, 320
Thornton, Francis II, 320
Thornton, Francis III, 319
Thornton, Francis, Jr., 319
Thornton, Mildred, 12, 45, 53, 55, 125, 131, 320
Thornton, William, 319
Three Forks of the Missouri, 278
Todd, Dolley, 178, 208
Todd, John, 208
Todd, Payne, 208
Treaty of Paris, 180, 209
Treaty of Paris in 1763, 70
Treaty of San Ildefonso, 240
Treaty of St. Louis, 274
Treaty of Tripoli, 209
Treaty of Vincennes, 274
Tribble, Rev. Andrew, 101
Tripoli, 209, 210, 226, 269, 274
Tuckahoe, 25, 26, 27, 28, 31, 35, 41, 42, 44, 50, 52, 65, 69, 163, 170, 199, 220, 236, 289, 290
Turpin, Thomas, 138
Tuttle, Ebenezer, 258
Two Penny Act, 15, 71, 72, 73
U.S Army, 179
U.S. Army, 200, 223, 227, 242, 253, 254, 256, 258, 294, 315
U.S. Marines, 199
U.S. Navy, 269
U.S. Supreme Court, 199, 234, 238, 313
University of Virginia, *317, 318*
Vermont, 181
Versailles, France, 153, 169
Vincennes, IN, 274
Virginia House of Burgesses, 18, 20, 45, 49, 77, 85, 87, 94, 95, 96, 103, *105*, 106, 107, 320
Virginia Resolutions, 188
Walker, Capt. Thomas, 131
Walker, Dr. Thomas, 3, 7, 11, 12, 17, 28, 35, 45, 50, 52, 55, 56, 57, 58, 60, 62,

Walker, Betsy Moore, 55, 68,
   69, 70, 76, 77, 84, 87, 94, 124, 125,
   131, 141, 176, 177, 178, 199, 289,
   320
Walker, Elizabeth Simms, 125, 131, 177
Walker, Jane, 125, 131
Walker, John "Jack", 3, 4, 5, 6, 11, 12,
   14, 35, 45, 47, 49, 52, 56, 58, 62, 66,
   76, 94, 106, 107, 130
Walker, Lucy, 131
Walker, Mary, 125, 130, 177
Walker, Mary Peachey, 55, 84, 131
Walker, Mildred, 131, 320
Walker, Mollie, 15, 88
Walker, Peachy, 49, 125, 131, 177
Walker, Sarah, 131
Walker, Susanna, 49, 76, 125, 131, 177
Walker's Church, Albemarle Co., VA, 88
War, Revolutionary, 45, 111, 126, 135,
   151, 187, 240, 305
Warfington, Richard, 260
Washington D.C., 22, 45, 48, 49, 53,
   54, 55, 128, 138, 139, 140, 142, 143,
   153, 158, 159, 167, 168, 169, 170,
   179, 180, 181, 183, 184, 190, 191,
   198, 199, 200, 203, 205, 207, 208,
   209, 211, 215, 222, 227, 228, 229,
   232, 236, 237, 241, 242, 246, 247,
   258, 266, 268, 270, 271, 272, 278,
   279, 280, 291, 297, 298, 299, 300,
   306, 307, 310, 311, 315
Washington state, 234, 285
Washington, George, *15, 45, 47, 48, 49,
   53, 54, 55, 77, 99, 103, 106, 114,
   120, 124, 128, 133, 138, 139, 140,
   142, 150, 156, 157, 158, 163, 164,
   166, 171, 178, 179, 181, 191, 200,
   221, 223, 236, 239, 313, 314, 320*
Washington, Mildred, 320
Washita River, 308
Wayles, John, 92, 94, 97, 123
Wayles, Martha, 92
Wayles, Martha Eppes, 31
Weiser, Peter, 258
West Point, NY, 227, 260
Westmoreland County, VA, 139

Whiskey Rebellion, 179, 180, 200, 222
whiskey tax, 167, 179, 210, 223, 227
White House, 195, 202, 204, 205, 206,
   208, 209, 211, 212, 213, 216, 223,
   224, 225, 229, 233, 241, 243, 244,
   249, 251, 252, 265, 266, 267, 268,
   271, 272, 273, 279, 281, 290, 293,
   298, 300, 301, 302, 303, 307, 310,
   311, 312
White, Isaac, 258
Whitehouse, Joseph, 256
Whitfield, George, 80
Whitlough, Thomas, 190
Wilkes County, GA, 222
Wilkinson, Gen. James, 200, 294, 297, 314
Wilkinson, James, 294, 308, 314
Willard, Alexander, 258
William and Mary, College of, 11, 34, 66, 67, 75
Williamsburg, Virginia, 42, 55, 62, 64,
   65, 67, 69, 71, 74, 76, 78, 84, 89, 90,
   92, 94, 96, 99, 107, 108, 109, 110,
   111, 112, 113, 126, 128, 130, 133,
   134, 136, 137, 138, 140, 142, 156,
   236, 295, 313, 322
Wilson, Woodrow, 211
Windsor, Richard, 258, 259
Winston, Isaac, 80
Wistar, Caspar, 223, 243
Wood River, 259
Woods, Henry, 196
Wythe, George, 66, 67, 68, 69, 71, 72,
   74, 76, 77, 79, 87, 120, 126, 128,
   133, 134, 135, 138, 147, 199, 294,
   295, 296
XYZ affair, 187
Yankton Sioux tribe, 279
Yellowstone River, 282
York, 21
York - slave, 10, 21, 22, 164, 166, 252,
   253, 255, 258, 259, 263, 281, 299,
   305, 306, 316
York River, 65, 142
Yorktown, 65, 112, 131, 140, 142, 143,
   159, 236, 322

Son.

I hate seeing you put too much pressure on yourself, and even more I hate seeing you unhappy. You've given me&more than your parents could ever give you, and that alone makes you the best father I could ask for.

I know a lot of what is going on how is a result of troubles from you & mom's past, but I'm lucky to be your son no matter how the future shapes out.

(flip over)

Hey Dad,

You were exercising when I left so I just decided to write this instead.

I noticed the life lessons and poem hanging up.

I know you are going through tough times right now. I know finding a job to your standards is extremely hard to come by nowadays. I know having mom breathing down your back doesn't make anything easier either.

The only thing that matters in all of this is that you are trying. You could bag groceries for th

I just need you to know that you aren't in this alone, and you've given me most of the qualities that all of my friends love about me.

I believe in you no matter what happens. And I'm honored to be your son every day.

dad.

I love you ~~~~~~~~

-Ryan

CPSIA information can be obtained at www.ICGtesting.com
Printed in the USA
LVOW042000120912

298489LV00001B/7/P

9 781462 720521